Historical Dictionary of Lithuania

Saulius Sužiedėlis

European Historical Dictionaries No. 21

The Scarecrow Press, Inc.
Lanham, Md., & London
1997

SCARECROW PRESS, INC.

Published in the United States of America
by Scarecrow Press, Inc.
4720 Boston Way
Lanham, Maryland 20706

4 Pleydell Gardens, Folkestone
Kent CT20 2DN, England

British Cataloging in Publication Information Available

Library of Congress Cataloging-in-Publication Data

Sužiedėlis, Saulius, 1945–
  Historical dictionary of Lithuania / Saulius Sužiedėlis.
    p.   cm. — (European historical dictionaries : no. 21)
  Includes bibliographical references.
  1. Lithuania—History—Dictionaries. I. Title. II. Series.
DK505.37.S89   1997   947.93'003—dc21   97–12398 CIP

ISBN 0–8108–3335–2 (cloth: alk. paper)

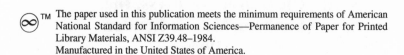

The paper used in this publication meets the minimum requirements of American
National Standard for Information Sciences—Permanence of Paper for Printed
Library Materials, ANSI Z39.48–1984.
Manufactured in the United States of America.

IN MEMORIAM

Simas Sužiedėlis (1903-1985)
Antanina Sužiedėlienė (1904-1995)

CONTENTS

EDITOR'S FOREWORD

Few countries have undergone vicissitudes as extreme as Lithuania. An expanding and thriving Grand Duchy in the 15th century, which dwarfed neighboring kingdoms, it lost territory and shrank during successive wars and partitions until it completely disappeared. Then, almost miraculously, it was resurrected after the First World War, only to be swallowed up again, and finally returned as an independent state only a few years ago. Obviously, even during its periods of absence from the community of nations, the essence of a Lithuanian state was preserved, as was the hope. Once again, we can see what the Lithuanians are capable of as they revamp their political institutions, reorganize the educational system, revitalize the economy and set out in new directions in foreign policy.

It is not easy to unravel Lithuania's history. But that has been done amazingly well here through an introduction, chronology and a multitude of entries on crucial persons, places and events. The institutions and traditions of Lithuania are described in equally useful entries. Others give us a feel for the people, the language and the culture. Not least important are those outlining the political, economic and social situation up to the present. This is already a significant first step toward knowing this new (and old) country. Further steps can be taken in desired areas by reading some of the books and articles listed in the selective bibliography.

The rebirth of an independent Lithuania was a pivotal event in the lives of many Lithuanians, both those who remained in their country and those who emigrated, including the author, Saulius Sužiedėlis. Although living in the United States, he devoted his studies and much of his career to learning and teaching about Lithuania in particular, and Eastern Europe in general: from a dissertation on the Lithuanian peasantry to a book on the Church in Lithuania, as a teacher of history at several colleges, and presently as associate professor at Millersville University of Pennsylvania. In addition, Dr. Sužiedėlis, as well as this *Historical Dictionary of Lithuania,* have also benefited from the new possibilities to learn and teach in Lithuania itself.

Jon Woronoff
Series Editor

PREFACE

Let me define at the outset the scope of the *Historical Dictionary of Lithuania*, which also, of course, means to acknowledge its limitations. No single volume can encompass all the complexity and nuances of a country whose very name has evoked different geographic, political and cultural connotations over the centuries. This *Dictionary* is intended, rather, as an introduction for the non-specialist who needs a guide to the most important mileposts of Lithuania's past. This immediately raises the difficult and sensitive problem of selection, which inevitably entails omissions, as one tries to distinguish between the more important and less significant personalities, events and institutions. Naturally, such selection is to some extent subjective, guided by the predilections and even prejudices of the author. I can only hope that my attempt at invoking common-sense considerations has succeeded and that three decades of study about Eastern Europe and Lithuania have left some mark in the form of recognizing the most important features of Lithuanian history.

First, I have tried to select the information that would be of most interest to the educated general reader and student unfamiliar with Lithuania's past but with some knowledge of general European history. One question I have asked as a guide is this: if someone were reading a general history of Europe, or one of Lithuania's neighbors, which terms would he or she be most (or least) likely to encounter? Second, I have tried to choose those items for the dictionary which are representative and informative, that is, those which tell us the most about the political, social and cultural life of Lithuania at different times in the country's history. Finally, I have tried, wherever possible, to demonstrate Lithuania's place in the history and life of her neighbors and in the general development of Europe, to place the Lithuanian past within its broader context of a unique position between East and West. Lithuania's political isolation during the last half-century has led many people, including some in Lithuania, to forget that, historically speaking, the country is as "European" as France and Italy. The Renaissance and the Reformation, the movements of national Romanticism and democracy, the Hapsburgs and the Angevins, are all component parts of Lithuania's past. At the same time, Lithuania played a major role in the history of her Orthodox, eastern Slavic Russian, Ukrainian, and Belarusan neighbors whose cultural roots are found in Byzantium. In the 16th century, the Roman Catholic Grand Duke of Lithuania, after attending a Latin Mass, would announce his decrees in a derivative of Old Church Slavic, the liturgical language of the Russian Orthodox Church. I have tried to convey this unique European cultural experience both in the text and in the choice of the *Dictionary*'s entries.

Lithuania's history is a multinational one, involving many languages and hence different versions of toponyms, personal names and institutional designations. Even the terms "Lithuania" and "Lithuanian" have meant different things at different times to different people. Once again, I have invoked common sense as a guide. With few exceptions, I have used the present-day spellings of place names as utilized by the National Geographic Society, which means employing the current official language of the region, hence always Vilnius, not Vilna; Suwałki, not Suvalkai. However, I have also provided alternative versions that are often encountered in the literature. In presenting surnames, I have tried to adhere to the spelling peculiar to a given person's nationality, except where widely utilized versions in English-language works dictated otherwise (hence Radziwiłł rather than Radvila or Radvilas). In my experience, attempts to observe absolute consistency at the expense of common sense, at least in this regard, can lead to what are unrecognizable concoctions for most Western readers.

It is my pleasure to thank a number of people who assisted me in the publication of this historical dictionary. Dr. Rasa Mažeika of

Toronto kindly shared her insights on some of the more complicated aspects of Lithuania's medieval past. Prof. William Urban of Monmouth College (Illinois) helped with his specialty, the Teutonic Knights and Prussia. Prof. K. Paulius Žygas of Arizona State University assisted me with the history of art and architecture. I am very grateful to the editor of the *Historical Dictionaries* series, Mr. Jon Woronoff, for his suggestions and his patience in accepting long delays in the preparation of the manuscript. Prof. Violeta Kelertas of the Endowed Chair of Lithuanian Studies at the University of Illinois-Chicago helped me with literary themes. Mr. Edvardas Tuskenis of the Lithuanian Embassy in Washington provided information on current Lithuanian politics. I would like to acknowledge the Geography Department of Millersville University for their assistance with the maps. But obviously I alone remain responsible for the facts, interpretations and errors found herein. I welcome constructive criticism from the readers in the spirit of learning.

Finally, there are two people who were crucial to my undertaking this task in the first place. This book is lovingly dedicated to my father, a medievalist trained at the University of Riga, who taught me curiosity and love of history, and to my mother, who was among the first women university graduates in independent Lithuania, and who always stressed a profound respect for learning. Together, both at home and in exile, they actually lived the joys and sorrows of the Lithuanian people in the 20th century, an experience I hope is at least partly reflected in this text.

Saulius Sužiedėlis
Millersville, PA

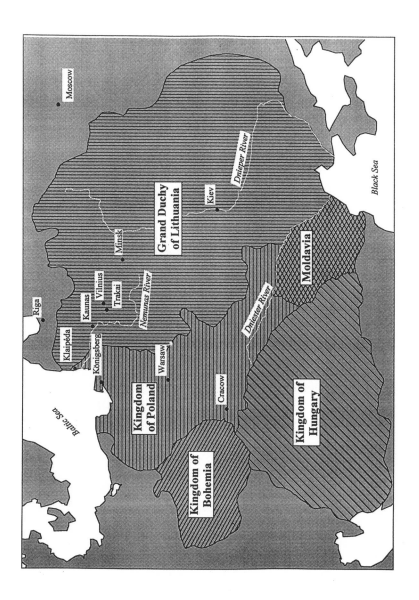

Grand Duchy of Lithuania in the Mid-15th Century

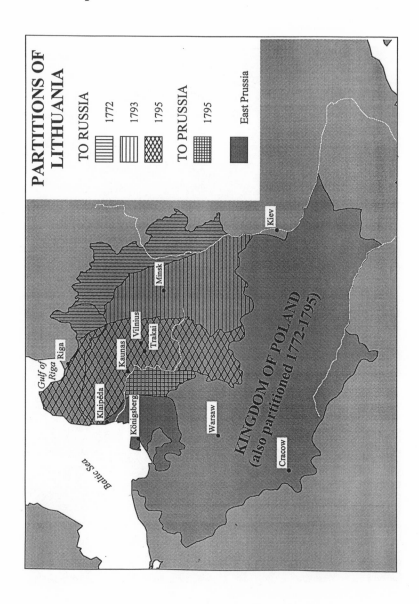

PARTITIONS OF LITHUANIA

TO RUSSIA
1772
1793
1795

TO PRUSSIA
1795

East Prussia

Kiev

Minsk

Vilnius

Trakai

Riga

Gulf of Riga

Kaunas

Klaipėda

Königsberg

Warsaw

KINGDOM OF POLAND
(also partitioned 1772-1795)

Cracow

Baltic Sea

The Polish-Lithuanian Commonwealth and
the Partitions of Lithuania 1772-1795

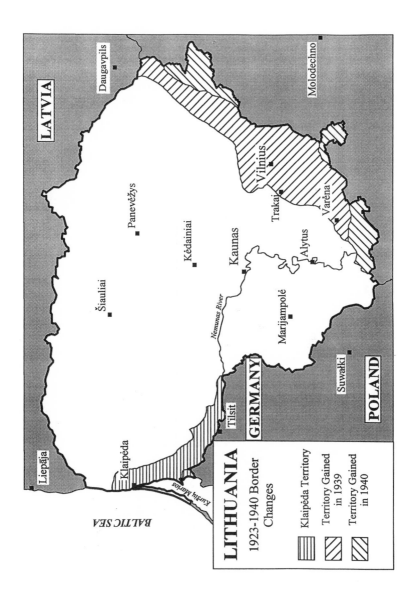

Lithuania: 1923-1940 Border Changes

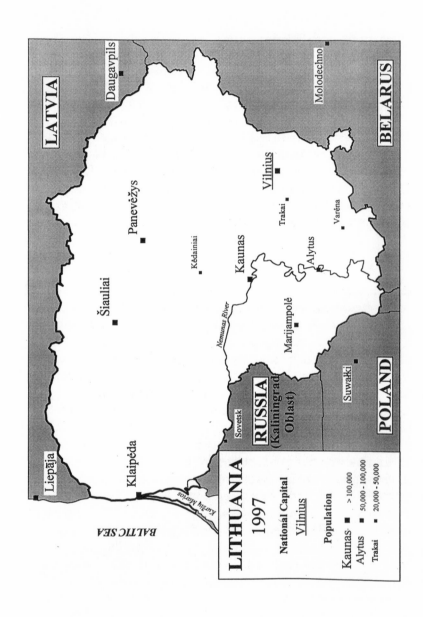

Lithuania 1997

ABBREVIATIONS AND ACRONYMS

Bel.	Belarusan
BDPS	Lith. Bendras Demokratinio Pasipriešinimo Sąjūdis (The United Movement of Democratic Resistance)
CPSU	Communist Party of the Soviet Union
CSA	Ger. Christliche Sozialistische Arbeitsgemein-schaft (The Christian Socialist Workers' Union)
FPO	Yiddish: Fareinikte Partizaner Organizatzie (United Partisan Organization)
Ger.	German
IE	Indo-European
IRO	International Refugee Organization
JBS	*Journal of Baltic Studies*
KGB	Rus. Komitet Gosudarstvennoi Bezopasnosti (Committee for State Security)
LAF	Lith. Lietuvių, Lietuvos Aktyvistų Frontas (Lithuanian Activist Front)
LAL	Lithuanian Airlines
LCP	Lithuanian Communist Party
LDDP	Lith. Lietuvos Demokratinė Darbo Partija (Lithuanian Democratic Labor Party)
LF	Lith. Lietuvių Frontas (Lithuanian Front)
Lith.	Lithuanian
LLA	Lith. Lietuvos Laisvės Armija (Lithuanian Freedom Army)
LLKS	Lith. Lietuvos Laisvės Kovotojų Sąjūdis (Lithuanian Freedom Fighters' Movement)
LMA	Lith. Lietuvos Mokslų Akademija (Lithuanian Academy of Sciences)
LNP	Lith. Lietuvių Nacionalistų Partija (Lithuanian Nationalist Party)
LPS	Lith. Lietuvos Persitvarkymo Sąjūdis (Lithuanian Movement for Restructuring)

LSDP	Lith. Lietuvos Socialdemokratų Partija (Lithuanian Social Democratic Party)
LTSR	Lith. Lietuvos Tarybų Socialistinė Respublika (Lithuanian Soviet Socialist Republic)
MOPR	Rus. Mezhdunarodnaya Organizatsiya Pomoshchi Revoliutsionerom (The International Organization for Assistance to Revolutionaries)
NATO	North Atlantic Treaty Organization
NKVD	Rus. Narodny Kommisariat Vnutrennykh Del (The People's Commissariat of Internal Affairs)
OMON	Rus. Otdely Militsii Osobennogo Naznacheniya (Special Assignment Militia Units)
Pol.	Polish
POW	Pol. Polska Organizacja Wojskowa (Polish Military Organization)
RAD	Ger. Reichsarbeitsdienst (Reich Labor Service)
RSDWP	Russian Social Democratic Workers' Party
RSFSR	Russian Soviet Federative Socialist Republic
Rus.	Russian
SA	Ger. Sturmabteilung (Stormtrooper Unit)
SS	Ger. Schutzstaffel (Security Staff)
SSR	Soviet Socialist Republic
UN	United Nations
UNRRA	United Nations Relief and Rehabilitation Administration
USSR	Union of Soviet Socialist Republics
VLIK	Lith. Vyriausias Lietuvos Išlaisvinimo Komitetas (The Supreme Committee for the Liberation of Lithuania)
VPMLL	Lith. Valstybinė Politinės ir Mokslinės Literatūros Leidykla (The State Publishing House for Political and Scholarly Literature)
YIVO	Yiddish. Yidisher Visenshaftliken Institut (Institute for Jewish Research)

GLOSSARY

Aukščiausioji Taryba	Supreme Soviet of the Lithuanian SSR 1940-1941 and 1944-1990; during 1990-1992 the legislature of the Republic of Lithuania, better known during this period as the Supreme Council (Lith.)
boyars	Class of nobility in Muscovy and the Grand Duchy of Lithuania descended from a feudal warrior class
grand hetman	Highest military rank in the Grand Duchy of Lithuania
gubernia	Province of the Russian Empire since the late 18th century
hetman	Military rank (field command) in the Grand Duchy of Lithuania
Lietuvos Respublika	Republic of Lithuania (Lith.)
litas	Unit of Lithuanian currency (in 1997: 4 litai = 1 USD)
nomenklatura	Term for the elite officialdom of the Communist Party (Rus.)
palatine	Head of a palatinate, one of the administrative divisions of the Grand Duchy of Lithuania
Sąjūdis	"Movement" (Lith.); popular name for Lietuvos Persitvarkymo Sąjūdis, or the Movement for Restructuring (Perestroika)
Seimas	Gentry diet of the Grand Duchy of Lithuania; also the parliament of the Republic of Lithuania, 1920-1940 and since 1992 (Lith.)

szlachta

Polish term commonly used to describe the petty, or lesser, gentry of Poland and Lithuania (Pol.)

Taryba

Lithuanian word for a council; used to denote the Lithuanian Council of 1917-1919; also the Lithuanian term for "Soviet" (Lith.)

CHRONOLOGY OF MAJOR EVENTS

ca. 3000 B.C.	Baltic tribes settled on the eastern Baltic coast.
ca. 2000 B.C.	Bronze Age in Lithuania. Greatest territorial expansion of the Baltic tribes.
997 A.D.	St. Adalbert (Vojtech) martyred in Prussia.
1008	First mention of Lithuania in the Querfurt Chronicle.
1251	Mindaugas adopts Christianity and is crowned King of Lithuania.
1263	Mindaugas' assassination.
1316-1341	Reign of Grand Duke Gediminas. Development of closer ties to the West.
1386	Grand Duke Jogaila (Pol. Jagiełło) is crowned King of Poland as Władysław II.
1387	Final conversion of Lithuanians to Catholicism begins. Diocese of Vilnius established.
1410	Teutonic Knights decisively defeated at the Battle of Grunwald/Tannenberg (Lith. Žalgiris).

1430	Death of Grand Duke Vytautas.
1529	Publication of the First Lithuanian Statute.
1547	Publication of the first known book in the Lithuanian language in Königsberg, East Prussia.
1569	Union of Lublin establishes the Polish-Lithuanian Commonwealth. Ukraine transferred from Lithuania to Poland.
1572	Death of King Sigismund Augustus ends the Jagiellonian Dynasty.
1579	Founding of the University of Vilnius.
1611-1612	Polish-Lithuanian forces occupy Moscow during the Time of Troubles in Muscovy.
1655	Treaty of Kėdainiai: Lithuania's attempt at union with Sweden.
1660	Treaty of Oliwa ends war with Sweden.
1700-1721	Great Northern War involving Russia, Poland-Lithuania and Sweden.
1708-1711	Famine and plague kill the majority of the population in Samogitia and East Prussia.
1772	First Partition of Poland and Lithuania.
1793	Second Partition of Poland and Lithuania.

1795	Final Partition of Poland and Lithuania. Most of Lithuania comes under the rule of the Russian Empire.
1807	Serfdom abolished in the Grand Duchy of Warsaw, including the Lithuanian-speaking districts in the north.
1812	Napoleon's army crosses the Nemunas River at Kaunas on the way to Moscow.
1830-1831	Armed uprising against Tsarist Russia in Poland and Lithuania.
1831	University of Vilnius closed. The beginnings of Russification and anti-Catholic policies under Tsar Nicholas I (1825-1855).
1840	The Lithuanian Statute is abolished and Russian law introduced into Lithuania.
February 1861	Tsar Alexander II announces the Emancipation Manifesto.
1861-1862	Anti-Russian demonstrations and agitation are on the increase throughout Poland and Lithuania.
January 1863	Armed struggle against Russians begins in Lithuania.
1863-1864	Insurrection against Tsarist Russia. M. N. Muravyev is appointed Governor-General of Vilnius and begins a massive suppression of the revolt.

1864   Governor-General Muravyev bans the publication of Lithuanian books in the Latin alphabet.

1869-70   Bishop Valančius of Samogitia begins organizing an illegal publication movement to circumvent the press ban.

1883   Publication of *Aušra* (The Dawn), the first modern Lithuanian periodical.

1889   Publication of *Varpas* (The Bell), the first Lithuanian secular political periodical, edited by Vincas Kudirka.

1893   Cossacks and Russian police massacre Catholic protesters at the monastery and church of Kražiai.

1896   Lithuanian Social Democratic Party established.

April 1904   The Russian government lifts the ban on Lithuanian publications in the Latin alphabet.

1905   Strikes and demonstrations erupt in Vilnius and other Lithuanian towns.

December 4-5, 1905   2,000 delegates attend the Great Lithuanian Assembly in Vilnius, the first Lithuanian political convention. Delegates demand an autonomous and democratic Lithuania within a new Russian federation.

1905-1906	The Revolution of 1905 spreads throughout the Lithuanian countryside. Peasants attack Tsarist institutions and demand an end to national and religious discrimination.
1906	Lithuanians and Jews elect a joint slate of deputies to the Duma in St. Petersburg.
August 1914	World War I begins. Lithuanian leaders declare loyalty to the Tsar.
September 1915	German Army occupies Vilnius. Tsarist authorities evacuate about a half-million inhabitants from Lithuania to the Russian interior.
1917	Formation of the Lithuanian National Council, the Taryba.
December 11, 1917	The Taryba declares the formation of a Lithuanian state allied to Germany.
February 16, 1918	The Taryba declares the restoration of an independent Lithuania without ties to any foreign state.
November 11, 1918	Formation of the first Lithuanian government headed by Augustinas Voldemaras.
February-April 1919	Lithuanian-Belarusan Soviet Republic established in Vilnius. Western Lithuania remains under the jurisdiction of the independence government.

May 1920

The Constituent Assembly (Lith. *Steigiamasis Seimas*) is elected.

July 12, 1920

Soviet Russia signs peace treaty with Lithuania and renounces all claims to Lithuanian territory.

October 7, 1920

Suwałki Agreement with Poland leaves Vilnius under Lithuanian administration.

October 9, 1920

Polish forces under General Lucjan Żeligowski occupy Vilnius.

January 1923

Lithuanian volunteers seize Klaipėda (Ger. Memel) from French garrison enforcing the Allied mandate.

March 15, 1923

Conference of Ambassadors announces recognition of Polish claims to Vilnius.

January 1924

Lithuania signs a convention with Britain, France, Italy and Japan providing for Lithuanian sovereignty over Klaipėda Territory.

December 17, 1926

Military coup overthrows the center-left government of President Grinius and Prime Minister Sleževičius after which Antanas Smetona is named President.

1927

Nationalist Union disbands the Seimas, bans political parties and consolidates its power. Authoritarian regime established under President Smetona.

1934-5

Trial of Klaipėda Nazis in Kaunas.

1935-6	Violent agrarian strikes erupt in southwestern Lithuania.
March 11, 1938	Polish ultimatum to Lithuania demands that diplomatic relations be established. Lithuania accepts on March 17.
March 22, 1939	German troops occupy Klaipėda Territory following Berlin's ultimatum.
August 23, 1939	German-Soviet Non-Aggression Treaty (Molotov-Ribbentrop Pact) signed in Moscow. Lithuania is assigned to the German "sphere of influence."
September 1, 1939	World War II begins. Lithuania declares neutrality.
September 28, 1939	German-Soviet Treaty of Friendship (Second Molotov-Ribbentrop Agreement) transfers Lithuania to the Soviet "sphere of influence."
October 10, 1939	Lithuania and the USSR sign Treaty of Mutual Assistance providing for Soviet military bases in Lithuania and the return of Vilnius.
October 28, 1939	Lithuanian troops enter Vilnius.
May 1940	First public expressions of Soviet dissatisfaction with Lithuania's enforcement of the mutual assistance pact.
June 7, 1940	Prime Minister Antanas Merkys is summoned to Moscow.

June 14, 1940	USSR issues ultimatum to the Republic of Lithuania demanding the establishment of a pro-Soviet government and the entry of an unlimited contingent of Soviet troops to ensure fulfillment of the mutual assistance pact.
June 15, 1940	Lithuanian government accepts the Soviet ultimatum and Soviet troops occupy Lithuania. President Smetona flees the country.
June 17, 1940	A new Lithuanian People's Government headed by leftist journalist Justas Paleckis is formed.
June 26, 1940	Lithuanian Communist Party is legalized. Leftist political prisoners released.
July 11-12, 1940	First widespread arrests conducted by the NKVD. Hundreds of political and cultural leaders are incarcerated or deported to the Soviet Union.
July 14-15, 1940	Hastily organized elections to the People's Diet. The Communist-led Lithuanian Labor Bloc announces that it has won 95% of a near total turnout.
July 21-22, 1940	The People's Diet convenes in Kaunas and proclaims the Lithuanian Soviet Socialist Republic. A resolution demands that Lithuania apply to join the USSR.

August 3, 1940	The Supreme Soviet of the USSR approves the application of the Lithuanian Soviet Socialist Republic to join the Soviet Union, thus formally annexing Lithuania.
November 1, 1940	Anti-Soviet manifestations during All Souls' Day in Kaunas.
November 3, 1940	Lithuanian Activist Front (LAF) is formed in Berlin.
June 14-17, 1941	NKVD and Communist activists carry out deportations of nearly 18,000 Lithuanian civilians.
June 22, 1941	Soviet-German war begins. German Army invades Lithuania.
June 23, 1941	Anti-Soviet rebellion breaks out and a provisional government announces the restoration of independent Lithuania.
July 25, 1941	German authorities announce the establishment of civilian administration (Ger. *Zivilverwaltung*) in Lithuania.
August 5, 1941	The Lithuanian Provisional Government resigns under German pressure.
July-October 1941	Nazi *Einsatzgruppen* or action squads carry out massive executions of over 100,000 civilians, primarily Jews. Surviving Jews are driven into ghettos in Vilnius, Kaunas and Šiauliai.

February 1943	German occupation authorities announce a drive to form a Lithuanian SS Legion, but the mobilization fails.
February 1944	Germans agree to allow the formation of a Local Force (Lith. *Vietinė rinktinė*) under Lithuanian command.
May 1944	The Local Force is disbanded.
July 13, 1944	Soviet Army enters Vilnius.
1944-1952	Period of active guerrilla war between the anti-Soviet resistance and USSR security forces. Over 120,000 more civilians deported to Siberia and points east.
March 5, 1953	Stalin dies.
February 1956	Khrushchev's secret speech denouncing Stalin's crimes at the 20th CPSU Congress. De-Stalinization begins in Lithuania.
November 1956	Anti-Soviet demonstration in Vilnius on the occasion of the Hungarian Revolution.
January 22, 1970	Antanas Sniečkus, the First Secretary of the LCP, dies in Vilnius.
November 1970	Seaman Simas Kudirka's attempt to defect to the Coast Guard vessel *Vigilant* near Martha's Vineyard creates an international incident.

May 14, 1972	The self-immolation of Romas Kalanta triggers anti-Soviet disturbances in Kaunas.
November 1976	The Lithuanian Helsinki Committee announces it will begin monitoring Soviet compliance with the Helsinki Accords of 1975.
November 1978	The formation of the Lithuanian Catholic Committee for the Defense of Believers is announced in Moscow.
March 11, 1985	Mikhail S. Gorbachev is appointed General Secretary of the CPSU.
August 23, 1987	A demonstration commemorating the anniversary of the Molotov-Ribbentrop Pact attracts hundreds of participants to St. Ann's Church in Vilnius.
May-June 1988	Popular demonstrations commemorating the Soviet deportations begin in Vilnius. The Initiative Group of the Movement for Restructuring in Lithuania is formed.
June 24, 1988	Mass demonstration demanding reform sends off Lithuanian delegates to the 19th Conference of the CPSU.
July 9, 1988	Massive pro-Sąjūdis demonstration of 100,000 in Vingis Park demands environmental protection, sovereignty and democracy for Lithuania.
July-October 1988	The Sąjūdis movement establishes chapters throughout Lithuania.

October 1988	The formal founding congress of the Sąjūdis movement opens in Vilnius. Algirdas Brazauskas appointed First Secretary of the LCP. The Cathedral of Vilnius is returned to the Catholic Church.
March 1989	Elections to the Soviet Congress of People's Deputies in Lithuania brings a Sąjūdis majority.
August 23, 1989	"Hands Across the Baltic" demonstration on the 50th anniversary of the Molotov-Ribbentrop Pact involves over a million demonstrators in the Baltic republics.
December 18, 1989	The 20th Congress of the LCP declares its independence from the CPSU.
January 11-13, 1990	Gorbachev visits Lithuania to campaign against secession. Mass demonstration in Vilnius demands independence.
February 1990	Elections to the Supreme Soviet of the Lithuanian SSR result in a Sąjūdis majority.
March 11, 1990	The Lithuanian Supreme Soviet in Vilnius votes 124-0 to restore the country's independence; Vytautas Landsbergis is elected Chairman of the Supreme Council.
March-April, 1990	Soviet government initiates economic boycott of Lithuania.

January 13, 1991	14 demonstrators are killed and hundreds wounded in a Soviet attack on the TV tower in Vilnius. Pro-Soviet hardliners fail to topple the Landsbergis government.
July 30, 1991	Six border guards are killed by Soviet secret service forces at the Medininkai border post during President Bush's visit to Moscow.
August 23-24, 1991	Hardline coup fails both in Moscow and Lithuania.
August-September 1991	The USSR and Western states recognize Lithuania. The Baltic States are admitted to the UN.
December 25, 1991	Gorbachev resigns as President, marking the formal demise of the USSR.
February 1992	Lithuania takes part in the Olympics for the first time since 1928 in Lilihammer, Norway.
May 13, 1992	French President François Mitterrand becomes the first head of state of a major power to visit Lithuania.
August 1992	Lithuanian men's basketball team wins the bronze medal at the Summer Olympics in Barcelona.
October 1992	The LDDP wins a surprising victory in the first elections to the Seimas.
February 14, 1993	Brazauskas wins the first popular election for President of Lithuania.

June 25, 1993   The litas is reintroduced as Lithuania's currency.

September 1, 1993   The last Russian troops leave Lithuania.

September 4-8, 1993   Pope John Paul II visits Lithuania.

January 27, 1994   Lithuania announces that it will join NATO's Partnership for Peace Program.

June 12, 1995   Lithuania signs an Association Agreement with the European Union.

December 20, 1995   Bank crisis erupts after Lithuania's two largest banks are declared insolvent and top bank officials are arrested and charged with fraud.

January-February 1996   Political crisis deepens after Prime Minister Adolfas Šleževičius admits withdrawing over $30,000 from a Lithuanian commercial bank only days before its closure. President Brazauskas calls for the premier's resignation.

February 8, 1996   The Seimas votes 94-26 to dismiss Šleževičius. Mindaugas Stankevičius is appointed prime minister.

August 1996   Lithuanian men's basketball team wins the bronze medal in the Summer Olympic Games held in Atlanta.

October-November 1996   Landsbergis' Conservatives win elections to the Seimas. Gediminas Vagnorius is again appointed prime minister.

INTRODUCTION

The Land and the People

The Republic of Lithuania is located on the eastern shore of the Baltic Sea, between 53° 54' and 56° 27' N latitude and between 20° 56' and 26° 51' E longitude. Historically, the country is treated as part of Eastern Europe, although in strictly geographic terms, Lithuania is actually in the center of the European continent. The nation's eastern upland region is equidistant between the Pyrenees and Urals; it is also halfway between northern Norway and southern Greece. Lithuania, together with Latvia and Estonia, are often referred to as the Baltic States. The country's neighbors are Latvia in the north, Poland in the south, Belarus (Byelorussia) in the east and the Kaliningrad Oblast of the Russian Federation in the west. The territory of Lithuania encompasses 65,200 sq. km. or 26,173 sq. mi.; by comparison, it is about the size of the Republic of Ireland and slightly larger than West Virginia.

Lithuania is part of the immense European plain stretching from the Urals to Western Europe. The country contains no significant mountains, although elevations are somewhat higher in the east: the tallest hill is Medininkai, 288 m. above sea level, located near the Lithuanian-Belarusan border. In general, Lithuanians divide their land into four major regions reflecting not only somewhat different topographies, but also distinct historical and dialectical characteristics. The western region of Žemaitija (Samogitia), literally meaning "The Lowland," ranges from Lithuania's 123-km. Baltic coastline to approximately the Nevėžis River. Aukštaitija, or the highland region, includes the central and northeastern area of the Lithuanian Republic. Dzūkija, a region which encompasses a part of eastern and southern Lithuania, is known for the peculiar dialect spoken in this area. Finally, the territory to the south and west of the Nemunas River is variously known as Sūduva, Suvalkija or Užnemunė (literally, the "land beyond the Nemunas"). Lithuania's climate is somewhat cooler than that of the corresponding latitudes

1

in Western Europe. The mean temperature is about 6°C. In general, winters are colder inland, where January mean temperatures reach minus 6° C, although harsher conditions are not infrequent. The warmest month is July with a mean temperature of about 17-18° C. Summers in Lithuania are relatively cool with abundant rainfall, especially in the west.

In 1997 Lithuania's population was estimated at 3,705,000 of which nearly 68 percent is classified as urban. Ethnic Lithuanians make up 81 percent of the country's inhabitants. The other major nationalities include the Russians (8.5 percent), Poles (7 percent) and Belarusans (1.5 percent), while the remainder consists of Ukrainians, Tatars, Jews and other small groups. The majority of Lithuanian believers are Roman Catholic, although there are Lutheran Evangelical and Reformed (Calvinist) communities in the north and west of the country. Among the minorities, virtually all Polish believers are Catholic, while Russians are predominantly Orthodox. There are also small groups practicing Judaism and Islam (mainly Tatars); in recent years, there has been growing interest in Christian fundamentalism and Eastern religions. Vilnius (1995 pop. est. 575,000) has been Lithuania's historic capital and cultural center since the 14th century. Other major urban centers and their population estimates for the mid-1990s: Kaunas, 430,000; Klaipėda, the major seaport, 210,000; Šiauliai, 150,000; Panevėžys, 130,000.

Lithuanian and Latvian are the only surviving members of the Baltic subgroup of Indo-European languages. Lithuanian, which utilizes the Latin alphabet, is the official language of the Republic and is the medium of instruction in the majority of primary, secondary and higher schools. There are also numerous schools with instruction in the minority languages, particularly Polish and Russian. Lithuanian is the native language of most ethnic Lithuanians and a part of the Lithuanian diaspora. It is also gaining ground as a second language among Lithuania's minorities. Polish is widely spoken in the eastern districts of the country and Russian is the native language of most Russians, as well as some Belarusans and Ukrainians. A half-century of Soviet rule (1940-1941, 1944-1990) has made the majority of adult Lithuanians conversant in

Russian to some degree, but the importance of the Russian language has declined rapidly since the restoration of Lithuania's independence in 1990.

The Government and Economy

On March 11, 1990 the newly-elected Supreme Soviet of the Lithuanian SSR formally declared the restoration of the Republic of Lithuania as an independent state. The country's legislature, which then became known in English as the Supreme Council (Lith. *Aukščiausioji Taryba*), elected Vytautas Landsbergis as its new chairman, with functions approximating those of president and head of state. Although the Supreme Council had been elected for a five-year term, the political crisis that deepened in 1991-1992 led to new elections in 1992. The Constitution adopted on October 26, 1992 provides for a 141-person legislature, a popularly-elected president for a five-year term, and a four-year term for the legislature, the Seimas, which has replaced the Supreme Council. Constitutional amendments require a two-thirds majority in the Seimas. During Soviet rule, Lithuania was divided into 44 regions (Lith. *rajonas*) and 11 municipalities. Administrative reforms after independence have redivided the country into ten districts (Lith. *apskritis*), which are subdivided into regions. The latter are split into rural counties (Lith. *valsčius*) which contain villages (Lith. *kaimas*), the lowest administrative units. Local affairs, including those of the major urban areas, are handled by elected self-governing bodies (Lith. *savivaldybė*).

Lithuania is the least industrialized of the Baltic States: agriculture and food processing have long been mainstays of the economy. Private farming has been permitted since 1989 and has grown steadily at the expense of the collectivized agriculture introduced by the Soviets after World War II. However, during the 1960s and 1970s Lithuania also developed some major industries, including electronics, wood processing, petroleum refining and machinery. Foreign trade, once oriented almost exclusively toward Russia, is increasingly directed towards Western countries. In 1996 about half of Lithuania's foreign trade was with the West: Germany has been the country's leading Western trade partner since independence. Germany, the United States and Great Britain accounted for more than one-half of the $359,000,000 of foreign investment in 1995. According to government estimates, the Gross Domestic Product grew by 1 percent in 1994 and 5 percent in 1995. In May 1996, the average wage was 614 *litai* per month, although public servants, for example teachers, are earning considerably less; many pensioners and poorly paid employees have slipped below the official poverty line. During the early 1990s disparity in income between a small wealthy elite and the rest of the population has continued to increase. Economic distress is also seen in the growing foreign debt (estimated in October 1995 at some $592,000,000) and the inability of the state and the private sector to pay skyrocketing costs for energy, still based mainly on petroleum and natural gas imports from Russia.

Inflation has declined from over 1,000 percent in 1992 to an estimated 35.6 percent in 1995. The unit of currency, reintroduced in 1993, is the *litas*, which in 1997 was valued at $.25 US and has remained remarkably stable despite pressure for devaluation. However, a serious banking crisis that erupted during the fall of 1995 and the outflow of hard currency from Lithuania have led to concern about a deepening monetary and economic crisis.

HISTORICAL SURVEY

From The Origins of the Lithuanian State Until 1569

Lithuanians and Latvians are Balts, that is, nations which speak Baltic languages. However, in addition to its ethnic and linguistic connotation, the term "Balts" has recently acquired a political meaning. It is sometimes used to denote the indigenous peoples of all three Baltic States, including Estonia, although Estonians are ethnic relatives of the Finns and speak a language unrelated to either Lithuanian or Latvian.

The exact origin of the Lithuanian people has been debated over the years, but it is clear that between 3000 and 2500 B. C. agricultural communities were well established in what is now Lithuania and Latvia. These central Baltic tribes were the direct ancestors of present-day Latvians and Lithuanians. The Baltic peoples achieved their greatest expansion during the Bronze Age (before 1500 B. C.) when they inhabited a vast area stretching from the Vistula to central Russia. However, after the collapse of the Roman Empire in the West, the Balts were caught between the westward movement of the Slavs and the Germanic expansion in northern Europe. As a result, most of the Baltic tribes disappeared through assimilation and conquest. The Latvian tribes were subdued by German crusaders during the 13th century. Only the Lithuanians managed to create an independent state when they united against the threat of the Teutonic Knights, a crusading order which had conquered Prussia and sought to establish control throughout the Baltic. During the middle of the 13th century Lithuania briefly became a Christian realm under King Mindaugas, but after his assassination in 1263, most of the country abandoned Christianity and returned to traditional religious practices.

After a short interregnum which followed Mindaugas' death, Lithuania established herself as an important East European state. The real founder of medieval Lithuanian power was Grand Duke Gediminas (1316-1341), who established Vilnius as the capital of the Lithuanian state, annexed many Slavic lands to the east and initiated diplomatic contacts with West European powers, including the papacy. However, Gediminas devoted most of his attention to the two problems that were to bedevil the Grand Duchy for centuries: defense against the powerful Teutonic Knights in the west and competition with emerging Muscovy for control of the predominantly Orthodox Slavic lands in the east, although the latter problem was not nearly as important for him as for his successors. Gediminas was followed by his son, Algirdas (1345-1377), who conquered additional eastern territories, including Kiev, and ruled in close cooperation with his brother, Duke Kęstutis of Trakai. In 1386 Algirdas' son Jogaila (Pol. Jagiełło) accepted the Polish crown: The Grand Duchy of Lithuania and the Kingdom of Poland now entered into a dynastic alliance which provided the military power to decisively defeat the Teutonic Knights at Grunwald in 1410. In 1387, after Jogaila's baptism, Lithuania once again formally accepted Roman Catholicism, which became the dominant religious and cultural force in the ethnographic Lithuanian lands. As Poland's King under the name Władysław II, Jogaila initiated a Polish-Lithuanian dynasty that was to rule much of Central Europe until 1572.

Lithuania reached the zenith of her power and influence under Jogaila's cousin, Grand Duke Vytautas (1392-1430), who ruled independently of Cracow. After his death, Polish culture became increasingly dominant in Lithuania, especially among powerful noble families, such as the Radziwiłłs (Lith. Radvila or Radvilas). Gradually, Polish language and culture penetrated most of the landowning and urban elite. By the early 19th century the Lithuanian language was, with few exceptions, preserved only among the peasantry and the lesser gentry in Samogitia or Žemaitija (western Lithuania). For this reason, until the 20th century, the country's nobility and urban dwellers viewed Lithuanian as a peasant dialect rather than as a national language.

Despite the Grand Duchy's loss of its easternmost Russian possessions and dependencies to the growing power of Muscovy, the period between the early 1500s and the middle of the 17th century was an age of considerable cultural and economic achievement. Catholic Lithuania maintained close ties to Central and Western Europe and was, thus, profoundly influenced by the Renaissance and the Reformation. The influence of the Renaissance was most visible in the country's architecture: many new churches in the Gothic and Baroque styles were constructed in Vilnius with the help of Italian artisans. The Grand Duke's court encouraged the dissemination of letters and the arts. The Reformation had an even greater impact on Lithuania's cultural life. Lutheranism became the religion of the people in the predominantly Lithuanian regions of East Prussia, while Calvinism engulfed much of the Grand Duchy during the late 16th and early 17th centuries. The spread of Protestantism encouraged the development of the vernacular. The first known Lithuanian-language book, a catechism written by the

Lutheran pastor Martynas Mažvydas, was published in 1547. In turn, the successful Counter-Reformation, led by the Jesuits and supported by the crown, not only restored the primacy of Catholicism, but was instrumental in encouraging the spread of education. The University of Vilnius began as a Jesuit academy in 1579 under a charter granted by King Stephen Batory and Pope Gregory XIII.

The 16th century was also a period of far-reaching legal and economic reforms. In 1529, the Grand Duchy issued the Lithuanian Statute, a comprehensive legal code that underwent several revisions and remained in force until 1840. By the standards of the age, the Lithuanian state tolerated considerable religious diversity among its Protestant, Catholic, Orthodox, Jewish and Muslim subjects: the Third Lithuanian Statute of 1588 explicitly mandated religious tolerance. In 1547 Sigismund Augustus initiated the great agrarian transformation known as the Volok Reform, named after the unit of land that the Grand Duchy assigned to an average peasant household. This agrarian reform determined the boundaries of the crown domains and established villages on the Western model, which stimulated agriculture by promoting the three-field system of cultivation on the manorial farms. The new forms of land tenure also encouraged grain exports, which became the mainstay of the Lithuanian economy and assisted the development of urban life. In general, the Grand Duchy of Lithuania encouraged the immigration of skilled craftsmen and merchants, particularly Germans and Jews, who became an important economic force in Lithuania.

The Polish-Lithuanian Commonwealth, 1569-1795

The major external threat to the Grand Duchy of Lithuania was the growing power of the Muscovite state. Under the reign of Casimir (Grand Duke 1440-1492; King of Poland 1447-1492) Lithuania experienced her first substantial territorial losses to Muscovy. During the 16th and 17th centuries, the Grand Duchy fought numerous wars against Muscovy, often concluded by short-lived treaties mandating "eternal peace." The military balance in this conflict favored the Muscovites who steadily rolled back the Grand Duchy's previous conquests. The growing Russian threat forced Lithuania to strengthen ties to Poland, despite the desire of the Lithuanian magnates to preserve the country's independence. In 1569, the Lithuanian and Polish diets negotiated the Union of Lublin under the aegis of King Sigismund Augustus (1548-1572), the last of the Jagiellonian monarchs. This treaty, which established the Polish-Lithuanian Commonwealth, limited Lithuania's independence and transferred Ukraine to the Kingdom of Poland. Many Poles viewed the Union as the formation of a single nation; however, until the Partitions of the late 18th century, the Grand Duchy maintained its own administrative, legal, military and monetary systems.

The Union of Lublin failed to stem Lithuania's political and military decline. The Jagiellonian dynasty was followed by two years of rule by Henry Valois, the brother of French King Charles IX, but he left in 1574 to assume the French throne. Sensing the weakness of the royal power, the gentry demanded ever increasing privileges at the expense of the monarchy which had become elective rather than hereditary. Valois was followed by the energetic and able Hungarian duke Stefan Batory (1576-1587) who successfully contained the expansionist plans of the Muscovite Tsar, Ivan the Terrible. After Batory, the nobility turned to Sigismund III Vasa (1587-1632) who was, for a time, also concurrently King of Sweden. Sigismund was followed by his son Władysław IV (1632-1648) and then a nephew, John Casimir (1648-1668).

The Vasa kings presided over the Commonwealth during an extraordinarily complex and volatile epoch in Eastern Europe. When Russia underwent the infamous "Time of Troubles" (1598-1613), Sigismund tried to seize the Muscovite throne and Polish-Lithuanian forces briefly occupied Moscow itself. However, with the accession of the Romanov dynasty in 1613, Russian power waxed again. In the mid-17th century a series of military disasters befell Poland-Lithuania. The Cossack incursions, particularly those led by Bohdan Khmelnitsky, destroyed much of Poland, but they also reached into Lithuanian-ruled Belarus. The Cossacks' decision to swear allegiance to Tsar Alexis in 1654 led the Commonwealth into a 13-year war with Russia. Lithuania's military fortunes reached a nadir in 1655 when Russian troops seized Vilnius and destroyed most of the city, the first time the country's capital had fallen to a foreign foe. The Treaty of Andrusovo in 1667 ceded Smolensk, Kiev and left-bank Ukraine to Russia.

King Sigismund Vasa's attempts to maintain his Swedish throne in absentia meant more travails for the already overburdened Commonwealth by drawing Poland-Lithuania into a war with the King's Lutheran enemies in Sweden. By 1629 the new Swedish ruler Gustavus Adolphus had won most of Livonia, then a vassal state of the Polish-Lithuanian Commonwealth. The Swedish advance resumed again in 1655 under Charles X and proved so inexorable that the leaders of the Lithuanian Grand Duchy, already devastated by the Russian attack, drew up an act of dynastic union with Sweden at the town of Kėdainiai. However, Charles X showed little interest in pursuing this alliance and, in any case, by the late 1650s, the Swedes were in retreat. The treaty of Oliwa in 1660 ended Swedish claims in Poland-Lithuania, although Sweden retained Livonia.

The military and diplomatic reverses of the Commonwealth during the 17th century were accompanied by the progressive weakening of Poland-Lithuania's political, economic and social structures. The power of the landed aristocracy grew at the expense of the elected kings. The reigns of Michael Wiśniowiecki (1669-1674) and John Sobieski (1674-1696) were marked by successful wars against the Ottoman Turks, but little was done to stem domestic chaos. By the end of the 17th century, the royal election had become the object of bribery, international intrigue and foreign coercion demonstrated by the choice of the ambitious but inept Augustus II of Saxony, whose rule from 1697 until 1733 was interrupted by the five-year reign of the enlightened Stanisław Leszczyński (1704-1709). Even more disturbing for the political stability of the Commonwealth was the "election" of Augustus III (1733-1763) who, despite yet another challenge from Leszczyński, was elevated to the throne in a session of the diet surrounded by Russian troops.

At the beginning of the 18th century, internal disorder became endemic as political alliances of nobles, called confederations, battled each other for influence. Economic decline was exacerbated by a series of plagues (1708-1711) and the destruction inflicted by marauding Swedish and Russian armies during the Great Northern War. In East Prussia the plague killed at least half of the predominantly Lithuanian-speaking population, leaving vast areas of vacant farmland available for subsequent German colonization, permanently altering the national balance in the region.

Despite these disasters, there were signs of recovery during the second half of the 18th century. In both Lithuania and Poland, agriculture and commerce revived as grain exports resumed. In addition, there were now serious calls for the reform of state and society, stimulated in part by the influence of the Enlightenment. Another important incentive for reform was the desire of the patriotic gentry to escape foreign domination which since the early 18th century took the form of a virtual Russian protectorate. However, Poland-Lithuania's neighbors, especially Russia, vigorously opposed any attempt to end the debilitating political anarchy in the Commonwealth. The reign of the last Polish-Lithuanian monarch, Stanisław August Poniatowski (1764-1795), was marked by external aggression and civil war as Commonwealth reformers sought to overcome foreign and domestic opposition to change.

Poniatowski's desire to establish an effective government in Poland-Lithuania surprised the Russians who expected this former consort of Catherine the Great to act as a loyal viceroy of St. Petersburg. The Empress' interference within the Commonwealth finally provoked an anti-Russian uprising in 1768, known as the Confederation of Bar. The conflict ended in the First Partition of 1772, when Russia, Prussia and Austria prevailed over Poland-Lithuania's cowed government and seized substantial shares of the Commonwealth's territory. The Grand Duchy lost Courland, Latgale, Polotsk, Vitebsk and a large area of Minsk province, regions which had been under Lithuanian rule for centuries.

This Partition of 1772 induced reform-minded Polish-Lithuanian gentry to undertake a campaign to save what remained of their state. The Commonwealth's Diet of 1773-1775 established a permanent governing council for Poland-Lithuania, which considerably restricted the autonomy of the Grand Duchy. However, the reform of the central government was offset by the fact that, during most of the late 18th century, Russia, Austria and Prussia exercised an informal veto over the government of Poland-Lithuania and even manipulated the country's new governing council for their own ends.

The turbulent last quarter-century of the Commonwealth's history was marked by attempts at reform against the opposition of Russia and the conservative aristocracy. The reform movement reached its peak during the historic session of the Four-Year Diet (1788-1792), which overhauled the Commonwealth's political system. The Diet abolished the Russian-controlled governing council, strengthened the Commonwealth's central government and greatly expanded the royal power. In April 1792 Polish-Lithuanian opponents of the Constitution formed the Confederation of Targowica and, supported by the Russian Army, attacked the Commonwealth's forces, led by the radical reformer and American Revolutionary War hero, Thaddeus Kościuszko, who was initially supported by the King. In August 1792 Russia's military superiority persuaded Poniatowski to abandon the struggle, whereupon Kościuszko went into exile, while the Polish-Lithuanian Army dispersed. Prussia and Russia seized the opportunity to carry out the Second Partition of the Commonwealth in 1793; the Lithuanian Grand Duchy lost most of Belarus, including Minsk. The disaster of 1793 provoked the more radical elements in the Commonwealth to call for a national uprising against foreign domination, which was launched in March 1794 with Kościuszko once again at the helm of the anti-Russian forces. Kościuszko's rebels briefly seized Warsaw and Vilnius, but after initial successes, the Polish-Lithuanian revolt was crushed by the combined might of Prussia and Russia.

The suppression of the 1794 uprising signaled the end of the Polish-Lithuanian Commonwealth. Stanisław August, its last King-Grand Duke, abdicated in November 1795. At the same time, Russia, Prussia and Austria agreed to the final dismemberment of Poland-Lithuania. The formal Treaty of Partition was signed in

January 1797 in St. Petersburg. The Hapsburgs seized much of south-central Poland, including Cracow. Prussia gained central Poland and the regions adjacent to East Prussia, including the ethnic Lithuanian areas south and west of the Nemunas River. Most of the Grand Duchy of Lithuania was incorporated into the Russian Empire.

Lithuania Under the Tsars

The dissolution of the Grand Duchy in 1795 at first did not profoundly alter Lithuania's cultural and social life. Under Tsar Paul I (1796-1801) and the relatively liberal Alexander I (1801-1825), the Lithuanian nobility preserved its power and influence within the society. More significant changes occurred in south-western Lithuania, the region on the left bank of the Nemunas River, which included about a fifth of the ethnic Lithuanian population and had passed under Prussian rule (1795-1807) following the final partition of the Commonwealth. This region, variously known as Užnemunė, Suvalkija or Suwałki, was later included in Napoleon's vassal state, the Duchy of Warsaw (1807-1815), and then remained a part of Congress Poland until 1874. Here the introduction of the Napoleonic Code resulted in the abolition of serfdom in 1807.

The Napoleonic invasion of Russia in 1812 briefly stirred hopes of liberation from Tsarist rule when some Lithuanian nobles launched a plan for restoring the Grand Duchy. Although Napoleon's defeat meant the return of Russian rule, the relatively relaxed Tsarist policy towards Lithuania during the first quarter of the 19th century permitted an impressive cultural renaissance. In 1803, prodded by his friend Adam Czartoryski, Alexander I had established the Vilnius Principal School as an imperial university and for the next three decades it became the seat of learning for the lands of the old Commonwealth and a major center of science and scholarship in Eastern Europe. While this unique period in Lithuania's intellectual history was primarily a contribution to the Polish national movement and its culture, it also stimulated interest among some of the country's scholars in the language and culture of the Lithuanian-speaking peasantry.

Despite the reality of Tsarist power, the Lithuanian gentry's desire to reestablish the Commonwealth persisted. The accession of the reactionary Nicholas I (1825-1855) to the Russian throne and attempts to curtail the autonomy of the Kingdom of Poland triggered an armed uprising in Warsaw in November 1830. The Polish uprising spread to Lithuania where the students at the University of Vilnius and officers of the Lithuanian Corps led the insurrection. The rebels proclaimed independence from Russia, promising to restore the federal union of Poland and Lithuania. The insurgents were decisively defeated in July 1831 and soon after anti-Russian guerilla activity also came to an end.

The Tsarist government had suppressed the insurgency with harsh methods and after the war Nicholas I instituted a policy of Russification aimed at transforming Lithuania into a Russian province in fact as well as in name. The University of Vilnius was closed in 1832. The Lithuanian Statute was abolished in 1840. About 40,000 members of the petty gentry were deprived of their charters of nobility and many were deported to the Caucasus and the Russian interior. For the first time in Lithuania's history, the Catholic Church was subjected to systematic persecution. As a result of Nicholas' policy of repression, hundreds of Lithuanians, primarily from among the nobility, fled to the West, including such well-known cultural figures as Adam Mickiewicz and Joachim Lelewel (1786-1861). Tsar Nicholas' doctrine of Official Nationality, a reactionary blend of autocratic power, religious intolerance and Russian nationalism, became the guiding light of Tsarist government policy.

The Origins of Modern Lithuanian Nationalism and Social Change After 1861

The Russian government's repressive policies coincided with the first stirrings of the modern Lithuanian national movement. The brief renaissance in the University of Vilnius had stimulated an interest in Lithuanian culture and language among the petty gentry of Samogitia. The foremost of the Samogitian literati were Dionizas Poška, who dreamed of introducing the Lithuanian language into public life, and Simonas Stanevičius, whose work displayed a national consciousness separate from that of the Poles. In 1845 the historian Simonas Daukantas (1793-1864) published the first historical work in the Lithuanian language. During the mid-19th century Motiejus Valančius (1801-1875), the Bishop of Samogitia between 1850 and 1875, laid the foundations of the modern Lithuanian national movement. Valančius published numerous secular and religious Lithuanian-language works for the peasantry. He also organized an extensive primary school system in the villages and founded the popular temperance societies, which were instrumental in encouraging the reading of popular literature in the Lithuanian language.

The reign of Nicholas' liberal successor, Tsar Alexander II (1855-1881), was a period of ferment in Lithuania. The Tsar's emancipation of the serfs in 1861 came at a time of renewed unrest which developed into a full-fledged revolt when, on February 1, 1863, an underground Lithuanian Committee declared itself the country's provisional government and called upon the populace to rise up against the Russians. Despite widespread support from virtually all strata of Lithuanian society, the insurrection was suppressed with a great deal of bloodshed by the Russian Army; hundreds were executed and thousands were deported to Siberia during a reign of terror engineered by the Governor-General of Vilnius, M. N. Muravyev. The Russian government severely restricted the Catholic Church and adopted an even harsher policy of cultural Russification. The Polish language was banned from Lithuania's secondary school system and the Catholic Lithuanian primary educational network was closed. At the same time, Muravyev tried to curry favor with the Lithuanian-speaking peasantry by improving the conditions of the Tsarist Emancipation, but this policy failed to create goodwill towards the Russian authorities.

The 1860s were a turning point in Lithuania's modern history. The insurrection of 1863-1864 marked the last time that Poles and

Lithuanians joined together in an attempt to restore the old Commonwealth. Politically, the most important development was the emergence of the Lithuanian-speaking peasantry as a social and economic force. Although interest in Lithuanian language and culture had been growing since the early 19th century, it was the subsequent appearance of the Lithuanian-speaking intelligentsia of peasant origin that initiated the modernization of Lithuanian society and culture.

This new educated elite, which gained prominence during the late 19th century, reaffirmed a national and cultural identity distinct from that of the Poles and Russians. The most prominent secular figures in the Lithuanian national movement of the 19th century were Dr. Jonas Basanavičius, widely considered the patriarch of the national cultural renaissance, and Vincas Kudirka, a skilled satirist and editor, who was instrumental in politicizing Lithuanian resentment of Russian rule. Lithuania's younger Catholic clergy also came under the influence of Lithuanian nationalism. Although the Tsar banned the publication of Lithuanian books in the Latin alphabet in 1864, the prohibition was circumvented by the publication of Lithuanian-language books in Prussia (and later in the United States). The distribution of the illegal publications through a clandestine international network involved many people in the national movement. The struggle against the book ban was so effective that the Russian government lifted it in 1904. The "book smuggling" movement provided Lithuanian nationalism with a cause, political cohesion and a sense of shared injustice that furthered political radicalization.

By the turn of the century, as Lithuanian nationalism spread among the intelligentsia, clergy and urbanites, Lithuanian culture emerged from its traditional village milieu, while the national movement became politically diverse. Eventually, it harbored conservative, clerical, liberal and socialist factions with differing political agendas. On December 4-5, 1905 a Lithuanian gathering of about 2,000 delegates, known as the Great Lithuanian Assembly (Seimas) of Vilnius, convened in Lithuania's historic capital. This first modern Lithuanian political conference proclaimed as its goal the establishment of an autonomous, democratic Lithuania with equal rights for all the country's nationalities. The Revolution of 1905 was suppressed in Lithuania and in the other parts of the Russian Empire within two years but the basis for modern Lithuanian politics had been laid. Some Lithuanian politicians were elected to the Duma, Russia's new parliament permitted by the Tsar's October Manifesto, where they lobbied for national autonomy and continually raised the "Lithuanian question" in St. Petersburg.

By the eve of World War I, Lithuanian society had undergone considerable change. While Lithuania's industrial development had been modest, the cultural and economic progress of the peasantry compared favorably with that in the Russian Empire as a whole. The growing political consciousness and economic importance of the Lithuanian-speaking majority changed the balance of power within Lithuanian society. The emergence of an ethnic Lithuanian professional and commercial stratum, as well as an urban working class, however small, hastened the social modernization of Lithuanian-speaking society, once largely trapped within the confines of the traditional village and beholden to the Polonized manor. Most of the landed gentry, contemptuous of the peasantry's emerging national consciousness, continued to cling to their aristocratic outlook and resisted the diminution of their role in the society.

Despite these significant social changes, Lithuania remained an economically underdeveloped region. The population of the ethnographic Lithuanian lands (including the Lithuanian-speaking areas of East Prussia), which had grown to nearly four million before the Great War, was overwhelmingly rural. Lithuania's towns and cities were largely populated by Poles, Jews and Germans, who made up a majority of those employed in the professions, commerce, trade and industry. Only 21.6 percent of the inhabitants of Kaunas, Lithuania's second largest city, were reported to be ethnic Lithuanians in 1909. Before the outbreak of World War I, ethnic Lithuanians made up scarcely 2 percent of the population in Vilnius, Lithuania's largest city and most important cultural and economic center.

The outbreak of the First World War in August 1914 did not immediately alter the political goals of the Lithuanian intelligentsia, the majority of whom supported the idea of national autonomy within a democratized Russian federation. Influential Lithuanian leaders, such as Jonas Basanavičius and Martynas Yčas, while dissatisfied with the government's response to these political demands, initially expressed loyalty to the Tsar. They hoped that a victorious and grateful Russia would unite the ethnic Lithuanian lands of East Prussia with those in Russian-ruled Lithuania. However, the early Russian military successes were soon reversed and in the spring of 1915 the German Army entered Lithuania; by year's end, the Russians had abandoned Vilnius, ending more than a century of Tsarist rule in Lithuania.

World War I and the Emergence of Independent Lithuania

The Russian retreat of 1915 and the subsequent German occupation of Lithuania inflicted destruction on a scale that the country had not seen since the wars and pestilence of the early 18th century. Nearly a half-million inhabitants either fled or were forcibly evacuated eastward. In November 1914 the Lithuanian Committee to Assist the Victims of the War was founded in Vilnius; after the Germans took the city in September 1915, a part of the group was moved to Petrograd. In Russia, this Committee became a kind of government-in-exile for Lithuanians displaced by the war. In Lithuania itself, the German military administration exploited the country for the war effort through agricultural requisitions and forced labor, arousing opposition among the populace.

Initially confident of victory, the Kaiser's government planned to annex Lithuania and other adjacent territories. However, the entry of the United States into the war and Germany's deteriorating military and economic situation forced the Kaiser to accommodate the national aspirations of the Lithuanians and the other East European peoples. The Kaiser's government sought to appease popular discontent in Lithuania by allowing the organization of a native advisory council. In September 1917 a Lithuanian political conference met in Vilnius and selected a Council, known as the Taryba, which represented the major non-Bolshevik political parties. On December 11, 1917, the Taryba proclaimed an independent Lithuanian state on the basis of close economic and military ties with Germany. However, by early 1918 the Taryba, hoping to preserve its credibility and Lithuanian political unity, began to distance itself from Berlin. On February 16, 1918, the Taryba issued a declaration announcing the restoration of the Lithuanian state based on a democratic political structure without mentioning relations with Germany. The Kaiser issued a qualified recognition of Lithuania on March 23, 1918; during the next few months there was complex political maneuvering between the Lithuanian authorities and Germany, whose forces still occupied Lithuania. The Lithuanian independence movement received crucial financial support from Lithuanians in the United States, while the Lithuanian intelligentsia in Western Europe lobbied the Allies to support their country's independence.

On November 11, 1918, the day the Germans signed the armistice with the Allies, the first Lithuanian cabinet under President Antanas Smetona and Prime Minister Augustinas Voldemaras took office. Lithuania's survival was in large part due to the able second Prime Minister Mykolas Sleževičius who, together with his center-left cabinets, hung on during the trying months of early 1919 as the new Lithuanian state slowly consolidated its position. The successive Lithuanian governments, protected by their own meager forces and a deteriorating German military umbrella, were able to survive a succession of emergencies during 1919-1920: a Bolshevik invasion and the subsequent creation of the short-lived Lithuanian-Belarusan Soviet Republic (Litbel) in the east; continued obstruction by the German military establishment; a devastating attack by well-equipped White Russian and German volunteers called Bermondtists in the west; a Polish invasion and attempted coup d'état; and recurrent financial crises. A combination of factors, including volunteer enthusiasm, German military assistance and the Allied presence in the Baltic, allowed the Lithuanian Army to drive out the Bolsheviks from most of Lithuania by late 1919 and to fend off the other threats to independence.

On July 12, 1920 Soviet Russia signed a peace treaty with the Republic of Lithuania in Moscow, renouncing in perpetuity all Russian claims to the country. The treaty granted Lithuania extensive territory, including the regions of Grodno, Suwałki, and Augustów, lands which had once been part of the Grand Duchy of Lithuania but were now inhabited primarily by peasants speaking Belarusan or Polish. Lithuania was never to acquire the boundaries established by the 1920 agreement with Moscow, primarily because of Polish power in the region. In 1919 the major Western powers had also extended de facto recognition to Lithuania and the other Baltic governments, and this was soon followed by de jure recognition. In 1921 Lithuania became a member of the League of Nations. The United States government, reluctant to violate the territorial integrity of Russia and skeptical of the viability of the Lithuanian state, delayed de jure recognition until 1922.

Struggles for Territory: Vilnius and Klaipėda (1918-1924)

Lithuania's conflict with Poland over Vilnius defined much of her foreign and domestic policy during the interwar period. To Lithuanians, Vilnius was their country's natural political center and historic capital. This ethnically divided city was one of the most important European centers of Jewish cultural life, and, in the 19th century, it became a stronghold of Polish culture and education. In 1917-1918 Vilnius was the seat of the Lithuanian Taryba and other Lithuanian institutions; on the other hand, Vilnius remained the hub of Polish influence in the Catholic lands of eastern Lithuania and western Belarus.

After the Germans withdrew from Vilnius in January 1919, the city changed hands a number of times among Lithuanians, Bolsheviks and Poles. As the Red Army retreated from the Polish counteroffensive in August 1920, clashes occurred between Polish and Lithuanian forces as both sides vied for control in the vacuum left by the Bolsheviks. On October 7, 1920 Polish and Lithuanian delegations signed an agreement at Suwałki which drew a demarcation line leaving Vilnius under Lithuanian administration.

However, within hours of the signing, Gen. Lucjan Żeligowski, under secret orders of the Polish government, led a force of alleged mutineers in an attack on the Lithuanian Army, seizing Vilnius and its environs. The Conference of Ambassadors recognized the Lithuanian-Polish armistice line established after the attack as the de jure frontier between the two states in March 1923. Lithuania never accepted this decision and persisted in claiming Vilnius as its capital. Vilnius was to remain part of Poland until 1939.

Another thorny territorial issue was the Baltic port of Klaipėda, which under the name of Memel, had been part of East Prussia since the 13th century. By the early 1900s, East Prussia was thoroughly Germanized, although a substantial Lithuanian-speaking population survived near Klaipėda and along the Prussian border with Russia. Article 99 of the Versailles Treaty detached the East Prussian lands on the right bank of the Nemunas River from Germany and placed them under an Allied mandate. In January 1923 a detachment of insurgents armed and encouraged by the Lithuanian government invaded Klaipėda and quickly overpowered the port's small French garrison. The Allies, preoccupied with the Ruhr crisis, accepted Lithuanian control of the region. On May 8, 1924 Lithuania signed a convention with the major Allied Powers (Britain, France, Italy, Japan), which transferred formal sovereignty over Klaipėda Territory to Lithuania. The Klaipėda Convention contained provisions ensuring the territory's autonomy and the rights of the German-speaking inhabitants. The issues of Vilnius and Klaipėda became sources of friction between Lithuania and her two powerful neighbors: Poland and Germany.

Domestic Politics: Parliamentary Democracy (1920-1926) and Authoritarian Rule (1926-1940)

The government announced elections to the Constituent Assembly in the spring of 1920, which returned a clear majority for a Catholic coalition led by the Christian Democratic Party. The Social Democrats and Populists provided the center-left opposition. The Chairman of the Assembly, Aleksandras Stulginskis, was elected President of the Republic. In October 1922 the Constituent Assembly ended its term after enacting the important Land Reform Act of 1922 and approving a new constitution which provided for a parliament, the Seimas, elected for a three-year term on the basis of proportional representation; in turn, the Seimas chose the President. The three dominant political movements during the next four years of democracy were the Catholic-dominated Christian Democratic Bloc, the Peasant Populists, and the Social Democrats, who espoused socialism but were also committed to Lithuania's independence and political pluralism. The antidemocratic parties of the right and left extremes were weak. The Communists had a small though vocal following, primarily among urban workers and the national minorities, especially Jews and Russians. On the right, the Nationalist Union gathered together the more conservative elements disenchanted with the feuding between the Catholic and anticlerical factions, but it did not win any seats to the Seimas until May of 1926.

Lithuania's parliamentary democracy, as in most of the other East European states, was beset by serious difficulties. The tradition of democratic political culture was weak and economic troubles led to social unrest. Official corruption became a major political issue. The election campaign during the spring of 1926 proved especially bitter. The center and left parties fanned anti-Church passions, while many Catholic Bloc politicians accused everyone to their left of Bolshevism. The elections brought to power a center-left coalition of Peasant Populists and Social Democrats led by two respected statesmen: Prime Minister Mykolas Sleževičius and President Kazys Grinius. The government abolished martial law, reduced the military budget and proposed to secularize education. Virtually from its inception, the new government faced virulent opposition from many quarters. The Army was angered by the government's intentions to cut the military budget. The sense of instability and disorder encouraged a right-wing reaction. On December 17, 1926 a group of rightist Army officers disbanded the Seimas and forced President Grinius to appoint Nationalist politician Augustinas Voldemaras to head a new government. After Grinius' resignation, a rump session of the Seimas dominated by

Nationalists and Christian Democrats elected Antanas Smetona President.

Smetona's failure to call for new elections as required by the constitution led to the Christian Democrats' withdrawal from the ruling coalition in March of 1927. Smetona dismissed the Seimas and for the next twelve years the Nationalists ruled alone. In May 1928 the government announced a revised constitution concentrating executive power in the presidency. Political activity was severely circumscribed and in 1935 political parties were banned altogether (the Nationalist Union claimed it was not a political party). After the President dismissed Voldemaras from the government in 1929, his followers attempted to return the former Prime Minister to power. The most serious conspiracy was a military mutiny in 1934 involving the Army's chief of staff. However, except for a part of the younger officer corps and nationalist students, Voldemaras' faction had little support in the society at large. Embarrassed by agrarian unrest in southwestern Lithuania during the economic crisis of 1935-1936, the Smetona government sponsored an indirect vote by a restricted electorate which effectively excluded the opposition. The Fourth Seimas approved the constitution of 1938, which further entrenched the Nationalist monopoly of power, which was not seriously tested until the spring of 1939.

The Nationalist ideology was a mixture of agrarian populism, the personality cult of Smetona as the "Leader of the Nation," a stress on national unity and some superficial borrowings from Italian fascism. However, Smetona shied away from those values which he thought were inconsistent with Western and Christian tradition. Most of the Nationalist leadership explicitly rejected racism and viewed Nazism with fear and suspicion. In principle, the Lithuanian Nationalists were favorably disposed toward religion; Smetona emphasized the importance of the Catholic Church as a partner in preserving Lithuanian national values and maintaining the moral health of the citizenry. While the Nationalists censored the newspapers, there was no serious attempt to challenge the country's tradition of ethnic, cultural and religious pluralism. Under Smetona,

Lithuania remained a relatively open society: there were few restrictions on the importation of foreign books, periodicals or ideas.

The international crisis that erupted in the late 1930s weakened the Nationalist dictatorship. The ultimatum from Poland in March 1938 caused widespread domestic dissatisfaction. The loss of Klaipėda in March 1939 and the prodding of the popular commander of the Lithuanian Army, General Stasys Raštikis, forced Smetona to appoint a coalition cabinet of national unity in March 1939, headed by General Jonas Černius. The Černius government stirred hopes for a democratization of the political system but it lasted only eight months. A new government under Prime Minister Antanas Merkys was formed in November 1939, which was more in the authoritarian mold acceptable to the Nationalists, most of whom resisted sharing power.

Society, Economy and National Culture Between the Wars

The population of Lithuania stood at about 2,250,000 during the early 1920s. More than 80 percent of the population were ethnic Lithuanians. The largest minorities were the Jews (7 percent), Germans (4 percent), Poles (3 percent), and Russians (2.7 percent). In the early 1920s about three-fourths of the population was engaged in agriculture. Lithuania underwent a steady, though modest, urbanization during the years of independence. By the late 1930s about a fourth of the country's people were classified as urban.

The ethnic structure of Lithuania's towns and cities experienced a major transformation between the wars. Before World War I, not a single city in Lithuania had a majority of Lithuanian speakers. During the first decade of independence, with the exception of Vilnius and Klaipėda, all of Lithuania's major cities acquired ethnic Lithuanian majorities. The predominance of Lithuanians in the cities reflected the change in the country's power structure. For the first time in centuries, ethnic Lithuanians controlled the political establishment. They also rapidly achieved prominence in the economy, professions and cultural life. The Land Reforms of 1922, the introduction of Lithuanian as the official language and the development of national education, had revolutionized the role of ethnic Lithuanians in the society and effectively modernized Lithuanian culture. This process signified a social revolution: A previously disenfranchised majority achieved political power and social influence proportionate to its numbers.

The economic reconstruction of Lithuania after the Great War was complicated by the need to wean industry away from Russian markets. Germany's trade embargo against Lithuania during the early 1930s, and the fall of agricultural prices during the worldwide depression exacerbated the problem. Despite these difficulties, Lithuania achieved considerable gains in farm productivity. After the land reform eliminated the old manorial system, medium-size and small farms predominated; in 1930 they made up an estimated 78 percent of all farms. During the 1930s, pork and dairy products, especially high grade butter, accounted for the majority of Lithuania's exports.

Despite these gains in productivity, Lithuanian agriculture still suffered structural weaknesses. Many peasants remained indebted and farm failures were frequent. In 1930 about 45 percent of the farms were under ten hectares in size; the smallest of these belonged to destitute peasants. Their conditions of life were difficult and explain the large Lithuanian emigration to South America, particularly Brazil and Argentina, during the 1920s. The mechanization of farming and the electrification of the villages proceeded slowly. The relationship of industrial and farm prices was extremely unfavorable to the peasantry. The social and economic problems of Lithuania's villagers gave rise to rural protest movements. However, during the late 1930s, the condition of the peasantry improved when limited welfare programs were introduced and day laborers' wages rose substantially.

Lithuania's most developed industries were textiles and food-processing, particularly the meat and dairy sectors. The Maistas Company, the nation's largest native concern, played an important role in developing the economy. Overall, between 1930 and 1938 industrial production more than doubled. In general, it can be said that Lithuania achieved a solid measure of economic progress during its two decades of independence despite the obstacles: the lack of investment capital; the weak industrial base; the worldwide depression of the 1930s and the need to reorient exports because of the 1932 German trade embargo.

Lithuania's major foreign trade partners were Germany and Britain, the latter acquiring an increasing share of Lithuanian exports during the middle and late 1930s. In 1938 Britain absorbed nearly 40 percent of Lithuanian exports, while Germany's share was 27 percent. Meat and butter constituted over a third of total exports; livestock (pigs and horses), grains, flax and lumber made up most of the rest. Manufactured products, particularly machinery, and raw materials (coal, oil, iron) made up most of the imports. After a shaky start in the early 1920s, the currency and finances of the Republic proved remarkably stable. Lithuania's foreign debt was small and domestic obligations totaled only 65,000,000 *litai*. The government's 1938 budget of 366,000,000 *litai* was practically balanced. The defense budget took the largest share, nearly a fourth of expenditures.

Lithuania's social welfare structure between the wars was relatively weak, although it was expanded and strengthened during the late 1930s. Infant mortality was reduced by more than a third between the mid 1920s and the later 1930s. While the number of doctors grew slowly, the number of hospital beds increased five-fold between 1920 and 1939. There was no unemployment insurance, although after 1927 the government periodically utilized public works projects to reduce the jobless rate. The greatest progress in independent Lithuania was made in the field of education and culture. The laws of the Republic of Lithuania mandated religious and ethnic equality, as well as cultural autonomy. During independence the illiteracy rate was reduced from 44 percent to less than 15 percent. While formal education in the native language had been extremely limited before independence, after 1918 the Lithuanian government systematically expanded education from the primary to the university level. Compulsory primary education was introduced in 1928 and an adult literacy campaign was begun. The number of primary schools quadrupled between the wars: by 1938 there were 2,599 primary schools with 300,000 pupils and nearly

100 secondary schools with over 20,000 students. A number of technical and specialized higher schools were established as well as a national university in Kaunas. In addition to public education, Lithuania possessed numerous private schools most of which were operated by the Catholic Church and the national minorities.

Cultural development expanded in new directions. Opera, theater, ballet and contemporary music were integrated into the national culture. Despite some official censorship, the number and variety of Lithuanian-language publications rose rapidly, including scholarly and literary journals that exposed the growing number of educated readers to the ideas current in the West. Sports became widely popular. During the mid 1930s a basketball craze swept the country after Lithuania, assisted by Lithuanian-American stars from the U. S. Olympic team, twice won the European championships: in Riga in 1937 and in Kaunas in 1939.

Crisis, War and the End of Independence (1938-1940)

During the last two years of interwar independence, Lithuania's larger neighbors, Poland, Germany and the USSR, gradually reduced Lithuania's diplomatic freedom of action through military and political pressure. The first major crisis came on March 17, 1938, when, after a border incident, Poland presented an ultimatum to the Lithuanian government demanding the commencement of diplomatic relations under the threat of military intervention. Lithuania accepted the ultimatum and diplomatic ties were established between Kaunas and Warsaw at the end of March 1938.

At the same time, the situation in Klaipėda Territory deteriorated. On March 20, 1939 Germany presented an ultimatum to the Lithuanian government demanding the immediate transfer of Klaipėda Territory to the Reich. Once again, faced with overwhelming force, Smetona's government retreated. The loss of Klaipėda provoked considerable domestic dissatisfaction with the Nationalist government, which had repeatedly promised to defend the country's territorial integrity.

The Soviet Union's position as a power broker in the approaching conflict between the Western Powers and Germany proved fatal to the independence of the Baltic States. When France and Britain proved reluctant to accommodate the Soviet demands for military access to Poland and a free hand in the Baltic States, Stalin struck a deal with Hitler. After some intense negotiations concerning mutual interests in Eastern Europe, the USSR and Germany signed the Soviet-German Treaty of Nonaggression, or the Molotov-Ribbentrop Pact, on August 23, 1939. The treaty contained a secret protocol, which divided most of Eastern Europe into spheres of influence. Lithuania, including the disputed Vilnius region, and the western half of Poland were assigned to Germany; the Soviets were to receive Finland, Estonia, Latvia and Bessarabia (Moldova).

After the German invasion of Poland on September 1, 1939, the USSR attacked eastern Poland on September 17. While the Germans initially pressed Lithuania to join in the attack and regain Vilnius, the Lithuanian government adhered to a position of neutrality. On September 28, 1939 Ribbentrop and Molotov signed the German-Soviet Borders and Friendship Treaty, which contained additional secret protocols, one of which transferred most of Lithuania into the Soviet sphere of influence, except for a slice in the southwestern region of the country that was assigned to the Reich.

In late September Stalin began to consolidate his gains by forcing the Baltic States to accept pacts of mutual assistance with the USSR. In early October the Lithuanian government and the USSR signed the Soviet-Lithuanian Treaty of Mutual Assistance and the Transfer of Vilnius on October 10, 1939. The Soviet-Lithuanian mutual assistance pact provided for the stationing of 20,000 Soviet troops in Lithuania for fifteen years, but guaranteed noninterference in the Republic's internal affairs. In Lithuania, the shock of accepting foreign military bases was, to a large degree, attenuated by the population's joy at the prospect of recovering Vilnius which, according to the treaty, was to be transferred to Lithuania.

The war and the acquisition of Vilnius posed difficult problems for the Lithuanian government. The internment of thousands of Polish troops who had fled to Lithuania and the care of tens of thousands of Polish civilian refugees strained a government budget amidst shortages caused by interruptions in international trade. Most of the Vilnius region was less-developed than the rest of Lithuania and its administration was complicated by tensions with the Polish-speaking population of the area who constituted a majority. Yet despite the hardships brought on by the war, the Soviet-Lithuanian relationship seemed tranquil until the spring of 1940.

On May 25, 1940 the Soviet government alleged that Lithuanian authorities were encouraging the desertion of Soviet soldiers in Lithuania and conducting espionage against the Red Army. The Kremlin charged that these activities proved Lithuania's hostile attitude towards the Soviet Union and its unwillingness to abide by the Lithuanian-Soviet mutual assistance pact. The Soviet government also undertook a broad propaganda campaign against the Baltic States in the spring of 1940 claiming that they were adopting a dangerously pro-British course. The Kremlin charged that Lithuania was conspiring with Latvia and Estonia to create a Baltic alliance directed against the Soviet Union. On June 11 Lithuanian Foreign Minister Juozas Urbšys brought to Moscow a personal letter from Smetona to President Kalinin of the USSR, promising strict Lithuanian adherence to the agreements undertaken the previous October. On midnight of June 14 Molotov delivered a Soviet ultimatum to Mr. Urbšys in the Kremlin, demanding the arrest of Lithuania's interior minister and security chief, the formation of a government satisfactory to the USSR and, most important, the entry of additional Soviet forces. An answer was demanded as of ten o'clock on the morning of June 15, in effect providing the Lithuanian government only a few hours to respond.

During the early morning hours of June 15 the Lithuanian cabinet met to discuss the Soviet ultimatum; despite the President's support for armed resistance, the cabinet accepted the demands. At about noon on June 15, over two hundred thousand Soviet troops, supported by tanks, aircraft and artillery, crossed the border into

Lithuania. On June 17 similar ultimatums were presented to the Latvian and Estonian governments; within hours over a half-million Soviet troops were firmly in control of the Baltic States.

Lithuania's Annexation by the USSR and the First Year of Soviet Rule, 1940-1941

Following the Soviet occupation, Lithuania's affairs were directed by Vladimir Dekanozov, Moscow's plenipotentiary who arrived with the invading troops, and Nikolai Pozdniakov, the Soviet Ambassador to Lithuania. At their insistence, Acting President Antanas Merkys appointed a leftist journalist, Justas Paleckis, the new Prime Minister on June 17. Upon Merkys' resignation, Paleckis also became Acting President, a change of leadership that was of doubtful legality according to the succession provisions of the Lithuanian Constitution. Paleckis' cabinet was declared the People's Government (Lith. *Liaudies Vyriausybė*) and included some well-known Lithuanian democrats as well as Communist sympathizers. Within two weeks of the Soviet occupation, the Communist Party was legalized, leftist political prisoners were released, and decrees separating Church and State were promulgated.

In mid-July 1940 the USSR accelerated the process of Lithuania's Sovietization in a two-pronged strategy of neutralizing potential opposition and then staging Lithuania's annexation as an expression of popular will. On July 11-12, Communist-controlled security forces arrested hundreds of prominent Lithuanians, many of whom were deported to the Soviet Union. Virtually all non-Communist organizations were either banned or placed under the supervision of Lithuania's tiny Communist Party. The elections to Lithuania's People's Diet on July 16-17 were rigged in favor of the only permitted political group, the hastily formed, Communist-controlled Lithuanian Union of Labor. Despite a smaller than expected turnout, the Communist authorities proclaimed that 99.5 percent of eligible voters had cast nearly 99.2 percent of their ballots for the Union of Labor. The People's Diet, which met in Kaunas on

July 21-24, 1940, voted to proclaim a Soviet Socialist form of government and chose a delegation to petition for Lithuania's membership in the USSR, a request granted on August 3, 1940, when the Supreme Soviet in the Kremlin admitted the Lithuanian SSR into the Soviet Union. Most governments refused to recognize the Soviet Union's forcible annexation of the Baltic States and continued to accredit Baltic diplomatic missions.

During the first year of Soviet rule, the government sought to eliminate or transform those Lithuanian institutions which made the country distinct from the USSR, but the Sovietization policies in Lithuania aroused opposition. When the Soviet regime announced a land reform that would benefit landless peasants and the poorest smallholders, it temporarily gained some support among the rural populace; however, this advantage was quickly squandered by harsh taxation measures and policies that foreshadowed collectivization. The expropriation of private enterprises and bank accounts, as well as the replacement of the *litas* with rubles at a confiscatory exchange rate, invited the opposition of the propertied classes. The increasingly repressive Communist policy toward the Church aroused resentment in one of Eastern Europe's most Catholic countries.

By the spring of 1941 the anti-Soviet opposition in Lithuania had coalesced into an underground movement. In November 1940 a group of Lithuanian diplomats and activists, some of whom had escaped into Germany after the Soviet takeover, met in Berlin and founded the Lithuanian Activist Front (LAF), a coalition of all the major Lithuanian non-Communist groups dedicated to the restoration of Lithuania's independence. By the spring of 1941 the LAF had developed an extensive underground network of anti-Soviet cells that would await the outbreak of a German-Soviet war, which most Lithuanians believed inevitable. The ideology of the LAF tended towards authoritarianism and intense nationalism.

During the spring of 1941, the political situation in Lithuania deteriorated even further. Thousands of persons had been arrested or deported for political reasons. Tensions between those collaborating with the Soviets and opponents of the regime grew as rumors of an approaching Russo-German war spread among the populace. The population was stunned when in the predawn hours of June 14, 1941, NKVD troops, assisted by local Communist activists, suddenly began large-scale deportations of so-called unreliable elements to the Soviet Union. Within 72 hours the Communist forces netted more than 18,000 men, women and children.

Lithuania Under Nazi Occupation, 1941-1944

On June 22, 1941 the German Army invaded the USSR. Except for the Communists and their supporters, few Lithuanians offered any resistance to the invaders. Lithuanian Red Army troops deserted by the thousands as Soviet forces retreated rapidly across Lithuania. On June 23, 1941 an anti-Soviet revolt inspired by the LAF engulfed Kaunas and parts of Vilnius. The rebels captured the radio station and announced the formation of a Lithuanian Provisional Government. During the first days of the war, a largely spontaneous uprising also spread through the provinces. As the Soviet forces retreated, the Red Army and various Communist units massacred hundreds of people, including prisoners they did not wish to transport eastward.

The rebels' Provisional Government could do little to affect events in the country because its jurisdiction was severely limited by the Nazi occupation. On July 25 the Reich announced the establishment of a civilian administration (Ger. *Zivilverwaltung*) in Lithuania; on August 5, 1941 the Provisional Government resigned in protest. The Reich's decree of July 25 created the General Commissariat (Ger. *Generalkommisariat* or *Generalbezirk*), of Lithuania, which, together with Estonia, Latvia and Belarus, constituted the Nazi province of Ostland. Some spheres of life, such as all matters dealing with ethnic Germans, Jews, and the military were placed exclusively under German control. Other matters, such as education, the local economy, communications, the ordinary police and the administration of law involving Lithuanians, were relegated to a body of native counselors under general German supervision. General Petras Kubiliūnas, a pro-German officer, was appointed to head this group as General Counselor.

The greatest single atrocity of the Nazi occupation was the mass murder of Lithuania's Jews of whom about 90 percent perished in the Holocaust. While Jews were killed throughout the German occupation, the majority were massacred during the summer and autumn of 1941. The killings were carried out by special Nazi action groups (Ger. *Einsaztgruppen*), which were assisted by auxiliaries recruited from the local population. The total number of Jews killed in Lithuania, including those brought in from other countries, will probably never be known, but it is estimated that the number approached a quarter of a million. Over 20,000 Jews escaped eastward in 1941 and another few thousand were rescued by Gentile Lithuanians.

While much of the population had initially greeted the German invasion as a liberation from Stalinist rule, the Nazi policy of economic expropriation and cultural repression soon provoked resistance among the Lithuanian populace. The major political issues were the Nazis' refusal to grant Lithuania significant autonomy, the harsh behavior of German officials and the Reich's increasing reliance on forced labor. On the other hand, the majority of the Lithuanian population feared another Soviet occupation. Most were distrustful of the anti-Nazi Polish and Soviet partisans concentrated in eastern Lithuania who were hostile to Lithuanian national aspirations and themselves often utilized terror against civilians. Tensions in Lithuania came to a head in the spring of 1943 with the executions of peasants and the German demand for manpower. In March 1943 the Lithuanian populace sabotaged the formation of a Lithuanian SS Legion. Nazi authorities blamed the intelligentsia for this failure and began a series of arrests. During the spring of 1944, German officials announced permission for the formation of a Lithuanian defense force, the so-called Local Force (Lith. *Vietinė Rinktinė*), that would guard the country against the approaching Soviet Army. However, when Reich officials suspected that the Lithuanians intended to use the army solely for their own ends, they arrested the Force's senior officers and inducted the volunteers into German units.

The German occupation devastated Lithuania. At least a quarter of a million people, predominantly Jews, were massacred by the Nazis. More than 75,000 young Lithuanians were pressed into the Reich Labor Service, thousands of whom were killed in Germany during Allied bombings or simply disappeared. Hundreds of villages were destroyed in the war. Vilnius, Klaipėda, Šiauliai and other major Lithuanian cities were heavily damaged.

Postwar Stalinism and Mass Repression, 1945-1953

In June 1944 the Red Army smashed through the Belarusan front in the largest land operation of the war. By mid-July the Soviets had taken Vilnius and on August 1 the Germans abandoned Kaunas. Upon their return, the Soviets mobilized about 100,000 young men into the Red Army. About 100,000 Lithuanian civilians attempted to flee West and more than 60,000 succeeded in making their way into Germany where they were liberated by the Western Allies. After V-E Day, most of these refugees eventually found themselves in Displaced Person (DP) camps operated by the United States and Britain.

After the German surrender in May 1945, Lithuania underwent one of the most violent periods in its history. Heavy population losses resulted from mass deportations, an intense anti-Soviet guerilla war, and agricultural collectivization. Between 1946 and 1953 Soviet authorities deported at least another 150,000 people to the USSR. Lithuania's anti-Soviet guerilla war, which lasted nearly eight years and reached its peak during the late 1940s, was especially destructive. Nearly 50,000 persons perished in the armed struggle between 1945 and 1953, including Lithuanian civilians who died at the hands of the various Soviet security forces suppressing the uprising, as well as thousands of Communist activists and Soviet collaborators who were killed by the resistance. The main armed resistance ended by 1953, although isolated bands were reported in Lithuania's forests as late as the mid-1960s. The collectivization of Lithuania drove many people in the countryside close to famine. By 1950 collectivized agriculture had largely displaced private farms in Lithuania.

The period of postwar Stalinist rule also introduced religious and cultural repression. A third of the country's Catholic priests were deported or killed after the war. Hundreds of churches and monasteries were closed. In 1946 the Communist Party, following the Soviet campaign against "cosmopolitan" trends in literature, began a purge of Lithuanian writers and artists who were perceived as too nationally-minded. The Communist Party itself began the postwar period as a Russian-dominated political machine. In the early 1950s, scarcely a fourth of the republic's Communists were ethnic Lithuanians.

After Stalin: The Khrushchev and Brezhnev Years, 1953-1982

Stalin's death on March 5, 1953 initiated important changes in the Soviet Union. The late 1950s under Khrushchev were marked by the period of the so-called "thaw," which softened some of Stalinism's most egregious policies. Gradually conditions for the thousands of Lithuanian deportees improved and some of them began returning to Lithuania during the mid and late 1950s. Another important change was the partial relaxation of the restrictions on Lithuanian national culture. The intelligentsia and even some Party members sought to reverse Lithuania's Russification. Persecution of the Catholic Church lessened, although atheist indoctrination continued unabated. In the early 1960s Moscow responded with a new crackdown on national assertiveness in the Baltics and some prominent Lithuanian leaders were expelled from the Party for "nationalist deviations." However, there was no return to mass terror.

In October 1964 Khrushchev was removed from power by a clique of Communist leaders who coalesced around Leonid Brezhnev, the new party secretary. In Lithuania, the Party was still dominated by the LCP First Secretary, Antanas Sniečkus, who had been its leader since the 1930s. After his death in 1974, Sniečkus was replaced by the conservative Petras Griškevičius. The 1970s and early 1980s saw renewed efforts at Russification. The major rationale behind this policy was outlined during the Tashkent Conference of 1975, which stipulated increased efforts in promoting the study of Russian in the Soviet Union's non-Russian schools. In general, official policy of the period promoted the consolidation (Rus. *sliyanie*) of the Soviet peoples into a single nation. The later Brezhnev years in particular witnessed an intensified campaign in favor of "internationalism," widely understood as the euphemism for Russification.

The Lithuanian economy underwent severe dislocations during the Brezhnev years. The number of large, polluting industrial enterprises controlled by the central planning agencies in Moscow increased dramatically, along with a corresponding rise in immigrant labor, primarily of Russian and other Slavic origin. The worsening ecological situation was a factor in the declining standard of living during the 1970s and 1980s.

During the early 1970s dissident activity against the Soviet regime in Lithuania became more pronounced. In November 1970 a Lithuanian sailor, Simas Kudirka, attempted to defect but was forcibly returned to a Soviet ship off the New England coast. Kudirka's trial in Lithuania galvanized dissident circles. In early 1972 a petition against religious persecution signed by 17,000 Lithuanian Catholics reached the UN; it elicited no official response but received press coverage in the United States. On May 14, 1972 a young student, Romas Kalanta, immolated himself in a Kaunas park in protest against Soviet rule in Lithuania, provoking several days of anti-Russian riots in Kaunas that were reported in the Western press.

A less spectacular but more significant event during the same year was the appearance of the *Chronicle of the Catholic Church in Lithuania*, a samizdat publication which collected and disseminated information about the persecution of Lithuania's Catholics and the suppression of national rights. A number of other underground periodicals also appeared. Two internationally known human-rights organizations were founded during the 1970s: the Lithuanian Helsinki Group and the Committee to Defend the Rights of Believers. Both groups organized the collection of signatures and appeals to free imprisoned dissidents, publicized the violations of human rights, and sought to defend the rights of national and religious dissidents in Lithuania.

The Soviet government met the new movements with harassment and selective repression, imprisoning the more active leaders. While the number of religious and national activists who were sentenced to imprisonment and exile was not great, at most several hundred, the harassment of nationally-minded youth, practicing Catholics and other "nonconformists" involved thousands of persons. The regime sought to block virtually all avenues of what it considered dangerous national expression. The KGB even disbanded popular ethnographic and historical student expeditions.

Glasnost, Perestroika and the Rebirth of the Lithuanian National Movement, 1982-1988

Brezhnev's death in October of 1982 and his replacement with Yuri Andropov (1982-1984) and, later, the senile Konstantin Chernenko (1984-1985), had little immediate impact on Lithuania. However, the early 1980s were a period of growing debate on ecological issues, which were to become a major factor in Lithuanian politics. Gradually, some relaxation in official policy became apparent during the mid-1980s. The regime's anti-Catholic campaign became less strident. New bishops were consecrated and the number of seminarians increased. The intelligentsia began to demand that constraints on scholarly and creative work be loosened and raised concerns about the fate of the Lithuanian language.

The tenure of the last General Secretary of the CPSU, Mikhail Gorbachev (1985-1991), began with promises of reform in the shape of perestroika (restructuring) and glasnost (openness). However, in Lithuania, the Party leadership reiterated the condemnations of bourgeois nationalism under the conservative party boss, Ringaudas Songaila, who had replaced Griškevičius in 1987. But the Lithuanian Communist Party was unable to stem the increasingly powerful current of national dissent. One of the most important issues that emerged during the mid-1980s was the recovery of the nation's history, when writers and literary critics began an unprecedented debate on Lithuanian historiography, criticizing the constraints that official circles had placed on research and writing. For their part, philologists protested against Russification and urged the authorities to protect the Lithuanian language. The disaffection of the intelligentsia spread to the population at large through a series of protests, demonstrations and political confrontations, which completely rearranged Lithuania's political landscape within two years.

On August 23, 1987 a large crowd gathered outside St. Anne's Church in Vilnius to commemorate the 48th anniversary of the Molotov-Ribbentrop Pact. In response, the Party and the official media launched a vituperative campaign against the organizers of the demonstration, but this action contrasted sharply and embarrassingly with Gorbachev's call for openness and democratic reform.

Distressed by the rise in national feeling, Lithuania's hardline Communists were determined to prevent demonstrations on February 16, 1988, the 70th anniversary of the restoration of Lithuanian independence. On that day most cities in Lithuania were under the watchful eye of the militia and their civilian auxiliaries. The government succeeded in preventing mass demonstrations; however, the regime's actions exposed the Communists' fears and provoked even more criticism. The growing popular disaffection with the Lithuanian government and Party in the republic was fueled by the example of the reformist Estonian Popular Front, which had the support of much of the Estonian Communist Party.

The Sąjūdis Movement and the Road to Independence, 1988-1990

Exasperated by the LCP's tepid response to Gorbachev's call for openness and restructuring, a group of concerned intelligentsia met on June 3, 1988 at the Lithuanian Academy of Sciences in Vilnius to discuss reform. The participants elected 35 persons to lead the Initiative Group to Support Perestroika in Lithuania. This was the core of what later became known as the Lithuanian Movement for Restructuring (Lith. *Lietuvos Persitvarkymo Sąjūdis*), or simply, Sąjūdis. About half of the Initiative Group were LCP members. The Initiative Group appeared in time to harness growing popular discontent. Ever larger pro-reform demonstrations occurred during the summer of 1988 as more and more people hoisted the banned prewar tricolor and other national symbols. The rallying cries of Lithuania's reform movement centered around demands for sovereignty, environmental issues, the defense of Lithuanian culture, and an end to officials' privileges. On July 9, 1988 about 100,000 people gathered at the outdoor amphitheater in Vilnius' Vingis Park to greet the delegates returning from the 19th CPSU Conference in Moscow. The sea of national banners, the obvious enthusiasm of the crowd, the numerous signs supporting the fledgling Sąjūdis, as well as the radical tone of the speeches, marked this demonstration as a turning point in postwar Lithuanian politics. During the summer of 1988, an ecological "March across Lithuania" by young people received an emotional welcome in many of Lithuania's small towns. At the same time, Sąjūdis activists began publishing unofficial periodicals reluctantly tolerated by the authorities.

The growth of the Lithuanian national opposition also received a boost from the prestige of the Catholic Church. On June 28, 1988 the president of the Lithuanian bishops' conference, Vincentas Sladkevičius, was named Lithuania's first modern cardinal. He issued increasingly assertive statements, demanding religious and national rights for Lithuanians. On August 23, 1988 one of the largest demonstrations in Lithuania's modern history convened in Vilnius when nearly a quarter of a million people gathered at Vingis Park to commemorate the 49th anniversary of the signing of the Molotov-Ribbentrop Pact. The "secret protocols" of the Pact became an increasingly sensitive political issue. Condemnation of the Nazi-Soviet Pact of 1939 inevitably led to criticism of its effects: the Soviet occupation of the Baltic states. In the late summer and fall of 1988 new chapters of Sąjūdis began to appear even in the smaller towns.

On September 28, 1988 Soviet internal ministry troops and local militia attacked a demonstration organized by the pro-independence Lithuanian Liberty League. The violence provoked an outcry and within days, Songaila was ousted and the more popular Algirdas Brazauskas became the LCP's new First Secretary. The installation of Brazauskas coincided with the founding congress of Sąjūdis on October 22-23, 1988, which was intended to provide a formal structure for the new movement. Brazauskas publicly opposed the increasingly vocal demands for the withdrawal of Soviet troops from Lithuania, but promised wide-ranging reforms and a new political era in the republic, albeit within the Soviet system. The Sąjūdis congress elected an executive council and chose Vytautas Landsbergis as its chairman. It adopted a program calling for the rule of law, economic autonomy, self-determination, the introduction of Lithuanian as the official language of the republic, as well as equal rights and cultural autonomy for the national minorities.

In November, 1988 the Lithuanian Supreme Soviet issued a decree confirming Lithuanian as the official language and declared February 16th, traditionally viewed as Independence Day, a national holiday. At the same time, Sąjūdis issued a statement which went beyond the goal of Lithuanian autonomy, calling for the eventual reestablishment of a neutral, democratic and independent Lithuanian state even though Brazauskas had declared that independence was out of the question.

The elections to the USSR's Congress of People's Deputies on March 26, 1989 proved an overwhelming victory for the pro-independence forces as Sąjūdis-supported candidates won 36 of the 42 Lithuanian seats to the Congress. On the weekend of May 12-14, 1989 in Tallinn the Estonian and Latvian popular fronts and Sąjūdis established the Baltic Assembly. The Assembly adopted resolutions calling for self-determination, the creation of a neutral Baltic demilitarized region, and an examination of the history of the Molotov-Ribbentrop Pact. On May 18, 1989 the Lithuanian Supreme Soviet met in Vilnius and proposed changes in the Constitution of the Lithuanian SSR which would give Lithuania the right to veto Soviet laws. The legislature also announced that the future relations of Lithuania with the USSR would have to be negotiated as international agreements.

The Baltic delegates to the Congress of People's Deputies, which convened in Moscow in May 1989, successfully utilized the issue of the Molotov-Ribbentrop Pact of 1939 to highlight the need to reevaluate the status of the Baltic republics. On June 11, 1989, Lithuania's Party and Government leadership announced that June 14, the anniversary of the deportations of Lithuanians in 1941, would be commemorated as a Day of Mourning and Hope to honor the victims of Stalinism. Stalinist crimes were equated with Nazi genocide and condemned in harsh terms never before used by the official media. The authorities admitted that Lithuania had been, in fact, invaded by the Soviet Army in June 1940. In late June 1989 the LCP's Central Committee dismissed a number of Russian and Lithuanian hardliners, replacing them with avowed reformers.

On August 22, 1989 a commission of the Lithuanian Supreme Soviet announced that the 1940 decree of the Lithuanian People's Diet requesting that Lithuania join the USSR, as well as the decree of the USSR Supreme Soviet of August 3, 1940, admitting Lithuania into the Soviet Union, were invalid because they had occurred under conditions of fraud, intimidation and military occupation. The next day, on the 50th anniversary of the Nazi-Soviet Pact, more than a million persons linked hands in a 370-mile human chain from Tallinn to Vilnius called the "Baltic Way." This was the largest political demonstration in Soviet history. A few days later, the Central Committee of the CPSU responded with a strong verbal attack on the Baltic national movements and signaled that it was losing patience with Baltic Communist leaders who were unable or unwilling to restrain "nationalist excesses."

In September 1989 the Lithuanian CP leadership announced a draft program before the convening of a special congress of the LCP later in the year. The Lithuanian Party's reformist leadership argued that if it was to stave off complete disaster in the elections to the republic's Supreme Soviet scheduled for February 1990, it had to gain credibility by reaffirming its independence from the Kremlin. On December 17, 1989 the Lithuanian CP opened its Twentieth Congress in Vilnius. Despite strong warnings from CPSU leaders, the LCP proclaimed itself an independent Marxist party with a social democratic orientation. A number of hardline delegates broke away from the reformist majority to establish the so-called LCP (CPSU) faction loyal to Moscow. On January 11-13, 1990 Soviet President Mikhail Gorbachev flew to Lithuania in a highly-publicized attempt to dampen Lithuanian fervor for independence, but his visit clearly failed to convince the Lithuanian public that their future lay within a reformed Soviet Union. In fact, the first multi-party elections to the Lithuanian Supreme Soviet in February 1990 brought a Sąjūdis majority with a clear mandate for the restoration of the republic's independence.

The Republic of Lithuania Since 1990

On March 11, 1990 the newly elected Lithuanian Supreme Soviet unanimously approved a declaration restoring the independence of the Republic of Lithuania and abolishing the Lithuanian SSR. The parliament now became known in English as the Supreme Council in order to distinguish it from the legislature of the Soviet period. On the same day, the new body elected Sąjūdis leader Vytautas Landsbergis as the Chairman of the Supreme Council and, in effect, head of state and named the economist Kazimiera Prunskienė as the new Prime Minister. Brazauskas agreed to serve as Prunskienė's deputy.

The Soviet government denounced the Supreme Council's declaration of independence as illegal and the Soviet military responded with repressive measures, such as rounding up Lithuanian deserters from the Soviet Army and occupying buildings belonging to the reformist LCP in the name of restoring CPSU property. In addition, Gorbachev imposed an economic blockade on Lithuania which lasted until the summer of 1990. In April 1990 the USSR Supreme Soviet approved detailed legislation enabling secession of Union Republics according to Article 72 of the Soviet Constitution, which actually made legal secession difficult, if not impossible, for most republics. Gorbachev initially refused Lithuania's requests for negotiations on implementing independence, later suggesting that the USSR would demand exorbitant reparation payments and even territorial concessions from an independent Lithuania.

The qualified support that the Lithuanian Prime Minister, Mrs. Prunskienė, received during her visit to the United States, Britain, France and Germany in May 1990, as well as some concessions by the Lithuanian Supreme Council, resulted in the lifting of the Soviet economic boycott of Lithuania. However, Gorbachev's turn to a more conservative course in the fall of 1990 led to a series of repressive measures against selected Lithuanian institutions by the special OMON, or Black Berets, units of the Soviet Interior Ministry, particularly against the new Lithuanian customs service. The Soviet government's policies were supported by the LCP (CPSU) with allied groups such as the Committee for Defending Soviet Power in Lithuania, the Yedinstvo (Rus. Unity) movement of recent Russian-speaking settlers, and segments of the Polish minority. However, the actions of Soviet authorities and their supporters simply reinforced the allegiance of the majority of Lithuanians to the Landsbergis government.

The Lithuanian crisis escalated after the resignation of Soviet Foreign Minister Eduard Shevardnadze on December 20, 1990, as Soviet troops began a series of actions aimed at reinforcing Soviet power in the republic. The Soviet authorities also encouraged opposition to the Landsbergis government by Yedinstvo, LCP (CPSU) supporters and other hardline elements, which culminated in a series of anti-government demonstrations in early January, 1991, leading to the resignation of Prime Minister Kazimiera Prunskienė and the appointment, after a brief interlude, of Gediminas Vagnorius as premier. However, the anti-government protests soon dissipated in the face of large pro-independence manifestations. In the predawn hours of January 13, 1991 Soviet troops stormed the Lithuanian TV tower and broadcasting facilities in Vilnius killing 14 civilians and wounding hundreds, while a little-known Committee of National Salvation, apparently headed by LCP (CPSU) stalwarts Juozas Jermalavičius and Mykolas Burokevičius, attempted to claim power. Western governments, preoccupied with the Gulf war, protested the

Soviet crackdown, but offered little or no practical support to Lithuania.

The coup against the Lithuanian government failed to dislodge Landsbergis and rallied considerable support for Lithuania from Russian radicals, such as Russian president Boris Yeltsin. In February, 1991 more than 90 percent of Lithuanians voted in support of establishing a democratic, independent Lithuanian republic. Nevertheless, during 1990-1991 Lithuania experienced a period of dual government; while the Republic of Lithuania under Landsbergis continued to administer the country, the republic received international recognition only from Iceland. At the same time, the Soviet military and KGB effectively controlled Lithuania's borders. The OMON continued its attacks against Lithuanian institutions; the most violent incident was the murder of six Lithuanian customs officers at the Medininkai border post on July 31, 1991.

The failure of the Communist hardline coup in Moscow of August 18-22, 1991 and the collapse of the CPSU led to the realization of Lithuania's independence. The OMON were withdrawn from the Baltic, while the KGB headquarters in Vilnius were seized by Lithuanian police. Western governments recognized the independent governments of the Baltic States and, finally, on September 6, 1991 the Federation Council of the USSR itself accepted the independence of Lithuania, Latvia and Estonia. The three countries were admitted to the United Nations in the following week.

The years 1991-1992 were marked by an increasingly bitter struggle between Landsbergis and the opposition, much of it drawn from the former LCP, now the Lithuanian Democratic Labor Party (LDDP). The Sąjūdis movement turned to the right, losing much of its appeal among the intelligentsia. The government of Prime Minister Gediminas Vagnorius (January 1991-July 1992) and his successor Aleksandras Abišala (July 1992-December 1992) carried out major fiscal reforms and a policy of privatization, but failed to reverse a deep slide in industrial production and living standards. In the elections of October 26, 1992 the LDDP scored a surprising victory, winning a majority (75 out of 141 seats) in the Seimas (parliament). In February 1993, Algirdas Brazauskas, the head of the LDDP, defeated Stasys Lozoraitis, Lithuania's Ambassador to Washington, for the presidency. Landsbergis became the leader of the opposition: his supporters coalesced into the Fatherland Union (Conservative) party in May 1993 with 24 seats in the Seimas, while the Union's political allies, the Christian Democrats, the Nationalists and the Union of Political Prisoners and Deportees, have another 20 seats. With seven seats, the Social Democrats became the only significant party of the left outside the LDDP. The caretaker government of Bronislavas Lubys (December 1992-March 1993) was replaced in March 1993 by one headed by Prime Minister Adolfas Šleževičius. In November-December 1995 the country was rocked by financial scandals involving the failure of three major banks. This led to the dismissal of the director of the state Bank of Lithuania, the police detention of several leading bankers and demands for the resignation of Premier Šleževičius who had withdrawn his private bank accounts before the collapse. On January 30, 1996 President Brazauskas demanded that the Seimas hold a vote of confidence on Šleževičius, precipitating a government crisis. On February 8, 1996 the Seimas voted to dismiss Šleževičius and replaced him with Mindaugas Stankevičius who was to head a caretaker government while the country prepared for parliamentary elections scheduled for October 1996.

While the currency, the *litas*, has remained stable, Lithuania is only slowly recovering from the economic depression that had begun in the late 1980s. The standard of living has plummeted for large segments of the population: at least half of the population live below the government's statistical poverty line. However, there has also emerged a middle class, variously estimated at between 15-25 percent, whose situation has either remained stable, or has improved. There is a small wealthy elite as well, which has gained during the privatization process; much of it, however, is known to have close ties to the various organized crime syndicates popularly termed "the mafia." Corruption and the failure of the judiciary and police to curb the activities of the underworld have become major political issues.

Economically, Lithuania has experienced the usual problems of unemployment tied to the inefficiency of the former large-scale Soviet industrial enterprises. The country is making a major effort to reorient economic activity towards the West with some success: over half of exports now go outside the former Soviet Bloc. Lithuania is also seeking to reduce its dependence on Russian oil and natural gas by continuing to operate the large Chernobyl-style reactor at Ignalina, and beginning construction of the Butingė oil terminal north of Klaipėda for the import of energy by sea. However, the energy picture has been clouded by a major dispute with Latvia over drilling on the Baltic Sea coast. Since 1995 the energy problems have been complicated by a serious debt crisis as the country's oil and natural gas users have fallen behind in their payments to the energy companies. In turn, Lithuania's gas and oil concerns have been unable to continue timely payments to their Russian suppliers. In November-December 1995 the country was shaken by the aforementioned financial scandal which led to the demise of Prime Minister Šleževičius. During 1996 there were growing concerns about the advisability of maintaining the stability of the *litas* and some economists predicted a devaluation of the currency, although by mid-1997 the government had as yet shown no signs of considering such a step.

In foreign policy, the Lithuanian government has been able to point to some notables successes. The negotiations concerning the withdrawal of Russian troops led to their departure by September 1993. Lithuania has developed closer ties to the other Baltic States and the Scandinavian countries, as well as to the member states of the European Union. In January 1994 Lithuania announced that it intended to join NATO's Partnership for Peace program, although the government's formal position is that the country should eventually become a full-fledged member of the North Atlantic alliance. Negotiations for membership in NATO are continuing, despite strong objections from Russia. At the same time, along with the other Baltic States, Lithuania has continued a policy aimed at both political and economic integration with the rest of Europe. In June 1995 the country signed an association agreement with the European Union and the hope is that Lithuania would join the

Union sometime in the next decade. In 1995, as part of its efforts
to participate in the solution of European problems, Lithuania sent
a small peace-keeping contingent to Bosnia. There is a growing
recognition that, despite the continued rhetoric about economic
integration with Europe, gaining membership in the European
Community will be a prolonged and difficult process. Recent
opinion polls have indicated rising skepticism in Lithuania about the
social and economic costs of integrating the country's economy with
that of western Europe.

The political situation changed dramatically when in October-
November 1996 Landsbergis' Conservatives and their political
allies won an impressive victory in the elections to the Seimas,
securing an absolute majority in the legislature at the expense of the
LDDP. The former Communists' failure to deliver on their promises
to raise the standard of living, and the aura of corruption
surrounding the Šleževičius government were major factors in this
startling political turnabout. On November 28, 1996 Gediminas
Vagnorius was once again appointed prime minister at the head of
a new government dominated by the Conservatives; for his part,
Landsbergis was elected chairman of the parliament.

THE DICTIONARY

- A -

ACADEMY OF SCIENCES. Lithuania's most prestigious and comprehensive institution of scholarly research established on January 16, 1941 by the Council of Commissars of the Lithuanian SSR. The initiative for founding the Academy and much of its scholarly personnel came from the Institute of Lithuanian Studies (Lith. *Lituanistikos institutas*) founded in Kaunas in 1939. The first president of the Academy, based in Vilnius, was the prominent writer and literary scholar Vincas Krėvė-Mickevičius (q. v.). Initially six institutes were established encompassing history, Lithuanian literature, Lithuanian language, ethnology, economics, and law. The Academy acquired an extensive library based on the renowned Vrublevskis (Pol. Wróblewski) collections. In 1945 the Academy of Sciences was reorganized and expanded to include the physical sciences. By 1967 the Academy had twenty institutes in three divisions: mathematics, physics and technology; biology and chemistry; and the social sciences. During the 1950s and 1960s, some of the Academy's work was transferred to government agencies and only ten institutes remained; on the other hand, the Academy coordinated the work of dozens of scientific institutions within the republic. During the 1970s the Academy employed about 3,000 people in a hierarchical structure headed by the academicians (Lith. *akademikai*), the most prestigious scholarly and scientific rank in the USSR, followed by corresponding Academy members, senior and junior associates (most with the equivalent of Ph. D's), and junior researchers. The Academy is administered by a presidium chaired by the President of the Academy and is empowered to grant the doctoral degree. In the Soviet system the Academies of Sciences generally emphasized advanced research, while the universities concentrated on teaching

47

although, since independence, this pattern has begun to change in Lithuania.

In 1988 the Academy was the site of the organizational meeting of Sąjūdis (q. v.); a number of the leaders of the independence movement were academicians. Since 1990 the structure and purpose of the Academy has changed. The Academy has been significantly depoliticized and many institutes have begun functioning autonomously from the Academy's governing body. The Lithuanian Academy of Sciences, like the other institutions of higher learning, has suffered from the severe economic situation of the 1990s and, thus, has lost much of its former political and academic influence. After 1990 a Council of Education (Lith. *Mokslo Taryba*) has been established to coordinate research and education in institutions of higher learning. See EDUCATION.

AGRICULTURE. Historically agriculture has been the mainstay of the Lithuanian economy and its development has largely mirrored the agrarian history of Eastern Europe in general. The beginnings of primitive agriculture in Lithuania can be traced to the Neolithic period (ca. 3000-1000 B. C.), while the systematic raising of livestock commenced during the Bronze Age (before 500 B. C.). Slash-and-burn cultivation, characteristic of heavily forested regions, predominated in Lithuania during this early period. Wooden ploughs and harrows, as well as iron hoes, made their appearance during the early medieval period. By this time, the predominant form of cultivation was the two-field system, in which one field was planted, while the other was left fallow.

The more sophisticated three-field system of crop rotation, in which only a third of arable land was left fallow, came to Lithuania some centuries after it had appeared in the more densely settled regions of western and central Europe. In 1547 King Sigismund Augustus (q. v.) initiated a series of measures, collectively known as the Volok Reform (q. v.), named after the unit of land (Rus. *volok*, Pol. *włóka*, Lith. *valakas*) that the Grand Duchy of Lithuania (q. v.) assigned to an average peasant household. This agrarian reform determined the boundaries of the crown domains and private estates, established villages on the Western model and provided each peasant household with a *volok* of land. Sigismund's reforms increased revenues for the Grand Duchy and systematized the obligations of the peasantry. They also expanded agricultural output by making the three-field system predominant on the large manorial farms. The reforms of the 16th century, as well as the gradual extension of the system of serfdom (q. v.) towards the peasantry, enabled Lithuania to become a major exporter of agricultural products to Western Europe. However, the wars and plagues of the 17th and early 18th centuries devastated the Polish-Lithuanian Commonwealth (q. v.). It was only during the second half of the 18th century that Lithuania began to recover from the devastation of the previous wars and again become an exporter of grains and flax.

During the late 18th century, new methods of cultivation and labor organization were introduced on some of the large estates, particularly the crown domains called economies (q. v.). Gradually, there also emerged a class of relatively prosperous peasantry, particularly in southwestern Lithuania. During the 19th century, the social struggle in the countryside resulted in the emancipation of the peasantry from serfdom and the gradual decline of the land-owning nobility. There were also important changes in agriculture itself, such as the development of improved tools, the gradual introduction of modern crop rotation and the emphasis on new crops, such as the potato and commercial crops, for example, flax, hemp and sugar beets. At the same time, traditional agriculture, including the two-field system, was still practiced in large parts of Lithuania, especially in the poorer eastern regions.

The Great War and, especially, the expropriations of the German occupation authorities, proved a disaster for Lithuanian agriculture, and brought the country to the brink of famine. However, the establishment of an independent Lithuanian state in 1918 transformed Lithuanian agriculture. The Land Reform Bill of 1922 placed land holdings of larger then 80 hectares into a Land Fund for distribution to the peasantry. In 1929 the maximum allowance for landowners was increased to 150 hectares. By 1930

Lithuania contained 287,380 farms, most of them small; less than three percent of the farms were over 50 hectares. Increasingly, Lithuanian farms were consolidated into individual homesteads (Lith. *vienkiemiai*). During the interwar period Lithuania became an exporter of dairy products, flax and animal products. Cooperatives and special farmers' societies were widespread.

The Second World War revolutionized the Lithuanian countryside. The Communist regime established in 1940 sought to foment class war in the countryside by reducing private holdings to 30 hectares and redistributing the excess to landless peasants and smallholders. Preparations for collectivization on the Stalinist model were interrupted by the German invasion of June 1941, but were resumed after the Soviet reoccupation of Lithuania in 1944-5. During 1947 the Communist regime launched an attack on the middle and prosperous peasants, deporting thousands of villagers to Siberia and the Far North. Collectivization was virtually completed by 1950; most peasants were now working in either collective farms (Rus. *kolkhozy*), or state farms (Rus. *sovkhozy*). The collectivization process transformed the rural landscape by destroying traditional individual homesteads and replacing them with collective rural housing projects. As a general rule, the productivity of collectivized agriculture in the socialized Lithuanian economy remained low: the tiny private "kitchen garden" plots kept by the collective farmers since the 1960s consistently produced a disproportionate amount of the republic's dairy products, meat and produce.

The disintegration of Soviet rule in Lithuania and the restoration of an independent state in 1990 initiated a new era in agriculture as the Landsbergis (q. v.) government decreed that the land should be parceled out to private owners. However, mismanagement and confusion during the privatization process, as well as the general economic crisis that afflicted virtually all former Soviet republics, has caused agricultural production to plummet during the early 1990s. See ECONOMY (ROYAL ESTATE); SERFDOM; VOLOK REFORM.

ALEXANDER, GRAND DUKE (1460-1506). Grand Duke of Lithuania, 1492-1506 and King of Poland, 1501-1506. Alexander was the fourth son of King Casimir IV (q. v.); his mother was Elizabeth Hapsburg, the daughter of the Holy Roman Emperor Albert. King Casimir appointed Alexander as his representative to Lithuania in 1490, but gave him no formal title. In July 1492 the Lithuanian Diet (q. v.) elected Alexander Grand Duke of Lithuania, but forced the new ruler to both grant the nobility additional privileges and reaffirm Lithuania's political independence. Alexander's reign coincided with the expansion of Muscovite power under Tsar Ivan III. In 1494 Alexander negotiated the peace treaty between the Grand Duchy and Muscovy (q. v.) in which Alexander ceded some of Lithuania's eastern territories. In 1495 Alexander married Elena, Ivan's daughter, but the marriage to an Orthodox princess failed to bring peace between Muscovy and Lithuania, producing religious and political conflicts. A new series of Russian-Lithuanian wars during 1500-1503 resulted in more territorial losses for the Grand Duchy.

In 1501 Alexander's brother King John Albert of Poland died and the Grand Duke succeeded to the Polish throne. Poland and Lithuania, while politically separate, found themselves once again under a single monarch, a situation that was to prevail until 1795. Alexander's armies did manage to defeat a Tatar invasion of Lithuania supported by Muscovy in 1506. In March 1505 Alexander granted Lithuanian Orthodox nobles equality with their Catholic counterparts. He did much to develop and beautify Vilnius, where he spent most of his time even after election as King of Poland. Alexander died in Vilnius on August 19, 1506 and was buried in the city's cathedral.

ALGIRDAS (Rus. Olgerd, Pol. Olgierd) (d. 1377). Grand Duke of Lithuania from 1345 to 1377, the third son of Gediminas (q. v.). After Gediminas' death in 1341, his youngest son, Jaunutis, briefly occupied the throne in Vilnius. However, Gediminas' other sons were dissatisfied with this arrangement and in 1345 removed Jaunutis, assigning him territory in Russia. Algirdas was installed as Grand Duke and conferred considerable authority on his brother Kęstutis (q. v.), the Duke of Trakai, whom some sources have described as Lithuania's co-ruler during Algirdas' reign. While Kęstutis was preoccupied with defending western Lithuania against the frequent incursions of the Teutonic Knights (q. v.), Algirdas, generally regarded as a shrewd and wily ruler, developed territorial ambitions in the east.

Algirdas seems to have envisioned Lithuania as the unifier of the East Slavic realm that had disintegrated after the collapse of Kievan Rus'; during his rule Lithuania's rivalry with the emerging Muscovite state escalated into a major confrontation that was to last several centuries. Algirdas led several military expeditions against Moscow, but failed to subdue Muscovite power. Nonetheless, he extended Lithuania's domain considerably with the annexation of Kiev, Podolia and other Russian principalities, laying claim to territory as far as the Black Sea. Algirdas attempted to acquire influence over the Russian Orthodox Church by persuading the Patriarch of Constantinople to appoint a Lithuanian-sponsored metropolitan for all Russia who would reside in Kiev rather than Moscow, however, his efforts to establish Lithuanian control over the Russian Church were ultimately unsuccessful.

While he never became a Christian, Algirdas showed favor to both Eastern and Western Christians, allowing Catholic and Orthodox churches in Vilnius. Algirdas' two wives, Maria of Vitebsk and Juliana of Tver, were Russian Orthodox. He left behind some twelve sons and seven daughters. Two of his sons by his second wife Juliana, Jogaila (q. v.) and Švitrigaila (q. v.), became important historic personages and future rulers of the Lithuanian Grand Duchy and adjacent lands.

ALYTUS. Town and district seat in southwestern Lithuania, located 52 km. south of Kaunas, pop. in 1995: 76,500. Alytus, the industrial and cultural center of the country's Dzūkija (q. v.) region, is situated on the Nemunas River, with the main part of the town located on the left bank. During the late 14th century, Alytus developed as an important fortified town, since it was located on the route frequently taken by the military expeditions of the Teutonic Knights (q. v.). Alytus was granted a town charter in 1581 and it soon became the administrative center of the region. During the 17th and 18th centuries, Alytus was the center of the large Alytus crown estate, the Alytus economy (q. v.) (Lith. *ekonomija*), which stretched west of the town to the Prussian border. During the period of Tsarist rule, the Nemunas River divided Alytus between the province of Augustów (since 1867 Suwałki) on the west bank and Kaunas gubernia on the east. During the interwar period of independence, Alytus was reunited and grew rapidly, but the town suffered heavy damage during World War II. In the years of Soviet rule, the introduction of new food processing, chemical and construction industries transformed Alytus into Lithuania's fifth largest city.

AMBER. Lithuania's most famous ornamental treasure and an important object of trade in ancient times. Amber is fossilized resin from a variety of pines which grew in the Baltic region 40-60 million years ago. During historic times, amber was collected as fragments, which had washed ashore on the Baltic coast, particularly during storms. The size of the yellow and bronze-like fragments ranges from a few grams to several kilograms, although the large ones are rare. Amber emits an electric charge when subjected to friction, and was known as *elektron* in Greek. Amber pieces containing inclusions, particularly prehistoric insects, are highly valued.

Since earliest times, amber was widely used by Baltic tribes as ornaments and for carving figurines. Amber from the eastern Baltic is easily identified and this has made it possible to trace prehistoric and ancient European trade routes. Baltic amber has been found in Asia Minor, Greece and Italy in archeological sites dating back to the Bronze Age. Amber is still one of Lithuania's best-known exports and a significant factor in the country's tourist trade. See TRADE.

AMBRAZEVIČIUS-BRAZAITIS, JUOZAS (1903-1974). Lithuanian literary scholar, Catholic activist and acting prime minister of the Lithuanian Provisional Government during June-August 1941, born in Marijampolė district on December 9, 1903. After studies at the universities of Kaunas and Bonn, he taught literature at the University of Kaunas from 1934 to 1943 and was a leader in Lithuanian Catholic intellectual circles. Ambrazevičius gained prominence as the acting prime minister of the six-week revolutionary Lithuanian Provisional Government proclaimed on June 23, 1941 in the wake of the German invasion of the USSR, a position he resigned on August 5, 1941. During the German occupation (1943-1944) he edited the underground periodical *Į Laisvę* (Towards Freedom) and, after fleeing to Germany in 1944, became one of the leaders of the Supreme Committee for the Liberation of Lithuania (VLIK) (q. v.). He emigrated to the United States in 1948 and worked as an associate editor of the Catholic newspaper *Darbininkas* (The Worker) under the name Brazaitis. During the 1960s and early 1970s Brazaitis came under attack in the Soviet press and from American Nazi hunters as a pro-German collaborator, charges he resolutely denied, publishing his own extensive account of the activities of the 1941 provisional government. He died in New York on October 28, 1974. See LITHUANIAN ACTIVIST FRONT (LAF).

ANGARIETIS, ZIGMAS (1882-1940). Prominent Lithuanian Communist leader, born as Zigmas Aleksa on June 25, 1882 in Vilkaviškis district. During 1902-1904 Angarietis studied at the veterinary institute of the University of Warsaw but was expelled for his involvement in radical activities. He joined the Lithuanian Social Democratic Party (q. v.) in 1906 and became a member of its Central Committee. During his imprisonment and exile to Siberia by Tsarist authorities in 1909-1917, Angarietis became close to the Bolsheviks and joined their Party in 1916. He worked in the bureau of the Lithuanian section of the Russian Bolshevik Party and was a member of the Litbel (q. v.) government, as well as the Lithuanian-Belarusan Communist Party Central Committee, in 1918-1919. After 1919 Angarietis served in various leadership positions within the Lithuanian Communist Party (q. v.) and then in the Communist International in Moscow. During his career, he published over a hundred Marxist-Leninist tracts on the situation in Lithuania. He was arrested in March 1938 during Stalin's purges and executed in Moscow on May 22, 1940. Angarietis was rehabilitated in 1956 during Khrushchev's de-Stalinization campaign.

ARCHEOLOGY. The first serious student of archeology in Lithuania was Count Eustach Tyszkiewicz (Tiškevičius) (q. v.) who published two substantial Polish-language surveys of Lithuanian archeology in 1842 and 1850. Since the mid-19th century, after the establishment of an Archeological Commission by the Tsarist government, the number of archeological excavations, collections of artifacts, and museums grew rapidly. Before World War I the most prominent investigators, among others, were Constantine Tyszkiewicz, Adam Kirkor, Feodor Pokrovski and Tadas Daugirdas. During the interwar period new work was initiated by Eduardas Volteris (Wolter) and Vladas Nagevičius and especially Jonas Puzinas, a professor at the University of Kaunas, who published numerous studies and accounts of excavations dealing primarily with the Bronze and early Iron Ages in Lithuania.

During the Soviet period archeological research on the national level was conducted by the Archeology and Ethnography Division of the Institute of History within the Academy of Sciences, and the Department of Archeology and Ethnography of the University of Vilnius, as well as regional museums and ethnographic societies. Among the most prominent archeologists of this period are Adolfas Tautavičius, Regina Kulikauskienė and Pranas Kulikauskas. Lithuania's best-known archeologist, however, is Prof. Marija Gimbutas (1921-1993), a long-time professor of archeology at UCLA, whose works dealt with Baltic and European prehistory. Her ground-breaking study, *The Civilization of the Goddess: The World of Old Europe*, which described a peaceful, matriarchal culture that was well-established before the invasion of warlike

Indo-European peoples, provoked much discussion and controversy within the archeological profession. See BALTS; PRUSSIA; RELIGION, PRE-CHRISTIAN; YOTVINGIANS.

ARCHITECTURE. Traditional Lithuanian architecture commonly utilized timber in construction. Before the late medieval period, stone and brick construction was found only in the larger towns requiring extensive fortification. Until the 16th century many Lithuanian castles were constructed of stone, interspersed with brick and wood. For the peasantry, the typical dwelling consisted of a log cabin, similar to rural structures elsewhere in central and eastern Europe, with elaborately decorated gables, window frames and doors. Thatched roofing was a common sight in the Lithuanian countryside until the Second World War. During the early medieval period, Byzantine architecture exercised some limited influence in eastern Lithuania: a few Orthodox churches were constructed in Vilnius during the 14th century.

With Lithuania's turn to the Latin West during the 14th and 15th centuries, Gothic architecture became increasingly prominent and was reflected in the construction of both castles and churches. By the early 16th century, the old towns and market squares of most of Lithuania's major cities, such as Vilnius and Kaunas, were completed in their present form. Builders turned increasingly to brick for construction. St. Anne's Church, built ca. 1495-1500, is a masterpiece of late Gothic architecture in Vilnius. Baroque architecture was introduced into Lithuania during the 17th century, partly under the stimulus of the Counter-Reformation, and is reflected in a number of monasteries and churches, such as St. Casimir's in Vilnius (built 1604-1618) and the ornate Pažaislis convent (built 1667-1681); there were also the Baroque mansions of the wealthy Radziwiłł (Lith. Radvilas) family, for example, in Biržai, which was built in 1589. Until the 18th century, Italian architects played an important role in the development of Lithuanian architecture.

Despite the political turmoil of the late 18th and early 19th centuries, neoclassical architecture, much of it inspired by native masters, came to Lithuania. The best-known example is the Cathedral of Vilnius, rebuilt in the late 18th century by Liudvikas Stuoka-Gucevičius, and located in what is now the center of the city, Gediminas Square. Under Tsarist rule in the 19th century, a kind of imperial classicism became the major architectural style for public buildings, while stone structures imitating Romantic and various other modes became popular on the estates of the wealthy landed nobility.

During the period of Lithuania's interwar independence (1918-1940), a new generation of architects, such as Vladas Dubeneckis (1897-1932) and Vytautas Landsbergis-Žemkalnis (b. 1893), made their mark by constructing numerous government and public buildings, especially in Kaunas, the country's provisional capital. The new buildings, particularly those built during the 1930s, utilized modern examples from Western Europe and the United States, eventually provoking a discussion about the adaptation of Lithuanian traditional architectural designs to modern architecture. Some of these traditional themes can be seen in the architecture and design of buildings constructed by Lithuanian émigrés in the West after World War II, such as the Transfiguration parish church in Maspeth, NY designed by architect Jonas Mulokas (b. 1907).

Meanwhile, the reconstruction of Lithuania after World War II was influenced by Soviet examples of architecture, which meant that most public construction during the late 1940s and early 1950s followed the Stalinist model. The collectivization of the country-side permanently altered the Lithuanian landscape as traditional peasant homesteads disappeared in most of the country. More creative styles were introduced in the 1960s, when modern themes were combined with some Lithuanian decorative elements. The notable designs of the post-Stalinist period include the Vilnius Sports Palace (1971) and the capital's Opera and Ballet Building (1974). One of the major concerns of the architecture of the Soviet period was the construction of large housing projects; in 1974 Lithuanian architects V. Čekanauskas and others received the Soviet Union's Lenin Prize for the design of the Lazdynai housing project in the suburbs of Vilnius.

ARMED FORCES. Little is known about the organization of military forces before the late medieval period, although it is known that Lithuanian military expeditions raided Prussia, Poland, Livonia and what is now Belarus well before the political unification of the Lithuanian state in the 14th century. During the early 15th century Lithuanian military units were centered on the mounted knights, usually drawn from the landowning class, supported by a retinue of lightly-armed foot soldiers. These knights were grouped into so-called battle-flag formations which consisted of between 50 and 80 heavily armed cavalry.

During the 16th century Lithuania's military establishment was institutionalized on the basis of feudal service tenure. However, by the 18th century, the reluctance of the nobility to serve had led to the increasing use of hired troops maintained through tax levies. The Lithuanian Army was led by the Grand Hetman, appointed by the Grand Duke, and operated independently of the Common-wealth's (q. v.) Polish forces. After 1795 Lithuania came under the Tsarist recruit system in which draftees often served as long as 25 years; however, many Lithuanians also fought in the rebel armies during the anti-Russian insurrections of 1831 and 1863 (q. v.). In general, most Lithuanians serving in the Tsar's Army did so in the ranks since few Lithuanian Catholics were admitted to the Russian Army's officer corps until the early 1900s. During World War I the disintegration of the Russian Army led Lithuanians to form their own military units but these were disbanded after the Bolshevik Revolution of 1917.

On November 23, 1918, the first government of independent Lithuania announced the formation of the Lithuanian Army staffed largely by volunteers and officers returning from Russia; in January 1919 the government began mobilization. During the struggle for independence between 1918 and 1920, when Lithuania confronted Bolshevik, Bermondtist (q. v.) and Polish forces, the Army acquired not only an infantry, but cavalry, artillery, armored car and tank units as well as a small air force. Later a miniscule navy was founded. Between the wars, Lithuania maintained armed forces of between 22,000 and 28,000 men, primarily equipped with French,

Belgian and Czech ordnance. Some of the military's weaponry and shells were manufactured in Lithuania. In 1938 the air force numbered some 100 aircraft. In addition to the regular army, Lithuania possessed a volunteer reserve force, the Riflemen's Union (Lith. *Šaulių Sąjunga*) (q. v.), which in 1940 numbered more than 60,000 men and women.

After the Soviet occupation in 1940, the Lithuanian Army was integrated into the armed forces of the Soviet Union as the Red Army's 29th Territorial Rifle Corps; many Lithuanian officers were arrested and some were executed by the Soviets. During the German invasion of June 1941 the majority of Lithuanian Red Army men deserted, while the remainder were evacuated to the Russian interior where some of them joined the Soviet 16th Lithuanian Division. In German-occupied Lithuania, the Nazi authorities organized as many as 20 Self-Defense battalions, the so-called *Schutzmannschaft* units, some of which saw action on the Eastern Front, while others were utilized for local police, security and punitive operations. There were, however, no Lithuanian Waffen SS units. After the return of the Soviets in 1944-1945, tens of thousands of Lithuanians were drafted into the Red Army; many other young men fled into the country's forests and joined the anti-Soviet partisans.

During the rise of the anti-Soviet dissident (q. v.) movement in Lithuania and the mass national protests of the late 1980s, the issue of the mistreatment and hazing of Lithuanian draftees in the Soviet Army became a highly emotional rallying cry in the campaign for independence. After the Lithuanian declaration of independence in March 1990, the new government began organizing the National Defense Service under Defense Minister Audrius Butkevičius. The Lithuanian Army was reestablished in 1991 and has been gradually building a rudimentary defense capability. In the mid-1990s the various Lithuanian security forces consisted of about 13,000-15,000 men including border guard, air support, coastal defense and rapid deployment commando units. There is a volunteer national guard known as the SKAT (Lith. *Savanorių Krašto Apsaugos Tarnyba*). According to a treaty between Vilnius and Moscow, the former Soviet, now Russian, Army completed its withdrawal from Lithuania by September 1993. See AVIATION; RESISTANCE MOVEMENTS; RAŠTIKIS, STASYS.

ART. Evidence collected from archeological excavations indicates that decorative art in Lithuania dates from the Neolithic period, consisting mainly of engraved sherds and pottery uncovered at gravesites. Metal ornaments date from the Bronze and Iron Ages. By about 500 A. D. the Baltic tribes inhabiting Lithuania had achieved considerable artistic sophistication, employing bronze, silver, gold and amber. Folk art utilizing perishable materials such as wood and cloth have not survived from these early periods, but some aspects of their style can be deduced from surviving artifacts collected during the past two centuries.

The first evidence of what can be called the fine arts are traces of frescoes in the castle of Grand Duke Vytautas dating from the early 15th century, but it has been impossible to determine their forms and style. The earliest surviving Lithuanian paintings and sculptures date from the 16th century and, while their authors are unknown, it is thought that, in addition to native artists, Flemish and Italian masters were then active in Vilnius. Most of the sculptures of the period are sepulchral monuments; the use of colored and white marble not found in Lithuania indicates that some of these monuments were foreign works. During the 17th century Italian artists, sponsored by the Grand Duke's court and the landed nobility, were the dominant influence in Lithuanian sculpture and painting. Michelangelo Paloni de Campo's works are still found in the Pažaislis monastery near Kaunas and in the Cathedral in Vilnius. During the 17th and 18th centuries wood sculpture and carving, often in the Baroque and Rococo styles, spread throughout Lithuania. Art was taught at the University of Vilnius from its inception as an Academy in the late 16th century until the closure of the University by the Tsarist regime in 1832.

The most prominent native painter during the last years of the Grand Duchy period was Pranciškus Smuglevičius (Pol. Smuglewicz) (1745-1798), the founder of the art department at the Vilnius Academy. Although a neoclassicist, Smuglevičius also left some realistic scenes of Lithuanian rural life. During the 19th century, Lithuanian painters, including the Vilnius-born Italian Elviro Andriolli, often took their themes from Lithuanian legends and history, seeking to inspire patriotic feeling. After the Revolution of 1905, Lithuania's artists increasingly reflected the cultural outlook of the Lithuanian national movement. The sculptor Petras Rimša (1881-1961) and the painter Antanas Žmuidzinavičius (1876-1976) based their work on folk themes emanating from the Lithuanian-speaking village. The best-known Lithuanian artist in modern times was Mikalojus Konstantinas Čiurlionis (1875-1911) (q. v.) who achieved an international reputation as a member of the *Mir isskustva* (Rus. World of Art) avant-garde group in St. Petersburg during the early 1900s.

Lithuanian art of the interwar independence period reflected both a turn to the West and an emphasis on folk art. The Kaunas School of Fine Arts established in 1924 became the major center for the development of painting and sculpture. Among the leading artists of this time were the painters Adomas Galdikas (1893-1969) and Adomas Varnas (1879-1979), the sculptor Juozas Zikaras (1881-1944) and the engraver Vytautas K. Jonynas. The Kaunas school and the influence of Western Europe encouraged new trends among the younger generation of artists, for example, expressionism, impressionism and primitivism. In general, it can be said that the interwar years witnessed the evolution of a distinct Lithuanian style of art, reinforced by the general Lithuanianization of the country's cultural institutions.

World War II and the consequent Soviet occupation drastically altered the development of Lithuanian art. In Lithuania itself, the Stalinist form of socialist realism dominated until the early 1950s. During the relaxation of Soviet cultural policy that followed Stalin's death, Juozas Mikėnas became one of the best-known sculptors in the Soviet Union, while Gediminas Jokūbonis was acclaimed for his monument to the victims of a 1944 Nazi massacre in the village of Pirčiupis. Painting has languished somewhat, but engraving was highly developed. During the war, some of the most prominent prewar artists fled to the West, including Jonynas, Varnas, Galdikas and the painter Kazimieras Žoromskis, who later returned to Lithuania. One of the most interesing of the Lithuanian émigré artists was Prussian-born Pranas Domšaitis (Ger. Franz Domschat), an expressionist painter who settled in South Africa in 1949, and was acclaimed for his landscapes of both the Lithuanian countryside and the Karoo region of his adopted country.

ATEITIS. An influential Roman Catholic (q. v.) organization, primarily of Lithuanian students and intelligentsia, founded in 1908, as well as the name of the organization's journal. The first issue of *Ateitis* (The Future) was published in 1911 and was aimed at contesting socialist influence among Catholic secondary school and university students. In 1927 this Catholic movement, known as the *ateitininkai*, adopted an organizational structure formally known as the Ateitis Federation; it was divided into three separate branches representing secondary school pupils, university students and alumni. The Ateitis Federation emphasized religious and national values which appealed to Lithuania's Catholic intellectual elite. Although the secondary school organization of Ateitis was proscribed by Lithuania's Nationalist (q. v.) government in 1930, it never ceased functioning and numbered about 10,000 members in 1940. Ateitis was banned by the Soviet authorities after 1940 and most of its leaders either fled West or were repressed by the Communists. The Ateitis Federation was reconstituted in the West after World War II; in 1967 there were about 3,000 *ateitininkai*, mainly in the U. S. and Canada. With the restoration of religious freedom in the late 1980s, Ateitis has once again become active in Lithuania. See CATHOLIC CHURCH.

AUGUSTUS II, "the Strong," (1670-1733). King of Poland and Grand Duke of Lithuania from 1697 to 1706 and from 1709 to 1733, also Elector of Saxony as Frederick Augustus I from 1694 to 1733, born on May 12, 1670 in Dresden. Augustus, an heir of the Saxon House of Wettin, succeeded his brother as Elector of Saxony in 1694 and became known as a generous patron of the arts. After the death of John III Sobieski (q. v.), he was able to win election to the Polish-Lithuanian throne as Augustus II through bribes and the assistance of Russia and Austria in June 1697. With help from Lithuanian magnates who opposed the powerful Sapieha (q. v.) family, Augustus persuaded Lithuanian leaders to support his ambition of instituting an absolute monarchy in the Grand Duchy, but this proposal met with vigorous opposition in Poland. Augustus' attempts to instill an absolute monarchy in Lithuania with the help of the Saxon army were derailed by his defeats in the Great Northern War (q. v.) with Sweden. Augustus was deposed in July 1704 and in 1706 was forced by the Swedes to formally abdicate, but his fortunes revived after the decisive Russian victory over Charles XII at Poltava in 1709. Having regained the throne in 1709, Augustus again attempted to increase royal power, but was stymied by the Russian-supported Confederation of Tarnogrod. The so-called Silent Diet of the Commonwealth in 1717 forced the withdrawal of Saxon troops from Poland-Lithuania, thus undercutting Augustus' power and initiating a period of Russian interference. For Lithuania, the reign of Augustus II was one of the most disastrous periods in the country's history, featuring the Great Northern War, the plague of 1708-1711 and Russian invasions. Although ambitious, intelligent and politically astute, as well as an able military commander, Augustus was also known for his dissolute ways. He received the epithet, "the Strong," on account of his size and physical strength (reportedly fathering some 300 children). Augustus died in Warsaw on February 1, 1733.

AUGUSTUS III (1696-1763), King of Poland and Grand Duke of Lithuania, also Elector of Saxony as Frederick Augustus II from 1733 to 1763, born in Dresden on September 17, 1696, the son of Augustus II, the Strong (q. v.). His election to the Polish-Lithuanian throne in 1733 was largely engineered by the Saxon minister Count Heinrich von Brühl with the support of Austria and Russia against the strong opposition of the Polish nobility who actually chose Stanisław Leszczyński (q. v.) as King on September 12, 1733. Russian troops, with reluctant Lithuanian assistance, then forced the election of Augustus III in a second vote of the

Commonwealth's Diet on October 5, 1733; however, the dispute between Augustus' and Leszczyński's supporters dragged on until 1736. During Augustus' 30-year reign the Polish-Lithuanian Commonwealth fell ever more under foreign control and became virtually defenseless against its neighbors: during the Seven Years' War Prussian, Austrian and Russian armies traversed Poland-Lithuania freely. Internal politics were dominated by the struggle between the Czartoryski (q. v.) family, which leaned toward Russia, and the Potocki party, which looked to France. While members of the nobility increasingly called for social and political reform, royal government remained weak and the gentry diets often dissolved in chaos. Spending most of his time in Saxony, Augustus III lacked the political skills and ambition of his father, although he was a generous patron of the arts. He died in Dresden on October 5, 1763.

AUKŠTAITIJA, AUKŠTAIČIAI. Term meaning "Highland Region," the name for the hilly central and northeastern region of Lithuania. The lands of Aukštaitija are generally considered to include the territory east of the Nevėžis and Nemunas Rivers; the inhabitants are called *aukštaičiai, aukštaitis* in the singular (although the plural term for the people can also signify the land of Aukštaitija). The eastern highlands are in contrast to western Lithuania known as Žemaitija, or the Lowland region, often referred to in English-language texts as Samogitia (q. v.). Various versions of the term, Aukštaitija, have been used in chronicles and other sources since the 13th century; unlike Samogitia, however, Aukštaitija never formed a single distinct political or ecclesiastical province. The *aukštaičiai* comprise one of the four major Lithuanian ethnographic and dialectical subdivisions, known for their distinct folk architecture. The region is also known for the cultivation of flax and the prominence of weaving in the local peasant economy. The folk costumes and other woven materials from Aukštaitija are valued for their artistry.

AUŠRA, (Old Lith. *AUSZRA*). Lithuanian-language monthly published in East Prussia between 1883 and 1886. *Auszra* was the first secular Lithuanian periodical, which also gave its name to an entire generation of nationally-minded Lithuanian intelligentsia. *Auszra* (Lith. The Dawn), later spelled *Aušra*, proclaimed an agenda of romantic nationalism whose avowed purpose was to save the Lithuanian language from extinction and to develop a sense of national pride derived from Lithuania's history and culture. *Aušra*'s founder and guiding spirit was Jonas Basanavičius (q. v.), widely regarded as the patriarch of the modern Lithuanian national renaissance.

The first issue of *Aušra*, dated March 20, 1883, was published in Ragnit (Lith. Ragainė), East Prussia in April of 1883; later in the year, the journal was issued from Tilsit (q. v.), the major town on the Prussian border with Russia. Because of the Tsarist press ban on Lithuanian publications, *Aušra* was mailed to subscribers in unmarked envelopes; some issues were smuggled into Russian-ruled Lithuania from East Prussia along with other illegal publications. Two of the periodical's editors, Jonas Šliūpas (q. v.) and Martynas Jankus (1858-1946), were prominent leaders of the Lithuanian national movement. Forty issues of *Aušra* appeared between April of 1883 and the summer of 1886.

Despite *Aušra*'s limited circulation of only about 1,000, it had an important impact on the development of the modern Lithuanian nation. While much of Lithuania's influential Catholic establishment objected to the secular and liberal tone of the journal, it proved popular among the nationalistic younger clergy and the growing number of Lithuanian-speaking intelligentsia with roots in the countryside. The leaders of this intelligentsia, who generally supported the goals of *Aušra*, became known as the "*Aušra* movement" (Lith. *aušrininkai*). This movement is widely regarded as the immediate precursor to modern Lithuanian political nationalism, which eventually articulated the goal of an independent Lithuanian state under a democratic form of government.

AVIATION. The development of military and civil aviation received an impetus during Lithuania's struggle for independence following the Great War. The Lithuanian Air Force began as an engineering company of the army in 1919; its first equipment was a British Sopwith captured from the Bolshevik forces. The Air Force participated in the battles with the Soviets and Poland in 1919-1920. By 1940 Lithuania's Air Force numbered over 100 reconnaissance, fighter and bomber aircraft. The major base was located in Aleksotas, a suburb of Kaunas. The Lithuanian designer Jurgis Dobkevičius (1900-1926) built three training types (the DOBI series). The best-known Lithuanian engineer was General Antanas Gustaitis (1898-1941) who designed the ANBO series of trainers, reconnaisance craft and light bombers.

Civil aviation received a major boost with the creation of Lithuania's Aero Club in 1927. During the 1930s gliding became a popular sport and a gliding school was established in Nida on the Baltic coast. On June 15, 1933 two Lithuanian-American pilots, Stepas Darius and Stasys Girėnas, attempted a record-breaking non-stop flight from New York to Kaunas in a modified single-engine Bellanca J-6, a journey of over 7,000 km. Unfortunately, both men perished when their plane crashed in Soldin (now western Poland), on June 17. The Darius-Girėnas episode became a national epic in Lithuania and greatly stimulated interest in aviation. Lithuania's first commercial airline was organized in 1937, operating flights from Kaunas to the Baltic coast. In 1940 Lithuania's civil and military aviation came under Soviet control. After World War II Vilnius became the hub of the Lithuanian section of the Soviet airline, Aeroflot, with numerous connections to major Soviet cities. In December 1991, Lithuanian Airlines (LAL) was founded and began operating separately from Aeroflot. By 1996 LAL had acquired three Boeing 737 aircraft and upgraded 11 of its Soviet-made YAK-42 jetliners for service to the major capitals of Scandinavia, central and western Europe. A new passenger terminal for Vilnius International Airport was completed in 1994.

- B -

BALTIC ENTENTE. An alliance established by Lithuania, Latvia and Estonia in 1934 to promote political cooperation and to coordinate the foreign policies of the Baltic States. There had been attempts to form a larger Baltic bloc of states that would include Finland, the Scandinavian states and Poland since the end of World War I. In 1920 conferences in Helsinki, Finland and in Bulduri, Latvia failed to form such a larger alliance because of the Polish-Lithuanian conflict over Vilnius, as well as Finland's reluctance to be involved in its southern neighbors' potential problems with Germany and Russia.

In 1934 the Lithuanian government proposed a smaller entente with the other two Baltic States, Latvia and Estonia. The text of the treaty was negotiated during the summer of 1934 in Kaunas and Riga. The final document, the Treaty of Friendship and Cooperation, was signed on September 12, 1934 at Geneva and was ratified on November 13 of that year in Riga. The Baltic Entente provided a forum for political cooperation through the Foreign Ministers' Conferences, of which nine were held during the 1934-1940 period. The alliance also created a number of commissions to expand cooperation in legal, cultural and economic matters. During the late 1930s there were attempts to expand cooperation in defense matters as well, but these attempts were cut short by the Soviet occupation of the Baltic States in June 1940, which put an end to the Baltic Entente. The spirit of the Baltic Entente was restored in 1989 with the creation of the Baltic Council to coordinate the activities of Sąjūdis (q. v.) and the Latvian and Estonian Popular Fronts. Since 1990 the Baltic States have sought to enhance their cooperation in the military, economic and cultural fields. See LATVIA.

BALTRUŠAITIS, JURGIS (1873-1944). Lithuanian poet and diplomat, born on May 2, 1873 in Raseiniai District. A graduate of the University of Moscow, he began to contribute to Russian literary magazines during the 1890s. He was one of the founders of the Russian avant garde Skorpion publishing house established in 1899. Baltrušaitis' first collection of Russian poetry, *Zemnye stupeni* (Earthly Steps), was published in 1911 and gave him recognition as a force in the Russian Symbolist movement. Baltrušaitis also became known as a Russian translator of French and German literature. In 1914 he and his wife befriended the young Boris Pasternak, the future author of *Doctor Zhivago*, who tutored Baltrušaitis' son. In 1919 Baltrušaitis was elected chairman of the Soviet Union of Writers, then entered public service in 1920 when he was appointed Lithuanian minister plenipotentiary to Moscow. In 1934 he made unsuccessful efforts to save the Russian poet Osip Mandelstam from Stalinist repression. Baltrušaitis remained Lithuania's envoy to the USSR until 1939 when he was transferred to the Lithuanian Legation in Paris, where he died on January 3, 1944.

While Baltrušaitis wrote primarily in Russian, he also contributed several collections of Lithuanian poetry later in life, primarily written from 1939 to 1943. His thorough immersion in both the Russian and Lithuanian cultural worlds has made him a unique fixture in the history of Lithuanian literature. See LITERATURE.

BALTS. A name that has acquired two distinct meanings: (1) as a political and geographic term of recent popular usage denoting the native inhabitants of the Baltic States of Lithuania, Latvia and Estonia; (2) as an ethnolinguistic term originating in the 19th century signifying speakers of the Baltic group of the Indo-European family of languages. In utilizing the first term, it should be noted that Estonians speak a Finno-Ugric language close to Finnish but unrelated to Lithuanian and Latvian, which are the only living Baltic languages. Strictly speaking, in historic and linguistic literature, only the second usage is acceptable. "Baltic peoples" is the better designation for the natives of the three Baltic States if one disregards ethnolinguistic criteria.

Most archaeologists and linguists who have studied material culture and the distribution of Baltic toponynms conclude that the ancestors of the Balts, that is, the speakers of Baltic languages, lived in the central regions of what is now European Russia and along the eastern shore of the Baltic Sea about 3000 B. C. In the west, some of the Baltic tribes reached the Vistula River. In addition to archeology, additional evidence for this comes from the study of Finno-Ugric and Slavic loanwords in the Baltic languages. The differentiation of the Baltic speakers into distinct tribes and dialects is dated from about 1000 B. C. Generally, scholars divide the Balts into the Western Baltic group, which included the Old Prussians (q. v.) and Yotvingians (q.v.), and the Eastern Balts, who included the Couronions, Semigallians and the other ancestors of today's Latvians (q.v.) and Lithuanians. The Western Balts were essentially exterminated or assimilated by the Teutonic Knights (q. v.). The easternmost Balts, including the Galindians, who are mentioned in historical sources, were overrun and assimilated by the Eastern Slavic peoples by the early medieval period. The remaining Baltic tribes coalesced into the modern Lithuanian and Latvian nations. See ARCHEOLOGY; LATVIA; LANGUAGE.

BAR, CONFEDERATION OF. One of the most important of the confederations (q. v.) formed by the nobility of the Polish-Lithuanian Commonwealth (q. v.), proclaimed at the town of Bar in the Podolia region of Ukraine on February 29, 1768. The purpose of the Bar assembly was to organize resistance against Russian interference in the internal affairs of Poland-Lithuania, which had become increasingly irksome to the patriotic gentry after the so-called Silent Diet of 1717. The gentry resented the way in which King Stanisław August Poniatowski (q. v.), the former lover of Catherine the Great, submitted to the dictates of the Russian ambassador in Warsaw, Nikolai Repnin. The Confederation of Bar was proclaimed under the slogan, "For country, faith and freedom," and was essentially a movement to preserve the independence of the Commonwealth. It was led by the Polish hetman Michael Krasiński and the Pulaski family. The King, supported by Russian troops, non-Catholic dissidents (q. v.) and the conservative nobility of the Confederation of Radom (q. v.), dispersed the Bar Confederates in the summer of 1768 and the remnants of the rebel army retreated to Moldova, then under Ottoman control. Despite initial setbacks, the Bar movement spread throughout the Commonwealth, including Lithuania, where it was spearheaded by the Radziwiłł, Pac, Ogiński and Sapieha magnate families. The Confederation of Bar led to international conflicts by precipitating a war between Russia and Turkey; it also received limited support from Austria and France. However, the Confederates' announcement of King Stanisław August's deposition, at a time when he was considering joining the movement, hurt the rebels' cause. General Suvorov defeated the Confederate army in Poland in the spring of 1771; in September the Russians destroyed the Confederate force in Lithuania led by Michael Ogiński. The defeat of the Confederation of Bar is historically important because it precipitated the first of the Partitions (q. v.) of Poland-Lithuania by Russia, Prussia and Austria which were determined not to allow the revival of a genuinely independent Commonwealth.

BARANAUSKAS, ANTANAS (1831-1902). Catholic bishop and poet, one of the leading literary figures of the Lithuanian national renaissance of the 19th century. Baranauskas was born on January 17, 1831 in Anykščiai. He entered the Theological Seminary at Varniai in 1856 and continued his religious studies at the Theological Academy in St. Petersburg, graduating in 1862. During the next two years he studied in Munich, Innsbruck and Rome. After a brief teaching stint at the St. Petersburg Academy, Baranauskas was assigned to the Theological Seminary in Kaunas where he taught until 1884. That year he was appointed auxiliary bishop of Samogitia and in 1897, Bishop of Sejny (Lith. Seinai).

Baranauskas was an extraordinarily gifted and somewhat eccentric personality, an accomplished philologist and grammarian of the Lithuanian language who also published works in mathematics and philosophy. However, Baranauskas is best known for his poetry, especially for the poem, *Anykščių šilelis* (Lith. The

Grove of Anykščiai), considered by some the best example of Lithuanian lyrical poetry of the period, as well as the patriotic collection *Kelionė Petaburkan* (Lith. Journey to St. Petersburg). Initially an enthusiastic supporter of Lithuanian national culture and much admired as a writer, Baranauskas became a political anachronism in his later years when he denounced the national movement for its anti-Polish separatism and endorsed a Polish-Lithuanian union. He died in Sejny on November 26, 1902. See LITERATURE.

BASANAVIČIUS, JONAS (1851-1927). The leading figure of the Lithuanian national movement in the 19th and early 20th centuries and founder of *Aušra* (q. v.). Jonas Basanavičius was born on November 23, 1851 in Ožkabaliai, Lithuania, the son of well-to-do peasants. Basanavičius graduated the Marijampolė secondary school in 1873 and then matriculated at the University of Moscow, receiving his medical degree in 1879. He was active in the circles of nationally-minded Lithuanian students in Moscow and, although he chose a medical career for practical reasons, devoted most of his life to the study of Lithuanian history. In 1880, Basanavičius accepted a position as a physician in newly-independent Bulgaria where he spent most of the next 25 years. In 1884 he married Elenora Mohl, a Bohemian German whom he met in Prague while furthering his medical studies and in the same year returned to Bulgaria with his new bride. Basanavičius actively participated in Bulgarian public life and politics as a member of the Bulgarian Democratic Party; he was also briefly Prince Ferdinand's palace physician. In 1891 Basanavičius was granted Bulgarian citizenship.

Remarkably, while in Bulgaria, Basanavičius provided the major impetus for the publication of *Aušra*, which signaled the emergence of modern secular Lithuanian nationalism. At the same time, Basanavičius wrote a number of scholarly works in which he traced the origins of the Lithuanian people to the Trojans and the region of Thrace. While many of Basanavičius' linguistic and historical assertions are now considered romanticized pseudoscience, his work played an important part in stimulating interest and pride in Lithuanian national culture. It was during his period of residence in Bulgaria that Basanavičius was widely acknowledged as the patriarch or dean of the Lithuanian national movement.

Basanavičius returned to Lithuania in 1905, finding the Lithuanian national movement he had inspired both politicized and much strengthened. He was elected chairman of the Great Lithuanian Assembly (q.v.) in Vilnius on December 4-5, 1905, the first modern Lithuanian political convention. However, Basanavičius' conservative concept of stressing national cultural values was soon superseded by a political agenda directed against Tsarist oppression and favoring an autonomous Lithuania. During the decade preceding the Great War, Basanavičius immersed himself in scholarly and cultural activities; his most important achievement was the founding of the Lithuanian Scholarly Society (Lith. *Lietuvių Mokslo Draugija*), which considerably enhanced scholarly work in the Lithuanian language and was an important center of Lithuanian cultural life in Vilnius. On February 16, 1918 Basanavičius became the most prominent signatory of Lithuania's Declaration of Independence, but afterwards he did not play a significant political role in the creation of the new state. After the Polish seizure of Vilnius in 1920, Basanavičius refused to evacuate to Kaunas and became the most prominent Lithuanian figure in the city. He continued his work with the Scholarly Society and took on the role of defending Lithuanian interests under Polish rule. Basanavičius died in Vilnius on February 16, 1927. See NATIONALISM, LITHUANIAN.

BASKETBALL. Considered by most Lithuanians as their national sport since the late 1930s. Modern sports became more popular after the establishment of an independent state, but basketball did not achieve prominence until the 1937 European championships in Riga, when the Lithuanian national team was reinforced by several excellent Lithuanian-American players, including the captain of the 1936 U. S. Olympic Team, Frank Lubin. Lithuania won the 1937 contest by achieving a stunning upset over such favorites as Italy and Latvia. As a result of the national enthusiasm engendered by this victory, basketball fever gripped Lithuania; in 1939 the Lithuanian team again won the European championships held in Kaunas.

After World War II, Lithuanians and other Balts played a key role in popularizing basketball in the USSR. Lithuanians figured prominently in the 1956 Soviet men's Olympic team in Melbourne and were a decisive factor in the 1988 Soviet victory over the U. S. which earned the USSR the gold medal at the Summer Olympics in Seoul. In the mid-1980s, Žalgiris of Kaunas won several Soviet men's basketball championships and was recognized as one of the best teams in Europe. In 1992 the Lithuanian Olympic team earned the bronze medal in men's basketball at the Barcelona Olympics and in 1995, the silver medal in the European championships held in Athens. In 1996 the Lithuanian basketball team once again won the bronze medal at the centennial Summer Olympics in Atlanta. Since independence, a number of Lithuanian basketball players have turned professional, most notably Arvydas Sabonis and Šarūnas Marčiulionis, who joined the National Basketball Association (NBA).

BATORY or BATHORY, STEFAN (1522-1586). King of Poland and Grand Duke of Lithuania from 1576 to 1586, born on September 28, 1533 in Somlyó, Hungary. In 1571 Bathory was elected Prince of Transylvania and, in March 1576, he was crowned King of Poland on the condition that he marry Anna, the daughter of Sigismund I (The Old) (q. v.). In June 1576 he was also named Grand Duke of Lithuania after promising to respect the Grand Duchy's political autonomy. By all accounts, Bathory was an intelligent, able and energetic monarch as well as a renowned military leader. After concluding a treaty in 1577 with the Ottoman sultan Murad III, who promised to restrain the Crimean Tatars from attacking the Commonwealth, he launched a successful campaign to reverse the Muscovite conquest of Livonia, concluding a peace with Ivan IV (The Terrible) in 1582. Bathory then became the ruler of most of Livonia and, during his reign, strengthened Catholicism in the region. In 1579 he granted the charter of higher learning to the Jesuit college in Vilnius, thus founding the University of Vilnius. Bathory reformed the Lithuanian judiciary by establishing a supreme tribunal and inspiring the third revision of the Lithuanian Statute (q. v.). He is known to have planned an ambitious military campaign, utilizing Polish-Lithuanian forces, to liberate Hungary from Ottoman rule and to reconquer Lithuanian lands lost to Muscovy. However, Bathory died on December 12, 1586 in Grodno (q. v.) before any of his plans could be realized.

BELARUS (also BELORUSSIA, BYELORUSSIA, and in older usage, WHITE RUSSIA). Since 1991 Lithuania's eastern neighbor and a member of the Commonwealth of Independent States, area 207,600 sq. km., population est. 10,400,000 in 1994, capital Minsk, pop. 1,700,000. Since 1991 the country's formal name is the Republic of Belarus, literally meaning "White Rus'." East Slavic tribes, the best-known of whom were the Krivichi, migrated to what is now Belarus beginning about the fifth century A. D., pushing aside or assimilating the eastern Baltic tribes then living in the region. The original Lithuanian cognate for the Belarusans is *gudai*, a term that may be derived from the word for "Goths," who swept through the area during the late Roman Empire. Before Lithuanian rule in the 13th century, much of Belarus was subject to the principality of Polotsk, which was a part of Kievan Rus'. All of Belarus came under the Grand Duchy of Lithuania during the reigns of Gediminas (q. v.) and Algirdas (q. v.) between 1316 and 1377, and remained under Lithuanian control until the Partitions (q. v.) of the Polish-Lithuanian Commonwealth (q. v.) in 1772-1795 when the country came under Russian rule. The centuries-old political separation of Belarus from Muscovy and Russia was the predominant factor in giving rise to a separate Belarusan national identity. The form of Old Church Slavic utilized in Belarus and west Russia became the official language of the Lithuanian Grand Duchy until 1697. The first book ever published in Lithuania (Vilnius) was Francis Skorina's *Apostol* (The Apostle) and *Malaya podrozhnaya knizhitsa* (The Little Travel Book), printed in the Belarusan version of Old Church Slavic in 1525. The first Slavic loanwords came into the Lithuanian language from the Belarusans, while the latter adopted numerous Lithuanian terms. Much of the population of eastern Lithuania was assimilated to Belarusan speech during the second half of the 19th century. Folklore, folk art and the customs of western Belarusans in particular are historically close to those of the Lithuanians. The long cultural and political affiliation of Belarus and Lithuania has led Belarusan nationalists to regard their country as a successor state to the Lithuanian Grand Duchy. However, in contrast to Lithuania and Ukraine, the Belarusan intelligentsia was weak and unable to launch a strong national movement, although there was an attempt to create an independent state in 1918-1919.

Like Lithuania, western Belarus was heavily influenced by the Polonization (q. v.) of its upper classes, a process reinforced in 1920-1939 when much of the area was part of Poland (the eastern half became the Byelorussian SSR). Western Belarus has remained the easternmost outpost of Roman Catholicism in Europe to this day. Belarus in its current borders resulted from the destruction of Poland in September 1939 and the border adjustments of Lithuania with the USSR during 1939-1941. During Soviet rule most of Belarus, especially the cities and its educational system, were thoroughly Russified. Although Belarus achieved formal independence with the dismantling of the Soviet Union in December 1991, its armed forces and foreign policy are closely tied to Russia. In 1995 the Russian Federation took over the Lithuanian-Belarusan customs functions and border crossings. In 1995 a Lithuanian-Belarusan treaty established normal relations and finalized border issues. While both countries have formally accepted their current borders, some Belarusan nationalists still claim Vilnius on historic grounds, while Lithuanians have complained about the lack of cultural autonomy for the Lithuanian minority in western Belarus in the so-called historic "islands" (Lith. *salos*) of Lithuanian settlement. See GRAND DUCHY OF LITHUANIA.

BERMONDTISTS (Lith. *bermontininkai*), or Bermondt's Army. A combined German-Russian force, formally called the West Russian Army, that invaded the Baltic region in 1919, better known under the name of its commander, the White Russian Colonel Pavel Bermondt-Avalov (1877-1941). Under the terms of the Armistice of November 11, 1918 that ended World War I, Germany was required to retain, as long as the Allies considered necessary, a force in the eastern Baltic sufficient to repel the expected Bolshevik advance. The German commander in the east, Gen. Rüdiger von der Goltz, sought to retain Germany's influence in the Baltic even after the Allies ordered the withdrawal of the German Army in the summer of 1919. Before his recall to Germany in October 1919, Goltz allowed German "volunteers" to transfer to the command of Colonel Bermondt-Avalov, who also brought in Russian fighters, mostly POW's released by the Germans. The newly created West Russian Army that was formed in Latvia (q. v.) under Bermondt-Avalov was actually designed to evade the Allied requirement for German withdrawal, although some Allied officers hoped it would constitute an effective anti-Bolshevik force.

The Bermondtists invaded Lithuania in July 1919 and, taking advantage of Lithuania's preoccupation with resisting the Red Army, occupied most of northwestern Lithuania, looting much of the countryside. The Lithuanian Army defeated the Bermondtists in a fierce battle at the town of Radviliškis on November 21-23, 1919, capturing an enormous cache of military hardware, including aircraft, that proved instrumental in the Lithuanians' success in future military operations. The Bermondtists reluctantly evacuated Lithuania under the supervision of the Allied Military Mission in December 1919. At the same time, they were forced out of Latvia by Estonian and Latvian troops supported by the British Navy. The collapse of Bermondt-Avalov's adventure put an end to the hopes of the German High Command of gaining Germany a military foothold in the Baltic region and maintaining the position of the Baltic German nobility in Latvia and Estonia.

BOOK-SMUGGLING MOVEMENT, BOOK SMUGGLERS (Lith. *knygnešiai*). See PRESS BAN.

BRAZAUSKAS, ALGIRDAS MYKOLAS (1931-). Former First Secretary of the Lithuanian Communist Party (1988-1990), leader of the Lithuanian Democratic Labor Party during 1990-1992, and President of Lithuania since February 1993. Brazauskas was born in Rokiškis, Lithuania on September 22, 1931. After his graduation from the Kaunas Polytechnic Institute in 1956, Brazauskas worked as an engineer and in 1959 joined the CPSU. He soon became one of the rising young stars within the Communist Party bureaucracy, earning his reputation as a manager in the state construction industry. In 1965 Brazauskas was appointed Minister of Construction of the Lithuanian SSR, one of the youngest members in the Republic's government. In 1966 he became the Deputy Chairman of the Lithuanian SSR's State Planning Commission. In 1974 Brazauskas received the candidate degree in economics.

In 1977 Brazauskas was appointed Secretary of the Lithuanian Communist Party (q.v.) Central Committee, which placed him near the top of Lithuania's party leadership. Brazauskas achieved political prominence during the summer of 1988 when he distanced himself from the Republic's aging Party leadership and showed willingness to cooperate with the rapidly emerging Sąjūdis (q. v.) reform movement. On October 21, 1988 Brazauskas was elected to head the LCP as First Secretary and attempted to steer a middle course between the program of Sąjūdis and pressure from Moscow to halt the growing demand for Lithuanian independence. In response to such demands, Brazauskas led the LCP to declare itself independent from the CPSU during its Twentieth Party Congress in December 1989. As a result, Soviet authorities accused the Party leader of fomenting separatism.

Although Brazauskas was elected a deputy to the Lithuanian Supreme Soviet in the February 1990 elections, the Sąjūdis movement won a majority and chose Vytautas Landsbergis (q.v.) to lead the legislature (hence called the Supreme Council). On

March 11, 1990 Brazauskas, along with the other deputies, signed Lithuania's declaration formally restoring the country's independence. At the same time he was appointed Deputy Prime Minister in Kazimiera Prunskienė's (q.v.) government. In 1990 Brazauskas took the leadership of the newly-formed Lithuanian Democratic Labor Party (q. v.), the successor to the reformist LCP, and during the following two years he led the political opposition to the rightist political groups supporting Landsbergis, who headed the Supreme Council. The October 1992 elections to Lithuania's new parliament, the Seimas, gave a majority to Brazauskas' LDDP, in effect returning him to power. In Lithuania's first popular presidential elections of February 14, 1993, Brazauskas defeated rival candidate Stasys Lozoraitis (q. v.), claiming 60 percent of the vote. See COMMUNIST PARTY, LITHUANIAN.

BREST, UNION OF (1596). The union of the Eastern Orthodox and Roman Catholic Churches within the Polish-Lithuanian Commonwealth, proclaimed by a church synod at the town of Brest. Brest (also known as Brest-Litovsk, literally, the Lithuanian Brest), was an important cultural and trading center of the Commonwealth, located near the Polish-Lithuanian border. The establishment of the Moscow Patriarchate by Tsar Fedor in 1589 led to fears of Russian domination among many of the Orthodox bishops of Poland-Lithuania and, as a result, Metropolitan Michal Rahoza of Kiev petitioned Pope Clement VIII for union with Rome. In October 1596 the Orthodox bishops of the Commonwealth met at the Synod of Brest where a bitter schism developed between the advocates and opponents of union with Rome. The Uniates who accepted Catholicism were allowed to retain their Slavic Eastern Rite and a married clergy, but were compelled to adopt the Roman Catholic doctrine of the Eucharist and to promise obedience to the Holy See. The Uniates were viewed by the Orthodox Church as schismatics and traitors; the struggle between the two churches has lasted into the 20th century. In the 19th century the predominantly Uniate lands of eastern Galicia, centered around the city of Lviv, became the nucleus of the modern Ukrainian national movement.

Historically, the Uniates have often been referred to as "Greek Catholics," although "Eastern Rite Catholics" (distinguishing them from Latin Rite or Roman Catholics) would be a more useful term.

BUND. Name commonly used for the General Jewish Workers' Union in Lithuania, Poland and Russia (Yiddish: *Algemeiner Yidisher Arbeter Bund in Lite, Poiln un Rusland*). The Bund was established in September 1897 by Jewish Social Democrats to represent the interests of the Jewish workers in the cities and towns of the former Polish-Lithuanian Commonwealth and the Jewish Pale of Settlement in the Russian Empire. In 1898 the Bund, which was centered in Vilnius, joined the Russian Social Democratic Workers' Party (RSDWP) as an autonomous organization. During the early 1900s it was the strongest and most numerous revolutionary socialist organization in Lithuania. The Bund published the Yiddish-language underground newspaper, *Arbeter shtime* (Voice of the Workers), from 1896 to 1905. At the Second Congress of the RSDWP in Brussels and London, Lenin engineered the expulsion of the Bund from the Party, accusing it of narrow nationalism and rejecting the Bund's claim to be the sole representative of Jewish workers in Russia. After the Revolution of 1917 a part of the Bund joined the Bolsheviks, while the moderate faction continued its activities outside the USSR. See SOCIAL DEMOCRATIC PARTY, LITHUANIAN.

- C -

CASIMIR IV (1427-1492). King of Poland and Grand Duke of Lithuania, born in Cracow on November 29, 1427, the youngest son of King Władysław II Jogaila (q. v.) and his fourth wife, Sophia. After the assassination of Grand Duke Sigismund Kęstutaitis (q. v.) in 1440, the Lithuanian magnate families chose the thirteen-year-old Casimir over Sigismund's son, Michael, who was supported by the nobility of Samogitia (q. v.). Despite Polish objections, Casimir was formally proclaimed Grand Duke in Vilnius in 1440 and subdued the rebellious Samogitians, while his brother Władysław III ruled in Poland. The latter was killed in a campaign against the Turks near Varna, Bulgaria in 1444. After protracted disputes with the Poles, who threatened to elect a non-Jagiellonian ruler, the Lithuanian nobility agreed to Casimir's election to the Polish throne in 1447, but only after extracting a guarantee of Lithuania's political autonomy and territorial integrity. In domestic affairs, Casimir's reign was marked by bitter disputes between Poland and Lithuania over the control of Podolia and Volynia in Ukraine as well as over the nature of the Polish-Lithuanian dynastic alliance. Because of Casimir's long stay in Cracow and his neglect of Lithuanian affairs, there were several conspiracies which aimed to put another Grand Duke on the Lithuanian throne and even a foiled plot to assassinate Casimir in 1481. Casimir's support for legal reform and education considerably advanced Lithuania's cultural Westernization. Casimir was probably the last Grand Duke of Lithuania to have had a command of the Lithuanian language.

In foreign affairs, Casimir was faced with the growing power of Muscovy. Vasilii II (1425-1462) checked Lithuanian expansion in the east, while under the rule of Ivan III (1462-1505), Muscovy began to detach the Grand Duchy's easternmost territories from Lithuania and to conquer Lithuania's Russian allies, such as Novgorod (1471). Through his marriage to Elizabeth Hapsburg of Austria, which produced six sons and five daughters, Casimir considerably expanded the power of the Jagiellonian dynasty: his oldest son, Władysław, was elected both King of Bohemia (1471-1516) and Hungary (1490-1516). Casimir died in Grodno (q. v.) on June 7, 1492. See CASIMIR, SAINT.

CASIMIR, SAINT (1458-1484). The patron saint of Lithuania, the third child of Casimir IV (q. v.), born in Cracow on October 3, 1458. Casimir was educated at the royal court by the Polish chronicler Jan Długosz and the Italian humanist Callimachus

Buonacorsi. In 1471, bolstered by the claims of his mother, Elizabeth of Hapsburg, he was sent to Hungary in an unsuccessful bid to seize the throne from King Matthias Corvinus. From 1481 to 1483 Casimir administered Poland when his father began making frequent trips to Lithuania. In 1483 he arrived in Lithuania, residing mainly in Vilnius and Trakai (q. v.) as his father's viceroy in Lithuania, in charge of the Grand Duchy's Chancellory. Casimir died in Grodno (q.v.), probably of tuberculosis, on March 4, 1484, the date celebrated as his feast day. He was buried in the Cathedral of Vilnius.

Having gained a saintly reputation for his religious devotion and ascetic lifestyle, Casimir was canonized by Pope Leo X in 1521. The cult of St. Casimir received considerable impetus from reports of his miraculous interventions in Lithuania's wars against the Muscovites in the 16th century. In 1953 his coffin was moved from the Cathedral of Vilnius to the Church of SS. Peter and Paul, but was returned to its place in the Cathedral in 1988. Numerous Lithuanian churches and religious institutions have been named in his honor. Casimir (Lith. masc. Kazimieras or Kazys, fem. Kazimiera) is one of the most popular given names in Lithuania.

CATHOLIC CHURCH. Catholicism is the religious affiliation of the vast majority of Lithuanian-speaking people, both in Lithuania and outside the country. The Roman Catholic Church also exercised enormous cultural, economic, social and political influence in the history of the Lithuanian nation. In the tenth century, Christian missionaries came to Prussia; by the early 13th century, Danish and German missionaries were active in what is now Estonia and Latvia. The conquest of the Prussian tribes by the Teutonic Knights (q. v.) confronted the Lithuanians, who until then practiced their own traditional religion, with the need to respond to the Christian challenge.

It is thought that the first Christian churches appeared in Lithuania by the early 13th century. By the mid-13th century, the Lithuanian prince Mindaugas (q. v.) managed to unite the feuding Lithuanian tribes and in 1251 was baptized and crowned King of

Lithuania. However, Mindaugas' baptism failed to deter attacks by the Teutonic crusaders and there is speculation that Mindaugas may have become an apostate before his assassination in 1263. Between 1263 and 1387 Lithuania's rulers were once again pagans and most of the country returned to traditional religious practices. Grand Duke Gediminas (c. 1316-1341) (q. v.) employed Franciscans in his chancery and allowed Christian churches in Lithuania. His diplomatic correspondence indicated a willingness to accept Christianity but attempts to reconvert the realm came to naught. Gediminas' son Algirdas (1345-1377) (q. v.) took a Russian Orthodox wife; Kęstutis (q. v.) was the Grand Duchy's last non-Christian ruler. In 1386 Algirdas' son Jogaila (Pol. Jagiełło) accepted the Polish crown, creating dynastic ties between the Grand Duchy of Lithuania and the Kingdom of Poland. In 1387, after Jogaila became King of Poland as Władysław IV, Lithuania, now ruled by his cousin Vytautas (1392-1430) (q. v.), once again formally accepted Roman Catholicism, which became the dominant religious and cultural force in the ethnographic Lithuanian lands. Despite attempts at union with Rome, Lithuania's East Slavic lands, which encompassed Ukraine and much of central Russia, remained Eastern Orthodox.

The penetration of Catholicism into the general Lithuanian population proceeded slowly. Christianization was hampered by the lack of clergy fluent in Lithuanian; the first Capitula was made up of Poles, Germans and Czechs. Despite problems, Catholicism became an important political and cultural force in Lithuania. Christianization accelerated the processes of Polonization (q. v.) and Westernization, particularly in the area of education. The Reformation (q. v) was a significant event in Lithuanian history, but its influence was relatively short-lived. While Calvinism engulfed much of the Grand Duchy during the second half of the 16th century, its success was only temporary. In 1564 King Sigismund Augustus of the Polish-Lithuanian Commonwealth endorsed the Tridentine Reforms. The educational and religious activities of the Jesuits, who established an Order in Lithuania in 1608, helped make the Counter-Reformation (q. v.) successful in the Grand Duchy.

During the 18th century, the Church undertook not only religious indoctrination among the lower classes, but encouraged reform of elementary education under the leadership of Ignacy Massalski (q. v.), the Bishop of Vilnius. The Partitions (q. v.) of the Polish-Lithuanian Commonwealth between 1772 and 1795 did not seriously affect religious life until the anti-Russian uprising of 1830-1831. After the rebellion, Tsar Nicholas I (1825-1855) adopted an increasingly oppressive policy: the Catholic Church was attacked as a bastion of Polish, and hence anti-Russian agitation. Despite government obstructionism, the Church, under the leadershop of the Bishop of Samogitia, Motiejus Valančius (1801-1875) (q. v.), took a more active part in the education and social life of the peasantry, especially through the parish schools and temperance societies. Between 1864 and 1904 printing the native language in Latin letters was banned as part of the Russification campaign. In response the Catholic clergy initiated the *knygnešiai* or book-smuggling movement (q.v.). At times, Russian religious persecution turned violent: in 1893 at the town of Kražiai (q. v.), popular resistance to the closure of the local monastery and church resulted in a punitive Cossack rampage that killed nine people and injured many others.

The emergence of the Lithuanian national movement in the 19th century inspired a struggle between the Polonized hierarchy and the Lithuanian-oriented younger clergy. The latter gradually gained the upper hand, a process completed with the coming of independence and majority rule to Lithuania in 1918. Catholics made up about 80 percent of the population during the interwar period. After 1926, the authoritarian Nationalist regime suppressed some Catholic youth organizations as potentially subversive, but the state continued to accord the Church a privileged position. Before 1940 Lithuania had no civil registry; all births and marriages were recorded by the clergy of the various religious communities. Lithuania's relations with the Holy See were exacerbated by the Polish-Lithuanian dispute over Vilnius, Lithuania's historic capital, which was under Polish control between 1920 and 1939, and which the Vatican had recognized as part of the Polish ecclesiastical province. Normal relations with the

Holy See were established only in 1925. In 1926 Lithuania was named an ecclesiastical province and a Vatican-Lithuanian concordat was signed in 1927, but tensions with Rome over the Vilnius issue persisted. The concordat abolished the historic diocese of Samogitia (Žemaitija) (q. v.). The Archdiocese of Kaunas became the metropolitan see with Juozas Skvireckas (1873-1959) as its first head. The rest of the country was divided into the dioceses of Telšiai, Panevėžys, Kaišiadorys, Vilkaviškis and the prelature of Klaipėda, the seaport Lithuania acquired from Germany in 1923. Three seminaries, the Catholic faculty of theology and philosophy of the University of Kaunas, and the Catholic Academy of Sciences were established. Catholic cultural, intellectual and charitable organizations enrolled hundreds of thousands of members. There were in 1940 over 1,400 secular and monastic Catholic clergy, about 400 seminarians, and more than 700 churches. Between 1914 and 1940 the number of priests grew by about 40 percent and the number of seminarians fourfold. In addition to religious institutions and religious communities, the Lithuanian Church maintained numerous lay organizations, which enabled Catholicism to exert a powerful influence in virtually every aspect of Lithuanian life, such as the *Ateitis* (q. v.) Catholic Federation representing the intelligentsia and the students; for rural youth, the *Pavasaris* (Lith. Spring) association; the Union of Catholic Women's Organizations and the national Catholic children's organization, the *angelaičiai* (Lith. Angels). Although difficult to quantify, the impact of Catholicism on Lithuania's cultural life was probably even more important than its organizational power. Lithuania's foremost Catholic daily, *XX Amžius* (The Twentieth Century), published between 1936 and 1940, had a large following outside traditionally Catholic circles. The monthly journal *Židinys* (Lith. Hearth), the illustrated cultural weekly *Naujoji Romuva* (Lith. The New Romuva) and the Faculty of Theology and Philosophy periodical *Athenaeum*, were the most prestigious academic periodicals.

In 1940 Lithuania became the first Roman Catholic country to come under Soviet rule. The new Communist regime abolished religious instruction in public schools, ended government support for religious institutions, instituted civil marriage, legalized divorce and abolished religious holidays. The government nationalized the Catholic press, outlawed Catholic societies, closed virtually all Catholic institutions and took over the Theological Seminary in Kaunas. Communist repression of religion intensified during 1940-1941 when the NKVD began to recruit priests to work for the political police. During the German occupation, when Nazi authorities showed relatively little interest in purely religious matters, some seminaries were reopened and religion was allowed back into the schools. In March 1942 the Germans deported Archbishop Romuald Jałbrzykowski (1876-1955) of Vilnius and a number of Polish religious, thus marking the end of Polish control of this historic diocese. The Lithuanian Catholic Church, like most of the population, viewed the return of the Soviet armies in 1944 with alarm. Lithuania's metropolitan Skvireckas and hundreds of religious fled or were evacuated westward. Mass deportations between 1945 and 1953 sent thousands of Lithuanian citizens to Siberia and other remote regions of the USSR. Collectivization and a particularly bitter anti-Soviet guerrilla war raged in Lithuania during the later 1940s and early 1950s. Prohibitive taxes were levied against the Church and in 1948 religious instruction outside the home was banned by the Soviets; at the same time, all Church properties were nationalized and the buildings "leased" to the religious communities. A new system of supposedly self-governing religious communities responsible to the government was introduced in an attempt to subvert the traditional Catholic parish system and undermine the clergy's leadership of the faithful. In February 1946 the NKVD arrested and executed Bishop Vincentas Borisevičius (1887-1946) of Telšiai and deported his auxiliary, exiled Archbishop Mečislovas Reinys (1884-1953) and then imprisoned the most outspoken opponent of the regime, Bishop Teofilis Matulionis (1873-1962) of Kaišiadorys. By the middle of 1947 Lithuania's only active bishop was Kazimieras Paltarokas (1875-1958). About a third of Lithuania's Catholic clergy were killed, imprisoned or deported during the late 1940s. This period also witnessed an intensification of Soviet atheistic propaganda.

However, the regime's attempts to cut the Lithuanian Church's links with the Vatican were unsuccessful.

The policies of Stalin's successor, Nikita Khrushchev (1953-1964), signaled an abandonment of mass terror and a temporary relaxation of controls. A number of deported priests and two bishops, Matulionis and Ramanauskas, returned from exile. In 1955 two new bishops, Petras Maželis (1894-1966) and Julijonas Steponavičius (1911-1992) were consecrated and assigned to Telšiai and Vilnius respectively. For the first time since the war, limited official contact with the Holy See was permitted and some Lithuanian clergy were allowed to attend the Second Vatican Council. Khrushchev's "thaw," as it was known, was short-lived and repressive policies were activated by the late 1950s without, however, reverting to the mass terror of the Stalin years. By 1961 Bishops Matulionis, Vincentas Sladkevičius (q. v.) (b. 1920) and Steponavičius were exiled from their dioceses and a number of priests were arrested. Even as the Soviet government attempted to normalize relations with the Vatican, and the Holy See sought an "opening to the east," the Lithuanian Soviet regime launched an anti-Catholic campaign which reached its height in the 1960s and 1970s.

In response to Soviet repression a Catholic dissident movement gained strength in the 1970s. Its main vehicle was the *Lietuvos Katalikų Bažnyčios Kronika* (Lith. The Chronicle of the Lithuanian Catholic Church) which began to circulate in 1972, one of the most important samizdat publications in the Soviet Union until the late 1980s. Along with the Catholic Committee for the Defense of the Rights of Believers organized in 1978, it detailed abuses of religious freedom, as well as the violation of human and national rights in Lithuania. Despite arrests and harassment of Catholic activists by the KGB, Soviet authorities were unable to eliminate the dissident movement. Catholic resistance to Soviet religious policy also opened up a split within the Lithuanian Church between elements in the hierarchy and clergy favoring accommodation with the Soviet regime, and the Catholic dissident groups, which were closely allied to the growing Lithuanian movement to restore national sovereignty.

The reforms and upheavals of the Gorbachev era (1985-1991) in the Soviet Union transformed the public role of religion in Lithuania. The most egregious restrictions on religion were lifted in the late 1980s and effectively eliminated by 1990. Imprisoned Catholic activists and exiled prelates were released and allowed to resume their work. In June 1988 Bishop Vincentas Sladkevičius (q. v.) was named Lithuania's first modern cardinal and actively supported the movement for greater religious and national rights. In October 1988 the Cathedral of Vilnius, which had been turned into an art gallery by the Soviets, was returned to the Church. By 1989 most legal restrictions on the Church were removed and, after independence was proclaimed in March 1990, the Lithuanian government has continued the process of restoring Church property seized under the Soviets. The Theological Seminary in Kaunas has been expanded and a new one has opened in Telšiai. The Holy See opened its nunciature in Vilnius in 1991. Optional Catholic and other religious instruction has been permitted in public schools and a number of private Catholic primary and secondary schools opened during the early 1990s. The Catholic press now publishes several popular periodicals, the largest being *Katalikų pasaulis* (Lith. Catholic World). In 1992 the Vatican appointed a career Vatican diplomat, Audrius Bačkis, as Archbishop of Vilnius, who was also elected president of the Lithuanian bishops' conference of nine members (in 1995). With the restoration of Lithuania's independence and the re-establishment of diplomatic relations, the Vatican also recognized the Archdiocese of Vilnius as part of the Lithuanian ecclesiastical province. In September 1993 Pope John Paul II visited Lithuania. See JESUITS; REFORMATION; RELIGION, PRE-CHRISTIAN; RESISTANCE MOVEMENTS; ŠALKAUSKIS, STASYS; TEUTONIC KNIGHTS; VALAN-ČIUS, MOTIEJUS.

CENTRAL LITHUANIA (1920-1922). A small state created after the seizure of Vilnius and its environs by the troops of Gen. Lucjan Żeligowski (q. v.) with the silent assent of the Polish government in October 1920. Mindful of the initial international disapproval of Żeligowski's move, the Polish government eschewed immediate annexation of the region. In addition, since Żeligowski claimed that he had occupied Vilnius in order to allow the local inhabitants to freely choose their own political future, any precipitous incorporation of the territory would have proved embarrassing. As political cover for his operation, Żeligowski proclaimed the establishment of the formally independent state of Central Lithuania (Pol. *Litwa Środkowa*) on October 12, 1920, naming himself as the head of its government and army. Central Lithuania, which encompassed over 13,000 sq. km. with about 600,000 primarily Polish, Lithuanian, Belarusan and Jewish inhabitants, received immediate diplomatic "recognition" from Warsaw. The elections to the Central Lithuanian diet on January 8-9, 1922 were boycotted by much of the non-Polish population and electoral registration rules heavily favored Polish-speaking voters. On February 20, 1922 the newly-elected diet voted to request that Central Lithuania be made an integral part of Poland. In March 1922 the Polish government and parliament approved the incorporation of Central Lithuania into the Polish republic. Despite Lithuanian protests, the Conference of Ambassadors formally recognized the existing boundary of Poland and Lithuania as the international border between the two countries on March 15, 1923, thus, in effect, sanctioning Polish sovereignty over Vilnius. See POLAND; VILNIUS; VILNIUS QUESTION; ŻELIGOWSKI, LUCJAN.

ČERNIUS, JONAS (1898-1977). Lithuanian general and statesman, born on January 6, 1898 in Panevėžys district. Among the first graduates of the Lithuanian military academy in 1919, he studied military engineering in Belgium and France in the late 1920s and early 1930s. From 1935 to 1939 he was chief of staff of the Lithuanian Army, reaching the rank of brigadier general. During the political crisis following the loss of Klaipėda (q. v.) to Nazi Germany in March 1939, the embattled Smetona (q. v.) regime sought to placate public opinion by asking General Černius, a respected career military officer, to head a coalition cabinet called the "Government of Unified Work." However, Černius' attempts to liberalize the political atmosphere, ease censorship and encourage broader participation in politics ran afoul of Nationalists (q. v.) who feared losing their grip on power. Černius resigned his premiership on November 22, 1939 and was assigned to command the Lithuanian Army's First Infantry Division. He died in Claremont, California on July 3, 1977. See ULTIMATUMS.

CHODKIEWICZ (Lith. Chodkevičius, also Katkevičius). A Samogitian noble family, which dominated Lithuanian politics during much of the 16th and early 17th centuries and produced a number of famous military leaders. **Jerome Chodkiewicz** (ca. 1500-1561), the Elder of Samogitia (q. v.) and a Count of the Holy Roman Empire led the Lithuanian forces against Ivan IV ("The Terrible") in Livonia in 1560. His brother, **Gregory Chodkiewicz** (1505-1572), served as Palatine of Vitebsk and Kiev between 1554 and 1558; he distinguished himself as the Grand Hetman of Lithuania in campaigns against the Tatars, Swedes and Muscovites, defeating the latter at the Battle of Ula in 1564. **John Jerome Chodkiewicz** (ca. 1525-1579), the son of Jerome, served as Administrator of Livonia from 1566 to 1578; he led the Lithuanian delegation to the talks that resulted in the Union of Lublin (q. v.). The most illustrious of the Chodkiewicz clan was his brother, **John Karol Chodkiewicz** (1560-1621), who held various high administrative posts in the Grand Duchy, but was best known as a skilled military leader. He gained his reputation first by defeating numerically superior Swedish armies in Livonia in 1604-1605. Chodkiewicz was given command of the Polish-Lithuanian forces in 1611-1613 during Russia's Time of Troubles, but was unable to maintain the Commonwealth's garrison in Moscow. In 1621 Chodkiewicz died while leading a final campaign against Sultan Osman II in Moldavia in September 1621, when the Polish-Lithuanian forces managed to repel a large Ottoman army on the right bank of the Dniester River.

CHRISTIAN DEMOCRATIC PARTY, LITHUANIAN (Lith. *Lietuvos Krikščionių Demokratų Partija*). The Lithuanian Christian Democratic Party emerged from the Catholic wing of the national movement in the 19th century and gained important support from the younger clergy who had rejected the leadership of the Catholic Church's (q. v.) Polonized hierarchy. The biweekly newspaper *Apžvalga* (Lith. Review), published from 1894 to 1896, and the monthly *Tévynes Sargas* (Lith. The Guardian of the Fatherland), from 1896 to 1904, formulated a national political program which became the basis of Lithuanian Christian Democracy. In 1907 the Catholic political movement was named the Lithuanian Christian Democratic Union; it was heavily influenced by the encyclicals of Pope Leo XIII, especially *Rerum Novarum* (Latin: Of New Things). Prominent clergy were the first leaders of the Lithuanian Christian Democrats, for example, the statesman Msgr. Mykolas Krupavičius (q. v.) and Bishop Pranciškus Būčys (1872-1951). In 1920 the Christian Democratic Party and the Peasant Union formed a Catholic Bloc which won 59 out of 112 seats to the Constituent Assembly, and then won a majority in the First (1922-1923) and Second (1923-1926) Seimas (q. v.). However, the Christian Democrats became a minority during the bitterly contested elections to the Third Seimas in May 1926.

Most Christian Democrat leaders supported the right-wing coup of December 17, 1926 but they fell out with the Nationalists in April 1927 and withdrew from government. Like the other political parties, the Christian Democrats were restricted by the Smetona (q. v.) regime; they returned to the government in March 1939 when two Christian Democratic ministers were included in the coalition cabinet of General Jonas Černius (q. v.). The leadership and the rank-and-file of the Christian Democratic movement were decimated by Soviet arrests and deportations after 1940, but the party continued its activities in emigration after World War II, particularly within the Supreme Committee for the Liberation of Lithuania (q. v.); it also maintained contacts with the international Christian Democratic movement. The Lithuanian Christian Democratic Party was reestablished in Lithuania after the restoration of independence in 1990. During the October 1992 elections to the Seimas, the Christian Democrats won 12 out of 141 seats in parliament, but lost ground in the October 1996 election.

ČIURLIONIS, MIKALOJUS (1875-1911). Lithuanian painter and composer, born on September 10, 1875 in Varėna. Čiurlionis began his training as a musician in Plungė, Samogitia, at the private school of Prince Ogiński who supported the young man's studies at the Warsaw Conservatory from 1893 to 1899 and at the Leipzig Conservatory in 1901-1902. During his musical studies Čiurlionis grew increasingly fascinated by cosmology, as well as the history of culture and poetry. He attempted to convey his appreciation of the harmony of the universe in his cantatas, sonatas and short pieces for the piano. Čiurlionis' symphonic poem *In the Forest* became his best-known and most frequently performed orchestral composition in Lithuania, while *The Sea* is his most popular composition for the piano.

However, it was in painting that Čiurlionis achieved artistic prominence. He began to paint after he had already become a skilled composer. Čiurlionis gave his works musical themes and titles; for example, one popular cycle of paintings was entitled *The Sonata of the Sea*. He attended the Warsaw Academy of Art from 1904 to 1906 and is considered to have created his finest paintings in Vilnius and St. Petersburg between 1907 and 1909. He held public exhibitions in Vilnius in 1906 and 1907. Čiurlionis joined the avant-garde Russian *Mir isskustva* (Rus. World of Art) movement during the so-called Silver Age of Russian culture on the eve of World War I. Towards the end of his life Čiurlionis' work grew increasingly more mystical. In addition to his own artistry, Čiurlionis organized Lithuanian choral groups to encourage public performance of folk music and did much to foster an appreciation for Lithuanian culture and folk art. In 1909 he married Sofija Kymantaitė (1885-1958), a writer and public figure in her own right. Despite his talent, Čiurlionis was in financial straits much of the time and towards the end of his life suffered from mental illness. He died in a hospital near Warsaw on April 10, 1911. Čiurlionis received greater recognition both in Lithuania and internationally only after his death; today he is regarded by most Lithuanians as the country's most gifted artist. See ART; MUSIC.

COMMONWEALTH, POLISH-LITHUANIAN. The term widely used for the Polish-Lithuanian state from the 16th to the 18th centuries. After the Act of Krėva, or Kriavas (Pol. Krewo) (q. v.) in 1386 the Kingdom of Poland (q.v.) and the Grand Duchy of Lithuania (q. v.) functioned as two separate states under the same Jagiellonian ruling house: after 1501 the King of Poland was invariably chosen as Grand Duke. The two states entered into a more closely-knit confederation at the Union of Lublin (q. v.) in 1569 which stipulated a common diet and a coordinated foreign policy, while allowing each state to maintain a separate judicial system and military establishment. The term Commonwealth is an English translation of the Polish term *Rzeczpospolita* (derived from the Latin *res publica*), which is often used in Lithuanian as well (Lith. *Žečpospolita*). Because of the Latin root of this term, some English-language works employ the concept of the "Gentry Republic," to describe the Polish-Lithuanian state between 1569-1795. The revolutionary Constitution of May 3, 1791 abolished the confederate structure of the Kingdom and Grand Duchy in favor of a unitary state, but this plan was never realized because the Third Partition (q. v.) of Poland-Lithuania in 1795 ended the Commonwealth.

COMMUNIST PARTY, LITHUANIAN (Lith. *Lietuvos Komunistų Partija*). The ideas of revolutionary socialism came into Lithuania through Marxist study circles founded during the last quarter of the 19th century. Initially, most of the Marxists were members of the Lithuanian Social Democratic Party (q. v.), the Jewish Bund (q. v.), and other revolutionary socialist groups. In 1917 the leftist social democrats who supported Bolshevism, led by Vincas Mickevičius-Kapsukas (q. v.), Zigmas Angarietis (q. v.) and Pranas Eidukevičius (1869-1926), organized a Lithuanian section of

Leninist wing of the Russian Social Democratic Workers' Party, which in 1918 formally became the Russian Communist Party (Bolsheviks). The occupation of eastern Lithuania by the Red Army encouraged the formation of local Bolshevik groups. These were later consolidated as the Lithuanian and Belarusan Communist Party, which succeeded briefly in establishing a Lithuanian-Belarusan Soviet Republic in Vilnius, the so-called Litbel (q. v.), in late 1918 and early 1919. Soviet Russia's recognition of Lithuania's independence in 1920 led to the creation of a separate Lithuanian Communist Party which was a member of the Communist International from 1921 to 1940. Since the LCP was banned in Lithuania, most of the Old Bolshevik leadership of the Party lived in the USSR and attempted to coordinate clandestine activities in their homeland. The LCP's Politburo worked in the USSR, while an underground Organizational Bureau directed Party activities within Lithuania. During the Stalinist purges of the 1930s a number of prominent Lithuanian Communists residing in the USSR, including Angarietis, were executed.

In Lithuania the LCP operated with only minor restrictions until the military coup of December 1926 when, after the execution of four Communist leaders for treason, the Party was driven underground. Between 1926 to 1940 LCP membership fluctuated between a few hundred to several thousand and had little popular appeal. In addition, the LCP enjoyed the support of MOPR (Rus. acronym for the International Organization to Assist Revolutionaries), which raised money for imprisoned Communists and their families. Most Lithuanians came to view the Party as an alien political force: a third to a half of the membership were non-Lithuanians (primarily Jews and Russians), while the Communists' open admiration for the USSR gained them a reputation as foreign agents.

The occupation of Lithuania by the Soviet Union on June 15, 1940 brought the LCP to power through the establishment of the People's Government (q. v.) and the incorporation of Lithuania into the USSR in August 1940, after which the LCP became a constituent part of what was then known as the All-Union

Communist Party (Bolsheviks). At the same time, Antanas Sniečkus (q. v.) was appointed First Secretary and remained in that post for the next three decades. In February, 1941, when the LCP's Fifth Party Congress outlined Lithuania's Sovietization program, the membership of the LCP stood at less than 2,000; during the spring of 1941 the Party increasingly came under the direct control of the NKVD, the Soviet secret police. During the German occupation of 1941-1944 the LCP suffered severe losses both as a result of executions and in guerrilla warfare against the Nazis. During 1944-1953 the Party was heavily involved as an ally of the Soviets in the pacification of postwar Lithuania; as a result, thousands of Party activists were killed by anti-Soviet partisans. During this period the LCP was thoroughly Russified and dominated by outsiders; in 1953 only about a fourth of its membership were ethnic Lithuanians. This situation changed after Stalin's death; as a part of the CPSU, the LCP's membership on the eve of Gorbachev's reforms was about 80 percent Lithuanian. However, it was common practice to appoint an ethnic Russian in a supervisory capacity as Second Secretary of the LCP. During the late 1950s, a number of prominent Party members, including the rector of Vilnius University, were purged for "nationalist deviations," that is, attempts to bring a measure of cultural autonomy to the Lithuanian SSR. After the death of Sniečkus in 1974, the Party secretaries were Petras Griškevičius (q. v.), Ringaudas Songaila and Algirdas Brazauskas (q.v.).

The LCP came under severe pressure as a result of the ferment that seized Lithuania in the late 1980s. Initially, the party leadership resisted the changes that were already sweeping the other Baltic republics, but in October 1988 the new (and last) party leader Algirdas Brazauskas proved more amenable to change. On December 6, 1989, the LCP officially renounced its "leading role" that had been enshrined in the Constitution of the Lithuanian SSR. As sentiment for Lithuanian independence swelled, the LCP responded by formally withdrawing from the CPSU at its Twentieth Congress in Vilnius on December 20, 1989 and proclaiming a social democratic platform, despite intense pressure from the Kremlin. A pro-Soviet minority faction, led by Juozas

Jermalavičius and Mykolas Burokevičius, opposed the separation and formed a breakaway party committed to Moscow, the so-called Lithuanian Communist Party (CPSU), but it was banned after the failed anti-Gorbachev coup of August 1991. Despite its attempts to accommodate the new political realities, the LCP lost the February 1990 elections to the Lithuanian Supreme Soviet and became the minority opposition in the legislature. In December 1990 the LCP declared itself a workers' party of a social democratic type, renamed the Lithuanian Democratic Labor Party (Lith. *Lietuvos Demokratinė Darbo Partija*) (q.v.). Opponents of the LDDP have charged that this party was simply a political vehicle for the former LCP's elite, the so-called nomenklatura, to retain its power. Nevertheless, the LDDP won a majority in the Seimas in October 1992.

CONFEDERATIONS. A term denoting temporary political and military alliances of the *szlachta*, or gentry, during the period of the Polish-Lithuanian Commonwealth (q.v.), especially after the end of the Jagiellonian dynasty in 1572. Generally, any member of the gentry could initiate a confederation by proclaiming a political cause and then presenting formal Articles of Confederation to which the gathered assembly would give its support. Special diets of the Commonwealth were known as Confederal Diets, during which decisions were made by majority vote which could not be obstructed by the infamous *liberum veto* (see DIETS). Some confederations were formed to protect local interests, while others aimed to solve problems of the entire Commonwealth. At first, the confederations were an important means by which the gentry could protect their interests against royal power. During the 18th century several confederations, especially those of Radom (q. v.), Bar (q. v.) and Targowica (q. v.), attempted to tackle the perennial crises caused by social and political anarchy as well as foreign intervention.

CONSTITUENT ASSEMBLY (Lith. *Steigiamasis Seimas*). Lithuanian representative body, elected on April 14-15, 1920, which laid the constitutional foundations for the Republic of Lithuania, whose independence had been proclaimed in 1918. The first democratic elections in Lithuanian history chose 112 representatives: 59 Christian Democrats, 28 members claiming allegiance to the Socialist Populists and the Peasant Union, 12 Social Democrats (q. v.), 11 members of national minorities (7 Jews, 3 Poles, one German), and two non-partisan deputies. The Constituent Assembly, which convened in Kaunas on May 15, 1920, elected Aleksandras Stulginskis (q. v.) head of state or president in his capacity as the chairman of the Assembly, and approved a Christian Democrat-Populist coalition government headed by Kazys Grinius (q. v.). The Constituent Assembly was a youthful body: 29 members were under 30 and only eight were more than 50 years old. The most important achievement of the Assembly was the approval of the Republic of Lithuania's first constitution (q. v.) on August 1, 1922. In addition, the Assembly enacted a sweeping land reform act in April 1922, which essentially ended the old manorial system in agriculture (q. v.). It also ratified a number of important treaties, notably the July 12, 1920 Soviet Russian-Lithuanian peace treaty. The Constituent Assembly ended its work in the fall of 1922. On October 10-11, elections were held to the first regular Seimas (Diet) as required by the new constitution. See DIETS; CONSTITUTIONS; TARYBA.

CONSTITUTIONS. The ideal of constitutional government first came to Lithuania under the influence of the French Revolution in the late 18th century. Following are the constitutional arrangements in modern Lithuanian history:

The Constitution of May 3, 1791. This document was much influenced by the writings of the Polish Enlightenment thinkers Hugo Kołłątaj (1750-1812) and Stanisław Staszic (1755-1826), and by the admiration of reform-minded gentry for the French and American Revolutions. Taking advantage of Russia's war with the Ottomans, radical deputies of the Four-Year Diet (q. v.) approved the "Law of Government" (Pol. *Ustawa Rządowa*) which separated executive, legislative and judicial functions in the Polish-Lithuanian Commonwealth. Executive authority was vested in a hereditary King, the Primate of the Catholic Church, and a Council of Ministers. Decisions of the Diet were by majority vote, thus eliminating the *liberum veto* (see DIET). Confederations (q. v.) were banned and the right to vote was tied to property qualifications. However, serfdom was still legal, although the peasants were to be protected. Most important for Lithuania, the "Commonwealth of Two Nations" was formally abandoned and a unitary state proclaimed, eliminating the Grand Duchy's separate judiciary, treasury and army. At the insistence of Lithuanian representatives, in October 1791 the Diet passed an act of "Mutual Assurance of the Two Nations," which restored some measure of political autonomy to Lithuania. In the end, Poland-Lithuania was never really governed by the May 3rd Constitution because of Russian intervention (see TARGOWICA, CONFEDERATION OF).

The Constitutions of the Republic of Lithuania, 1918-1940. After the proclamation of Lithuanian independence in February 1918, the country was governed by the Temporary Constitution of November 2, 1918, which placed power in the hands of a three-person Presidium, the State Council and the Cabinet. This temporary basic law was amended in April 1919 by creating the office of President and introducing the State Control Agency. Another temporary constitution was approved on June 10, 1920 after elections to the Constituent Assembly (Lith. *Steigiamasis Seimas*) (q. v.). The Seimas placed most of the power in the hands of the legislature with a weak executive President elected by parliament.

On August 1, 1922 the Constituent Assembly adopted a permanent constitution. The President of the Republic was elected for a three-year term by the Seimas but the power of the presidency was limited. Actual executive power was vested in the government (the premier and cabinet), but the greatest authority was reserved for the unicameral Seimas, elected by universal and direct suffrage. After the Nationalist (q. v.) seizure of power in December 1926, the

Seimas adopted a considerably less democratic constitution on May 15, 1928, which greatly strengthened the executive power of the President, who was now to be chosen indirectly by an electoral college for a seven-year term and could not be removed from office by the Seimas. The basic law of 1928 severely limited the prerogatives of the legislature. On May 12, 1938 the Seimas and President ratified a new constitution, which better reflected the authoritarian principles of the Nationalist regime and, in practice, entrenched the dictatorship of Antanas Smetona (q. v.). The Constitution of 1938 enumerated a series of obligations of the citizens to the state and gave the President power to rule by decree. All three constitutions of independent Lithuania (1922, 1928 and 1938) provided for an independent judiciary, protection of all religions under the law, and mandated the equality of all nationalities.

Constitutions of the Lithuanian SSR (1940-1990). On August 3, 1940 Lithuania was proclaimed a Union Republic of the USSR by the Supreme Soviet in Moscow. On August 25, 1940, the People's Diet (q. v.) announced the Constitution (Basic Law) of the Lithuanian SSR, thus completing the legal Sovietization of the country. The legislature (Seimas) now became the Supreme Soviet of the Lithuanian SSR (Lith. *Lietuvos TSR Aukščiausioji Taryba*), which elected a governing Presidium. On December 26, 1951 the Supreme Soviet of the Lithuanian SSR amended the 1940 basic law to realign it more closely with that of the other Soviet republics. Following the lead of the All-Union Soviet government, the Lithuanian SSR adopted a new constitution on April 20, 1978 which reflected the realities of a society under "mature socialism," mandated a closer legal integration of the Republic into the All-Union economic, social and political structures, and formally proclaimed the Communist Party as the "leading force" in society (the latter provision was abandoned in December 1989). While the Constitutions of the USSR and the Lithuanian SSR provided for legal secession from the Soviet Union, this article was viewed as a dead letter.

Constitutions since 1990. In February 1990 Sajūdis (q. v.) defeated the Lithuanian Communist Party (q. v.) in the elections to the Supreme Soviet of the Lithuanian SSR. On March 11, 1990 the legislature, now better-known in English as the Supreme Council of the Republic of Lithuania (Lith. *Lietuvos Respublikos Aukščiausioji Taryba*) declared null and void the Lithuanian SSR Constitution of 1978 and abrogated the USSR Constitution of 1977 in Lithuania. In an unusual constitutional move, the Supreme Council voted to restore, and then immediately suspend, the May 12, 1938 Constitution, thus emphasizing the continuity of the pre-1940 Republic of Lithuania with the independent state of 1990. In place of the authoritarian 1938 constitution, the Supreme Council enacted the Provisional Basic Law of the Republic of Lithuania, which served as the country's temporary constitution. Supreme authority was vested in the Council and its chairman served as de facto head of state; executive power was granted to the Council of Ministers. On October 25, 1992 the Supreme Council replaced the Provisional Basic Law with a permanent constitution, providing for a popularly elected president (five-year term) and a unicameral legislature, the Seimas (four-year term), consisting of 141 deputies. The head of government, the prime minister, can be removed by the president only with the concurrence of the Seimas. See BAR, CONFEDERATION OF; DIET; SMETONA, ANTANAS; TARGOWICA, CONFEDERATION OF.

COUNTER-REFORMATION. After the Protestant Reformation (q. v.) swept much of Lithuania, the Catholic forces in the Grand Duchy attempted to roll back the Lutheran and Calvinist gains. As elsewhere in Europe, the Catholic revival in Lithuania was inspired by the Council of Trent (1545-1563). The Tridentine Reforms reaffirmed Church teachings regarding Scripture, rationalized Catholic dogma and improved the training of the clergy. In Lithuania, even when Lithuanian Protestantism was at its height between the mid-16th and mid-17th centuries, the Catholic hierarchy resisted. Paul Holszański, the bishop of Vilnius from 1536 to 1555, warned King Sigismund Augustus (q. v.) against accommodating Protestants and urged him to use force against the Church's enemies. For their part, King Sigismund the Old (q. v.)

and Queen Bona Sforza (q. v.) had opposed the Reformation with bans and decrees. In 1564 Sigismund Augustus endorsed the Tridentine Reforms, while disunion within Protestant ranks began to weaken the forces of the Reformation. Influential nobles, such as the sons of Nicholas Radziwiłł (q. v.) "the Black," converted to Catholicism and John Chodkiewicz (q. v.) also broke ranks with the Protestants.

The arrival of the Jesuits in 1569 (q. v.) furthered Catholic revival. The first diocesan seminary was established in Vilnius in 1582; in Samogitia, Bishop Merkelis Giedraitis (ca. 1536-1609), an educated and vigorous prelate who took office in 1574, established new parishes, supervised the publication of religious literature in Lithuanian and initiated court cases to recover ecclesiastical property seized by the Calvinists. The reign of Stefan Batory (q. v.) (1572-1586) saw the monarchy turn decisively towards Catholicism, and anti-Protestant feeling increased markedly under his successor, Sigismund III Vasa (q. v.) (1587-1632), who steadily eliminated Protestants from government positions. During the late 17th and early 18th centuries the rights of non-Catholics, the so-called dissidents (q. v.), within the Commonwealth were curtailed, although religious strife in Lithuania never escalated to the type of religious warfare prevalent in western and central Europe. For most Lithuanian Catholics, the victory of the Church in Lithuania is symbolized by the cult of Our Lady of Šiluva, the country's most popular shrine. Samogitian Calvinists were reportedly routed here after a miraculous appearance of the Blessed Virgin in 1608. The Grand Duchy's Counter-Reformation was highly successful: the only significant Lithuanian Protestant communities that remained were the Lutherans in or near East Prussia, and small Reformed congregations around the Radziwiłł (q. v.) stronghold of Biržai in northern Lithuania. See CATHOLIC CHURCH; REFORMATION.

COURLAND (Ger. Kurland, Lith. Kuršių žemė). Duchy and vassal state of the Polish-Lithuanian Commonwealth (q.v.), which bordered the Grand Duchy of Lithuania in the north from the 16th to

18th centuries. The term Courland derives from the native Baltic tribe, the Couronians (Lith. *kuršiai*), known to have lived in the region until medieval times. Courland encompasses the territory of present-day western Latvia, including the coast north of Klaipėda (q. v.) and Palanga. In 1562 the last Master of the Livonian Order, Goddert Kettler, became the vassal of Sigismund August (q. v.) as Duke of Courland and established a secular dynasty. The Duchy was dominated by the Lutheran Baltic German nobility who ruled over the predominantly Latvian serfs. Courland was an important battlefield in Lithuania's wars with Sweden in the early 17th century. Courland's most renowned ruler was Duke Jacob Kettler, who ascended the ducal throne in 1642. Jacob fostered ambitious naval, mercantilist and colonial schemes, briefly acquiring for Courland small colonies in Africa (The Gambia) and the Caribbean (Tobago), but his work was destroyed by the Swedish invasion of 1658. Although formally a vassal state of Poland-Lithuania, Courland fell increasingly under Russian influence during the 18th century. In March 1795, on the eve of the last Partition (q. v.), the Courland diet abrogated its vassalage to the Commonwealth and placed the Duchy under Russia's protection. With the advent of Latvia's independence in 1918, the local German nobility lost their preeminent political status and the region was integrated into the modern Latvian state. See LATVIA.

CZARTORYSKI. Noble family prominent in the political life of the Polish-Lithuanian Commonwealth in the 18th century, originating from Volynia in Ukraine. **Alexander Czartoryski** (Chartorysk), was prince of Pskov (1443-1447) and Novgorod (1447-1455). Originally Orthodox, the Czartoryskis converted to Catholicism in the 16th century. **Florian Czartoryski** (1620-1674) became archbishop of Gniezno and primate of Poland. The Czartoryski family achieved their greatest influence in Poland and Lithuania at the end of the 18th century and were supporters of reforms to strengthen the Commonwealth. **Michael Czartoryski** (1696-1775) was chancellor of the Grand Duchy from 1752 to 1775. **Adam Czartoryski** (1770-1861) achieved the greatest fame as a Russian statesman and patron of education in Lithuania. From 1798 to 1801 Adam Czartoryski served as the Russian ambassador to the Kingdom of the Two Sicilies and as foreign minister of Russia from 1803 to 1806. Czartoryski was a close advisor and long-time friend to Tsar Alexander I. He took part in the negotiations at the Congress of Vienna and was instrumental in drawing up the plans for an autonomous Kingdom of Poland under the Russian crown. From 1803 to 1824 Czartoryski was curator of the Vilnius (q. v.) educational district and under his tutelage the University of Vilnius became the most important center of Polish culture in the lands of the old Commonwealth. Czartoryski was head of the revolutionary Provisional Government of Poland during the insurrection of 1830-1831 (q. v.) after which he emigrated. He lived in Paris from 1832 to 1861, mainly at the Hotel Lambert, which became the focus of Polish-Lithuanian émigré political activity. Czartoryski's memoirs and correspondence with Alexander I were published in French and English in 1887-1888.

- D -

DAUKANTAS, SIMONAS (1793-1864). Lithuanian historian and writer, born in Samogitia on October 28, 1793. He studied law, history and languages at the University of Vilnius from 1818 to 1825. Between 1825 and 1835 Daukantas worked as a government translator in Riga and then moved to St. Petersburg where he conducted most of his scholarly research in the archives of the Russian Senate. He returned to Lithuania in 1850 and developed a close friendship with the Bishop of Samogitia, Motiejus Valančius (q. v). Daukantas died in the town of Papilė on November 24, 1864.

Daukantas was the first author to publish scholarly history in the Lithuanian language, albeit in a colorful Samogitian dialect. In 1822 he wrote *Darbai senovės lietuvių ir žemaičių* (Lith. The Deeds of the Ancient Lithuanians and Samogitians), which was, like most of his works, published posthumously (1929). However,

Daukantas' best-known work, *Būdas senovės lietuvių kalnėnų ir žemaičių* (Lith. The Character of the Ancient Lithuanians: Highlanders and Samogitians) was published in St. Petersburg in 1845 and had a considerable impact on the emerging Lithuanian-speaking intelligentsia and literate peasantry. Because of his romanticized and idealized version of Lithuania's past, Daukantas is more important for his literary contributions in the Lithuanian language rather than as a historian. In addition to his historical interests, he also compiled and published folk-songs and popular stories. Daukantas is also important as the first major figure of the modern Lithuanian national movement to publicly excoriate the Polonization (q. v.) of Lithuania's cultural life and to portray Poland as a historic enemy of Lithuania.

DAUKŠA, MIKALOJUS (d. 1613). Catholic priest and early figure in Lithuanian literature. Little is known of his early life, except that he was probably born near Kėdainiai (q. v.) sometime after the late 1520s. It is clear, however, that Daukša was educated in the spirit of Renaissance humanism and had a distinguished career in ecclesiastical administration: he worked in the diocesan office of Samogitia (q. v.) from 1585 to 1592 and in 1609 was appointed administrator of the diocese. He died in Varniai on February 13, 1613.

Daukša wrote several Lithuanian religious works and is the first prominent published writer in the language from the Grand Duchy (previous Lithuanian-language works had been published in East Prussia). In 1595 he issued a Lithuanian translation of the Spanish author J. Ledesma's catechism, but Daukša is best known for his *Postilla Catholicka*, an explanation of the Gospels published in Vilnius in 1599. The preface to the *Postilla* contains a ringing appeal for the wider use of Lithuanian in public life and among the upper classes, contradicting the notion of some scholars that there was no resistance to cultural and linguistic Polonization (q. v.) in Lithuania until modern times, or that it was confined to the lower classes. Daukša's texts, which eschewed Slavic loanwords and preserved many archaic grammatical and morphological features, are also useful in the study of the history of the Lithuanian language. See LANGUAGE; LITERATURE.

DEMOCRATIC LABOR PARTY, LITHUANIAN (Lith. *Lietuvos DemokratinéDarbo Partija*). Political party founded in December 1990 primarily by the membership of the reformed Lithuanian Communist Party (q. v.). It proclaimed a platform based on Western social democratic principles and formally rejected Marxist-Leninist doctrine. The LDDP currently has an estimated membership of 30,000 and in the mid-1990s was considered the largest and best-organized political party in the country. Its leader from 1990 to 1993 was Algirdas Brazauskas (q. v.), the former head of the LCP, who resigned the post of party leader when he assumed the presidency in February 1993. Adolfas Šleževičius, Lithuania's prime minister from March 1993 to February 1996, was then chosen to head the LDDP. See NATIONALISM, LITHUANIAN.

DEMOCRATIC PARTY, LITHUANIAN (Lith. *Lietuvių Demokratų Partija*, after 1905: *Lietuvos Demokratų Partija*). Lithuanian liberal political party established in 1902. The LDP grew out of Vincas Kudirka's (q. v.) monthly *Varpas* (The Bell) (q. v.), which was the focus of political action and anti-Tsarist agitation for the Lithuanian secular nationalist intelligentsia at the turn of the century. The initial party program demanded a democratic, autonomous Lithuania with equality of rights for all nationalities and an emphasis on the economic plight of the Lithuanian peasant majority. Among the early leaders of the LDP were a number of future Lithuanian statesmen such as Jurgis Šaulys (q. v.), Ernestas Galvanauskas (q. v.), Kazys Grinius (q. v.) and others. In 1905 the LDP began to split between more radical members concerned with social problems and conservative nationalists, like Antanas Smetona (q. v.). In 1920 the LDP amalgamated with the centrist Peasant Populist Union (q. v.).

DEPORTATIONS. See POPULATION AND DEMOGRAPHY.

DIET (Lith. *Seimas*), MEDIEVAL AND EARLY MODERN PERIOD. Generally, the term diet signifies the representative assemblies of the nobility and gentry during the medieval and early modern periods. During the reign of Grand Duke Vytautas (1392-1430) (q. v.) it was the practice to call together assemblies of notables to conclude peace treaties and decide important matters of state without, however, establishing any formal advisory council. After the election of Jogaila (q. v.) as King Władysław II of Poland, the Lithuanian and Polish nobility assembled at Horodło in 1413 and agreed to call joint diets; however, it did not become common practice to convoke such gatherings until the 16th century. In 1492 Grand Duke Alexander (q. v.) granted Lithuania's Council of Lords formal consultative powers, especially in foreign policy. The Council was composed of princes, magnates, palatines, ministers of state, bishops, high-ranking military commanders and other dignitaries. The Council constituted the higher chamber, a House of Lords, while the representatives of the lower gentry, who in 1447 had been given the right to assess taxes, made up a kind of lower house. The periodic Lithuanian diets did not pass laws; however, by giving or withholding their assent to war and taxes, they gradually acquired real power.

The administrative reforms of the 1560s and the Union of Lublin (q. v.) in 1569 drastically altered the nature of the Grand Duchy's politics. Lithuania's diets were made to conform to the Polish pattern. The Grand Duchy's Council of Lords was merged with the Commonwealth's newly created Senate and a joint Polish-Lithuanian diet was formed. The Diet of the Polish-Lithuanian Commonwealth consisted of the King-Grand Duke, the Senate appointed by the ruler, and the gentry's representatives gathered in the Chamber of Deputies. Ordinary diets were convoked every two years in either Warsaw (Poland) or Grodno (Lithuania). The King presided over the Senate, while the Marshall of the Diet chaired sessions of the Chamber of Deputies. Generally, the gentry of the

Lithuanian Grand Duchy met separately to decide matters not pertaining to Poland, or to prepare their political position vis-à-vis the Poles before the convening of the joint diet, but after the early 17th century, separate Lithuanian assemblies became rare.

One of the most unusual features of the Polish-Lithuanian Diet was the *liberum veto*. Since the decisions of the Diet had to be unanimous, any deputy could halt legislation by simply announcing his opposition, a practice which led to much confusion and chaos. The administrative reforms of the 1560s also established the institution of the so-called "dietines" or, literally, "minidiets" (Lith. *seimeliai*), local assemblies of the gentry, which elected representatives to the Commonwealth's Diet and dealt with local matters. With the weakening of the central power in the late 17th and 18th centuries, these local *seimeliai* assumed increasing legislative and executive authority; little could be accomplished without their approval. The local gentry diets survived into the Tsarist period but were abolished after the 1863 anti-Russian insurrection (q.v.). See CONFEDERATIONS; CONSTITUTIONS.

DISPLACED PERSONS (DP's). Term given to the refugees, primarily from Eastern Europe and the Soviet Union, after World War II. There may have been as many as ten million such persons in Germany and Austria in 1945, including about a quarter million refugees from the Baltic States. The majority of the displaced Lithuanians had been either forced laborers under the Nazi *Reichsarbeitsdienst* (RAD), or were among the approximately 100,000 persons who fled westward from the advancing Red Army in the summer and fall of 1944, hoping for eventual Western Allied protection. Baltic DP's, including Lithuanians, were not Soviet citizens and, thus, could not be forcibly repatriated, even though Soviet representatives were allowed to attempt to persuade refugees to return home. Most Baltic refugees were housed in DP camps in the British and American zones under the jurisdiction of Allied military authorities and the United Nations Relief and Rehabilitation Administration (UNRRA). After 1947 they were under the authority of the UN's International Refugee Organization

(IRO). The largest Lithuanian DP camps were in Hanau, Hamburg, Lübeck and Seedorf; in all, there were about 60,000 Lithuanians in such settlements in 1946-1947. During the 1940s Lithuanian DP's established hundreds of schools, cultural organizations and religious societies, published dozens of periodicals and, together with the other Baltic communities, operated the Baltic University at Hamburg-Pinneberg. During the late 1940s and early 1950s, the DP camps were disbanded and most of the refugees left Europe. Some 30,000 Lithuanians came to the United States under the Displaced Persons Act of 1948; most of the others who left Germany found a home in Canada (ca. 20,000) and Australia (ca. 10,000). See EMIGRATION; POPULATION AND DEMOGRAPHY.

DISSIDENTS, in the Grand Duchy of Lithuania. A legal term used to denote non-Catholic subjects in early modern Lithuania. When Catholicism became the state religion of Lithuania after 1387, the government was forced to deal with the issue of the predominantly Orthodox Slavic lands which made up most of the Grand Duchy. Formally, only Catholics were allowed to be officials in the central government, although this stricture was often ignored in practice. In 1563 and again in 1568 Sigismund Augustus (q. v.) declared the equality of Catholic, Orthodox and Protestant nobles. The religious tolerance that had characterized the Grand Duchy of Lithuania began to fade in the late 16th century. Protestants became known as dissidents, or dissenters (Lat. *dissidentes de religione*), even though the Lithuanian Statute (q. v.) of 1588 prohibited religious persecution. Orthodox believers who rejected the Union of Brest (q. v.) were also called dissidents or disunionists (schismatics). The civil rights of these non-Catholic dissidents were increasingly curtailed after the early 17th century. In 1673 non-Catholics were banned from entering the nobility. Religious discrimination was formalized by the Commonwealth's Diet of 1733, which mandated freedom of worship but withdrew most political rights from non-Catholics. The domestic conflict between Catholics and non-Catholic "dissidents" provided Orthodox Russia and Lutheran

Prussia opportunities to interfere in the Commonwealth's internal affairs and was a major source of domestic conflict in the later history of the Polish-Lithuanian state.

DISSIDENTS (ANTI-SOVIET). See RESISTANCE MOVEMENTS.

DONELAITIS, KRISTIJONAS (Ger. Christian Donalitius) (1714-1780). Lutheran pastor and classical Lithuanian poet, born on January 1, 1714 in the district of Gumbinnen (Rus. Gusev), East Prussia. He studied theology and Lithuanian culture at the University of Königsberg from 1736 to 1740, then served as pastor in the village of Tolminkiemis (Rus. Chystye Prudy) in his native district, where he became known as a defender of the rights of his parish's Lithuanian serfs. He died in Tolminkiemis on February 18, 1780.

Donelaitis is considered Lithuania's most important literary figure before the emergence of the modern Lithuanian national movement in the 19th century. His first Lithuanian-language works consisted of a version of Aesop's fables, but he is best-known for the epic poem, *Metai* (Lith. The Seasons), a remarkable description of the life, work and customs of East Prussia's Lithuanian peasants, or *būrai* (from the Ger. *Bauer,* or peasant). The first edition of *Metai* was edited and published with a German translation by the Lithuanian scholar Liudvikas Rėza (Ger. Ludwig Rhesa) in Königsberg in 1818. *Metai* is recognized as a unique masterpiece of Lithuanian literature. See LITERATURE; PRUSSIA.

DZIERŻYŃSKI, FELIKS (1877-1926). Belarusan-born Bolshevik who achieved fame as the head of the notorious Cheka, the precursor of the KGB, born to a Polish family on September 11, 1877 in Minsk district. He joined the Lithuanian Social Democratic Party (q.v.) in 1896 and worked in the revolutionary underground in Kaunas, where he published a Polish-language newspaper, *Kowieński Robotnik* (Pol. The Kaunas Worker), in

1897. In 1902-1903 Dzierżyński briefly worked in the Social Democratic Party of the Kingdom of Poland and Lithuania, before joining the Bolsheviks. After serving as an underground organizer in Warsaw and St. Petersburg, and stints in Tsarist prisons, he came into the Bolshevik Party's central committee and was one of the organizers of the October Revolution (1917). During the Russian Civil War of 1918-1921, Dzierżyński carried out tens of thousands of executions during the Red Terror as head of the infamous Cheka, the Soviet secret police. He died in Moscow on July 20, 1926.

DZŪKIJA. One of the four major ethnographic and dialectic regions of Lithuania, located in the east and south of the country. In medieval times the land of the *dzūkai* was called Dainava, literally, the land of songs. The present name of the people and the region comes from the tendency of the inhabitants to palatalize the consonant d- to form a dz- sound. The boundary of this dialect stretches from the Latvian border in the northeast in a broad belt to the west, beyond the town of Alytus (q. v.). The core of Dzūkija includes the Merkinė and Ula Rivers and its center is near the railroad junction of Varėna, southwest of Vilnius. The region of Dzūkija has been economically less developed than the rest of Lithuania; partly for this reason, village life and traditional customs have persisted longer here than in the more urbanized regions. See AUKŠTAITIJA; SAMOGITIA; SUVALKIJA.

- E -

ECONOMY, or ROYAL ESTATE (Pol. *ekonomja*). An important feature of the agrarian structure of the Grand Duchy of Lithuania, the so-called economies provided most of the income for the royal house in early modern times. The Volok Reform (q. v.) of the 16th century separated state and private lands; until then, the lands of the Grand Duke and private estates had been intermingled in a complex patchwork. In 1589 the royal estates were consolidated into six large economies within the Grand Duchy: Šiauliai and Alytus in present-day Lithuania; also Grodno (q. v.), Brest-Litovsk, Kobrin and Mogilev in what is now Belarus (q. v.). Until the mid-18th century, the economies were subdivided into rural districts called "keys," each containing a number of estates, villages, towns and even manufactories. After the mid-18th century a larger administrative sub-unit called the *gubernia*, consisting of several "keys," was introduced. At the end of the 18th century, the Šiauliai (q. v.) Economy contained three *gubernias*, 26 "keys," 50 estates, five towns and 321 villages; the Mogilev Economy had a population of nearly 120,000. The economies were either administered by royal stewards or were rented to private landowners, usually wealthy magnates. See AGRICULTURE; SERFDOM.

EDUCATION. There is little information on education in medieval Lithuania, although it is known that Grand Duke Gediminas (q. v.) employed Franciscan scribes for correspondence with the Latin West and it is certain that 14th-century Lithuanian rulers employed scholars familiar with the form of Old Church Slavic utilized in Lithuania's Russian lands. Some Lithuanian nobles attended the University of Prague, but when Jogaila (q. v.) became King of Poland in 1387, he revived and expanded the University of Cracow, which then attracted an increasing number of students from the Grand Duchy of Lithuania. In Lithuania itself, the first Latin school was attached to the cathedral in Vilnius no later than 1397. While some documents indicate that the Grand Duke authorized the establishment of schools in new parishes in the early 15th century, a wider network of primary and cathedral schools emerged only in the 1600s. In 1539 Abraomas Kulvietis (q. v.), who had been educated abroad, founded a school of classics in Vilnius, but it was closed in 1542 because of its Calvinist tendencies. Until the late 16th century hundreds of Lithuanians who possessed the means studied in universities abroad. The German schools, such as Frankfurt, Basel, Freiburg, Wittenberg, Heidelberg and Königsberg proved the most popular.

In 1570 a Jesuit college was formally established in Vilnius; in 1579 King Stefan Batory and Pope Gregory XIII granted it a university charter and privileges. The Jesuit academy founded in that year is considered the beginning of the University of Vilnius (q. v.), which achieved, by the mid-17th century, a fine reputation for studies in theology, philology and history and for its numerous scholarly publications. However, the Muscovite sack of Vilnius in 1655 and the subsequent wars and famines led to the University's decline. The Jesuits established a number of smaller colleges in the rest of the Lithuanian Grand Duchy, in Kaunas, Kražiai, Grodno, Brest-Litovsk and elsewhere. The Reformation and Counter-Reformation greatly expanded education in the Lithuanian-speaking lands. In 1547 the Lutheran pastor Martynas Mažvydas (q.v.) published the first known Lithuanian-language book in East Prussia (q. v.) (or Lithuania Minor), a catechism.

An important force for popular education in the Catholic, Lithuanian-speaking lands of the Grand Duchy were the Piarists (or Pietists), who established a network of three-year schools, and, under the leadership of Jerzy Ciapiński, produced an educational program aimed at the lower gentry and peasantry. The Pietists' increasing use of Polish rather than Latin considerably hastened Lithuania's cultural Polonization, despite some interest in expanding the use of the Lithuanian language by such men as Mikalojus Daukša (q. v.). Until the mid-19th century education among the peasantry was confined to the publication of poorly written and heavily Slavicized Lithuanian devotional literature and a few primary schools attached to the parishes. The banning of the Jesuit Order in 1773 led to a major educational reform in Lithuania: the establishment of the National Educational Commission established by the Polish-Lithuanian Diet and headed by Bishop Ignacy Masalski (q. v.) of Vilnius, the first state ministry of education in Europe. The Commission divided the entire Commonwealth into school districts and introduced a modernized secular curriculum which emphasized civics and encouraged the study of Polish.

Under Tsarist rule (1795-1918) public primary schooling reverted mainly to the parishes, while overall supervision of

Lithuania's education was exercised by the newly-created Vilnius Educational District, one of six in the Russian Empire. Vilnius University became a major educational center in the lands of the former Polish-Lithuanian Commonwealth but as a result of the repressions following the insurrection of 1830-1831 (q. v.), the University and a majority of the lower schools were closed. During the 1840s and 1850s the Bishop of Samogitia, Motiejus Valančius (1801-1875) (q. v.), founded an extensive primary education system for the peasantry in western Lithuania, the first such system with Lithuanian as the language of instruction. Valančius' school system contributed to a dramatic increase in peasant literacy during the 19th century. The suppression of the insurrection of 1863 (q. v.) led to the closing of hundreds of parish schools in Kaunas and Vilnius gubernias. The press ban (q. v.) on Lithuanian publications in the Latin alphabet and the establishment of Russian-language government primary schools (Rus. *narodnye shkoly*) were part of the general policy of Russification (q. v.) encouraged by Ivan Kornilov (1811-1901), the curator of Lithuanian education between 1864 and 1868. By 1900 there were 264 government primary schools with over 18,000 pupils, primarily peasant children. At the same time, several important factors mitigated the Tsarist Russification campaign. In the Suwałki region of southwestern Lithuania, the government permitted limited Lithuanian-language instruction and the training of Lithuanian teachers in order to offset Polish influence. In the Sejny Catholic seminary Lithuanian-language instruction was also gradually instituted after 1870. For their postsecondary education, most Lithuanian students attended the Universities of Moscow and Warsaw where they formed groups interested in Lithuanian studies. In addition, secret or family schools flourished among the peasantry where literate villagers called "directors" (Lith. *daraktoriai*) taught reading and writing skills. Finally, beginning with the 1870s, numerous illegal publications in the Latin alphabet were brought into Lithuania by the book-smuggling movement (q. v.), further encouraging literacy in the native language.

One of the major Lithuanian demands during the Revolution of 1905 (q. v.) was an end to Russification in the educational system. Between 1906 and 1914 the Russian authorities permitted limited Lithuanian-language instruction. During the retreat of 1915 the Russians evacuated many schools to the Russian interior where a number of Lithuanian secondary institutions were reestablished. During the German occupation of 1915-1918 native-language instruction was introduced in all primary schools and the study of German was encouraged.

The advent of independence transformed the Lithuanian educational system as Lithuanian-language instruction, except in minority schools, became the norm. Compulsory primary education was introduced by 1930. The Ministry of Education estimated that in the 1929-1930 school year there were 2,386 primary schools of which 90 percent were Lithuanian schools; there were 155,288 pupils. By 1940 there were an estimated 341,000 primary school pupils. During the 1937-1938 school year there were 31 state and 29 private gymnasiums; of the latter, 14 were Jewish schools. In 1939 there were over 26,000 secondary school students in Lithuania. In 1922 the government established the University of Lithuania in Kaunas, which was renamed the University of Vytautas the Great (q. v.) in 1930. By 1939 the University enrolled about 3,000 students in the faculties of theology and philosophy, humanities, law, mathematics and natural science, and technology. During Polish rule in Vilnius (1920-1939), the University of Vilnius was known as the Stefan Batory University; after Lithuania's recovery of the Vilnius region in 1939, it became the second Lithuanian university. The universities, along with the Agricultural Academy in Dotnuva, the Institute of Art and the conservatory, the military academies, as well as the teachers' colleges, made up the higher education system of independent Lithuania. By the end of the independence period, it was estimated that illiteracy would be eliminated within a generation.

The Soviet invasion of 1940 initiated the Sovietization of Lithuanian schools. Religious instruction was abolished and replaced with courses in Marxism-Leninism; the Russification of the curriculum was reintroduced and the Jewish schools were closed. A Lithuanian Academy of Sciences (q. v.) on the Soviet model was established as the primary research institution. Some of the Soviet restrictions were lifted during the Nazi occupation of 1941-1944; however, most higher education institutions were closed in 1943 and the secondary schools suffered from the forced labor requisitions of young people. During the second Soviet period (1944-1990) the Lithuanian educational system was thoroughly Sovietized. During the 1964-1965 school year the Soviet government estimated that there were nearly 4,105 schools of various types enrolling over a quarter million pupils and employing some 30,000 teachers. The major institution of higher education was the Vincas Kapsukas University of Vilnius, along with the Kaunas Polytechnic Institute, the Vilnius and Šiauliai Pedagogical Institutes, and the Agricultural Academy, as well as the art and music schools. After the 1975 Tashkent conference of teachers of Russian, linguistic Russification was intensified; as a result, the Soviet government stipulated that all theses for advanced degrees be written in Russian.

The second period of independence (since 1990) has been marked by attempts to reform the Sovietized school system. Voluntary religious instruction has been reintroduced and private schools, primarily Catholic, have been founded. With the help of the Lithuanian diaspora, the University of Kaunas has been reestablished as Vytautas Magnus University with a Western-style curriculum; in addition to the University of Vilnius, there is now the Vilnius Pedagogical University and the University of Klaipėda. After 1990, Lithuania's educational system struggled with serious institutional and financial crises: rapid inflation undermined student scholarships and teachers' salaries, while Soviet-era bureaucrats in the Ministry of Education and local school administrations have tended to be lukewarm about educational reform, especially decentralization. On the other hand, the government and the educational establishment maintain that they are committed to reforming Lithuania's educational system along Western lines. See COUNTER-REFORMATION; LANGUAGE, LITHUANIAN; POLONIZATION; REFORMATION; RUSSIFICATION.

ELIJAH BEN SOLOMON ZALMAN (1720-1797). Better-known as the Vilna Gaon and considered one of the greatest Jewish intellectuals of modern times, was born in Grodno district. As a child he reportedly gave a homily in a Vilnius synagogue at the age of six. Elijah studied at Kėdainiai (q. v.), one of the centers of learning for Lithuanian Jewry, where he married and acquired a considerable knowledge of the Torah and Scripture through self-study. After travels to Poland and Germany, Elijah settled in Vilnius, where he gained fame for his asceticism and commitment to learning. He encouraged study of the natural sciences and was a bitter opponent of the mystical Hasidic movement then sweeping the Jewish communities of the Grand Duchy, making his scholarly group in Vilnius the center of opposition to Hasidism. During his lifetime, the Gaon wrote over 70 works and commentaries, the majority of which were published. More than any other figure, Elijah Ben Solomon influenced the development of 19th-century Lithuanian Jewish culture and laid the basis for the reputation of Vilnius as the "Jerusalem of Eastern Europe." See JEWS.

EMIGRATION. In proportionate terms, the Lithuanian nation has one of the largest diasporas in the world. Following the insurrection of 1830-1831 (q. v.), hundreds of Lithuanian rebels, especially gentry, fled to Western Europe, mostly France, where they agitated for the restoration of the Polish-Lithuanian state. More followed the insurrection of 1863 and some of these refugees are known to have reached the United States.

While a few Lithuanians came to the New World as early as the 17th century, large-scale emigration to America began only after the Civil War and reached a peak in the two decades before World War I. While evasion of the Tsarist military draft and political persecution were factors, economic considerations were most important in forcing many landless peasants and smallholders to seek employment. It is estimated that between 1869 and 1898 somewhat less than 100,000 ethnic Lithuanians and Jews left Lithuania for the United States. During 1899-1914, when Lithuanians were counted separately, some quarter of a million Lithuanians came into the U. S. At first, most Lithuanian immigants settled primarily in Pennsylvania's coal belt and then in urban centers like Chicago where there was work in the stockyards. The plight of the latter Lithuanian emigrants was depicted in Upton Sinclair's classic novel, *The Jungle* (1904). Officially, the 1930 U. S. Census counted 439,255 Lithuanian-Americans, of whom 45 percent were foreign-born.

During the turn of the century about 15,000 Lithuanians arrived in the United Kingdom; another few thousand left for Canada, Brazil, Argentina and South Africa. The latter country also became the destination for thousands of Lithuanian Jews; it is estimated that there are nearly 50,000 persons of Lithuanian Jewish origin in South Africa, some of whom, like the Progressive anti-apartheid activist, Helen Suzman, and long-time Communist Party leader, Joseph Slovo, became quite prominent. During the period of independence economic conditions in the 1920s and 1930s led to the emigration of nearly 30,000 Lithuanians to Brazil, another 17,000 to Argentina, 5,000 to Uruguay and about 7,000 to Canada. The U. S. Immigration Act of 1924 effectively ended large-scale immigration from Lithuania until after World War II. Another historically important exodus of Lithuanians went to the industrial centers of the Russian Empire during the late 19th and early 20th centuries: on the eve of World War I there were about 40,000 Lithuanians in St. Petersburg, 35,000 in Riga and 7,000 in Odessa.

Another great exodus from Lithuania came at the end of World War II. In 1944 at least 100,000 persons fled in the wake of the Soviet advance, of whom about three-fourths successfully reached the West. Of the postwar Displaced Persons (q. v.), or DP's, the vast majority emigrated to the United States, Canada and Australia. The postwar emigration was largely made up of political refugees, many of whom were members of the intelligentsia, the professions and the clergy. Most of the DP's settled in the urban centers of the United States and Canada which already had well-established Lithuanian communities: mainly Chicago, but also New York, Philadelphia, Boston, Baltimore, Cleveland, Toronto and Montreal. According to the U. S. Census of 1990, 526,089 persons reported their ancestry as Lithuanian of whom 34,523 were listed as foreign-born. Canada had an estimated 35,000 Lithuanians at the beginning of the 1990s. After Chicago, the largest single settlement of Lithuanians was in Sao Paulo, Brazil, but Latin America's Lithuanian immigrants assimilated rapidly and established relatively few churches, schools and other cultural institutions compared with their counterparts in North America. During the Soviet period after World War II (1945-1990), very few people were allowed to emigrate from Lithuania. An increasing number of legal and illegal immigrants entered the United States after 1990; while estimates are in the thousands, there is no accurate way to gauge the number of these new arrivals. See POPULATION AND DEMOGRAPHY.

- F -

FEBRUARY 16, 1918 DECLARATION OF INDEPENDENCE. See TARYBA.

FOUR-YEAR DIET (1788-1792). See CONSTITUTIONS; DIET; KOŚCIUSZKO; PARTITIONS; TARGOWICA, CONFEDERATION OF.

FRANCISCANS, Catholic religious order which first came to Lithuania during the medieval period and played an important role in the country's educational and cultural development. The Franciscan Order established communities in Prussia and Livonia during the first half of the 13th century. Chronicles indicate that during the reign of Lithuania's first king, Mindaugas (q. v.), who ruled from ca. 1251-1263, Franciscans were active as advisors to the court; they were thus the first Catholic monastic order to gain a foothold in Lithuania. The Franciscans served as intermediaries with the Teutonic Order (q. v.) and the Archbishop of Riga during the reign of Grand Duke Vytenis (1295-1316) (q. v.) and proved invaluable as clerks in the Grand Duke's chancery during Gediminas' (q. v.) diplomatic moves vis-à-vis the papacy and the Christian West, especially in composing the ruler's Latin correspondence in 1322-1323. Most of these earlier Franciscans came from Central Europe; two Bohemian monks are reported to have been killed in Vilnius in the early 14th century. The Franciscan community in Lithuania expanded rapidly after Lithuania's formal conversion to Christianity in 1387 and provided the first two bishops of Vilnius, Andrew (1388-1398) and Jacob (1398-1407).

The period of the Polish-Lithuanian Commonwealth (q. v.) saw the emergence of two branches of the Franciscan Order emerged: The Friars Minor Conventual and the Friars Minor Observants. In the Commonwealth the latter group were known as the Bernardines; they established an independent Lithuanian province in 1731. During the 17th and 18th centuries the Franciscans were heavily involved in education. The Bernardine botanist Jurgis Ambraziejus Pabrėža (1771-1849) was among the best-known Lithuanian scholars who left behind descriptions of peasant life in Samogitia (q. v.). During the Russification (q. v.) policies and violent suppressions of the insurrections (q. v.) of 1831 and 1863, the Franciscan monasteries were closed but the community revived in the early 20th century. In 1931 the Province of St. Casimir was reestablished and by 1940 numbered over 100 religious, while the lay Third Order of St. Francis counted almost 50,000 members. Lithuania's Franciscan Order was banned by the Communist government after the Soviet occupation of the country in 1940, but the Order has become active once again since the restoration of Lithuanian independence in 1990. Dozens of Lithuanian Franciscans fled to the West during World War II. The Franciscan house in New York, which published the newspaper *Darbininkas* (The Worker), and the large monastery in Kennebunkport, Maine established in 1947, became important cultural centers for the Lithuanian diaspora in the eastern United States. See CATHOLIC CHURCH; EDUCATION.

- G -

GALVANAUSKAS, ERNESTAS (1882-1967). Lithuanian statesman born in Panevėžys district on November 20, 1882. After studying engineering in St. Petersburg, he became prominent in the Lithuanian national movement in 1905 and was one of the organizers of the Peasant Populist Union (q. v.). After a brief stint in Russian prisons for his anti-Tsarist political activities, Galvanauskas studied at the University of Liège, Belgium and, after graduation in 1912, worked for several years in Serbia. In 1919 he assisted the Lithuanian delegation to the Versailles Peace Conference, then returned to Lithuania where he served in a number of government posts, most importantly as prime minister from 1919 to 1920 and foreign minister from 1922 to 1924. A skilled diplomat, Galvanauskas was instrumental in negotiating the Klaipėda (q. v.) Convention which transferred the port and surrounding territory to Lithuania in 1924. From 1924 to 1927 he was Lithuanian minister to London and then moved to Klaipėda, where he lived until 1939. Galvanauskas was minister of finance during 1939-1940. He was also briefly finance minister in the Soviet-controlled People's Government (q. v.) in June and July 1940. In 1947 Galvanauskas moved to Madagascar, where he was director of a secondary school, and lived there until the mid-1960s. He died in France on July 24, 1967.

GEDIMINAS (Rus. Gedimin, Pol. Giedymin) (d. 1341). Grand Duke of Lithuania and the founder of a dynasty that ruled Lithuania and Poland until 1572. Gediminas was born about 1275; some scholars think that his family originated from the region around Veliuona (q. v.). He succeeded his brother Vytenis (1295-1316) (q. v.) in 1316 and during the next two decades greatly expanded Lithuanian power and his personal political influence. Gediminas' policy was focused on protecting Lithuania from the Teutonic Knights (q. v.) in the west and expanding the territory of the Lithuanian state in the east. In his struggle with the Knights, Gediminas relied on both military and diplomatic means. In 1319 and again in 1329 he invaded the Teutonic Order's lands, but most of the fighting took place along the Nemunas River; the crusading attacks were particularly intense in 1336-1338. On the other hand, Gediminas also undertook diplomatic initiatives intended to strengthen Lithuania's position in Europe. With the support of the Archbishop of Riga, then involved in a conflict with the Livonian (q. v.) branch of the Teutonic Order, Gediminas sent a number of letters to Pope John XXII and western European rulers accusing the Teutonic Order of hindering Lithuania's Christianization by its violent assaults. Although their authenticity was once questioned by historians, Gediminas' letters are now considered one of the most important and reliable sources for the early 14th-century history of Lithuania. Gediminas was never able to resolve the conflict with the Order, which intensified in the latter years of his reign. However, he did invite Christians to settle in Lithuania and insisted in one of his letters that both pagans and Christians "all have one God."

In the east Gediminas pursued a successful policy of mostly peaceful expansion into the Russian lands. He established close ties to Pskov, Novgorod and Tver in order to offset the growing power of Muscovy (q. v.). Through a series of diplomatic marriages of his numerous children, including seven sons, Gediminas managed to acquire for Lithuania the lands of Vitebsk, Novogrodek and Pinsk and other West Russian principalities. His relations with Poland were enhanced by the marriage in 1325 of his daughter Aldona (christened as Anne) to the future King Casimir of Poland, apparently to engage the Poles as allies against the Teutonic Knights.

The circumstances surrounding Gediminas' death are obscure, but it is likely that he died during the winter of 1341. There is no doubt, however, that he was one of Lithuania's most important historical figures. While Mindaugas (q. v.) had briefly introduced Christianity and unified the Lithuanian tribes in the mid-13th century, Gediminas was the true founder of the Grand Duchy of Lithuania as the polity which played an important role in Eastern

Europe during the late medieval and early modern periods. Gediminas' plans regarding Lithuania's Christianization are unclear, but his tolerant attitude towards Catholicism, his employment of monks in the Grand Duke's chancery, and Lithuania's conquest of Orthodox Slavic lands brought increasing Christian influence into the Grand Duchy. He founded Vilnius (q. v.) as the capital and cultural center of Lithuania and today the central square of the city bears his name. Gediminas greatly expanded Lithuania's political and commercial ties to the West, stimulated urban life and trade, and attempted to systematize the country's administration and army. His legacy of holding the line against the Teutonic Order in the west, while seeking new conquests in the east was continued by his successors. See ALGIRDAS; IRON WOLF; KĘSTUTIS.

GORBACHEV, MIKHAIL (b. 1931). General Secretary of the CPSU (1985-1991) and Soviet President (1989-1991) during the period of the postwar movement for Lithuanian independence of 1988-1991. Initially, the conservative leaders of the Lithuanian Communist Party (q.v.) reacted coolly to Gorbachev's call for reform under the programs of *glasnost* (openness) and *perestroika* (restructuring). Much of the Lithuanian public, however, reacted positively to Gorbachev's reform proposals until 1988-1989 when it became apparent that the Sąjūdis (q. v.) reform movement and changes within the LCP were evoking calls for Lithuania's independence. In December 1989 Gorbachev tried unsuccessfully to persuade the LCP to stay within the CPSU. Gorbachev's conflict with Lithuanians was also fueled by the Soviet leader's growing animosity towards Vytautas Landsbergis (q. v.), the Sąjūdis leader and, later, Lithuania's president. On January 11-13, 1990 Gorbachev became the first Soviet leader to actually visit Lithuania while in office. His well-publicized tour and passionate pleas for Lithuanians to abandon their quest for independence were front-page news around the world, but proved a failure. After denouncing Lithuania's March 11, 1990 declaration of independence as unconstitutional, Gorbachev instituted an economic boycott of Lithuania in April 1990. During his visit to the U. S. and Canada in May 1990, he threatened the republic with the loss of Vilnius and Klaipėda, as well as huge costs if Lithuanian leaders insisted on independence. A final bitter break between the Soviet President and Lithuanians came during the violent attack on the Landsbergis government during December 1990-January 1991, which culminated in the massacre of 14 civilians at the Vilnius television tower on January 13, 1991, as part of a plot to place a pro-Soviet regime in power. Gorbachev denied blame for the killings, but did not condemn the violence and, contrary to his rival Boris Yeltsin, who publicly supported the Baltic movements, issued inflammatory statements against the Baltic governments. Since that time, despite their initially positive reaction to the reforms of the mid-1980s, many Lithuanians have nursed bitter feelings against Gorbachev, creating an image of the Soviet leader in Lithuania quite different from his reputation in the West as a liberal reformer. Gorbachev formally resigned as President of the USSR on December 25, 1991.

GOŠTAUTAS (Pol. Gasztold). Lithuanian noble family, which achieved prominence in the 15th and 16th centuries. The Goštautas clan owned lands east and southeast of Vilnius but, according to some sources, were Samogitian in origin. **John Goštautas** (d. 1458) is considered the founder of the family's power. He was chancellor of Lithuania from 1443 to 1458 and was an important power broker in the struggle for the grand ducal throne between Sigismund Kęstutaitis (q. v.) and Švitrigaila (q. v.) during the 1430s. In the 16th century the most illustrious member of the Goštautas clan was **Albert Goštautas** (d. 1539) who was chancellor of Lithuania from 1522 to 1539 and also achieved fame as a military commander against the Tatars (q. v.) and Muscovites (q. v.).

GRAND DUCHY OF LITHUANIA. The formal title of the Lithuanian state for most of the period between the early 13th century and 1795, sometimes referred to as the Grand Principality. The Lithuanian word for duke or prince, *kunigaikštis*, is derived from *kunigas*, and probably of Germanic origin. Until the late 14th century, Lithuanian rulers claimed a number of different titles, including the Slavic *velikii kniaz* (grand prince) and the Latin *rex*. However, since only Mindaugas (d. 1263) (q. v.) had been baptized, anointed and then given a crown through the mediation of the Church, the term "king," as it was used during the High Middle Ages, is not generally applicable to the Lithuanian rulers. During the 14th century, the Latin term *magnus dux* (grand duke) came into official use and remained until 1795.

The territory and administrative status of the Grand Duchy changed markedly during the more than six centuries of its existence. Gediminas (q. v.), and especially his son Algirdas (q. v.) and grandson Vytautas (q. v.), expanded the Grand Duchy to its greatest extent. The Lithuanian state stretched from the Baltic to Black Seas, including most of Ukraine and, for a time, Moldavia (Moldova). In the east, the Lithuanian lands bordered Moscow. During the 16th century, as a result of Muscovite pressure and the Union of Lublin (q. v.) in 1569, the territory of the Grand Duchy shrank to include essentially the territories of ethnographic Lithuania and Belarus (q. v.), leading some Belarusans to claim that the Republic of Belarus is a successor state of the Grand Duchy. Between 1386 and 1569 the Grand Duchy was in dynastic alliance with Poland through the Jagiellonian dynasty (or the House of Gediminas); the Lithuanian nobility elected the Grand Duke with the consent of the King of Poland. After 1501 the Kingdom and Grand Duchy were invariably ruled by the same monarch. The Union of Lublin changed the dynastic alliance of the two states into a more closely-knit Commonwealth (Pol. *Rzeczpospolita*) (q. v.) with an elected monarchy; however, the Grand Duchy still maintained its own army, postal service and currency. The Partitions (q. v.) of 1772-1795 led to the final demise of the Grand Duchy of Lithuania. Under the revolutionary Constitution of May 3, 1791 (q. v.) adopted by the Polish-Lithuanian Diet, the "Commonwealth of Two Nations," as it was known, was to be transformed into a unitary state, eliminating the Grand Duchy as an autonomous unit; however, it had little historical significance for Lithuania since the final Partition of 1795 formally ended the Grand Duchy and placed most of its lands under Tsarist rule. See MUSCOVY; PARTITIONS; POLAND.

GREAT ASSEMBLY (DIET) OF VILNIUS (Lith. *Didysis Vilniaus seimas*), the first modern Lithuanian political convention held on December 4-5, 1905. The Revolution of 1905 (q. v.) in Lithuania was accompanied by widespread agrarian unrest and national protest against Tsarist Russification (q. v.). In October 1905 a Lithuanian committee was established under the auspices of the first Lithuanian daily, *Vilniaus Žinios* (Lith. Vilnius News), to organize a Lithuanian conference. The response exceeded all expectations as about 2,000 delegates arrived in Vilnius in early December not only from Lithuania, but from Lithuanian communities in Russia, Ukraine, Poland, Latvia and East Prussia. The delegates were peasants, clergy, a few urban workers and intelligentsia; about half of them were elected or responsible to some constituency, while the others simply came on their own. The conference was formally chaired by Jonas Basanavičius (q. v.), the acknowledged patriarch of the national movement, who hoped for a cultural affairs agenda and planned only a mild memorandum to Sergei Witte, the Russian prime minister. However, a presidium representing the major political factions (the Social Democrats, Christian Democrats and peasant representatives) actually directed the proceedings and politicized the meeting. While there were disagreements between leftist and rightist agendas, the conference eventually agreed on a radical final resolution, published in *Vilniaus Žinios*, that was the most coherent expression of the political will of the Lithuanian people up to that time: it called for national autonomy, a democratic political structure based on universal suffrage, and the equality of all nationalities in Lithuania. In later years, in recognition of its historic importance, Lithuanians came to call this political convention the "Great Diet" of Vilnius. See NATIONALISM, LITHUANIAN.

GREAT NORTHERN WAR (1700-1721). One of the most destructive conflicts in Lithuania's history, involving Sweden, the Polish-Lithuanian Commonwealth and Russia but, at times, also involving Denmark, Saxony and Prussia (q. v.). The war began when Augustus II (q. v.) of Poland-Lithuania, in alliance with Denmark and Russia who hoped to end Swedish hegemony in northern Europe, invaded Livonia and sought to drive out the Swedes. However, Augustus failed in his campaign, while his Russian allies suffered a disastrous defeat at Narva. A military alliance between Tsar Peter I and Augustus was negotiated at Biržai in Lithuania, but the Swedes defeated both the Commonwealth and Russian forces. The armies of Sweden's King Charles XII invaded Lithuania, occupying Vilnius in 1702. Lithuania suffered greatly as Swedish forces and the Commonwealth's Russian allies swept through the country, plundering and ravaging the countryside. After the decisive defeat of Charles XII by Peter the Great at Poltava in 1709, the Russian army in effect occupied most of the Grand Duchy for several years. The Treaty of Nystadt of 1721, in which the Swedes ceded Estonia and northern Latvia to Russia, ended the war.

The Great Northern War had disastrous demographic and political consequences both for the Lithuanian people and the Commonwealth as a whole. In the plague of 1708-1711 which accompanied the war, as much as a third of the entire Lithuanian population perished, although in the west, Samogitia (q.v.) and East Prussia (q. v.), the death rate was even higher. In political terms, the decline of Swedish influence in the Baltic and the assertion of Russia's power increasingly transformed the Polish-Lithuanian Commonwealth into a Russian protectorate. See RUSSIA.

GRINIUS, KAZYS (1866-1950). President of the Republic of Lithuania from June 7, 1926 until December 17, 1926 and a prominent leader of the Lithuanian national movement in the late 19th century, born in Marijampolė district on December 17, 1866. After completing secondary school in the town of Marijampolė, he went on to study medicine at the University of Moscow where he graduated in 1893. Grinius was the president of the Lithuanian Student Association in Moscow and, upon his return to Lithuania in 1894, became engaged in anti-Tsarist activities. He was one of the leaders of the national movement centered around the monthly *Varpas* (Lith. The Bell) (q. v.) and edited the journal after the death of its founder, Vincas Kudirka (q. v.), in 1899. Grinius was instrumental in founding the Lithuanian Democratic Party (q. v.), which later formed the basis of the Peasant Populist Union (q. v.). Because of his political activities, Grinius was arrested by the Tsarist police in 1906 for the first of several times. In 1915 he was evacuated to Russia and at the end of the Great War made his way to France where he headed Lithuania's repatriation effort.

In 1920 Grinius was elected to Lithuania's Constituent Assembly (q. v.) and served as prime minister of the Republic from 1920 to 1922. When a coalition of Peasant Populists and Social Democrats won the 1926 parliamentary elections, Grinius was chosen president, naming Mykolas Sleževičius the prime minister. His left-of-center administration provoked considerable opposition from the Christian Democrats (q. v.) and rightist elements who accused the government of, among other things, tolerating Communist activity, hostility to the Church and an overly permissive attitude to the minorities. On the night of December 16-17, 1926, a group of army officers, supported by students and some Christian Democrats, overthrew the government and forced Grinius' resignation on December 19, after which they established a regime headed by the leader of the Nationalists, Antanas Smetona (q. v.).

After the coup (q. v.) Grinius worked in the city government of Kaunas as the director of health services and published numerous articles on public health issues. In 1942 he was detained and held under house arrest by German authorities for protesting Nazi occupation policies. In 1947 he came to the United States. Grinius died in Chicago on June 4, 1950.

GRIŠKEVIČIUS, PETRAS (1924-1987). First Secretary of the Lithuanian Communist Party (q. v.), from 1974 to 1987, born on

July 19, 1924. In 1940 he joined the Komjaunimas, the Lithuanian Communist youth organization, and, during the Second World War, fought with the Soviet guerrillas. In 1948 he began work in the propaganda section of the Lithuanian Communist Party's Central Committee and in the 1950s began to rise in the Vilnius city Party apparatus. In 1964 he was promoted to head the Lithuanian CP Central Committee's organizational section and in 1971 became city Party boss in Vilnius. When long-time Party chief Antanas Sniečkus died in 1974, Griškevičius was chosen first secretary of the Lithuanian CP. During his years as Lithuanian party boss, Griškevičius gained a reputation as a Kremlin loyalist and a stolid supporter of Brezhnev's conservative policies, including Russification (q.v.), as well as a staunch enemy of the religious and national dissident movement, which had arisen in Lithuania during the 1970s and 1980s. Griškevičius died on November 14, 1987. His death coincided with the intensification of the independence and reform movements in Lithuania. See RESISTANCE MOVEMENTS.

GRODNO (Lith. Gardinas, Bel. Horodna). Historically important economic, cultural and administrative center of the Grand Duchy of Lithuania, pop. 1994: 270,000, located on the Nemunas River southeast of Vilnius, part of the Republic of Belarus since 1991. The original inhabitants of the region were the Yotvingians (q. v.). Grodno is mentioned for the first time in 1198 in the Volynian Chronicle; it came under Lithuanian rule in the mid-13th century and remained part of the Grand Duchy until 1795. The city was a favorite of many Lithuanian rulers, such as Vytautas (q. v.) and King Stefan Batory (q. v.), who died here in 1586. Under the provisions of the Union of Lublin (q. v.), every third Diet of the Polish-Lithuanian Commonwealth was mandated to meet in Grodno. After the region came into the Russian Empire, Grodno became the capital of one of the two provinces (Rus. *gubernias*) into which Lithuania was divided, the other being Vilnius. Most of the population of the area was Slavicized by the early 20th century, with only small and isolated Lithuanian-speaking communities surviving in the region. The Soviet-Lithuanian Peace Treaty of July 12, 1920 (q. v.) granted Grodno to Lithuania, but the city became part of the Republic of Poland in 1920-1939, after which it was incorporated into the Belorussian SSR. Grodno is the birthplace of the well-known Polish writer, Eliza Orzeszkowa (1841-1910), whose writings describe the lives of the Polish, Belarusan, Lithuanian and Jewish people of the region, and who became a literary model for Lithuanian women writers in the late 19th and early 20th centuries.

GRUNWALD (Ger. Tannenberg or Grünwald, Lith. Žalgiris). Site of one of the decisive battles of medieval Europe, fought on July 15, 1410 between an allied Polish-Lithuanian force and the Teutonic Knights (q. v.), located in Prussia near the villages of Tannenberg and Grunwald. The latter name, meaning "Green Woods," has been incorporated into Polish and Lithuanian historiography. In the fall of 1409 King Władysław II Jogaila (q. v.) of Poland and his cousin Grand Duke Vytautas (q. v.) met to plan a war against the Teutonic Knights. The two rulers organized a combined Polish-Lithuanian force, which eventually included Russians, Tatars and Czech volunteers, and invaded Prussia in the summer of 1410. On July 15, this force, variously estimated by historians between 30,000 and 100,000 troops, confronted a somewhat smaller but better-equipped army of Teutonic Knights and their West European volunteers. After a vicious battle of some ten hours, the Knights' army was destroyed and much of its leadership killed, including the Grand Master, Ulrich von Junginen. Most scholars consider the Battle of Grunwald one of the turning points of medieval Baltic history: it initiated the downfall of the military power of the German Teutonic Knights and secured the Polish and Lithuanian states for several centuries against threats from the west. The site is now in Poland, where a monument has been constructed to celebrate the event. See PRUSSIA; TEUTONIC KNIGHTS.

- H -

HENRY OF VALOIS (1551-1589), son of Henry II and Catherine de Medici, and the brother of French King Charles IX, he briefly ruled the Polish-Lithuanian Commonwealth. Henry was the first ruler to follow the extinction of the Jagiellonian line of kings, which ended with the death of Sigismund Augustus (q. v.). He was elected to the Polish throne in May 1572 and was crowned in Warsaw on February 21, 1574. Henry's election caused consternation among the Commonwealth's Protestants because of Henry's mother's role in the infamous St. Bartholomew's Day massacre of the Huguenots in 1572. Having learned of his brother Charles IX's death in France, Henry secretly left Cracow for Paris in June 1574. Attempts by Polish-Lithuanian nobles to persuade him to return were unsuccessful. Henry was murdered in Paris during a struggle for the French throne in 1589.

HOLOCAUST (1941-1944). During the German occupation of Lithuania, the vast majority of the country's Jewish community was effectively annihilated. The total number of Jews killed in Lithuania, including those brought in from other European countries, as well as Lithuanian Jews killed outside the country, is estimated between 200,000 and a quarter of a million. Over 20,000 Jews escaped eastward in June 1941 and another few thousand were rescued by Lithuanian Gentiles. The Holocaust was the single largest massacre of civilians in the modern history of Lithuania.

The Holocaust in Lithuania occurred in several stages. The Nazi plan of destruction was initiated during the very first days of the German invasion of the USSR. The killings were supervised by special Nazi action groups (Ger. *Einsatzgruppen*). During the first weeks following the German invasion, the Nazi action groups organized a number of murderous actions against Jews. In the latter part of June, 1941, several thousand Jews were murdered in

pogroms and executions inspired by the German Security Poli
and with the participation of some local armed formation
primarily in Kaunas, other large cities and border areas. Accordir
to German documents, genuinely spontaneous pogroms were rar
Some of the killers were recruited from the local population or fro
local police units, but it was the Nazi authorities which inspired ar
led the actions. During the period between mid-July 1941 and tl
end of the year, the massacres reached their peak. The notorio
Einsatzkommando 3 of the action group, *Einsatzgruppe A*, statione
in the Baltics organized the murder of the majority of Lithuania
Jews in the period between mid-July and December 1, 1941. C
that day its commander, SS Colonel Karl Jäger, reported that ov
137,000 people, mostly Jews, had been shot in operations heade
by his men with the assistance of local auxiliaries (whom h
incorrectly termed "partisans").

During the phase of destruction which followed the initial ma
shootings, the survivors were herded into the ghettos of Vilniu
Kaunas and Šiauliai where many Jews were gradually worked t
death during the remainder of the Nazi occupation. Periodicall
mass killings reduced their numbers until the ghettos were final
liquidated in 1943 (Vilnius) and during the German retreat of 194
(Kaunas and Šiauliai). The most notorious of the Nazi killing fiel
in Lithuania was Paneriai (Pol. Ponary), where nearly 100,00
people, mostly Jews, were shot and buried in mass graves durin
the 1941-1944 period. Much of the killing at Paneriai was carrie
out by the so-called Special Platoon (Lith. *Ypatingas Būrys*), a un
of between 50 and 100 mostly volunteers under the supervision c
the German Security Police. Another large graveyard of th
Holocaust was the Ninth Fort in Kaunas, where an estimate
30,000 people, mostly Jews, were murdered between 1941 an
1944. The Fort, which is now Lithuania's best-known Holocau
site, houses a museum and is the site of a large monument to th
victims.

During the period of Soviet rule, the Jewish specificity of th
Holocaust was rarely acknowledged and most killing sites wer
commemorated as places where peaceful "Soviet people" had bee
murdered. Since the restoration of independence in 1990, th

Lithuanian government has acknowledged the Holocaust as a genocide of the Jews. On the other hand, the issue of restoring the property of the victims, and allegations that the Lithuanian authorities were pardoning some of the still-surviving perpetrators, have complicated Lithuanian-Jewish relations. During a state visit to Israel in March 1995, Lithuanian President Algirdas Brazauskas (q.v.) formally expressed regret over the participation of some Lithuanians in the Holocaust. See JEWS; NAZIS; POPULATION AND DEMOGRAPHY.

HORODŁO, ACTS OF. Agreements concluded by the nobility of Poland and Lithuania in October 1413 at the town of Horodło on the Bug River near the Lithuanian-Polish border. The Acts of Horodło were intended to solidify the dynastic alliance of Poland and Lithuania of 1386 in order to provide a stronger front against the Teutonic Knights. The first act of Horodło drawn up by King Jogaila (Władysław II) (q. v.) of Poland and his cousin Vytautas (q. v.) provided that after the death of the latter, Lithuania would choose its own ruler subject to the approval of Poland. Conversely, a new Polish King could not be selected without Lithuanian approval. Two other documents, one ratified by the Lithuanian nobility and the other by the Polish nobility, provided for similar administrative patterns in both countries and granted 47 Lithuanian families Polish coats-of-arms. The Acts of Horodło had little immediate practical effect on Lithuania since the Grand Duchy's rulers and nobility tended to run the country's affairs with scant regard for Polish wishes through much of the 15th and 16th centuries. However, historians consider that, in the longer term, the Horodło agreements initiated a process of gradual Polonization (q. v.) of Lithuania's social, cultural and political institutions. See KRĖVA, ACT OF; POLAND.

- I -

INDUSTRY. For most of the country's history, agriculture (q. v.), which employed nearly 90 percent of Lithuania's population until the 20th century, had been the mainstay of the Lithuanian economy. During the medieval period most manufactured goods, especially weaponry and luxury items, were imported from Western Europe, primarily by German merchants of the Hanseatic League which included many Baltic towns, as well as Novgorod, places with which Lithuanians had long-standing ties. Some of the earliest manufacturing consisted of weapons production and other crafts, such as leather-processing, performed in large part by foreign craftsmen and blacksmiths invited to Lithuania by the Grand Dukes. Gediminas (q. v.) invited foreign artisans to settle in Lithuania during the early 14th century. Grand Duke Vytautas (q. v.) invited construction specialists from Prussia in the early 15th century and it is known that a number of German specialists worked in Kaunas, producing wax and textiles as well as constructing mills. By the 16th century an arsenal in Vilnius produced artillery pieces and bells. The destructive wars with Muscovy (q. v.) of the mid-17th century and the plague that accompanied the Great Northern War (q. v.) during 1708-1711 devastated Lithuania's fledgling manufacturing centers.

During the mid-18th century the Grand Duchy's crown treasurer, Antoni Tyzenhauz (q. v.), attempted to revive industry by establishing manufacturing concerns on the royal economies (q. v.) utilizing compulsory peasant labor, but this policy provoked social protest and eventually proved counterproductive. Lithuania's industrial development in the modern sense began after the imposition of Tsarist rule in 1795 but it proceeded exceedingly slowly and proved unable to absorb the growing class of underemployed and landless villagers. There was only one large factory (employing 60 workers) in Lithuania before the late 1850s. Only a half-dozen of the traditional manorial manufactories were of comparable size and a third of the work force in these enterprises consisted of serfs. The most important "industrial" pursuit was distilled liquor, mostly from tiny manorial manufactories: there were nearly 1,800 distilleries and 300 breweries in 1858. Most of the rest of Lithuanian industry of the early 19th century consisted of tiny manufactories employing skilled craftsmen and peasant labor producing glass, paper and textiles. Steam power was little known in Lithuania before the 1850s.

Lithuania's first railroad became operational in April 1861 only a month after Tsar Alexander II's historic Emancipation Manifesto which seemingly ushered in an era of modernization. However, real industrial expansion began only during the last quarter of the century; in Lithuania, the proportion of industrial workers to the general populace at the turn of the century was at least three times lower than for Russia as a whole, although the standard of living of the peasantry was higher than in Russia. By 1879 the output value of larger enterprises had increased ten-fold since 1860 and then tripled between 1880 and 1900; however, much of the production remained in the traditional areas of distilling, food processing and leather. At the same time, financed largely by German capital and stimulated by railroad construction, the metal works industry grew appreciably, for example, the Westphalia and Tillman Bros. firm in Kaunas. Industrial development expanded unevenly: some parts of the country, such as southwestern Lithuania, experienced almost no industrialization. In the Klaipėda region, which was part of Prussia, wood processing emerged as an important industry. Until the Great War the majority of the urban proletariat in Lithuania was Jewish and Polish.

After the restoration of Lithuania's independence in 1918 industrial growth was initially hampered by the separation from the Russian transportation and marketing infrastructure, despite the addition of the industries of the formerly German Klaipėda territory, which produced cellulose and paper products. However, between 1929 and 1939 Lithuania's industrial production expanded by some 350%, led by the rapid development of food processing which accounted for over 40% of the value of industrial output by 1937, much of it from the large Maistas concern in Kaunas. Wood processing was centered in Klaipėda; in addition, the older industries, such as textiles and leather, also expanded their production. There were nearly 100,000 industrial workers employed in Lithuania by 1940. About a third of industry was financed by foreign investment, primarily British and German. Some 400 power stations supplied electricity, about half of it produced from coal. The seizure of Klaipėda by Nazi Germany in March 1939 and the outbreak of World War II, which greatly reduced exports, dealt a blow to the fledgling Lithuanian industry. Virtually all of the country's industrial establishments were nationalized following the Soviet occupation of Lithuania in June 1940 and the subsequent entrenchment of Communist rule. The Nazi occupation of 1941-1944, wartime destruction and postwar violence occasioned a sharp decline in production; it was only in 1950 that industrial output reached prewar levels.

An extremely rapid period of industrialization followed and by 1970 nearly half of Lithuania's population was employed in industry. An influx of over 300,000 primarily Russian and other Slavic arrivals from the Soviet Union after 1945 helped fill the republic's labor force, which had been depleted by deportations and other population (q. v.) losses. Special emphasis was placed on the development of heavy industry, such as chemicals (in Kėdainiai) and metallurgy, while energy was enhanced by huge new power plants: a fuel-based new complex in Elektrėnai just outside Vilnius and the enormous Ignalina nuclear power plant of the Chernobyl type in the northeastern corner of the country. While the new industry produced some relatively high-quality consumer goods, especially televisions and other appliances, the Soviet industrialization program came at a great cost. In addition to the demographic changes and the subjugation of Lithuanian industry to the demands of the Soviet economy rather than to local needs, environmental damage became a serious issue by the 1980s. Finally, the construction of the wasteful and inefficient Soviet industrial infrastructure meant that much of Lithuania's economic capacity consisted of what some Western businessmen have called "industrial museums." Since the late 1980s industrial production has declined sharply with a consequent rise in unemployment. The general collapse of the Soviet economy meant that, after the restoration of independence in 1990, Lithuania was faced with the challenge of upgrading its industry to compete in new markets. (For current statistics on the economy, see "Introduction: The Government and Economy," pp. 3-4). See AGRICULTURE; TRADE.

INSURRECTION OF 1830-1831. Uprising against Tsarist rule in Poland and Lithuania which sought to restore the Polish-Lithuanian Commonwealth. The relatively liberal reign of Tsar Alexander I (1801-1825) had allowed the proliferation of secret patriotic societies influenced by liberal and romantic ideas, particularly among university students and army officers, many of whom were dissatisfied that the Lithuanian lands did not enjoy the same autonomy provisions granted to the Kingdom of Poland (q. v.) by the Congress of Vienna. The July Revolution of 1830 in France and the military preparations of the reactionary Tsar Nicholas I (1825-1855) in response to European revolutions provoked an anti-Russian coup among liberal Polish army officers in Warsaw on November 29, 1830. The Polish revolt stimulated unrest in Lithuania and during the spring of 1831 a number of Lithuanian gentry, such as Anupras Jacevičius (Pol. Anupry Jacewicz) from Telšiai and the charismatic commander Emilia Plater (1806-1831), organized forces to fight the Russians. Between March and June of 1831 the Lithuanian rebels captured a number of towns, including Šiauliai, Panevėžys, Ukmergė and Kėdainiai. In April 1831 the insurgent forces managed to surround Vilnius itself but were unable to seriously threaten the city; however, in much of the countryside the rebels had succeeded in temporarily establishing their own local authority. In June 1831 Polish rebels under the command of General Disiderius Chłapowski and a joint Polish-Lithuanian force under Antoni Giełgud reinforced the Lithuanian insurgents, who then seized Kaunas and stormed Vilnius. The rebels were defeated here by a superior Russian force on June 19 and the insurgent army was pushed westward into East Prussia in the following month, while the Russian Army rapidly pacified the rest of the country. Guerrilla bands were active in Lithuania until the fall of 1831, but the rebellion came to an end with the surrender of the Polish rebels in November 1831. It is estimated that, at their peak, the Lithuanian rebel forces numbered as many as 30,000 persons. Aside from the military superiority of the Russians, weakness of leadership, disunity and the failure to garner sufficient support from the peasantry were contributing factors to the rebels' failures.

INSURRECTION OF 1863-1864. The second of the large-scale armed uprisings against Russian rule during the 19th century. Russia's defeat in the Crimean War and the plans of Tsar Alexander II (1855-1881) to abolish serfdom encouraged much of the gentry and intelligentsia to hope for reforms, such as increased administrative autonomy, restoration of the University of Vilnius, as well as an end to the Russifying and anti-Catholic policies pursued by Nicholas I. There was an increase in agrarian unrest and a period of patriotic marches called "manifestations," which intensified after Russian troops killed five Polish demonstrators in Warsaw in February 1861. On August 18, 1861 between sixty and eighty demonstrators were killed by Cossacks in Vilnius and martial law was declared in Vilnius, Kaunas and Grodno gubernias by Governor-General Vladimir Nazimov. By 1862 a secret Lithuanian Provincial Committee was organized by Konstanty Kalinowski (Lith. Kalinauskas) (q. v.) dominated by a radical faction known as the "Reds." The more socially conservative Lithuanian gentry within the anti-Russian movement came to be known as "Whites."

On January 22, 1863 the clandestine Polish National Central Committee in Warsaw proclaimed an insurrection against the Russians and on January 29 issued a manifesto to the Lithuanians urging them to join in a fraternal struggle for liberation. On February 1, 1863 the Lithuanian Committee proclaimed a revolutionary Provisional Government for Lithuania and Belarus, promised land to those who joined the uprising, and pledged equal civil rights for all citizens. At the end of February the conservative "White" faction led by Jakob Gieysztor (Lith. Goštautas) gained more influence in the revolutionary government.

By the spring of 1863 the rebellion had engulfed most of Lithuania; it is estimated that the rebel forces numbered over

15,000 men, facing a Russian army of nearly 100,000. The rebels were under the overall command of Zygmunt Sierakowski (q. v.) whose own detachment grew to a force of over 2,000 men; however, his forces were defeated at Biržai on May 9, 1863. Sierakowski was captured and hanged on June 27. Among the most important rebel units were the Lithuanian peasant forces in Samogitia commanded by the radical priest, Antanas Mackevičius (q. v.). Although much of the peasantry supported the insurrection, the Lithuanian rebels were unable to concentrate their forces or gain significant support from outside, despite considerable sympathy for the Polish and Lithuanian struggle in western Europe. By the end of 1863 the insurgents had been decisively defeated and had lost their leaders: Mackevičius and Kalinowski were executed on December 28, 1863 and March 23, 1864 respectively. The last clashes of the insurrection were reported in October 1864 in western Lithuania. The rebellion was followed by a wave of repression masterminded by Governor-General Mikhail N. Muravyev (1796-1866) (q. v.) who arrived in Vilnius in May 1863 and directed hundreds of executions, as well as the deportation of thousands of rebels and their sympathizers to Siberia.

The insurrection of 1863 differed substantially from the uprising of 1830-1831. Most noticeable was the participation of the Lithuanian and Belarusan peasantry, whose leaders emphasized the villagers' national aspirations along with those of the Poles. The events of 1863 signaled the emergence of the Lithuanian-speaking peasantry as a political force and marked the last time that Poles and Lithuanians fought together for a restoration of the old binational Commonwealth (q.v.). See NATIONALISM, LITHUANIAN; PRESS BAN; RUSSIFICATION; VALANČIUS, MOTIEJUS.

IRON WOLF (Lith. *Geležinis vilkas*). A medieval Lithuanian historic symbol and story, also a radical paramilitary organization established in the 1920s.

In Lithuanian **legend**, a howling iron wolf appeared in Grand Duke Gediminas' (q. v.) dream while he slept in one of the valleys in what is now Vilnius (q. v.). His high priest, Lizdeika, interpreted the apparition as a sign to build an impregnable castle and a city on the site which would become world famous. The legend explaining the founding of Vilnius, which bears some resemblance to the story of Romulus and Remus, probably originated in the early 16th century when theories of the Roman origins of the Lithuanian people had gained credence among the nobility.

The **Iron Wolf** nationalist organization originated in the mid-1920s, primarily among young right-wing army officers and students, dissatisfied with the left-of-center government of President Kazys Grinius (q. v.) and Prime Minister Mykolas Sleževičius (q. v.). After the Nationalist Union (q. v.) took power in December 1926, most of the members of the Iron Wolf became ardent supporters of Augustinas Voldemaras (q. v.) and grew increasingly critical of President Smetona's relatively moderate policies. The Iron Wolf enjoyed a brief period of legality as a sporting association, which served as a front for vigilant radical nationalists engaged in clandestine opposition to Smetona and elements in Lithuania viewed as insufficiently nationalist. In the eyes of many people, the members' penchant for violent intimidation of opponents and a secret initiation ceremony, which included swearing an oath on a dagger, gave the organization a sinister image. The ideology of the Iron Wolf had similarities to Italian fascism. Soon after the German invasion of Lithuania in 1941, former Iron Wolfers hoped to control the country through the openly fascist Lithuanian Nationalist Party (Lith. *Lietuvių nacionalistų partija*) (q.v.), but this group proved unpopular and the movement was banned by the Nazis because the LNP insisted on the eventual establishment of an independent Lithuanian state. See SMETONA, ANTANAS; VOLDEMARAS, AUGUSTINAS.

- J -

JAGIEŁŁO. See JOGAILA.

JESUITS, The Society of Jesus. Catholic religious order founded in 1534 which played an important role in Lithuania's cultural history. The Jesuit presence in Lithuania dates from 1569 when four Jesuits arrived in the country to found the college which later grew into the University of Vilnius and eventually to establish a number of new schools throughout the Grand Duchy. In their efforts to halt the spread of Protestantism, the Jesuits sponsored the publication of the gospels, hymnals and other religious literature in Lithuanian. In 1608 a Lithuanian Jesuit province was established, which included Livonia and Prussia. The Lithuanian province had over 1,000 members when the Order was suppressed in 1773 by the Vatican. The Jesuits returned to Lithuania in 1923, opening a prestigious secondary school in Kaunas and in 1936 establishing a Jesuit vice-province in Lithuania. Before the Soviet occupation there were over 100 Jesuits in Lithuania. Many of the Jesuits fled to the West in 1944, while the Soviet regime persecuted those remaining in Lithuania. In the West, the Lithuanian Jesuits have ministered to the Lithuanian diaspora, establishing religious centers in Chicago, Uruguay and Brazil. Since 1990 the Jesuits have once again become active in Lithuania. See COUNTER-REFORMATION; EDUCATION; REFORMATION.

JEWS, in Lithuania. While it is clear that some Jews lived in Lithuania as early as the 13th century, large-scale Jewish settlement dates from the reign of Grand Duke Vytautas (1392-1430). Most early Jewish settlers hailed from Poland and Germany; for the most part, their native tongue was Yiddish. The first known charters of settlement, or privileges, were issued by Grand Duke Vytautas to the Jews of Trakai, Grodno, Brest and Lutsk in 1388-1389, and were modeled after similar documents in Central and Eastern Europe, mandating Jewish religious and cultural autonomy. There was a brief period of expulsion between 1495 and 1503 as well as tensions between the nobility and Jewish communities, but on the whole, Lithuania's government did not systematically persecute the Jews. It is estimated that in the mid-16th century there were some 120,000 Jews in the Grand Duchy of Lithuania. Many Jews were killed or fled the country as a result of the rebellion of the Cossack leader Bohdan Chmelnicki (Khmelnytski) and the Muscovite invasion of the mid-17th century. By the end of the 18th century the number of Jews in the Grand Duchy may have reached 250,000; however, only between 10,000 and 15,000 lived in the Lithuanian-speaking lands, that is, the territory which approximates the current borders of the Republic of Lithuania. Vilnius became one of the most important centers of Talmudic scholarship and Jewish learning in general, mainly because of the work of the famous Gaon of Vilna, Elijah Ben Solomon (1720-1797) (q. v.). This gained Vilnius a reputation as the "Jerusalem" of Europe.

The imperial Russian government, which occupied most of Lithuania in 1795, intended to drive the Jews from the countryside into the cities, as was the practice in the Empire's Pale of Settlement; however, the Napoleonic invasion interrupted this movement. Most of Lithuania's Jews eventually did settle in urban areas or engaged in small trade or crafts in the villages. On the eve of World War I there were only a few hundred Jewish farmers. In 1900, Vilnius had some 150,000 inhabitants of whom a plurality, or about 40 percent, were Jews. The majority were conservative Orthodox; Hasidism was another powerful strain among Lithuanian Jewry. During the turn of the century strong secular trends also emerged: for example, the Socialist Bund (q.v.) and the Zionist Movement.

The establishment of independent Lithuania transformed the country's national relationships, as the Lithuanian-speaking majority ruled the country for the first time since the early medieval period. The support of much of the country's Jewish leadership for an independent Lithuanian state with its capital in Vilnius ensured a promising start for the Jewish community. The government census of 1923 indicated that there were over 154,000 Jews in the Republic, or 7.2 percent of the population, the largest national minority in Lithuania. During the early 1920s, Lithuania's official policy toward the Jewish minority emphasized autonomy. A Minister of Jewish Affairs was part of the Lithuanian Cabinet until 1924 after which Jewish political autonomy was curtailed. However, even after the abolition of the Jewish Ministry and the

Nationalist (q. v.) seizure of power in 1926-1927, the Jews maintained communal autonomy in religious and educational affairs. In 1936 there were 108 elementary schools and 20 secondary schools, partly subsidized by the government, with Hebrew or Yiddish as the languages of instruction. Before 1940 the government also contributed to rabbinical salaries. However, economic problems led to the emigration of nearly 14,000 Lithuanian Jews between 1928 and 1939, of whom the majority went to South Africa (35 percent) and Palestine (25 percent). At the same time, Jews lost some of their former preeminence in commerce and industry. Ethnic Lithuanians increased their share of the country's commercial and retail establishments from 13 percent in 1923 to 43 percent by 1936. By this time Lithuanians had also come to own about 60 percent of the industrial and handicraft businesses compared to a Jewish figure of 32 percent, although the latter enterprises tended to be somewhat larger. The Lithuanian cooperative movement acquired an increasing share of the agricultural markets previously dominated by Jewish merchants. The growing participation of Lithuanians in business did not eliminate the important role that the Jews played in the country's economic life: it is estimated that in 1936 Jews still operated slightly over 54 percent of small retail establishments, despite considerable inroads by Lithuanian shopkeepers. Shortly before World War II, Jews still operated about 20 percent of Lithuania's export trade and 40 percent of the import business. Members of the Jewish community remained well-represented in the professions: in 1937 42.7 percent of the country's doctors were Jews. During 1935-1936 there were, reportedly, 486 Jews out of 3,223 students in Lithuania, about twice the proportion of Jews in the total population, although this represented a two-fold decline in the number of Jewish university students since 1928-1929.

The Jews of the interwar Republic of Lithuania were predominantly Orthodox and Zionist with a high degree of proficiency in Hebrew. Jewish cultural life was remarkably diverse with five daily newspapers and numerous theater and sports associations. While there was an increase in anti-Semitism during the 1930s, largely as a result of economic competition and the proximity of Nazi Germany, violent pogroms were rare and there is no record of any fatalities in such outbreaks before 1939. At the same time, a growing number of Jews began to shift from Russian to Lithuanian as their second language. In the Vilnius region ruled by Poland between 1920 and 1939, the Jews suffered official discrimination but still managed to maintain a vigorous cultural life, including the world-famous YIVO research institute.

The outbreak of World War II and Lithuania's recovery of the Vilnius region in October 1939, as well as a flood of refugees from Nazi-occupied Poland, increased the number of Jews in Lithuania from about 160,000 (est. 1937) to over a quarter million people. The Soviet occupation of June 1940 resulted in strained relations between Lithuanians and Jews as traditional anti-Semitism grew, partly because the unpopular Soviet-installed Lithuanian Communist Party (q. v.) leadership, particularly in mid-level Party posts and in the Communist Youth League, contained a disproportionately large number of Jews and Russians, who thus became perceived as supporters of foreign occupation in the eyes of much of the populace. The German attack on the USSR on June 22, 1941 initiated Lithuania's Holocaust (q. v.), the most violent and thorough massacre of civilians in Lithuania's modern history. About 90 percent of Lithuania's Jews perished, resulting in the effective destruction of the country's historic Jewish community. Many Jews fought in anti-Nazi partisan units and in the 16th Lithuanian Riflemen's Division of the Soviet army. Following the reoccupation of Lithuania by the Soviet Army in the summer of 1944, thousands of Jews returned to the country but the total number of Lithuanian Jews in the republic continued to decline. In 1970 there were less than 25,000 Jews in Lithuania, of whom about three-fourths lived in Vilnius; it is estimated that less than half of this number were Lithuanian Jews. Vilnius became an important way station during the massive emigration of Soviet Jews to Israel and the West during the 1970s and 1980s; an estimated 15,000-17,000 Jews left Lithuania between 1959 and 1990. The present Jewish population in Lithuania is less than 10,000. Several prominent Jews, including Emanuelis Zingeris, who served as the chairman of the parliament's foreign affairs committee, and the writer Gabrielius Kanovičius, took part in the independence movement, Sąjūdis (q.v.). In 1988 the Cultural Association of Lithuanian Jews was established and in 1989 began publishing the newspaper, *Lithuania's Jerusalem*, in Yiddish, Lithuanian and Russian. The revival of Jewish cultural life since the national movement of the late 1980s has, however, been undermined by continuing emigration. See BUND; ELIJAH BEN SOLOMON; HOLOCAUST; NAZIS; VILNIUS.

JOGAILA (Pol. Jagiełło). Grand Duke of Lithuania from 1377 to 1381, and 1382 to 1387; King of Poland as Władysław II from 1386 to 1434. Jogaila was born about 1350, the oldest son of Grand Duke Algirdas (q. v.) and his second wife, Juliana of Vitebsk. In 1377 Jogaila ascended the grand ducal throne in Vilnius as decreed by Algirdas. Jogaila's rule in Lithuania was marked by civil war and internecine intrigues as he first had to suppress a challenge to his authority by his half-brother, Andrew of Polotsk, and then became embroiled in a conflict with his uncle Kęstutis (q. v.), who alleged that Jogaila's dealings with the Teutonic Order (q.v.) and his interest in accepting Christianity were undermining Lithuania's struggle with the Knights. Kęstutis seized Vilnius in August 1381 and proclaimed himself Grand Duke, while Jogaila was confined to the lands of Krėva, or Kriavas (Pol. Krewo), and Vitebsk. However, Jogaila's brothers and supporters managed to regain Vilnius and a full-scale war was averted with the death of Kęstutis under suspicious circumstances in August 1382. Kęstutis' son Vytautas (q. v.) escaped to the Teutonic Order from whence he waged a war against his cousin between 1382 and 1384 when a truce granted Vytautas lands in Grodno and Podłasie.

During the early 1380s, Jogaila sought to gain support against the Teutonic Order through an alliance with a major Christian power. He briefly considered marriage to Sophia, the daughter of the famed Muscovite ruler Dmitrii Donskoi, but eventually turned to the Poles. In 1385 a large Polish delegation arrived in Krėva to finalize ongoing negotiations concerning a Polish-Lithuanian dynastic union. On August 14, 1385 the Act of Krėva (q. v.)

mandated Jogaila's accession to the Polish throne through marriage to Jadwiga, the young Queen of Poland, and the union of the Polish Kingdom with Lithuania. In the spring of 1386 Jogaila traveled to Cracow where he was baptized as Władysław, married Jadwiga and was crowned King of Poland. Jogaila's coronation initiated the Christianization of Lithuania. In 1387 Jogaila returned to Lithuania with a large retinue of Polish nobility and clergy to begin the mass baptism of the Lithuanian people and this date is generally celebrated as the country's conversion to Christianity.

Jogaila hoped to rule Lithuania directly from Cracow, but this provoked another struggle between 1389 and 1392 with the ambitious Vytautas who again enlisted the help of the Order against his cousin. This period of Lithuania's internal strife finally ended in 1392 when Jogaila granted Vytautas all of Lithuania and then in 1401 recognized him as Grand Duke for life. The reconciliation of Jogaila and Vytautas laid the basis for their successful campaign against the Teutonic Order which culminated in the Knights' decisive defeat at Grunwald (q. v.) in 1410. New problems between Jogaila and Vytautas were created by the latter's plans to crown himself King of Lithuania, thus disrupting the Polish-Lithuanian dynastic alliance. Vytautas' death in 1430 allowed Jogaila to formally remain supreme ruler of Lithuania, although in practice the Grand Duchy operated independently.

Jogaila's rule as Władysław II of Poland was marked by the granting of extensive new privileges to the Polish nobility and the strong influence of Zbigniew Oleśnicki, the Bishop of Cracow. Between 1397 and 1400 Jogaila was instrumental in revitalizing the University of Cracow which now bears his name. After the death of Queen Jadwiga in 1399, he married three more times, finally fathering three sons by his last wife, Sophia, a relative of Vytautas. He died in Cracow on May 31 1434. Jogaila's descendants constituted the Jagiellonian Dynasty, or branch of the House of Gediminas (q.v.) (1386-1572), which played an important role in the history of East Central Europe. More than most medieval Lithuanian rulers, Jogaila proved a controversial figure, criticized by nationalist Lithuanian historians for his initiation of the union with Poland and, on the other hand, portrayed as a primitive, pagan character by medieval and early modern Polish chroniclers. However, later Polish historians have viewed Jogaila favorably. See ALGIRDAS; CATHOLIC CHURCH; KĘSTUTIS; POLISH-LITHUANIAN COMMONWEALTH.

JOHN CASIMIR VASA (1609-1672). King of Poland and Grand Duke of Lithuania, son of King Sigismund III Vasa (q. v.), born on March 22, 1609. During the 1640s John Casimir lived in Italy, where he was made a cardinal. He returned to Poland in 1648 to succeed his brother Władysław Vasa (q. v.), eventually marrying his brother's widow. John Casimir's reign was marked by disastrous wars, first with the Cossack rebel Bohdan Khmelnytski (Chmielnicki), and then against the combined Cossack and Muscovite forces. The Swedes invaded the Grand Duchy, but were forced to retreat. The Peace of Andrusovo in 1667 ended the war with Muscovy (q. v.), but the King faced stiff internal opposition and even armed uprisings. After his wife, Queen Louise Marie, died in 1667, the dispirited John Casimir abdicated the throne the following year and left for France where he died on December 16, 1672. John Casimir was the last of the Vasa rulers in Poland-Lithuania. See KĖDAINIAI, TREATY OF.

- K -

KAIRYS, STEPONAS (1878-1964). Prominent Lithuanian Social Democratic leader, born in Ukmergė district on December 20, 1878. He received his higher education at the Institute of Technology in St. Petersburg and between 1908 and 1911 worked as an engineer in central Russia. In 1901 he became a member of the Central Committee of the Lithuanian Social Democratic Party (q. v.) and supported the creation of an independent, non-Bolshevik Lithuanian socialist movement. In 1917 Kairys was elected to the Lithuanian Council or Taryba (q. v.) which was drawing up plans for the creation of a Lithuanian state. Along with other leftists, he opposed attempts to formally tie a Lithuanian state to Germany. On February 16, 1918 Kairys became one of the signatories of Lithuania's declaration of independence. In 1919-1920 he served as minister of industry and trade and in 1920 was elected to Lithuania's Constituent Assembly. In 1926 Kairys was appointed deputy speaker of the Seimas (q. v.), Lithuania's parliament. After the Nationalist (q. v.) coup of 1926, Kairys opposed the new regime as a democratic socialist. He was also active in anti-Soviet and anti-Nazi underground organizations. In 1944 he joined the Supreme Committee for the Liberation of Lithuania (VLIK) (q. v.) and, while living in the United States after 1952, was the acknowledged leader of Lithuanian Social Democrat émigrés in the West. He died in New York on December 16, 1964.

KALANTA, ROMAS (1953-1972). Student born in Kaunas in 1953. On May 14, 1972 Romas Kalanta immolated himself in a park across from the main theater in Kaunas in protest against Soviet rule in Lithuania. Kalanta's funeral on May 18, 1972 became the occasion for two days of violent anti-Soviet and anti-Russian demonstrations by young people supporting Lithuanian independence. The disturbances were eventually suppressed by Soviet security forces. Many persons were injured and arrested and a number were imprisoned. Soviet authorities attempted to portray Kalanta as mentally ill and a drug addict, charges later revealed to be groundless. Kalanta's suicide encouraged several other self-immolations and, for many Lithuanians, his act became a symbol of national resistance to the Soviet occupation. See RESISTANCE MOVEMENTS.

KALININGRAD DISTRICT (OBLAST). See PRUSSIA.

KALINOWSKI (Bel. Kalinoŭski, Lith. Kalinauskas), KONSTANTY (1838-1864). Radical leader of the 1863 anti-Russian insurrection of 1863-4 (q. v.) in Lithuania and Belarus, born in Grodno (q.v.) or

January 21, 1838. He graduated from the Vilnius secondary school and briefly attended Moscow University, then finished the University of St. Petersburg with a law degree in 1860 after which he was employed as a clerk working in peasant administration in his native Grodno gubernia. Here he began organizing like-minded revolutionaries for a struggle against the Tsarist regime. In 1862 Kalinowski began the publication of the clandestine newspaper *Mużyckaja prauda* (The Peasant's Truth), the first Belarusan-language publication aimed at the peasantry, in which he urged villagers to rise up against what he termed "Muscovite oppression." Kalinowski was one of the radical "Red" leaders of the Lithuanian Committee which led and organized the 1863 insurrrection (q.v.); after its defeat he was arrested and executed on March 10, 1864. Although Kalinowski as a publicist denounced Russian rule and proclaimed the liberation of Lithuania, his attachment to the cause of the Belarusan peasantry's national and social liberation makes him an important figure in the Belarusan, rather than the Lithuanian, national movement in the 19th century. See MAC-KEVIČIUS, ANTANAS.

KAPSUKAS, also MICKEVIČIUS-KAPSUKAS, VINCAS (1880-1935). One of the founders and prominent leaders of the Lithuanian Communist movement. Kapsukas was born as Vincas Mickevičius in Vilkaviškis district on April 7, 1880 into a well-to-do peasant family. He enrolled in the Marijampolė secondary school in 1890 and in 1897 matriculated at the Seinai Theological Seminary but was expelled in 1898 for anti-Tsarist activities. Between 1902 and 1904 Kapsukas attended classes at the University of Bern in Switzerland. Until 1902 he was a follower of the Lithuanian liberal national movement associated with the newspaper *Varpas* (The Bell) (q. v.), but in 1903 Kapsukas joined the Lithuanian Social Democratic Party and became one of its more radical activists, sympathetic to Lenin's wing of the Russian Social Democrats. In 1907 Kapsukas was arrested but he escaped from Siberian exile in 1913, then briefly worked for the pro-Bolshevik Lithuanian newspaper *Vilnis* (Lith. The Wave). Between 1914 and 1917

Kapsukas organized radical Lithuanian socialists in Galicia, Scotland and the United States. He returned to Russia after the February 1917 Revolution and in April formally enlisted in the Bolshevik Party; Kapsukas then became the head of its Lithuanian section and one of the editors of *Tiesa* (Lith. The Truth), the Lithuanian Bolshevik newspaper. After the Bolshevik Revolution, Kapsukas worked in the Soviet Russian government as head of Lithuanian affairs within the Commissariat of Nationalities.

In November 1918 Kapsukas arrived secretly in Vilnius and took over the fledgling Lithuanian Communist Party's (q. v.) Central Committee. Between December 8, 1918 and February 27, 1919 he was the Chairman of the Lithuanian Provisional Government of Workers and Peasants, and from February 27 to July 14, 1919, while eastern Lithuania was occupied by the Red Army, headed the Soviet Socialist Republic of Lithuania and Belarus, the so-called Litbel (q. v.) Republic. At the same time in 1919-1920 Kapsukas was a candidate member of the Russian Communist (Bolshevik) Party's Central Committee. With the collapse of Soviet rule in eastern Lithuania, Kapsukas for a time engaged in underground Party work but from the end of 1921 lived in Moscow where, along with Zigmas Angarietis (q. v.), he organized the Communist activists who had fled Lithuania. From 1928 until his death in 1935 Kapsukas worked as the head of the Comintern's secretariat for Poland and the Baltic States. Kapsukas was on the editorial staffs of virtually all Lithuanian Communist underground publications and was the most prolific author of Marxist literature in the Lithuanian language. He is credited with over forty brochures and books and more than 2,000 articles, primarily on Marxist-Leninist ideology, the class analysis of Lithuanian society and proletarian literature. Kapsukas died in Moscow on February 17, 1935. After 1940 a personality cult developed around Kapsukas: in addition to numerous monuments celebrating his person, the city of Marijampolė (q. v.) was named in his honor between 1955 and 1990 and, until the collapse of Soviet rule, the University of Vilnius (q.v.) also bore his name.

KARAIM (Lith. *karaimai*). Turkic people of the Judaic faith who settled in Lithuania in the 14th century, possibly descendants of the Khazars who ruled a khanate centered in the lower Volga region until the 10th century. Hundreds of Karaim were brought to Lithuania from their homeland near the Black Sea by Grand Duke Vytautas (q. v.) in 1397-1398 and served as the ruler's personal bodyguard. During the 17th century there were as many as 5,000 Karaim in Lithuania, but gradually their numbers were reduced through assimilation. The major cultural center of the remaining Lithuanian Karaim is in Trakai (q. v.); there are larger communities in Poland, Ukraine and Crimea. The Karaim espouse the religion of the Karaites, derived from a Judaic theological base, but distinct from Judaism proper. The term "Karaite," sometimes incorrectly applied to the Karaim, refers to practitioners of this faith, without regard to ethnicity. The Karaim houses of worship are called *kinese*; there is a newly-restored one in Vilnius and another in Trakai. Until the 19th century, the Turkic Karaim utilized the Hebrew alphabet and, afterwards, the Latin script. Despite the attempts of the Lithuanian Karaim to discourage marriage to outsiders and efforts to preserve the language, prospects for the continued existence of this group, now estimated at less than two hundred, are considered uncertain.

KAUNAS. Lithuania's second largest city and provisional capital between 1920 and 1939, pop. in 1995: 433,000. Located at the confluence of the Nemunas and Neris rivers, Kaunas is the gateway to central Lithuania and points east. It is one of the oldest fortified settlements which became an important defense installation against the incursions of the Teutonic Knights (q. v.). Kaunas is first mentioned in the chronicles in 1361. In 1408 the city was placed under the Magdeburg laws and grew in importance as a commercial center in the Hanseatic system, since the Nemunas River was navigable to the port of Klaipėda (Memel) on the Baltic. During the 17th and 18th centuries Kaunas contained paper manufactories, mints and other industrial enterprises. The population of Kaunas remained quite small (about 5,000 in 1825) until the mid-19th century. In 1843 the town became the capital of Kaunas (Rus. Kovno) gubernia and in 1864 it became the seat of the Diocese of Samogitia (Lith. Žemaitija). By 1897, together with the suburbs of Šančiai, Aleksotas and Vilijampolė, Kaunas contained 86,500 inhabitants of whom the vast majority were Jews, Poles and Germans. Lumber products, metal factories and railroad connections stimulated industrial development. At the turn of the century, the city attracted increasing numbers of Lithuanian villagers who constituted almost a fourth of the townspeople by 1914. During the late 19th and early 20th centuries, the Tsarist government developed Kaunas as one of its major western outposts, constructing an elaborate system of defensive fortifications around the city and building a large Orthodox church in the city's center as a symbol of Russian cultural dominance.

During the years of independence (1918-1940) Kaunas was transformed. After the loss of Vilnius (q. v.) to Poland in 1920, Kaunas became the provisional capital of Lithuania and the center of Lithuanian cultural life. The city's main avenue was named Laisvės Alėja (Lith. Freedom Boulevard). During the 1920s and 1930s numerous government buildings and schools were built, including the University of Kaunas. By 1923 Lithuanians made up slightly more than one-half of the inhabitants; by 1940 the city numbered 154,000, of whom Lithuanians were about three-fourths, while the Jews made up the largest minority (about 20 percent). Although Vilnius was recovered by Lithuania in October 1939, Kaunas remained the administrative center of the country until after World War II when most government institutions were transferred to Vilnius. During the Nazi occupation of 1941-1944 the Jews of Kaunas were confined to a ghetto in Vilijampolė (Yiddish: Slobodka); subsequently, most of them were massacred at the city's Ninth Fort.

Under Soviet rule, Kaunas grew rapidly as industries, especially metals, textiles and electronics, expanded and a polytechnic institute was established; by 1970 the city had grown to 306,200 inhabitants. Since the population of the city was 90 percent Lithuanian, Kaunas also became the site of periodic nationalist unrest against Soviet rule: the most violent incident was the anti-

Russian outbreak of May 1972 following the self-immolation of the student Romas Kalanta (q. v.). The Sąjūdis (q. v.) section in Kaunas developed a reputation as a radical pro-independence faction of the movement in 1989-1990.

KĖDAINIAI. Historic Lithuanian town located 45 km. north of Kaunas in the geographic center of Lithuania, on the Nevėžis River, pop. in 1995: 31,000. The town is first mentioned in chronicles in 1372; in the 15th and 16th centuries Kėdainiai began emerging as an important trading center. In 1590 the town was placed under the Magdeburg laws. In 1614 the Kėdainiai region came under the rule of the Radziwiłłs (Lith. Radvila) (q. v.) and flourished as an administrative and cultural center. During the Reformation the town was dominated by the Calvinists who established a well-regarded school. Under the leadership of the Radziwiłł family a paper manufactory and Lithuania's first pharmacy were established, and Kėdainiai attracted German, Dutch and Scotch merchants, some of whose homes have recently been restored. Kėdainiai declined after the wars of the mid-17th century; however, it grew rapidly during the independence period after World War I. In the 1960s a large chemical plant was constructed and the population increased to 24,500 by 1974. Kėdainiai is known for its unique architectural monuments, particularly the 17th-century Reformed Church which contains the tomb of John Radziwiłł, and the Catholic Church of St. Joseph built in 1766.

KĖDAINIAI, TREATY OF (1655). An agreement signed by Lithuanian leaders and Sweden, often referred to as the Union of Kėdainiai. The defeats suffered by the Polish-Lithuanian Commonwealth during the wars with Muscovy (1654-1667) persuaded many Lithuanian leaders, particularly the Grand Duchy's hetman John Radziwiłł (q. v.), that only a radical political reorientation could ensure the security of Lithuania against the Muscovite onslaught. During the summer of 1655 Radziwiłł carried on difficult negotiations with Gabriel de la Gardie,

Sweden's treasurer and the administrator of Livonia, about a possible dynastic union of the Lithuanian Grand Duchy with Sweden. On October 20, 1655, Radziwiłł, the bishops of Vilnius and Samogitia, and 1,134 Lithuanian gentry signed the Treaty of Kėdainiai, naming Sweden's King Charles X the Grand Duke of Lithuania, thus formally breaking off the country's union with Poland. However, the Union of Kėdainiai remained a dead letter, since, to the disappointment of the Lithuanian signatories, it became apparent that the Swedes were exploiting the Kėdainiai agreement simply to strengthen their military position in the Baltic, and because the behavior of the Swedish troops in Lithuania provoked a popular rebellion in Samogitia and elsewhere. In Lithuanian historiography the Kėdainiai incident is seen as an attempt by the Lithuanian nobility to reassert the Grand Duchy's independence from Poland, while Polish historians have viewed the agreement as a betrayal of the Commonwealth.

KĘSTUTIS (Pol. Kiejstut, Rus. Kestovt). Duke of Trakai, ca. 1338-1382 and Grand Duke of Lithuania, 1381-1382. Kęstutis was born about 1300 and was the fourth or, according to some sources, the fifth son of Gediminas (q. v.). While little is known of his early life, it is well established that by the time of his father's death in 1341, Kęstutis was the ruler of Samogitia, Trakai, and Grodno. In 1345 he led his brothers in a coup that removed Gediminas' ineffectual youngest son Jaunutis from the throne in Vilnius and transferred power to Algirdas (q. v.). Kęstutis was given the task of defending Lithuania's western border against Polish and, especially, Teutonic attacks. During the nearly four decades of his rule, he cooperated closely with his brother, Grand Duke Algirdas, and some historians consider the period 1345-1377 as practically one of joint rule, although this has been disputed by other scholars.

Between 1345 and 1380 the chronicles recount almost one hundred incursions by the Prussian and Livonian branches of the Teutonic Order (q. v) into western Lithuania, and forty campaigns by Kęstutis and the Lithuanians against the Knights. In 1361 Kęstutis was reportedly captured by the Knights but escaped the following year. Kęstutis was also involved in several campaigns against the Poles who competed with the Grand Duchy for the lands of Volynia and Galicia; about 1362 he also assisted Algirdas in the latter's victorious battle against the Tatars (q. v.) at the Blue Waters (Rus. Sinye Vody) in present-day Ukraine. In addition to his military campaigns, Kęstutis attempted to deflect the Order's attacks by negotiating the Christianization of Lithuania; the most serious of these proposals was in 1358 when Algirdas and Kęstutis offered to accept baptism on the condition that the lands seized by the Order since the 13th century be returned to the Lithuanians, and that the Knights be transferred to the east to defend Christendom against the Tatars. The Lithuanians later broke off these negotiations.

With the death of Algirdas in 1377, Kęstutis became involved in a struggle for power with Jogaila (q. v.) and in November 1381 seized Vilnius and proclaimed himself Grand Duke, accusing his nephew of secret dealings with the Teutonic Knights. Jogaila continued the struggle against Kęstutis and his son Vytautas (q. v.) but a full-scale war was averted in July 1382 when a truce was proclaimed as a prelude to negotiations. About mid-July Kęstutis died under mysterious circumstances: some chroniclers claim he was treacherously murdered by Jogaila who had violated a solemn pledge of safe conduct, while others suggest suicide. In any case, Kęstutis' death triggered a decade-long civil conflict between Jogaila and Vytautas. Kęstutis' passing marked the end of an era: he was Lithuania's last non-Christian ruler and the last to be ritually cremated according to ancient custom.

KLAIPĖDA (Ger. Memel). Lithuania's seaport and third largest city, located at the delta formed by the mouth of the Nemunas River, pop. in 1995: 210,000. In 1252 a fortress was constructed here by the Teutonic Knights (q.v.) to defend the coast connecting the Prussian and Livonian (q.v.) branches of the Order. The settlement was called Memel, the name the Germans also gave to the Nemunas River. Between 1323 and 1409 the castle and town were destroyed several times as a result of the Teutonic-Lithuanian wars. The

Treaty of Melno Lake in 1422 assigned Klaipėda and a strip of land stretching to the east and south of the town on the right bank of the Nemunas River to the Teutonic Order. In 1466 Klaipėda became part of the Duchy of Prussia (q.v.), a vassal state of the Polish crown; after 1660 the town was administered as part of Brandenburg Prussia. In the early 18th century Klaipėda had about 3,500 inhabitants, some 6,000 by the time of the Napoleonic wars, and over 30,000 by 1910. The city developed leather and wood-processing industries, the latter utilizing lumber floated to the port via the Nemunas River from the interior. By the end of the 18th century the growing importance of Klaipėda for the Baltic trade led to the establishment of British, French, Danish and Swedish consulates in the town.

The period of Prussian and German rule (1660-1914) resulted in the Germanization of much of the predominately Lutheran population of the Klaipėda region. The city became predominately German-speaking, while the countryside was mostly Lithuanian. Article 99 of the Treaty of Versailles (1919) recognized Klaipėda Territory, consisting of some 2,848 sq. km. and 140,000 inhabitants on the right bank of the Nemunas, as part of Lithuania, but the Territory was then placed under French administration on behalf of the Allied Powers pending the clarification of the situation in the region. On January 10, 1923 local rebels, reinforced by Lithuanian troops and encouraged by the Lithuanian government, staged an armed uprising, overwhelmed the French garrison and demanded annexation by Lithuania. On May 8, 1924 the major Allied Powers (Britain, France, Italy and Japan) signed the Klaipėda Convention with Lithuania. This treaty transferred sovereignty over Klaipėda Territory to Lithuania, but included international guarantees concerning local autonomy and bilingualism to protect the rights of the German population. The Territory's executive authority was vested in a Governor appointed by the President of Lithuania and assisted by a five-person Directory; legislative power was exercised by an elected Diet. The 1925 census of Klaipėda counted 141,645 inhabitants, including 41.9 percent Germans, 26.6 percent Lithuanians, 24.2 percent Memellaenders (or ethnic Klaipėda residents who were predominately Lithuanian-speakers), and 7.3

percent others. It is estimated that by the early 1930s Lithuanian-speaking residents made up nearly 60 percent of the population in Klaipėda Territory, including post-1923 immigrants from the rest of Lithuania. However, centuries-long German cultural influence and the autonomy conferred by the Klaipėda Convention enabled pro-German elements to dominate local politics.

The Lithuanian government considerably expanded Klaipėda's port facilities and industry during the period of independence but failed to stem the growing power of local German elements who demanded union, or *Anschluss*, with Germany; such agitation became particularly strong after the Nazis (q. v.) came to power in Berlin. In 1934 the Lithuanian authorities banned the pro-Nazi groups and declared martial law leading to a crisis in German-Lithuanian relations. On March 23, 1939 Germany seized Klaipėda Territory after an ultimatum to the Lithuanian Government. In January 1945 Klaipėda was captured by Soviet forces after heavy fighting which destroyed much of the city. Most of the German population fled during the war; by 1970 the population of the city alone was 140,000, primarily Lithuanians (60 percent) and Russians (30 percent). During the same period Klaipėda was developed as a military base and port; it also became the base of a large Soviet Lithuanian fishing fleet. In 1989 the issue of Klaipėda Territory was raised by Soviet leader Mikhail Gorbachev who asserted that Lithuania had no legal claim to the area. However, during the early 1990s the Russians abandoned their naval and military installations as part of their agreement with Lithuania. See GALVANAUSKAS, ERNESTAS; NAZIS; PRUSSIA.

KLIMAS, PETRAS (1891-1969). Lithuanian statesman and historian, born in Marijampolė district on February 23, 1891. After receiving a law degree from the University of Moscow in 1914, he became a prominent political leader of the Lithuanian independence movement. As a member of the Taryba (q. v.), he signed Lithuania's Declaration of Independence in 1918 and began a career in the Republic's foreign ministry. From 1925 until August 1940 he was Lithuania's envoy in Paris. In 1942 he was incarcerated by the

Nazis, but managed to return to Lithuania in 1943. Klimas was deported to Siberia in 1944 where he served a ten-year sentence. He died in Kaunas on January 16, 1969. In addition to his diplomatic career, Klimas was highly regarded for his erudite studies of Lithuanian history, both medieval and modern. Before his death, Klimas left memoirs, which are an important source for the study of Lithuania during the first decades of the 20th century.

KOŚCIUSZKO, TADEUSZ or THADDEUS (Lith. Koščiuška, Tadas) (1746-1817). Polish-Lithuanian and American revolutionary leader, born in the district of Brest in present-day Belarus on February 12, 1746 into a Lithuanian family of petty gentry. He enrolled at the Warsaw Military Academy during the 1760s and then studied in France, Italy and Germany. In 1776 he came to America and enlisted as an engineer in the service of the Continental Congress. Kościuszko served under George Washington at the Battle of Saratoga and during the Yorktown campaign, after which the Continental Congress made him a brigadier general. He returned home in 1784 and in the spirit of Enlightenment liberalism freed some of his serfs. Kościuszko became a prominent radical during the Commonwealth's Four-Year Diet (1788-1792) and in 1789 was appointed a general in the Polish Army. During the Prussian and Russian invasion of the Commonwealth in 1792 Kościuszko commanded forces under Józef Poniatowski and, after their defeat, he fled to France where he sought to enlist the support of the French revolutionary government for the Polish-Lithuanian cause.

Kościuszko became the acknowledged leader of the Polish-Lithuanian revolution which was proclaimed on March 24, 1794 in order to save the Commonwealth's independence and establish a liberal government in Poland-Lithuania. He was wounded and taken prisoner in October 1794; soon after, Warsaw surrendered to the Russians on November 18, 1794. Kościuszko was imprisoned in the Peter and Paul fortress in St. Petersburg but was released by Tsar Paul I in 1796. He traveled to the United States in 1797 but returned to Europe in 1798 where he continued his revolutionary efforts. Kościuszko helped organize Polish legions in Europe;

however, he declined to cooperate with Napoleon. He continued to publicly advocate the abolition of serfdom and the creation of a liberal Polish-Lithuanian state until his death in Switzerland on October 15, 1817. He was buried in the Wawel Castle in Cracow. Although Kościuszko often referred to himself as a Lithuanian, his cultural and political attitudes were typical of the Polonized gentry and, thus, he has usually been associated with Polish, rather than Lithuanian, history. See COMMONWEALTH, POLISH-LITHUANIAN; PARTITIONS; PONIATOWSKI, STANISŁAW AUGUST.

KRAŽIAI MASSACRE (Lith. *Kražių skerdynės*). Attack on Catholic demonstrators by Russian troops in the historic town of Kražiai in November 1893, which helped galvanize the Lithuanian national movement. The town of Kražiai was an important Catholic center since the conversion of Samogitia (q. v.) in the 14th century. In 1891 the Tsarist authorities ordered the closing of the local Benedictine convent as well as the parish church. In protest, local Catholics occupied the endangered buildings, while awaiting a response to a petition they had sent the Tsar. On November 9, 1893 General N. Klingenberg, Governor of Kaunas, arrived with a detachment of sixty police in order to carry out the eviction orders, but his force was outnumbered and overwhelmed by local protestors. On November 10 Cossack reinforcements stormed the Church, dispersed the faithful, carried out extensive public floggings and then attacked neighboring villages. The Lithuanian press and other sources documented at least nine dead, as well as scores of rapes and other injuries. Local peasants claimed a higher toll since some victims died soon after the floggings.

During the ensuing trial of 71 mostly peasant Catholics (55 men and 16 women), the defense team of liberal Russian lawyers embarrassed the Tsarist government by making clear that the authorities were responsible for the killings. The defense won acquittals for 34 of the defendants; eventually most of the remainder won an amnesty from the new Emperor, Nicholas II. The

Kražiai incident was important in further alienating the predominantly Catholic Lithuanian population from Russian rule. See
CATHOLIC CHURCH; RUSSIFICATION.

KRĖVA, also KRIAVAS (Pol. Krewo, Rus. Krevo), ACT OF (1385).
Polish-Lithuanian treaty which laid the basis for the eventual
dynastic union of the Kingdom of Poland and the Grand Duchy of
Lithuania. The location of the treaty is now in Belarus near the
town of Oshmyany. Historians think that sometime in 1383-1384
serious negotiations were under way between Grand Duke Jogaila
(q. v.) and the Polish nobility about the possibility of offering
Jogaila the Polish crown. Many Polish nobles were determined to
prevent the marriage of the young Angevin princess and future
Queen of Poland, Jadwiga of Hungary, to William of Hapsburg,
Prince of Austria. A Lithuanian alliance offered the advantage of
assistance against the Teutonic Knights (q.v.) and the prospect of
acquiring lands in the east. From Jogaila's point of view, a Polish
dynastic alliance and the acceptance of Roman Catholicism offered
Lithuania vital help against the Teutonic Order. In January 1385
a Lithuanian delegation headed by Jogaila's brother Skirgaila
traveled to Cracow, while other Lithuanian envoys journeyed to
Buda to negotiate with Jadwiga's mother, Queen Elizabeth of
Hungary. In Cracow the main conditions for the marriage of
Jogaila and Jadwiga were set out, including the Lithuanian
acceptance of Latin-rite Christianity, the return of Polish prisoners
of war, a compensation for the jilted William of Hapsburg, the
attachment of Lithuania to Poland, and the assistance of the
Lithuanians in recovering lands lost by Poland.

These conditions were confirmed on August 14, 1385 at the
Krėva castle by Jogaila, his brothers Skirgaila, Kaributas and
Lengvenis, as well as his cousin Vytautas (q. v.). While historians
consider that the Act of Krėva began the process of creating the
Polish-Lithuanian union which survived until the end of the Polish-
Lithuanian Commonwealth in 1795 and laid the basis for
Lithuania's turn to Roman Catholicism, there is no unanimity as to
its legal and political significance at the time. Some Polish

historians, such as Oscar Halecki, have maintained that the Krėva treaty meant Lithuania's incorporation into Poland, but the more acceptable view now is that the Lithuanian Grand Duchy continued as a practically autonomous, if not independent state until the Union of Lublin (q. v.) in 1569. See COMMONWEALTH, POLISH-LITHUANIAN; JOGAILA; POLAND.

KRĖVĖ-MICKEVIČIUS, VINCAS (1882-1954). Lithuanian writer and public figure, acting prime minister and foreign minister of Lithuania from June 17 until July 12, 1940. Vincas Mickevičius, better known by his pen name Vincas Krėvė, was born on October 19, 1882 near Merkinė in the Dzūkija (q. v.) region of southeastern Lithuania. In 1904 Krėve graduated from the gymnasium in Kazan, Russia and then briefly studied at the University of Kiev. In 1908 he obtained a doctorate in Indo-European philology from the University of Lviv; he also did research in Oriental studies. In 1909 he began teaching in Baku, Azerbaijan, and in 1919-20 served there as Lithuanian consul. During the 1920s and 1930s Krėvė taught Slavic literature at the University of Kaunas where he also served as Dean of the Faculty of Humanities. In 1904 he began his literary career. Krėvė's best-known works include *Dainavos šalies senų žmonių padavimai* (Lith. Legends of the Old People of the Land of Dainava) (1912), the dramas *Šarūnas* (1912) and *Skirgaila* (1925), recounting the dramatic lives of legendary Lithuanian medieval princes, and the collection of short stories of village life, *Šiaudinėj pastogėj* (Lith. Under the Thatched Roof) (1922-1923). These and numerous other publications totaled ten volumes. In June 1940 Krėve was persuaded to join the Soviet-sponsored People's Government (q. v.) as acting prime minister and foreign minister. Krėvė's memoir of his dramatic conversation with Soviet Foreign Commissar Vyacheslav Molotov in Moscow on July 1, 1940 is one of the most vivid accounts of the Soviet occupation and the Kremlin's annexationist policy toward Lithuania. In January 1941 Krėve was appointed the president of the newly-formed Lithuanian Academy of Sciences (q. v.). In 1944 Krėve fled the Soviet advance and came to the United States in

1947 where he obtained a position as professor of Slavic language and literatures at the University of Pennsylvania. He died in Philadelphia on July 7, 1954.

Krėvė-Mickevičius is considered one of the masters of the Lithuanian language and most literary scholars consider that his lyrical style, a kind of prose poetry, is unique and unrivaled in Lithuanian literature. Krėvė's knowledge of Eastern cultures and Lithuanian folklore enriched his style and subject matter, at times lending an exotic and mystical air to his work. See LITERATURE.

KRUPAVIČIUS, MYKOLAS (1885-1970). Monsignor, statesman and long-time leader of the Lithuanian Christian Democratic (q. v.) movement, born on October 1, 1885 near Marijampolė. Krupavičius graduated from the Veiveriai Teachers' Institute in 1905, then attended the Seinai Theological Seminary from 1908 to 1913 and the St. Petersburg Theological Academy until 1917. Krupavičius was influenced by the social teachings of Leo XIII and wrote extensively on the social mission of Catholicism. He returned to Lithuania in 1918 and joined the Ministry of Agriculture, first as head of the land reform program, and then as minister of agriculture during 1923-1926. Krupavičius is best-known in Lithuanian history as the architect of the country's Land Reform Act of 1922 which broke up the landed estates of the Polonized gentry and distributed over 400,000 hectares to landless peasants and smallholders. After the Nationalist coup of 1926, Krupavičius studied in France, and upon his return to Lithuania in 1929, engaged in pastoral work and teaching. In 1942 Krupavičius was arrested and deported to Germany for protesting Nazi policies. Between 1945 and 1957 he headed the Supreme Committee for the Liberation of Lithuania (Lith. VLIK) (q.v.). In 1957 Krupavičius came to the United States where he was a prominent member of the émigré community until his death in Chicago on December 4, 1970. See AGRICULTURE.

KUBILIŪNAS, PETRAS (1894-1946). Military leader and first general counselor during the Nazi occupation of Lithuania 1941-1944, born on May 16, 1894 in Rokiškis district. He graduated from the Vilnius military school in 1914 and served in the Tsarist Russian Army with distinction during World War I. Kubiliūnas returned to Lithuania in 1919 and quickly rose to become the Lithuanian Army's Chief of Staff in February 1929. He was arrested in May 1934 for supporting a right-wing military coup intended to bring Augustinas Voldemaras (q. v.) to power and imprisoned for two years. In 1940-1941 Kubiliūnas was arrested by Soviet authorities, but was liberated at the outbreak of the Nazi-Soviet war in June 1941. In August 1941 he agreed to head the Nazi-sponsored General Council of native advisors to the German Generalkommissar Adrian von Renteln with the title of First Counselor, thus becoming the highest-ranking Lithuanian official during the German occupation. Kubiliūnas was frequently excoriated by anti-Nazi Lithuanians for his compliant attitude towards the German authorities, as well as for his calls to fulfill German demands to supply youth for the Reich Labor Service (RAD) and German auxiliary military units. In 1944 he retreated to Germany. In December 1945 Kubiliūnas was kidnapped by Soviet operatives in the British occupation zone, brought back to Lithuania, thoroughly interrogated and executed on August 22, 1946.

KUDIRKA, VINCAS (1858-1899). Lithuanian publicist, editor and leader of the 19th-century national movement, born on December 31, 1858 in Vilkaviškis district. He attended the Marijampolė secondary school from 1871 to 1877 when, under parental pressure, Kudirka enrolled in the Seinai Theological Seminary only to be dismissed for lack of a vocation. In 1879 he returned to the Marijampolė secondary school and, after graduating with distinction, was admitted to the University of Warsaw in 1881 where he studied medicine. Kudirka had been sympathetic to a Polish cultural orientation until 1883 when he became a reader of the nationalist *Aušra* (q. v.), which transformed him into an ardent Lithuanian patriot. The account of his dramatic conversion to the nationalist cause became one of the best-known stories in the history of the 19th-century national movement. Kudirka was briefly associated with Marxist circles in Warsaw for which he was temporarily suspended from his studies, but managed to receive his medical degree in 1889. That same year Kudirka established the monthly *Varpas* (Lith. The Bell) for the Lithuanian intelligentsia and in January 1890 founded *Ūkininkas* (Lith. The Farmer), a paper aimed at the peasantry. In 1890 Kudirka moved to the town of Šakiai in southwestern Lithuania where he opened a medical practice, but much of his time was devoted to his editorship of *Varpas*, political writings and literary creation, which included fiction, poetry and satirical works. In 1895 he moved to Naumiestis (Rus. Vladislavov) where, under the watchful eye of the Tsarist police, he lived until his death from tuberculosis on November 6, 1899. In 1934 the Lithuanian government changed the name of Naumiestis to Kudirkos Naumiestis; a monument to Kudirka dominates the town square .

Along with Motiejus Valančius (q. v.) and Jonas Basanavičius (q. v.), Kudirka is the most important figure in the Lithuanian national movement of the 19th century. He imbued the Lithuanian movement, hitherto dominated by the Catholic Church and driven by cultural concerns, with a political content whose theme was national injustice. Kudirka was the author of some of the best Lithuanian satirical writing in which he excoriated Tsarist officialdom, especially in his *Viršininkai* (Lith. The Bosses) and *Lietuvos tilto atsiminimai* (Lith. Memoirs of a Lithuanian Bridge). In 1898 Kudirka published the words and music to *Tautiška giesmė* (Lith. The National Song) which was to become the Lithuanian national anthem. His writings took up economic, social and national issues, criticizing the wave of Lithuanian emigration to America, urging Lithuanians to resist the Tsarist regime and to assert themselves outside their traditional village milieu, for example, by entering commerce and the professions. Kudirka' secular attitude and liberalism provoked the enmity of much of the Catholic clergy, while his attacks on the economic role of the Jew revealed strains of anti-Semitism. Kudirka's politicization of the Lithuanian national movement was instrumental in leading to the formation of the major Lithuanian political currents, which resulted in the development of political parties. The movement centered around his periodical *Varpas*, which eventually alienated both clerical and socialist elements. The more moderate wing of the *varpininkai* grew into the Lithuanian Democratic Party (q. v.), while the more radical faction formed the basis of the Lithuanian Peasant Populist Union (q. v.). Kudirka's influence on Lithuania's political development has led many scholars to consider him the father of modern Lithuania nationalism. See NATIONALISM; *VARPAS*.

KULVIETIS, ABRAOMAS (ca. 1510-1545). Educator and leader of the early Lithuanian Reformation, born in Jonava district ca. 1510. In 1529 Kulvietis received the bachelor's degree from the Cracow Academy and in 1530 began studies in western Europe. Some historians have claimed that he studied under Erasmus although this now seems doubtful. About 1535 Kulvietis returned to Lithuania and in 1536 arrived in Prussia where Prince Albert of Brandenburg, one of the first rulers in the Baltic region to adopt Lutheranism, became his protector and sponsored Kulvietis' studies at the universities of Leipzig, Wittenberg and Siena. With the help of Bona Sforza (q. v.), the influential Italian wife of Sigismund the Old (q. v.), Kulvietis established a school of classical languages in Vilnius in 1539, but his propagation of Protestant doctrines soon led to his expulsion from Lithuania. He went again to Prussia where records indicate that he taught Greek and Hebrew at the newly opened University of Königsberg in 1544. In 1545 Kulvietis returned again to Lithuania when conditions for Protestants had improved, but he died of tuberculosis on June 6, 1545. Kulvietis was one of the earliest translators of religious literature, including Lutheran hymns and the Psalms of David, into the Lithuanian language. His earliest known published texts appeared post-humously in 1570. See REFORMATION.

- L -

LANDSBERGIS, VYTAUTAS (1932-). Leader of the Lithuanian independence movement Sąjūdis (q.v.) and Lithuania's head of state 1990-1993, born on October 18, 1932 in Kaunas. In 1955 Landsbergis graduated from the Lithuanian state conservatory as a pianist and received his doctorate in musicology in 1969. During the 1960s and 1970s, he taught at the Lithuanian conservatory and the Vilnius Pedagogical Institute. Landsbergis is known as a specialist in the music of the composer and artist Konstantinas Čiurlionis (q. v.) and has published a number of studies on the subject. In 1988 Landsbergis was elected the chairman of the Lithuanian Reform Movement, Sąjūdis, which under his leadership adopted a political program aimed at the restoration of Lithuania's independence. In March 1989 Landsbergis was elected to the USSR Congress of People's Deputies, and in May 1989 he led a walkout of Lithuanian representatives from the Congress in protest over Gorbachev's resistance to Lithuanian autonomy; as a result, he began to receive increasing attention in the West as the de facto leader of the Lithuanian independence movement. After the February 1990 elections to the Lithuanian Supreme Soviet won by Sąjūdis, Landsbergis was elected Chairman of the Lithuanian parliament, now called the Supreme Council, on March 11, 1990, the day the legislature declared Lithuania's independence from the Soviet Union. As chairman of the parliament, Landsbergis became Lithuania's head of state and was usually referred to as the country's president.

Between March 1990 and August 1991 Landsbergis directed most of his efforts at preserving Lithuania's fragile independence, culminating in his steadfast defiance of Moscow during the January 13, 1991 Soviet military attacks aimed at toppling his government. Internally, Landsbergis was increasingly drawn into conflict with the Supreme Soviet, which he claimed was a pro-Communist force obstructing his policies. His supporters eventually formed the Fatherland Union (Lith. *Tėvynės Sąjunga*) (Conservative) Party to oppose Algirdas Brazauskas' (q. v.) Lithuanian Democratic Labor Party (q.v.) (Lith. LDDP). In October 1992 the LDDP won the first elections to the Seimas, Lithuania's new parliament. After Brazauskas' victory over Stasys Lozoraitis (q. v.) in the presidential elections of February 1993, Landsbergis became the acknowledged leader of the opposition to the ruling Democratic Labor Party. When the Conservatives and their allies gained a majority in the October-November 1996 elections to the Seimas, Landsbergis was again elected chairman of the legislature, thus regaining much of his former political influence and stature.

LANGUAGE, LITHUANIAN. The official language of the Republic of Lithuania is classified as a member of the Baltic branch of the Indo-European (IE) language family, which includes most European languages. Linguists consider Lithuanian one of the most conservative, or oldest, languages of the IE family still spoken; thus, it has been of great interest to scholars of comparative philology. In some language classification schemes, the Baltic languages are included within a more general Balto-Slavic subdivision of IE. Lithuanian and Latvian are the only living Baltic languages, but the Baltic branch also included, among others, the extinct Old Prussian, Couronian, Zemgalian, Selonian and Yotvingian (q. v.) languages. More than 3.5 million people speak Lithuanian in the Republic of Lithuania as either a native or second language; Russian and Polish are the most important minority languages. While the Lithuanian diaspora numbers a million people of Lithuanian extraction, the majority in the United States, it can be estimated that only about 10-20 percent of this population has any command of the Lithuanian language. The Lithuanian language has always used the Latin alphabet (see Appendix 1), except during the period of the official Russian press ban (q. v.) of 1864-1904 which, however, had little success. There are two basic dialects: the Samogitian (q. v.), or *žemaičiai* (Lith. Lowlander) dialect, and the dialect of the Aukštaitija (q. v.) region, or the *aukštaičiai* (Lith. Highlander); the latter includes the subdialects of Dzūkija (q. v.) and Suvalkija (q. v.).

The Development of Modern Lithuanian. The first book in Lithuanian was the catechism of Martynas Mažvydas published in Königsberg in 1547, although a written text of a prayer found in a Latin book published in 1503 was discovered at the University of Vilnius and is now considered the oldest known text in the language. A number of catechisms, dictionaries, religious texts and poems were published in the 16th and 17th centuries, the majority in East Prussia (q. v.). During the 18th century the literary level of the Lithuanian language deteriorated when didactic catechisms and prayer books aimed at the peasantry utilized Slavic loanwords; little attention was paid to standardized grammar and usage. The national revival of the early 19th century increasingly stressed the importance of the Lithuanian language, and the quality of publications improved under such writers as Simonas Daukantas (q. v.), Bishop Motiejus Valančius (q. v.), Mikalojus Akelaitis (1829-1887) and Antanas Tatarė (1805-1889). At the same time, foreign scholars began to pay increasing attention to Lithuanian as one of the oldest languages of the IE family. One of the most important studies of the Lithuanian language in the 19th century was the prominent philologist August Schleicher's *Litauische Grammatik* (1856). Modern standard Lithuanian emerged during the late 19th and early 20th centuries largely through the efforts of such scholars as the comparative philologist Kazimieras Būga (1879-1924) and, especially, the practical linguist Jonas Jablonskis (1860-1930), known as "Rygiškių Jonas" (Lith. John from Rygiškiai). Most Lithuanians credit Jablonskis with creating a standard language based in large part on the *kapsai* idiom of the *aukštaičiai* (spoken in Suvalkija). This is the language now used in government and education, and is dominant in urban areas. The dialects still survive in the countryside.

Political and Social Factors. During the 19th century, scholars and ethnographers feared that Lithuanian would become extinct because of its low social prestige as a peasant idiom. The linguistic division of Lithuanian society into a Polish-speaking upper class and a Lithuanian-speaking peasantry was a long and complex process. The last Grand Duke known to have spoken Lithuanian was King Jogaila's (q. v.) son, Casimir (q. v.) (1440-

1492). Spoken Polish came into wider use in the Grand Duke's court by the middle of the 16th century. The upper nobility and magnates began accepting Polish language and customs soon after, while the lesser boyars, or *szlachta* as well as Gentile townspeople, continued to speak Lithuanian well into the 18th century. By the 19th century, except in Samogitia, they began to accept Polish, which became the language of public life and social prestige in Lithuania. Lithuanian became the means of communicating with and among peasants, thus, becoming the language of a social class rather than a nation.

One of the reasons for this process was the historic exclusion of the Lithuanian language from affairs of the Church and State. The official language of the Grand Duchy of Lithuania's chancery was an old Belarusan/West Russian form of Old Church Slavic; from the late 14th century diplomatic correspondence was increasingly conducted in Latin. Polish and Latin became the official languages of the Grand Duchy in 1697. Written Lithuanian was rarely used in ecclesiastical offices. Although spoken Lithuanian was still widely used in court cases in the 17th century, official decrees were handed down in Polish, Latin or the Belarusan form of Old Church Slavic. Only a few people, for example, Mikalojus Daukša (q. v.), called for the wider use of Lithuanian. The situation was different in Lithuanian East Prussia (q. v.), where, until the late 19th century, royal edicts were published in Gothic-scripted Lithuanian, which was recognized as an official language in local schools, churches and district government offices. Lithuanian was also studied extensively at the University of Königsberg.

During the 19th century, Lithuanian came into wider use as the Church, the government and various political forces sought to influence or mobilize the peasantry. Despite Tsarist efforts at Russification, literacy in standard Lithuanian increased before World War I. The postwar independent Republic of Lithuania was the first state to proclaim Lithuanian an official language and it rapidly came to dominate governmental, educational and commercial institutions. During the years of Soviet rule (1940-1941, 1944-1990) Russian was introduced as a compulsory second language in Lithuanian schools and became dominant in industry and government; bilingualism was declared the official policy. Until 1989 meetings of the Lithuanian Communist Party (q.v.) Central Committee and those of most central government offices were conducted in Russian, even though the majority of officials were native Lithuanians. In the Soviet census of 1979, while 97.7 percent of Lithuanians indicated Lithuanian as their first, or native, language, almost 38 percent indicated fluency in Russian. After the restoration of Lithuania's independence in 1990, official bilingualism was abandoned: Lithuanian was declared the official language of the central government and the compulsory teaching of Russian as a second language was halted. Minority-language schools, primarily Polish and Russian, are also permitted: these languages are given official status alongside Lithuanian in locales with a significant minority population. Increasingly, young educated Lithuanian-born Russians and Poles are acquiring a mastery of Lithuanian, essential to participating in the country's life. In 1990-1993 Russian-language commercial and official signs, including road and street signs, were removed as unnecessary and reminiscent of foreign occupation. See LITERATURE; POLONIZATION; RUSSIFICATION.

LATVIA. Baltic nation bordering Lithuania on the north, area 63,700 sq. km., population est. 2,740,000, capital Riga, pop. 917,000. The Republic of Latvia declared its independence from the USSR in 1991. Latvian and Lithuanian are the only two surviving languages (q. v.) of the Baltic branch of the Indo-European linguistic family. It is generally thought that the western region of present-day Latvia was inhabited by the Couronians (in Latvian, *kurši*), their land known as Courland (q. v.), or *Kuržeme* in Latvian. To the east the major Baltic tribes were the Semgalians, Letgallians and Selians. In the late 12th century, German traders and missionaries began arriving at the Gulf of Riga. Unlike the Lithuanians, the various Latvian tribes failed to unite against the threat of Germanic colonization and were subdued by the so-called Knights of the

Sword. Most of the region became known as Livonia (q. v.) and was ruled by the Teutonic Knights until the 16th century.

The arrival of Lutheranism and the division of the Latvian lands into the Duchy of Courland (q. v.) and Livonia (q. v.) created the basic contours of Latvian society until the 19th century. The secularization of the Teutonic Order (q. v.) led to the creation of a powerful landowning minority of Baltic Germans who dominated the Latvian-speaking majority, most of whom became hereditary serfs over the next two centuries. At the same time, the Reformation (q. v.) period produced the first Latvian-language books beginning in the 1580s. The Duke of Courland became a nominal vassal of Poland-Lithuania; for their part, the Radziwiłłs (q. v.) made efforts to attach Courland and Livonia to Lithuania. During the 17th century the city of Riga, Courland and Livonia became objects of struggle between the Polish-Lithuanian Commonwealth (q. v.) and Sweden, which occupied Riga and Livland in the early 1600s. As a result of the Treaty of Nystadt (1721) which ended the Great Northern War, Livland became part of the Russian Empire. In 1772 the eastern part of Latvia, Latgale, was annexed by Russia as a result of the First Partition (q. v.) of Poland-Lithuania, and was eventually attached to the gubernia of Vitebsk. In 1795 the remainder of the Latvian lands were incorporated into the Russian Empire. The Latvian and Estonian lands of the Russian Empire (Courland, Livland and Estland) are usually known in history as the "Baltic provinces" of the Russian Empire.

An increasingly assertive Latvian national movement emerged during the 19th century, partly stimulated by the emancipation of the serfs of the Baltic provinces during 1817-1819. The educational work of Lutheran pastors, many of whom were Germans, resulted in the Latvian peasantry achieving one of the highest rural literacy rates in Europe by the end of the 19th century (over 90 percent). The increasing urbanization of the Latvian people, the growth of industry and the development of the Latvian language under the leadership of persons such as Krišjānis Barons (1835-1923), the editor of the newspaper *Peterburgas avīzes*, and Atis Kronvalds (1837-1875), gradually undermined the social power and cultural monopoly of the Baltic Germans in Latvia. As in Lithuania, World War I, the Russian Revolution, and the assistance of the British Navy in 1918-1919 provided Latvia with the opportunity to declare independence in 1918 and by 1920 successfully establish a viable, democratic state based on majority rule. Land reform and emigration considerably reduced the power of the Baltic German landowners between the wars. In foreign policy, Latvia strove to avoid involvement in Lithuania's territorial quarrels with Poland and Germany. In 1934 Latvia joined Lithuania and Estonia in forming the Baltic Entente (q. v.), but this proved of limited use in enhancing the security of the Baltic States.

On June 17, 1940 the Soviet Army occupied Latvia, and on August 5, 1940, the country was incorporated into the USSR. As a result of Soviet rule and rapid industrialization, hundreds of thousand of immigrants, primarily Russians, were brought to Latvia as industrial labor, drastically changing the demographic structure of the Latvian SSR. The Latvian proportion of the population fell to just over 50 percent by the early 1990s and to about 30 percent in Riga, the largest city in the eastern Baltic. Soviet repression, as well as concern over the survival of the Latvian people and their environment, led to a resurgence of the Latvian independence movement during the late 1980s. The establishment of the pro-independence Latvian Popular Front proved an inspiration for reform in Lithuania. Since 1990 the Latvian and Lithuanian governments have followed a similar foreign policy; however, disagreements have erupted over oil drilling rights on the Baltic Sea shelf adjoining the two countries.

Lithuanians have long played a role in the history of Latvia. The burgeoning metropolis of Riga attracted tens of thousands of Lithuanian workers before the Great War; in addition, many Lithuanian students studied at the secondary schools of Jelgava (Ger. Mitau) and Liepāja during the turn of the 20th century. Between the wars the Lithuanian minority operated a secondary school in Riga as well as primary schools in the districts close to the Lithuanian border.

Law / 171

LAW. See CONSTITUTIONS; LITHUANIAN STATUTE.

LITBEL, or LITHUANIAN-BELARUSAN SOVIET SOCIALIST REPUBLIC. In 1919 the Bolsheviks established a short-lived Soviet Republic in Lithuania and Belarus, popularly known as the Litbel Republic. In December 1918 the Bolshevik leader Vincas Mickevičius-Kapsukas (q. v.) visited Lithuania to organize a Soviet authority in expectation of the arrival of the Red Army which was approaching eastern Lithuania in the wake of the German retreat. On December 8, 1918 the Lithuanian Communist Party (q. v.) created the Provisional Lithuanian Government of Workers and Poor Peasants headed by Kapsukas and on December 16 this government published a manifesto proclaiming the establishment of a Soviet republic in Lithuania. Lenin recognized the fledgling Soviet Lithuanian state on December 22, 1918 and the Red Army entered Vilnius on January 5, 1919. On January 7 Kapsukas arrived in Vilnius from Daugavpils to organize the country's Soviet administration. Since the Lithuanian Bolsheviks proved too weak to stand on their own, on February 27, 1919 a consolidated Lithuanian-Belarusan Soviet Republic, known as the Litbel, was proclaimed in Vilnius at the insistence of the Russian Bolsheviks.

The Litbel government survived only briefly. The prominence of non-Lithuanians in the Soviet regime and its refusal to parcel out the landed estates to villagers antagonized the Lithuanian peasantry. The defeats of the Red Army at the hands of German, Lithuanian and Polish forces doomed the Litbel: on April 21, 1919 Polish forces entered Vilnius and the Soviet government fled to Minsk. In July 1919 the Litbel regime liquidated its defense council and the government ceased functioning. On September 11, 1919 Soviet Russia proposed armistice negotiations to the Lithuanian government in Kaunas, thus granting de facto recognition to the Republic of Lithuania and confirming the end of the Lithuanian-Belarusan Soviet Republic. In later years, the brief Litbel episode provided the Bolsheviks with a historical reference point which served as a legitimizing rationale for later Communist activity and for the Soviet annexation of Lithuania in 1940, when the invasion was portrayed by Party ideologues as the "restoration" of the Soviet rule interrupted in 1919 rather than a foreign occupation. Furthermore, after World War II, Communist historians maintained that Kapsukas' manifesto of December 16 constituted the authentic reestablishment of the Lithuanian state, rather than the Declaration of Independence proclaimed on February 16, 1918. This interpretation is rejected by serious scholars. See BELARUS.

LITERATURE, LITHUANIAN. **Earliest Writings.** The Lithuanian people, as well as the other Balts, possessed a rich oral folk tradition, best expressed through the ubiquitous songs (Lith. *dainos*) which accompanied virtually all aspects of life: work, play, love, marriage, death. At least several hundred thousand of these lyrical songs have been recorded by Lithuanian and foreign researchers during the 19th and 20th centuries. Among the oldest Baltic written texts are scattered Old Prussian-language terms and phrases from the 14th and 15th centuries, written down by German scribes accompanying the Teutonic Knights (q. v.). Medieval Lithuanian chronicles appeared in a Belarusan form of Old Church Slavic, which was the first official language of the Grand Duchy of Lithuania. Latin assumed increasing importance during the 15th and 16th centuries under the influence of Renaissance (q. v.) humanism. One of the first significant Latin works was the historical survey of Michael the Lithuanian (Lat. Michalonus Lituanus) entitled *De moribus Tartarorum, Lituanorum et Moschorum* (Lat. On the Customs of the Tatars, Lithuanians and Muscovites). During the 16th century a number of Latin poets, such as the Spaniard Peter Roisius (1500-1571) and Nicholas Husovianus (ca. 1475-1540), brought the Renaissance style to Lithuania.

The first Lithuanian-language publications appeared during the Reformation (q. v.). In 1547 the Lutheran pastor Martynas Mažvydas published his 79-page *Catechismuṣa prasty shadey* (Old Lith. The Catechism in Plain Words) in Königsberg, East Prussia (q. v.); this is the first book known to have been published in the

Lithuanian language. Until the 17th century most Lithuanian-language publications were issued in Lutheran East Prussia, utilizing the Gothic-style Latin alphabet. Among the most talented of the Reformation period's Lithuanian literati were Jonas Bretkūnas (1536-1602) whose *Postilė* (Lith. Postylla) was published in 1591, Simonas Vaišnoras (ca. 1545-1600) and the grammarian Danielius Kleinas (1609-1666), a pastor from Tilsit (q. v.), whose *Grammatica Lituanica* set the standard for the systematization of the Lithuanian language. Secular Lithuanian-language literature of the 17th century was limited to dedications, epithets and praise of illustrious personages: the most notable example of this genre was the *Postylla* of Mikalojus Daukša (q. v.), one of the early proponents of public use of the Lithuanian language. The rather slow development of Lithuanian literature, despite the promising start of the 17th century, was in large part caused by the progressive relegation of the language to an idiom of the lower social strata. Polish and Latin came to predominate among the nobility and upper-class townspeople, as well as in the governmental and educational institutions of the Grand Duchy.

As a result, the most important achievement of Lithuanian literature in the 18th century came from East Prussia where Lithuanian was recognized as an official language on the local level until the middle of the 19th century: this was the epic poem *Metai* (Lith. The Seasons) by the Lutheran pastor, Kristijonas Donelaitis (q. v.). Another important literary figure of the period was the translator and folklorist Liudvikas Rėza (1776-1840) who published both Donelaitis' epic and the first collection of Lithuanian folk songs, the *dainos.* By contrast, the most popular publication in the Roman Catholic Grand Duchy was the prominent devotional tract, *Broma atverta ing viecznasti* (Lith. The Gates Opened to Eternity), whose heavily Slavicized vocabulary and pseudoreligious content revealed the decline of literary Lithuanian.

Developments Before the Late 19th Century. The revival of Lithuanian literature began in the first half of the 19th century under the influence of a "Lithuanian movement" (Lith. *lituanistinis sąjūdis*) among the Samogitian (q. v.) gentry, led by the poets Antanas Klementas (1756-1823), Dionizas Poška (q. v.), Simonas

Stanevičius (q. v.) and Silvestras Valiūnas (1789-1831). One of
the best-known poets among the Lithuanian peasantry was the
Catholic priest Antanas Strazdas (1760-1833), a true poet of the
people, whose verses became popular religious hymns. At the
same time, the Lithuanian language slowly gained social importance and intellectual respectability: Simonas Daukantas (q. v.)
and Motiejus Valančius (q. v.), the Bishop of Samogitia, were the
first to utilize Lithuanian in scholarly works. The expansion of the
Lithuanian-language primary school system fostered by Valančius
and the remarkable spread of the temperance brotherhoods during
the 1850s and 1860s stimulated both an increase in peasant literacy
and an outpouring of popular and devotional literature. Laurynas
Ivinskis (1811-1881) published a series of Lithuanian almanacs
(Lith. *Kalendoriai*) for the peasantry, which, in addition to practical
information and religious material, included poetry and history.
Mikalojus Akelaitis (1829-1887) played an important role in
propagating the use of the Lithuanian language in the educational
system and society and promoting the spread of popular literature.
Antanas Tatarė (1805-1889), the most prominent 19th-century
author from Suvalkija (q. v.), published a number of short stories
and didactic tales during the 1850s. Undoubtedly, the greatest
influence on Lithuanian literature before the emergence of the
modern national movement in the last quarter of the 19th century
was Bishop Valančius, whose *Palangos Juzė* (Lith. Juzė from
Palanga), detailing the travels of a folksy itinerant tailor, was
probably the most widely read work of secular prose in 19th-
century Lithuania. Valančius' brilliant mastery of style and folk
tradition also revealed the limited scope of Lithuanian literature
before the emergence of modern Lithuanian nationalism: its appeal
was restricted to the confined environment of the village and did
not reflect the transformation of Lithuanian society, particularly the
aspirations of the emerging Lithuanian-speaking intelligentsia of
the late 19th century. The work of Antanas Baranauskas (q. v.), the
Bishop of Sejny, perhaps Lithuania's finest lyricist of the 19th
century, was secular and modern; however, his adherence to
traditional political and social norms mark him as an author of an
earlier era.

The Late 19th Century and the Period of Independence.
Between the late 1800s and 1940, Lithuanian literature escaped its village environment and emerged as the medium of educated Lithuanian-speaking society. Jonas Mačiulis, best-known under the name Maironis (q. v.), emerged as the unchallenged Lithuanian poet of the modern national movement; his prose counterpart was Juozas Tumas-Vaižgantas (q. v.). With the emergence of Lithuanian secular periodicals, such as Jonas Basanavičius' (q. v.) *Aušra* (q. v.), and a politicized native intelligentsia, as well as the development of a standardized literary language, social themes and a critical approach in prose appeared. Vincas Kudirka (q. v.), the founder and editor of *Varpas* (q. v.), wrote the first Lithuanian satirical polemics. An important pioneer in modern prose was Vincas Pietaris (1850-1902) who penned the first Lithuanian historical novel, *Algimantas*, in honor of a prince who struggled to unify Lithuanian tribes in the face of the Slavic threat. Social problems dominated the writings of Julija Žymantienė, or Žemaitė (q. v.), who was also the first to stress feminist themes. Jonas Biliūnas (1879-1907) authored some shorter works: a memorable portrait of the 1863 insurrection (q. v.) in *Liūdna pasaka* (Lith. A Sad Tale) and a vision of socialism in *Laimės žiburys* (Lith. The Torch of Happiness). Psychological realism was the defining element in the works of the popular Antanas Žukauskas-Vienuolis (1882-1957) who became a dominant force on the literary scene before the Great War. The first modern Lithuanian dramatist, Aleksandras Fromas-Gužutis (1822-1900), wrote historical dramas; the most frequently performed play in Lithuania during the decade before World War I was Juozas and Jonas Vilkutaitis' *Amerika pirtyje* (Lith. America in Hot Water), first performed in 1899. Vydūnas (q. v.), or Vilhelmas Storosta, wrote dramas of an entirely different genre, emphasizing national historical and mythological themes imbued with Eastern philosophy.

Literature and Women. One of the significant developments in Lithuanian literature at the turn of the century was the advent of a number of important women authors, marking the emergence of women as a factor among the Lithuanian intelligentsia. During this time, educated Lithuanian women often came to the national movement from the culturally Polonized petty gentry. Polish literature, especially the works of Eliza Orzeszkowa (1841-1910), whose emphasis was on service to the poor and descriptions of village and small town life in Belarus and eastern Poland, impressed women aspiring to serve society. Their social origins forced these women to confront the relations between the Polonized manor and Lithuanian villagers. In addition to the works of Žemaitė, social themes predominated in the work of Žemaitė and Gabrielė Petkevičaitė-Bitė (1861-1943). As a deputy on the Peasant Populist (q. v.) list and chairman of the first session of the Constituent Assembly (q. v.), the latter became the most prominent woman public figure in independent Lithuania. The most prominent woman writer of a Catholic orientation was Marija Pečkauskaitė, better known as Šatrijos Ragana (Lith. The Witch of Šatrija), whose autobiographical novel *Sename dvare* (Lith. At the Old Estate), was acknowledged as a classic depiction of the *fin-de-siècle* disintegration of Lithuania's manorial society and its ambiguous relations with the peasantry. An interesting literary phenomenon among women was the work of the sisters Sofija Pšibiliauskienė (1876-1926) and Marija Lastauskienė (1872-1957), who befriended Orzeszkowa and wrote under the collective pseudonym, Lazdynų Pelėda (Lith. The Owl of the Hazels). Sofija translated her sister's Polish works into Lithuanian. One of the most prominent women writers of the interwar period was Ieva Simonaitytė (1897-1978) whose works, including her prize-winning 1935 novel *Aukštųjų Šimonių likimas* (Lith. The Fate of the Šimonis Family of Aukštųjų), depicted the specific milieu of the Lithuanians of her native Klaipėda region, struggling to survive Germanizing influences. Salomėja Nėris (1904-1945), despite her eventual drift into the Communist camp, remains one of the country's most widely read poets of the interwar generation.

Independent Lithuania (Before 1940). Political independence between the wars greatly enhanced mass literacy in the national language and, thus, contributed to the further development and diversification of Lithuanian literature. Several authors, who had begun writing at the beginning of the century, achieved their creative pinnacle during the interwar years: Vincas Krėvė-

Mickevičius (q. v.), considered by many Lithuanians as the country's finest writer, the poet Liudas Gira (1884-1946) and the novelist Vincas Mykolaitis-Putinas (q. v.), whose controversial autobiographical novel, *Altorių šešėly* (Lith. In the Shadow of the Altars), stunned 1930s Lithuanian society by depicting the author's own abandonment of the priesthood. The diplomat Ignas Šeinius, author of what some consider the first modern Lithuanian novel, *Kuprelis*(Lith. The Hunchback), also published in 1934 the highly-regarded *Siegfried Immerselbe atsinaujina* (Lith. The Rejuvenation of Siegfried Immerselbe), which foresaw the dangers of Nazism. Prominent symbolist poets included Jurgis Baltrušaitis (q. v.), Faustas Kirša (1891-1964), Mykolaitis-Putinas and Balys Sruoga (1896-1947); the latter also left a devastating account of his experience in the Stutthof Nazi concentration camp entitled *Dievų miškas* (Lith. The Forest of the Gods).

The interwar period also saw the emergence of avant-garde literature under the iconoclastic Four Winds (Lith. *Keturi vėjai*) Movement, initiated in 1922 by a group of young writers, such as Kazys Binkis (1893-1942), who criticized contemporary Lithuanian literature as sentimental, naive and rustic. Kazys Boruta (1905-1965) embodied the angry young man of Lithuanian literature, serving time in a Nationalist prison. Jurgis Savickis (1890-1952) provided Lithuanian readers with a cosmopolitan individualism, honed by his diplomatic experience in European capitals. During the 1930s a leftist avant-garde movement, the Third Front (Lith. *Trečias frontas*), included the poets Antanas Venclova (1906-1971), and the dynamic Salomėja Nėris (1904-1945).

Literature since 1940. The Sovietization of cultural life after Lithuania's occupation and forcible incorporation into the USSR in 1940 transformed the literary scene. The Party took control of the Lithuanian Writers' Association as the only legitimate literary organization in Lithuania and utilized it to enforce the Stalinist line. Petras Cvirka (1909-1947) became a prominent exponent of the now obligatory current of socialist realism, while the literary critic Kostas Korsakas (1909-1986) sought to explain the history of Lithuanian literature in Marxist terms. Some former leftist members of the Third Front, such as Venclova, Neris and Cvirka, were prominent during the Stalinist period. The postwar Soviet campaign against "cosmopolitan" influences led to repression in Lithuania as well: a number of writers, such as Kazys Boruta (1905-1965), Sruoga and Mykolaitis-Putinas, were forced to "correct" their deviant ideas, others were imprisoned, while the dissident leftist poet Kazys Jakubėnas (1908-1950) was murdered by security agents.

The "thaw" of the post-Stalin period allowed some room for creative innovation, albeit under the watchful eye of the Party. During the period between the late 1950s and the mid-1980s, when the Soviet censorship apparatus weakened considerably, Eduardas Mieželaitis (b. 1919), the winner of the Lenin Prize, gained fame for his collection of verse, *Žmogus* (Lith. Man). Juozas Baltušis (1909-1991) autobiographical novel, *Parduotos vasaros* (Lith. Summers Which Were Sold), emphasized agrarian social issues from a perspective of class struggle. The post-Stalin era also opened possibilities for literature with national themes, as in the works of the popular Justinas Marcinkevičius (b. 1930), who penned a number of historical dramas depicting Lithuania's heroic past. Other prominent prose writers, such as Juozas Avyžius (b. 1922) and Romualdas Lankauskas (b. 1932), tackled contemporary themes, including man's alienation in industrial society. The irreverent younger writers of the 1980s who were critical of the regime and the "Soviet man" it had spawned included Saulius Tomas Kondrotas (b. 1953) and Ričardas Gavelis (b. 1950); Jurga Invanauskaitė (b. 1961), a popular iconoclastic novelist, was influenced by the Western counterculture movement. Many young writers, such as the poet Sigitas Geda (b. 1943), took an active role in the 1980s reform and independence movements. The collapse of the Soviet system had a serious impact on the work of Lithuanian writers: the drastic reduction in state support for the arts left many in an uncertain financial position. Ironically, the welcome end of censorship also reduced public interest in literature; it now ceased its role as a means of conveying subtle political criticism as it had during Soviet censorship.

Literature in Emigration. Much of the Lithuanian intelligentsia, including some of Lithuania's finest writers, fled to the West in 1944 where they were free of state censorship. Most émigré authors continued the trends they had initiated in Lithuania before 1940. Some older writers sought to recreate the lost homeland in their work; while others were more concerned with their alienating experience of war and exile. Bernardas Brazdžionis (b. 1907) gained acceptance as a national bard of resistance to the Soviet occupation both in emigration and in Lithuania. Other prominent poets included the lyricist Jonas Aleksandravičius-Aistis (1904-1973) and the younger avant-garde poets, like Alfonsas Nyka-Niliūnas (b. 1919) and Henrikas Radauskas (1910-1970). Jonas Mekas (b. 1922) also entered the American cultural scene as one of the founders, along with his brother Adolfas, of "underground cinema" in the United States. Of the prose writers, the most prolific were Jurgis Gliauda (1906-1996) and Birutė Pūkelevičiūtė (b. 1923). The innovative writer Marius Katiliškis (1910-1980) produced numerous short stories and four novels: his autobiographical work, *Išėjusiems negrįžti* (Lith. No Return), presented one of the most vivid accounts of the desperate experience of Lithuanians in 1944-1945. The playwrights Antanas Škėma (1911-1961) and Algirdas Landsbergis (b. 1924) experimented with what were, for Lithuanian theatre, new forms, although Kostas Ostrauskas (b. 1926) is, perhaps, the most daring dramatist, producing absurd drama and then turning towards postmodernist themes. While most émigré Lithuanian literature was produced in the United States, the novelists Kazys Barėnas (b. 1907) and Eduardas Cinzas (1924-1996) worked in Europe. One of the most unique Lithuanian writers of the postwar period is Icchokas Meras (b. 1934), currently living in Israel, who has utilized graphic accounts of his childhood in Lithuania during the Holocaust to examine the broader themes of human degradation and salvation. See LANGUAGE, LITHUANIAN; MIŁOSZ, CZESŁAW; POLONIZATION; RUSSIFICATION; REFORMATION; RENAISSANCE.

LITHUANIA MINOR. See PRUSSIA.

LITHUANIAN ACTIVIST FRONT (LAF). Anti-Soviet resistance organization founded in 1940. The origins of the Lithuanian Activist Front (Lith. *Lietuvių aktyvistų frontas*; in some sources: *Lietuvos aktyvistų frontas*) date to 1938 when a semi-clandestine coalition of groups, known as the Lithuanian Activist Movement (Lith. *Lietuvių aktyvistų sąjūdis*) and opposed to the Nationalist regime of Antanas Smetona (q. v.), was formed in Klaipėda (q.v.). The group advocated a populist, militantly nationalistic political line based on "authoritarian democracy" in Lithuania and a foreign policy friendly to the Axis powers. After the Soviet occupation in June 1940 a number of prominent Lithuanians escaped across the border into Germany. On November 3, 1940 Lithuanian leaders of most non-Communist political parties, and Lithuanian diplomats still accredited to the Republic of Lithuania, met in Berlin to establish the Lithuanian Activist Front (LAF) whose avowed purpose was to restore the independence of Lithuania. Colonel Kazys Škirpa (q. v.), the former Lithuanian envoy to Germany, was chosen to head the organization. The political philosophy of the LAF, as worked out by Škirpa and his associates, was rooted in the thinking of the right-wing opposition to Smetona which stressed populist nationalism with anti-Semitic overtones, economic policies modeled on a form of corporatism, emphasis on national will and discipline as opposed to bourgeois liberalism, and a "realistic" appraisal of the need to accommodate Germany's interests in the struggle for Lithuanian independence. However, there were also elements both within and outside the LAF opposed to Škirpa's pro-German stance and authoritarian ideology.

The LAF maintained sporadic contacts with the anti-Soviet resistance in Lithuania, which organizationally operated without much control from Berlin. The Soviet deportations (q. v.) of June 14-17, 1941 seriously disrupted the LAF's underground network within the country. After the German attack on the Soviet Union of June 22, 1941, an anti-Soviet uprising broke out in Kaunas and other parts of Lithuania. On June 23, the rebels proclaimed a Provisional Government in Kaunas headed by the LAF and announced the restoration of the country's independence. Disagreements with the German occupation authorities led to the disbanding of the Provisional Government on August 5, 1941 and the banning of the LAF the following month. During the German occupation the LAF was reorganized as the Lithuanian Front (Lith. *Lietuvių frontas*) and adopted passive resistance tactics against the Nazis. After the war former members of the LAF and some conservative Catholic-oriented groups formed the Friends of the Lithuanian Front (Lith. *Lietuvių fronto bičiuliai*) which became an influential factor in émigré politics. See RESISTANCE MOVEMENTS.

LITHUANIAN METRICA (Lith. *Lietuvos Metrika*, Rus. *Litovskaya Metrika*). One of the most important collections of manuscripts and registries of historical documents for the history of Lithuania and neighboring countries, essentially the surviving records of the chancellory of the Grand Duchy of Lithuania. Although many of the originals of treaties, ducal privileges, tax assessments, letters and other important manuscripts have been lost, the Grand Duke's office also maintained a meticulous registry of official documents sent out and received, often with descriptions of their contents. Most of the earlier documents and entries are in the West Russian or Belarusan form of Old Church Slavic. Systematic archival record-keeping in the Grand Duke's offices dates from the mid-14th century. In the early 1500s the archives were moved to Vilnius, but a considerable number of manuscripts perished during the Muscovite sack of Vilnius in 1655. Eventually, some of the original documents and many copies were transferred to private ownership, the largest number to the Radziwiłł (q. v.) estate in Nesvizh, Belarus from where they were transferred to Warsaw. In 1795, after the Partitions (q. v.) of the Polish-Lithuanian Commonwealth (q.v.), the records of the Lithuanian Metrica were moved to St. Petersburg where they were newly catalogued by a Tsarist commission in 1836-1837. In 1887 the Metrica was transferred to Moscow where the originals still reside. The Soviet-Lithuanian Peace Treaty of July 12, 1920 (q. v.) mandated the return of the records to Lithuania but the agreement was never honored; microfilm copies were sent to Vilnius after World War II.

The return of the Lithuanian Metrica is still currently a subject of negotiation between the governments of Lithuania and the Russian Federation.

LITHUANIAN STATUTE (Lith. *Lietuvos Statutas*, Rus. *Litovskii Statut*). Law code of the Grand Duchy of Lithuania, one of the few such comprehensive codes in medieval Europe. Until the 16th century the legal system of the Grand Duchy of Lithuania rested on local customary law in the ethnic Lithuanian parts of the Grand Duchy, and on the written and customary codes relevant to the Orthodox Russian lands. A number of privileges granting rights to nobles and town charters were issued during the 14th and 15th centuries.

In 1522 work began on the codification of a uniform law code for the entire Grand Duchy. The result was the First Lithuanian Statute, approved by the Grand Duchy's diet in Vilnius and proclaimed by Sigismund I (the Old) (q. v.) as the law of the land in 1529. In the preface to the Statute, the Grand Duke mandated the legal equality of Catholic and Orthodox Christians, one of the first examples of legalized religious tolerance in European history. The law code had 13 chapters and 243 articles. Some parts of it were a kind of constitution by which the ruler promised to respect Lithuania's interests and safeguard the Duchy's territorial integrity. The Statute detailed judicial procedures and laid down the basis for land tenure, including women's property rights.

In early 1566 a revised and more systematic law code, the Second Lithuanian Statute, was proclaimed, which broadened the personal rights of the nobility in general and enhanced the legal rights of the petty gentry in particular. The new code allowed landowners to freely dispose of their property, which also gave them increased power over their peasants. In January 1588 Sigismund III Vasa (q. v.) proclaimed the Third Lithuanian Statute, a more comprehensive code which reaffirmed religious equality and also included more sections reflecting local customary law. The Third Lithuanian Statute was the only one published, since the earlier Statutes were promulgated in manuscript form. It remained in force even after the annexation of most of Lithuania by Tsarist Russia in 1795. In 1840 Tsar Nicholas I annulled the Lithuanian Statute and placed Lithuania under Russian law.

LIVONIA. Historic region on the northern border of Lithuania, stretching east of the Gulf of Riga, now part of the Republics of Latvia (q.v.) and Estonia. The name of the region derives from the Finno-Ugric people known as the Livs, who inhabited the region during the 12th century, when the indigenous Baltic and Finno-Ugric tribes were conquered by the crusading German Knights of the Sword, and then came under the rule of the Livonian (q.v.) branch of the Teutonic Order. After the secularization of the Teutonic Knights (q. v.) in 1525, the head of the Livonian Knights was named a prince by the Holy Roman Emperor. In 1558-1559 large parts of Livonia were conquered by Ivan the Terrible's Muscovite forces; as a result, the Livonian nobility and the Archbishop of Riga obtained the protection of Sigismund Augustus of Poland-Lithuania in 1561. The southern part of Livonia was reorganized as the Duchy of Courland (q. v.) which became a vassal of the Polish-Lithuanian crown. In 1582 the Muscovites were finally expelled from the Livonian lands. The northern part of Livonia, including Riga, came under Swedish rule between 1629 and 1721 when much of the area was formally ceded to Russia by the Treaty of Nystadt. In 1918 most of historic Livonia became part of the newly independent Republic of Latvia (q. v.), while the northern section was incorporated into Estonia.

LIVONIAN ORDER, or Knights of the Sword. German crusading order which conquered Latvia and Estonia in the Middle Ages. The Livonian Order originated as the Fraternity of the Warriors of Christ (Latin: *Fratres militiae Christi*) founded by Bishop Albert of Riga in 1202-1203 to protect the German colonists who had arrived at the mouth of the Daugava River in Livonia at the end of the 12th century. They were widely known as the Knights of the Sword, referring to the symbol they used as their coat-of-arms. In

1207 the Order received from Albert the right to rule one-third of the lands they conquered and during the first half of the 13th century, the Knights proceeded to forcibly convert most of the population in what is now Latvia and southern Estonia. The Livonian Order then invaded the Lithuanian lands and Rus' but were decisively repulsed at the Battles of Saulė (Šiauliai) in 1236 (q. v.) and Lake Peipus (1242). In 1237 the Knights of the Sword amalgamated with the Teutonic Knights in Prussia and thus became the Livonian branch of the Teutonic Order (q. v.). The Master of the Livonian branch was usually elected by the high officers and representatives of the knights, priests and sergeants, and then confirmed by the Grand Master of the Teutonic Knights in Marienburg (Pol. Malbork). In 1346 the northern Estonian lands, previously ruled by Denmark, were transferred to the Livonian Knights whose territory now stretched to the Gulf of Finland. Much of the history of the Livonian Knights involved a bitter domestic struggle over land and political jurisdiction with the powerful Archbishop of Riga; the Lithuanian Grand Dukes frequently exploited the situation by intervening on behalf of Riga during the 14th century. The Livonian branch of the Order was secularized in 1562; some of the Knights then became landowners, known as the Baltic Germans, who became a strong Germanizing influence in the Latvian and Estonian lands until the 20th century. See TEUTONIC KNIGHTS.

LOZORAITIS, STASYS, Sr. (1898-1983). Lithuanian diplomat and foreign minister of Lithuania, 1934-1938, born on September 5, 1898 in Kaunas. After working in Lithuania's interior ministry and the chancery of the Council of Ministers, Lozoraitis entered the Lithuanian foreign service in 1923 as first secretary and later counselor in the Lithuanian Legation in Berlin. In 1929 he was transferred to the Lithuanian Legation at the Holy See where he became chargé d'affaires in 1931. He returned to Lithuania in 1932 as director of the political department of the Ministry of Foreign Affairs and became the foreign minister in June 1934. During the mid-1930s Lozoraitis was instrumental in shaping the

Baltic Entente (q. v.) with Latvia and Estonia and was an advocate of collective security as well as a rapprochement with Poland; however, he tendered his resignation following Poland's ultimatum (q.v.) of March 1938. In February 1939 Lozoraitis was appointed minister plenipotentiary to Italy. In May 1940 Foreign Minister Juozas Urbšys (q. v.) secretly authorized Lozoraitis to act as head of the Lithuanian diplomatic corps in the event of the country's occupation; thus, he was the senior Lithuanian diplomat abroad from June 1940 until his death in Rome on December 24, 1983.

LOZORAITIS, STASYS, Jr. (1924-1994). Lithuanian diplomat and presidential candidate, son of Stasys Lozoraitis, Sr. (q.v.), born in Berlin on August 2, 1924. Lozoraitis studied law at the University of Rome during 1944-1948. In 1947 he became an attaché at the Lithuanian Legation to the Holy See and served as first secretary there from 1964 to 1970 when he became Lithuanian representative to the Vatican. In 1983 Lozoraitis was appointed counselor to the Lithuanian Legation in Washington and in 1987 was appointed chargé d'affaires of the Lithuanian Legation in the United States. He became Lithuania's first ambassador to the United States in 1991. In the fall of 1992 Lozoraitis entered the presidential campaign in Lithuania but lost to former Communist Party leader Algirdas Brazauskas (q. v.) in the elections of February 1993, winning about 40 percent of the national vote. Afterwards, he was appointed Lithuania's ambassador to Italy but died in Washington on June 13, 1994 before he could assume his new duties. Lozoraitis is best remembered for his skillful representation of Lithuania's interests during the rise of the Sąjūdis (q. v.) movement and during the difficult first year of the restored Republic during 1990-1991.

LUBLIN, UNION OF (1569). Treaty which created the Polish-Lithuanian Commonwealth. Despite the dynastic alliance of Poland and Lithuania stipulated in the Act of Krėva (Pol. Krewo) (q. v.) in 1385, the Grand Duchy of Lithuania retained considerable independence in administrative, military, judicial and foreign affairs, even after 1501 when the thrones of the Kingdom of Poland and the Grand Duchy of Lithuania were occupied by the same person. A number of issues, particularly the common threat from Muscovy, the gradual cultural Polonization of the Lithuanian nobility and the approaching end of the Jagiellonian dynasty with the childless Sigismund Augustus (q. v.), persuaded most Polish and some Lithuanian leaders to press for closer ties between the two states. However, the King and Polish nobility had to overcome the reluctance of the Lithuanian magnates who wanted to preserve as much as possible of the Grand Duchy's independence and who resisted the notion of a common Polish-Lithuanian Diet, especially after the Lithuanian defeat of Muscovite forces at Ula and Orsha in 1564 which temporarily diminished the Russian danger.

At the end of 1568 Polish and Lithuanian delegates gathered in the eastern Polish town of Lublin for contentious negotiations concerning a new union. Some Poles demanded the elimination of the Grand Duchy and its replacement with a territory called New Poland, while the Lithuanians reacted by abandoning the Lublin talks in March 1569. The King's annexation of the southeastern part of the Grand Duchy, including Ukraine, to the Kingdom, and the reappearance of the Muscovite threat compelled the Lithuanians to return to negotiations in June 1569 under the leadership of the Samogitian elder statesman John Chodkiewicz (q. v.), who reluctantly accepted most of the Polish terms. The final act of the Union and its solemn oaths were enacted on July 1, 1569 and endorsed by the King during the following week. The Union declared Poland and Lithuania to be a Commonwealth (q. v) (Pol. *Rzeczpospolita*) constituting "one inseparable body" and joining two peoples into a single nation; established a common Polish-Lithuanian Diet (q. v.) and Senate which was to meet in Warsaw; foresaw the standardization of coinage, provided for a common foreign policy; and allowed Poles to own estates in Lithuania. On the other hand, the Grand Duchy maintained a separate legal system under the Lithuanian Statute (q. v.), as well as a separate army, treasury and coat of arms. Some of the provisions, such as the one stipulating common coinage and allowing Polish ownership of Lithuanian estates, were never enforced. Nonetheless, as a result of the Union of Lublin, Lithuania lost over a third of its territory and underwent more rapid cultural Polonization. The agreement of 1569 was a turning point in Polish-Lithuanian relations and established the constitutional basis of the Polish-Lithuanian Commonwealth which survived until 1795.

The Union of Lublin has elicited radically conflicting interpretations in the scholarship and popular histories of Poland and Lithuania. Poles have tended to value the Union as a triumph of wise statesmanship that inaugurated a unique federated state which, at least in the 16th century, experienced a golden age. After the Lithuanian national movement of the 19th century, Lithuanian scholars like Theodore Narbutt (q. v.), as well as the general public, began to see the Union of Lublin as an unmitigated disaster which severely limited the Grand Duchy's independence and hastened the Polonization of Lithuania's nobility. Thus, Polish and Lithuanian nationalists, in different ways, have come to view the Union of Lublin as a paradigm for the historic relations between the two peoples. See COMMONWEALTH, POLISH-LITHUANIAN; POLAND; POLONIZATION.

- M -

MACKEVIČIUS (Pol. Mackiewicz), ANTANAS (1828-1863). Lithuanian priest and revolutionary leader, born in Raseiniai district on June 14, 1828. Mackevičius studied at the University of Kiev and then enrolled in the Samogitian Theological Seminary at Varniai in 1850. After some minor postings as an assistant, Mackevičius was assigned to the parish of Paberžė. During his time there, Mackevičius became active in conspiratorial circles who were preparing for an anti-Russian uprising in Lithuania. Mackevičius and his radical friend, Konstanty Kalinowski (q. v.), stressed the importance of involving the Lithuanian peasantry in the rebellion. During the early 1860s, Mackevičius became known for his fiery sermons urging villagers to take up arms against the Tsar.

In one of the frequently cited dramatic moments of the insurrection, on March 8, 1863, Mackevičius read the rebels' manifesto from the pulpit of the Paberžė church and announced his own personal decision to join the revolt. He soon organized a military unit composed primarily of peasant guerrillas and became one of the 1863 rebellion's most charismatic military commanders. In April 1863 Mackevičius' unit reportedly enrolled almost 2,000 men. His forces were no match for the better-equipped Russian Army and on December 17, 1863 Mackevičius was captured; on December 28, 1863 he was publicly hanged in Kaunas.

Mackevičius is recognized as one of the important "Red" or radical leaders of the insurrection of 1863. He was also one of the first to raise the national issue, promoting the use of the Lithuanian language among his men and insisting that the Lithuanian people had a right to decide their own political future, although his conception of it was vague. Mackevičius believed that social justice for the peasantry also implied a recognition of their national and linguistic rights. In this respect, he differed from the pro-Polish orientation of most of the gentry leaders of the rebellion. See INSURRECTION OF 1863; KALINOWSKI, KONSTANTY.

MAIRONIS (1862-1932). Pen-name of the Lithuanian poet Jonas Mačiulis, the major literary figure of the Lithuanian national renaissance of the 19th and early 20th centuries, born on October 21, 1862 in Raseiniai district. After his graduation from the Russian secondary school in Kaunas, Maironis continued his education at the University of Kiev, the Kaunas Theological Seminary and the Theological Academy of St. Petersburg where he graduated with a doctorate in 1892. He taught moral theology there until his return to Lithuania in 1909, where he was appointed rector of the Theological Seminary in Kaunas, and later raised to the rank of prelate. Maironis taught theology at the seminary and the University of Kaunas until his death on June 28, 1932.

Maironis is Lithuania's most prominent poet and did much to shape the modern Lithuanian literary language. He published his first poem in *Aušra* (q.v.) in 1885 and is best known for his collection *Pavasario balsai* (Lith. Voices of Spring), which appeared in 1895 under the name Maironis, by which he became known throughout the country. This collection was published in six editions during his lifetime and contains many of the most popular poems in the Lithuanian language. Maironis' other major works included *Jaunoji Lietuva* (Lith. Young Lithuania), also in 1895, *Raseinių Magdė* (Lith. Magdė of Raseiniai) in 1909, *Mūsų vargai* (Lith. Our Troubles) in 1920, and a trilogy of historic dramas composed between 1921 and 1930: *Kęstučio mirtis* (Lith. Kęstutis' death), *Vytautas pas kryžiuočius* (Lith. Vytautas at the Teutonic Knights) and *Vytautas karalius* (Lith. King Vytautas). Much of Maironis' work is imbued with a spirit of romantic patriotism, extolling Lithuania's landscape and people, and emphasizing the country's heroic past. However, Maironis also contributed a number of satirical works, criticizing the venality of government officials and the intelligentsia of the early independence period. Several of his works were set to music: his composition to the Blessed Mother, *Marija, Marija* (Lith. Mary) is today the most popular Lithuanian religious hymn, while his poem *Lietuva brangi* (Lith. Dear Lithuania) served as a kind of unofficial national anthem during the Soviet period.

MASSALSKI (Lith. Masalskis), **IGNACY** (1729-1794). Lithuanian churchman and statesman, born on July 22, 1729 near Grodno. The Massalskis were an old and powerful noble family. Ignacy Massalski was educated in Rome and, after his return to Lithuania in 1748, he became a secretary in the Grand Duchy's Chancellory. Massalski rose rapidly within the Church administration and in 1762 became Bishop of Vilnius. He also joined the Lithuanian Senate and held various political posts. Massalski attempted to revitalize Lithuanian Catholicism by establishing new parishes and utilizing monastic orders, especially the Jesuits and Dominicans, for educational and missionary work; he expanded the diocesan seminary and strove to purify the liturgy. He reduced the obligations for the peasants on his estates and emphasized the need for educating the rural population. From 1773 to 1777 Massalski headed Lithuania's Educational Commission. He was also an important patron of the arts, commissioning the architect L. Stuoka-Gucevičius to build the new Vilnius Cathedral, which is now the major landmark in the heart of the city. Massalski also constructed the episcopal residence in Verkiai, where he stored valuable works of art. Politically, Massalski came to support the conservative pro-Russian forces in Lithuania and became a bitter opponent of the liberal May 3, 1791 Constitution, allying himself with the conservative Targowica Confederation (q. v.). In 1793 Massalski was a member of the Polish-Lithuanian delegation which negotiated the Second Partition of the Commonwealth with Prussia and Russia. Because of his pro-Russian sympathies, he was arrested by Polish rebels and hanged by a mob in Warsaw on the night of June 28, 1794. See EDUCATION.

MATULAITIS-MATULEVIČIUS (Pol. Matulewicz), JURGIS (1871-1927). Bishop of Vilnius and Lithuanian religious leader, a Blessed of the Roman Catholic Church and a candidate for canonization, born on April 13, 1871 near Marijampolė. He studied at the Theological Seminary in Kielce, Poland and continued his education in Warsaw and St. Petersburg. Matulaitis was ordained in 1899 and was assigned to a parish in central Poland, then continued his theological studies in Fribourg, Switzerland. In 1907 he was assigned to the newly-founded department of sociology at the Theological Academy of St. Petersburg. Matulaitis was a follower of the progressive teachings of Pope Leo XIII, who attempted to imbue Catholic doctrine with an emphasis on social activism. In 1909 he entered the Marian Order, which was on the verge of extinction in Lithuania, and was instrumental in restoring and expanding the Order when he became its Superior General.

In October 1918 Pope Benedict XV appointed Matulaitis Bishop of Vilnius, the first Lithuanian-speaking leader of the diocese in centuries. During this period of revolutionary change and the Polish-Lithuanian conflict engendered by the Vilnius Question (q. v.), Matulaitis consistently advocated ethnic tolerance among the Poles, Belarusans and Lithuanians of the diocese. His support for the linguistic rights of the Belarusan and Lithuanian Catholic peasantry aroused the animosity of Polish nationalists who saw Matulaitis as an obstacle in their efforts to maintain Poland's dominance over the cultural and spiritual life of the region. Under intense political pressure, Matulaitis resigned his position and went to Rome in 1925 to devote his energies to the Marian Order. In that same year Pope Pius XI appointed Matulaitis titular archbishop of Aduli and apostolic visitator to Lithuania. In his new capacity, Matulaitis led the planning to establish the Lithuanian ecclesiastical province with Kaunas as the metropolitan see, and played a crucial role in negotiating Lithuania's concordat with the Vatican. In the summer of 1926 Matulaitis visited the United States where he had helped establish Marian monasteries, but soon after his return from America, he fell ill and died on January 27, 1927 in Kaunas. Because of Matulaitis' reputation for spirituality, tolerance and charity, he was beatified by Pope John Paul II on June 28, 1987, gaining the title of "Blessed." If canonized, Jurgis Matulaitis would be Lithuania's first saint of modern times. See CATHOLIC CHURCH.

MEDININKAI, or Medninkai. Historic town in eastern Lithuania on the Lithuanian-Belarusan border located about 32 km. southeast of Vilnius. In medieval times it was an important fortress guarding the road to Vilnius from Oshmyany (Lith. Ašmena) and Krėva (also Kriavas, Pol. Krewo) and a favorite palace of the Lithuanian Grand Dukes Vytautas, Jogaila and Casimir. The area has been the site of numerous archeological excavations. The Juozapinė hill near Medininkai is the highest point in Lithuania at 294 m. above sea level. The town briefly captured world attention when on July 31, 1991, while President George Bush was visiting Moscow, Soviet special forces murdered six Lithuanian border guards and critically injured a seventh during a night raid on the Medininkai border post.

MERKYS, ANTANAS (1887-1955). Lithuanian military leader and statesman, born in Rokiškis district on February 1, 1887. Merkys studied law at the universities of Tartu and Kiev, then served as an officer in the Russian Army during World War I. In 1919-20 he served as Lithuania's Minister of Defense. In 1922 Merkys opened a law practice in Kaunas and soon became one of the founders of the Nationalist Union (Lith. *Tautininkų sąjunga*) (q. v.), as well as a close associate of Antanas Smetona (q. v.). After the Nationalist coup of December, 1926 Merkys once again entered government service as Minister of Defense in 1927 and then as Governor of Klaipėda Territory (q. v.) from 1927 to 1932. During 1933-1939 he was the mayor of Kaunas. After the takeover of the Vilnius region by Lithuanian forces on October 28, 1939, he briefly served as the area's administrator, but on November 21, 1939, he was called back to Kaunas and appointed Prime Minister. As Lithuania's last prime minister before the restoration of independence in 1990, Merkys led the government during the critical spring months of 1940 as relations with the Soviet Union deteriorated. On June 7, 1940 he traveled to Moscow hoping to persuade Stalin and Molotov that the Kremlin's charges concerning Lithuania's violations of the Soviet-Lithuanian Mutual Defense Treaty of 1939 were baseless and seeking clarification of Moscow's intentions. Merkys flew back to Kaunas on June 12 as the Soviet leaders adopted an increasingly threatening attitude. During the early morning hours of June 15, 1940 Merkys and President Smetona presided over the last cabinet session of independent Lithuania, which decided to accept the Soviet ultimatum of June 14 (q. v.), demanding the military occupation of the country. When the Soviet Army invaded Lithuania on June 15, President Smetona crossed into Germany, appointing Merkys acting president. At Soviet insistence, Merkys nominated the leftist journalist Justas Paleckis to head a new government on June 17, despite the questionable constitutional legality of such a step, and then resigned his position. On July 17, 1940 Merkys and his family were deported to the Soviet Union. He reportedly died in Russia on March 5, 1955. See NAZI-SOVIET PACT.

MICKIEWICZ (Lith. Mickevičius), ADAM (1799-1855). Polish writer and Romantic poet of Lithuanian extraction, born on January 4, 1799 in Novogrodek (Pol. Nowogródek, Lith. Naugardukas) district. Mickiewicz's family belonged to Lithuanian gentry who had settled in what is now Belarus. In 1815-1819 Mickiewicz enrolled at the University of Vilnius, then the major intellectual center of Polish cultural life in the lands of the old Commonwealth (q. v.). In 1817 Mickiewicz and his friends organized the secret Philomatic or Philaretic (Pol. *Filomaty*) Society (q. v.) in Vilnius, which propagated radical social and political views. In 1819 Mickiewicz became a teacher in Kaunas but in 1823 he and other Philomats were arrested by the Tsarist police for subversive activity and exiled to Russia; there he became active in the literary salons of St. Petersburg and Moscow. After a trip to Odessa, Mickiewicz left Russia in 1828 and traveled to Germany and Italy. In 1830 Mickiewicz went to Poznań to assist the insurrection of 1830-1831 (q. v.), which had broken out in Congress Poland; but after the rebellion's failure he joined thousands of Polish-Lithuanian rebels who emigrated to France. In 1839-1840 Mickiewicz taught Latin at the University of Lausanne and, during 1840-1844, Slavic literature at the Collège de France. At this time he briefly came under the influence of the messianism of the religious mystic Andrzej Towiański (1799-1878). In 1849 he began editing *La Tribune de Peuples*, a newspaper dedicated to the liberation and mutual friendship of oppressed European nations. When the Crimean War broke out in 1855, Mickiewicz went to Turkey to organize a Polish-Lithuanian unit to fight the Russians. He died in Istanbul on September 26, 1855. Mickiewicz is buried in the Wawel Castle in Cracow.

While most people regard Mickiewicz as Poland's greatest poet, he also influenced the cultural development of the Lithuanian national movement by choosing many of his themes from a romanticized vision of the Lithuanian past. His masterpiece, the epic *Pan Tadeusz, czyli ostatni zajazd na Litwie* (Pol. Lord Tadeusz, or the Last Raid in Lithuania), first published in 1834, which portrays Lithuania's Polonized gentry on the eve of the Napoleonic invasion, begins with the famous line: "Lithuania, my fatherland, you are like health!" Several other epics, notably, *Konrad Wallenrod* (1828), which depicted the Lithuanian struggle against the Teutonic Knights (q.v.), utilized themes from Lithuania's medieval past.

MIŁOSZ, CZESŁAW (1911-). Polish poet and Nobel Prize winner from Lithuania, born in Kėdainiai district on June 30, 1911. After a childhood in central Lithuania, Miłosz received his secondary and university education in Vilnius, graduating from the Stefan Batory University's law faculty in 1934. After 1936 he lived in Warsaw and during the German occupation was a member of the anti-Nazi underground. After the war Miłosz served in the Polish diplomatic corps in New York and Paris, defecting to the West in 1951 and finally settling in the United States, where he taught literature since the 1960s, most recently at the University of California-Berkeley. In addition to numerous literary awards in Europe and America, Miłosz was awarded the Nobel Prize for Literature in 1980.

Miłosz began his literary career while a student in Vilnius in the early 1930s, his poetry marked by a philosophical introspection concerning the human condition. In the West he became widely known for his collection of essays, *The Captive Mind*, both a literary commentary on totalitarianism and a survey of prominent Polish writers trapped under Stalinism. In 1955 he published the autobiographical novel, *Dolina Issy* (Pol. The Issa Valley), an account of the life of Lithuania's Polish gentry during the early 1920s, celebrating the mythology and folklore of the local peasantry. Much of Miłosz's poetry, fiction and literary history (such as *The Land of Ulro*, 1977) deal with Lithuanian themes and he has maintained close ties to Lithuania and the country's writers. In his public appearances, including his speech at the Nobel Prize award ceremony in 1980, he frequently asserted the right of the Lithuanian people to independence.

MILOSZ (Lith. Milašius), OSCAR V. DE LUBICZ (1877-1939). French poet of Polish-Lithuanian extraction, a cousin of Nobel

Prize winner Czesław Miłosz (q. v.), born in Mogilev province, Belarus, on May 29, 1877. In 1889 he went to Paris to study and lived in France for most of the remainder of his life. After his first collection of lyrical poetry, *Le Poème des Décadences*, was published in 1899, Milosz became progressively more interested in mystical philosophy and religion. Despite his Polish connections, during World War I Milosz began to support the idea of Lithuania's independence and became a member of the Lithuanian delegation to the Paris Peace Conference. From 1919 to 1925 he served as Lithuania's envoy to France. During the 1920s Milosz, in addition to more volumes of French poetry, published translations of Lithuanian folk songs and tales. He died in Fontainbleau on March 2, 1939.

MINDAUGAS (Rus. Mendovg, Pol. Mendowg or Mendog). King of Lithuania ca. 1253-1263, an early founder of the Lithuanian state and the first ruler to formally introduce Christianity into Lithuania. There is no reliable information about Mindaugas' birth or early life, although some medieval chronicles name his father as a powerful ruler. The first mention of Mindaugas is in the Volynian (or Ipatiev) Chronicle where he is mentioned as one of the most prominent of the 20 Lithuanian princes who signed a treaty with Roman of Volynia in 1219. Even before the reign of Mindaugas, the nucleus of an emerging Lithuanian state was centered around the region of Aukštaitija (q. v.) and included the areas around Kernavė, as well as the region around what is now Vilnius (q. v.) and Trakai (q. v.). Lithuania was then ruled by powerful princes in a loose military alliance. Mindaugas' achievement was to gather the Lithuanian lands, albeit temporarily, into a united kingdom, a process which he began sometime before 1240. Mindaugas also extended Lithuanian power eastward, taking advantage of the disintegration of Kievan Rus' following the Mongol invasions, and took control of the important settlement of Novogrudek (Pol. Nowogródek). Thus, Mindaugas initiated two important tendencies in Lithuanian history: the internal consolidation of the state and its expansion into the lands of the Orthodox Eastern Slavs. However,

Mindaugas is best remembered for his unsuccessful attempt to Christianize Lithuania and, thus, redefine his realm's relations with the Christian West.

The date and precise circumstances of Mindaugas' baptism are unknown, but it probably occurred sometime in 1251 as indicated by the letters of Pope Innocent IV who affirmed that Mindaugas was baptized along with his wife Martha, two sons, and "many pagans." The diocese of Lithuania was created by the Pope's decree of July 1251. The generally accepted date for Mindaugas' coronation as king of Lithuania is 1253; by this act, presided over by Bishop Henry Heidenreich of Kulm, Mindaugas was acknowledged as a Christian monarch. Although subsequent Lithuanian rulers were sometimes identified as *rex*, or king, Mindaugas was the only one to be crowned with papal approval according to the customary law of Catholic Europe and, thus, was Lithuania's only medieval ruler to truly deserve the royal title. Mindaugas' baptism and coronation can also be viewed as an early attempt to protect Lithuania from the fate of the Prussians (q. v.) who had been conquered by the Teutonic Knights (q. v.); he tried to accomplish this by developing diplomatic and ecclesiastical ties with the Livonian Order (q. v.). However, partly due to the fact that Samogitia (q. v.) remained outside Mindaugas' effective control, and to the difficulties of organizing an effective ecclesiastical administration under Lithuania's first bishop, Christian, Lithuania's Christianization proceeded only slowly. Mindaugas succeeded in his attempts to expand Lithuanian power to the east, but this policy required numerous and difficult military campaigns, while the Teutonic Order strengthened its position in western Lithuania.

Ultimately, Mindaugas failed to consolidate his power within the newly-founded and short-lived Lithuanian kingdom. The ambitious Samogitian rival of Mindaugas, Prince Treniota, favored military resistance against the Teutonic Knights; also, Mindaugas' policies of centralization and Christianization aroused resentment among many princes. Towards the end of his reign, Mindaugas was drawn into war against the Knights; there is some question as to whether he renounced Christianity at this time. In 1263

Mindaugas and his two sons were assassinated in a plot probably engineered by Treniota, although other sources ascribe his death to a personal quarrel over the wife of another prince, Daumantas. Mindaugas' demise triggered a period of political instability and violent struggle for power which lasted until the end of the 13th century. While Grand Duke Gediminas (q. v.) and his successors firmly established Lithuania as a power in Eastern Europe during the 14th century, Mindaugas played an important role in setting the precedent of supreme authority within the Lithuanian state and opening up relations with the Christian West. See CATHOLIC CHURCH; GEDIMINAS.

MIRONAS, VLADAS (1880-1954). Priest and statesman, born in Panemunis, Lithuania on June 22, 1880. After graduation from the St. Petersburg Theological Academy and ordination in 1904, Mironas became acquainted with Antanas Smetona (q. v.), the later president of Lithuania, and became active in fostering nationalist attitudes among the Lithuanian clergy. He joined the Taryba (q. v.) in 1917 and became one of the signatories of the Lithuanian declaration of independence in February 1918. In 1926 Mironas was elected to the Seimas as a member of the Nationalist Union (q. v.), becoming one of Smetona's closest advisors. In 1929 he was appointed chaplain of the armed forces and in March 1938 was called upon by Smetona to form a new government in the wake of the crisis over the Polish ultimatum (q. v.). Mironas' government resigned after another crisis precipitated by Germany's seizure of Klaipėda in March 1939. He was arrested during the first Soviet occupation of 1940-1941 and then again in 1947. Mironas died in the Soviet prison of Vladimir in 1954.

MOLOTOV-RIBBENTROP PACT. See NAZI-SOVIET PACT.

MURAVYEV, MIKHAIL NIKOLAYEVICH (1796-1866). Russian statesman and governor-general of Vilnius 1863-1865, born on

October 1, 1796. In 1825 Muravyev was involved in the abortive Decembrist Revolution against the Tsar; he was briefly imprisoned, abandoned his liberal views, and in 1828 began service in the Russian bureaucracy as governor of Mogilev. During the insurrection of 1831 (q. v.) Muravyev was in charge of pacifying southeastern Lithuania and Belarus. As the Tsar's Minister of State Domains, Muravyev opposed the abolition of serfdom and left the government after the emancipation of 1861. On May 1, 1863 Muravyev was appointed Governor of the Northwest Territory, including Lithuania and Belarus, which were then in the throes of rebellion. Muravyev ruthlessly suppressed the insurrection of 1863 (q. v.). He reinforced the local Russian garrisons and energetically pursued rebel detachments until most of Lithuania was pacified by late 1864. Muravyev ordered over 200 executions, including those of the important leaders of the rebellion. His forces burned entire villages and deported their inhabitants. By his own reckoning, Muravyev deported 1,427 persons to Siberia and exiled over 1,500 people to various parts of Russia. Another 4,000 were "resettled" outside Lithuania and several more thousands were jailed, forcibly recruited into the army or sentenced to forced labor. However, the actual toll of Muravyev's campaign of repression was probably higher.

Muravyev also introduced a program of Russification (q. v.) in Lithuania, intending to destroy the power of the Polonized Catholic Church and nobility, which he regarded as the main threat to Russian rule in Lithuania. The program included the closing of Catholic monasteries, restricting ecclesiastical administration, the elimination of the Polish language from Lithuanian schools, and the closing of the entire Catholic primary school system. Muravyev sought to strengthen the Russian position in Lithuania by introducing Russian primary schools, encouraging Orthodox missionary activity and bringing more Russian officials, land-owners and settlers to Lithuania. He hoped to curry favor with the Lithuanian peasantry and turn them against the Polish landowners by increasing their land allotments and utilizing other economic measures. However, Muravyev's press ban (q. v.) on Lithuanian publications in the Latin alphabet in 1864 eventually provoked a strong nationalist response, and his brutal pacification campaign, which earned him the epithet of "The Hangman" (Lith. *Korikas*), transformed this Tsarist official into a symbol of Russian repression. He died in St. Petersburg on August 31, 1866. See PRESS BAN; RUSSIFICATION.

MUSCOVY, relations with the Grand Duchy of Lithuania. The Muscovite state, which emerged as the leading Russian polity by the 15th century, played a decisive role in the history of Lithuania, primarily as the Grand Duchy's major rival for control of the western Russian lands. Since the early 14th century, especially during the reign of Grand Duke Gediminas (1316-1341), Lithuanian rulers had exploited the disintegration of Kievan Rus'. The Grand Duchy of Muscovy emerged as a power at about the same time that Lithuania was rapidly expanding into Belarus, Ukraine and western Russia. The prestige of the Muscovite princes was greatly enhanced by the transfer of the Kievan Russian metropolitanate to Moscow in 1328 and the success of the Muscovites against the Tatars under Dmitrii Donskoi (1359-1389). By the time of Grand Duke Algirdas (q. v.), Lithuania ruled most of west Russia and had allied itself with Muscovy's Russian enemies, such as Novgorod and Tver. Algirdas desired to rule all of Russia and twice besieged Moscow, but failed to capture the city; he also tried unsuccessfully to subject the Orthodox Church to his rule by establishing a separate Lithuanian metropolitanate. Algirdas' successors also made diplomatic attempts to gain a dynastic foothold in Muscovy. For a brief time, Grand Duke Jogaila (q. v.) considered marrying the Muscovite princess Sophia, while Vytautas (q. v.) married his own daughter (also named Sophia) to the Muscovite Grand Duke Vasilii I (1389-1425). In 1495 Grand Duke Alexander I (q. v.) married Ivan III's daughter Elena. However, in general, the centuries-long relationship between Muscovy and Lithuania was one of rivalry and conflict.

Lithuania's turn to Catholicism in 1386 sharpened the struggle between Moscow and Vilnius. Muscovite rulers claimed the Orthodox East Slavic lands of Rus' as their rightful patrimony to be liberated from Lithuanian Catholic hegemony. Under Ivan III (1462-1505), Muscovy gained a decisive advantage in the struggle with Lithuania by annexing Novgorod (1471) and Tver, declaring full independence from the Tatars and repeatedly asserting the right to rule all of Russia. The Lithuanian-Muscovite treaty of 1503 confirmed the loss of the easternmost lands of the Grand Duchy to Moscow. In 1514 Muscovite forces captured the important town of Smolensk. Under Ivan IV ("The Terrible") Muscovy engaged in a prolonged war with Poland-Lithuania over Livonia and the mid-16th century saw the loss of more Lithuanian lands, including Polotsk. Lithuania's losses against Muscovy were the major reason for concluding the Polish-Lithuanian Union of Lublin (q. v.), which turned Ukraine over to Poland. During Muscovy's interregnum, known as the Time of Troubles (1598-1613), Poland-Lithuania recovered some of the lost territories, including Smolensk (1611), and Polish-Lithuanian troops even briefly held Moscow. However, under the Romanovs, Muscovy recovered and once again resumed its western expansion. In 1655 Vilnius was captured and destroyed by the Muscovite forces of Tsar Alexis. The Peace of Andrusovo in 1667 gave Smolensk back to Muscovy, although Lithuania regained Vitebsk and Polotsk. The Lithuanian-Muscovite border established here remained unchanged until the Partitions (q. v.) of the Commonwealth in 1772.

The state of Muscovy formally became the Russian Empire under Peter the Great in 1721, ending the period of Lithuanian-Muscovite relations. The centuries-old Lithuanian-Muscovite struggle over the lands of western and central Russia had important historical consequences. The conflict shaped much of the legitimizing rationale for Russia's claims to its western borderlands. Also, the rule of much of Russia by the Lithuanians enhanced the political and cultural division of the Orthodox East Slavic peoples and promoted the development of Ukrainian and Belarusan ethnic and linguistic identities, separate from the Russians. See RUSSIA.

MYKOLAITIS-PUTINAS, VINCAS (1893-1967). Lithuanian writer and literary critic, born on January 6, 1893 in Marijampolė district.

He graduated from the Theological Seminary in Seinai in 1915, then studied at the Theological Academy of Petrograd and the Universities of Fribourg and Munich (1918-1923). Mykolaitis published his first collection of poems in 1917 and during the 1920s developed his reputation as a talented lyrical poet and dramatist under the pen-name of Putinas. From 1923 until 1929 he taught theology and philosophy at the University of Kaunas, then edited scholarly journals and briefly lived in France. In 1932-1933 he published his three-volume autobiographical novel, *AltoriŲ šešėly* (Lith. In the Shadow of the Altars), which created a literary sensation in Lithuania and went through numerous editions. The novel describes a young priest's inner conflict between his love for a woman and duty to the Church, a thinly-veiled confession of the writer's own struggle with his lack of a vocation. Mykolaitis married a former student in 1935 and, as a result, was excommunicated the following year. During the late 1930s Mykolaitis achieved a reputation as a literary historian and critic and was the president of the Lithuanian Writers' Union. Under the Soviet regime, he managed to continue publishing poetry and also wrote a popular historical novel about the 1863 uprising, *Sukilėliai* (Lith. The Rebels) (1957). In 1966 his excommunication was lifted by the Holy See. Despite the personal and ideological controversies that surrounded his life and work, Mykolaitis remains one of the most highly regarded and admired literary figures of 20th-century Lithuania. He died in Vilnius on June 7, 1967. See LITERATURE.

- N -

NARBUTT (Lith. Narbutas), TEODOR (1784-1864). Lithuanian historian born on September 8, 1784 in the district of Lida (Lith. Lyda). A mathematician and engineer who graduated from the University of Vilnius in 1803, Narbutt became interested in history as a student and began his own archeological work in 1810. Narbutt's writings were influenced by his romantic patriotism and exalted view of the Lithuanian past. His most famous work, the nine-volume *Dzieje narodu litewskiego* (The History of the Lithuanian Nation), was published in Polish between 1835 and 1841. Narbutt ended this study with a dramatic denunciation of the Union of Lublin as a tragic loss of Lithuania's independence. Although some of his work, especially that dealing with mythology and ancient history, is no longer regarded as reliable scholarship, Narbutt did introduce hitherto unknown sources and, like Simonas Daukantas (q. v.), with whom he corresponded, stimulated interest in Lithuanian history as an object of study separate from the Polish past. Narbutt died in Vilnius on November 26, 1864.

NARUTOWICZ (Lith. Narutavičius). Samogitian gentry family, which provided two prominent statesmen, one to Lithuania and another to Poland. As a student, **Stanisław Narutowicz** (1862-1932) became active in radical Russian and Polish socialist circles, but eventually gravitated to the Lithuanian national movement where he became better known by his Lithuanian name, **Stanislovas Narutavičius**. He was appointed to the Taryba (q. v.) and advocated a strong stand against Germany; he also was a signatory of the February 16, 1918 Lithuanian declaration of independence. In the 1920s Narutavičius participated in agricultural organizations and was a member of the town council of Telšiai in Samogitia. His younger brother, **Gabriel Narutowicz** (1865-1922), gravitated to the Polish national movement. He became Poland's foreign minister and was elected president of the country in December 1922. However, he was almost immediately assassinated by a Polish nationalist who opposed Narutowicz's liberal stance towards Poland's national minorities.

NATIONALISM, LITHUANIAN. As in the other countries of Eastern and Central Europe, Lithuanian nationalism underwent a number of transformations during its development. The first attempts to emphasize a separate Lithuanian national identity and consciousness are traceable to early modern times, during the

Lithuanian gentry's resistance to the Union of Lublin (q. v.) with Poland, and the emergence in the 16th century of the attempt to trace the origins of the Gediminas dynasty to Roman roots, a common practice in Renaissance Europe. The 17th-century Lithuanian publicist Mikalojus Daukša (q. v.) emphasized the importance of the Lithuanian language (q. v.), one of the first known attempts to publicly rally opposition to the cultural Polonization of Lithuania. The first signs of modern nationalism appeared in the early 19th century among the petty gentry of Samogitia, especially the poets Dionizas Poška (q. v.) and Simonas Stanevičius (q. v.), who fostered pride in the Lithuanian language, glorified Lithuania's medieval past, idealized traditional village life and opposed serfdom. The historian Simonas Daukantas (q. v.) was the first to formulate a coherent anti-Polish attitude, emphasizing the negative consequences of the Polish-Lithuanian union and cultural Polonization. These beliefs are among the hallmarks of the modern Lithuanian national movement. The Lithuanian language became more widely used and socially acceptable during the mid-19th century through the efforts of Bishop Motiejus Valančius (q. v.) and provided a means for mobilizing the peasant masses.

The collapse of the 1863 insurrection (q. v.) and the Russian press ban (q.v.) of 1864 laid the foundations for modern Lithuanian nationalism, which was primarily the result of the emergence of a secular Lithuanian-speaking intelligentsia, mostly from the well-to-do peasantry. This intelligentsia had few social ties to the Polonized gentry who, for the most part, were firmly opposed to this Lithuanian "peasant" movement. The first Lithuanian periodical *Aušra* (The Dawn) (q. v.), edited by Jonas Basanavičius (q. v.), emphasized romantic nationalism, but its successor, *Varpas* (The Bell) (q. v.), founded by Vincas Kudirka (q. v.) in 1889, formulated political goals based on ethnic separateness from the Poles and resistance to Tsarist oppression. Between 1890 and 1914 a number of Lithuanian political parties were founded, from the Social Democrats on the left to the Christian Democrats on the right. In December 1905 delegates to the Great Lithuanian Assembly of Vilnius (Lith. *Didysis lietuvių seimas*) (q. v.)

204 / Nationalism, Lithuanian
204 / Nationalism, Lithuanian

formulated the first Lithuanian national political program, calling for an autonomous democratic Lithuania based on universal suffrage and the equality of all national groups in the country. The creation of the independent Lithuanian republic in 1918 brought majority rule to Lithuania for the first time, inasmuch as the country was now dominated by ethnic Lithuanians. During the 20th century, the maintenance or recovery of an independent state became the major political goal of most nationally-conscious Lithuanians.

The period of rule by the Nationalist Union (Lith. *Tautininkų sąjunga*) (q. v.) between 1926 and 1940 greatly influenced the intellectual development of Lithuanian nationalism. Under the authoritarian leadership of President Antanas Smetona (q. v.), the government sought to establish a unified national state. Its ideology was a mixture of agrarian populism, the personality cult of Smetona as Leader of the Nation (Lith. *Tautos vadas*) and, later in the 1930s, emphasis on the "organic state" which, unlike parlia-mentary democracy, was best suited to express the national will. On the other hand, the Nationalist leadership explicitly rejected racism and many aspects of fascism. However, during the late 1930s a more militant nationalist stance emerged among right-wing opponents of Smetona's regime, such as the Iron Wolf (q. v.), supporters of Augustinas Voldemaras (q. v.), and the Lithuanian activist (q. v.) movements, as well as among younger Nationalist and Catholic intellectuals. The Soviet occupation of 1940-1941 strengthened these latter elements who came to prominence in the anti-Soviet and the non-Communist anti-Nazi resistance. During the period of postwar Soviet rule between 1945 and 1990, the Lithuanian diaspora was generally motivated by the struggle to restore independence and fight Communism. Within Soviet Lithuania, nationalism found expression in the armed guerilla struggle against the Soviet occupation (1944-1953) and, later, in the Catholic and nationalist dissident (q. v.) movements of the 1970s and 1980s. Lithuanian nationalism defined itself as a struggle for human rights, resistance to the Soviet Union's Russification (q. v.) policies and the preservation of national cul-ture. In the process, in contrast to the 1920s and 1930s, mainstream

Lithuanian nationalism, as it had done at the turn of the century, once again stressed democratic values. Since the restoration of independence in 1990 the more militant nationalism of the prewar variety has been confined to political parties of the right, primarily the reconstituted Nationalist Union and the Young Lithuania (q. v.) movement. See RESISTANCE MOVEMENTS; SĄJŪDIS.

NATIONALIST PARTY, LITHUANIAN (Lith. *Lietuvių nacionalistų partija*). An extreme nationalist Lithuanian political organization founded in 1934 by a radical faction of the *voldemarininkai*, or Voldemaras (q. v.) group, headed mainly by air force and army officers who had been active in the clandestine Iron Wolf (q. v.). Under the Nationalist regime of Antanas Smetona, when left and right-wing extremist groups were banned, the LNP operated as a clandestine organization. Some of its leaders fled to Nazi Germany when Soviet troops occupied Lithuania in 1940. With the outbreak of the Nazi-Soviet war and the German occupation of Lithuania in June 1941, the LNP began to operate openly, advocating a racist and totalitarian political line close to that of the Nazis, and utilizing a swastika in the party's emblem. Because it advocated an independent Lithuania, albeit allied to Germany, the LNP was banned by the Nazi occupation authorities along with all other political groups in September 1941. Some LNP members continued to collaborate with the Germans in the local police and administration, while others joined the non-Communist anti-Nazi underground.

NATIONALIST UNION (Lith. *Tautininkų sąjunga*). Lithuanian nationalist party which ruled the country between 1926 and 1940. The beginnings of this party date back to the establishment of the National Progress Party (Lith. *Tautos pažanga*) in 1916, which had formed around the periodical *Viltis* (Lith. Hope) founded in 1907. While the *Tautos pažanga* and its agrarian offshoot, the Agrarian Union (Lith. *Žemdirbių sąjunga*), did not have wide political appeal, the leadership of these groups was prominent among the founders of the Lithuanian state in 1918. In 1924 the two groups merged into the Lithuanian Nationalist Union (Lith. *Lietuvių tautininkų sąjunga*), commonly known as the Nationalists (Lith. *tautininkai*), and published the periodical *Lietuva* (Lith. Lithuania). The Union included a number of prominent intellectuals, including the first president of Lithuania, Antanas Smetona (q. v.). The Nationalists were fierce critics of both the Christian Democratic (q. v.) and left-of-center parliamentary Lithuanian governments of 1920-26. In 1926 the Nationalists won three seats in the parliament dominated by the Social Democrats (q. v.) and Peasant Populists (q. v.). On December 17, 1926, the leader of the Nationalists, Antanas Smetona, came to power in a military coup supported by, among others, students and elements of the Catholic Bloc. After Smetona dissolved parliament in April 1927, the Nationalists remained in power until the Soviet occupation of June 1940. The Union itself numbered nearly 15,000 persons in the mid-1930s, supported by its youth wing, the Young Lithuania (Lith. *Jaunoji Lietuva*) (q. v.) movement. While formally not a part of the Nationalist movement, the country's volunteer national guard, the Riflemen's Union (Lith. *Šaulių sąjunga*) (q. v.), generally supported the Nationalist regime's aims.

The Smetona government banned political parties, claiming that political factionalism had led to chaos and disunity. It formally presented the Nationalist Union as a patriotic organization rather than a political party. Throughout the 1920s and 1930s, the *tautininkai* were divided between a moderate faction led by President Smetona and younger radicals who rallied around Prime Minister Augustinas Voldemaras (q. v.), some of whom later formed the clandestine Iron Wolf (q. v.) organization. Smetona dismissed Voldemaras in 1929 and thus marginalized the radical fringe; however, a younger and more militant group of intellectuals coalesced around the Nationalist periodical *Vairas* (Lith. The Rudder). At first, the Nationalist Union envisioned an eventual return to democracy; eventually, Smetona's government and the official line of the *tautininkai* propagated a middle road between parliamentary democracy and an outright fascist dictatorship. The compromise was institutionalized in the Lithuanian constitution of 1938 (q. v.). Thus, while Smetona's regime had some superficial similarities to Italian fascism and suppressed political opposition, it explicitly rejected racism, banned Nazi and fascist groups, and allowed a considerable degree of religious, cultural and ethnic pluralism. After the Soviet occupation, the Lithuanian National Movement (Lith. *Lietuvių tautinis sąjūdis*) was established in Germany in 1945 as a replacement for the Union. In 1949 the Lithuanian-American National Union (Lith. *Amerikos lietuvių tautinė sąjunga*) was founded in the United States as the American branch of the former Nationalist Union. In 1990 the Nationalist Union was reestablished as a political party and chose Rimantas Smetona, a grand-nephew of the former President, as its leader. In 1992 the new Union won four seats to the Seimas, Lithuania's parliament. See NATIONALISM, LITHUANIAN; SMETONA, ANTANAS.

NAZIS, or the National Socialist German Workers' Party played a significant role in Lithuanian history as a subversive movement before World War II, and then as an occupying force in 1941-1944. In the 1920s the fledgling Nazi movement found sympathizers among the German-speaking population of Klaipėda (q. v.) Territory desiring a union, or *Anschluss*, of the region with Germany. In May 1933 the German pro-Nazi organization, known as the Christian Socialist Workers' Union (Ger. *Christliche Sozialistische Arbeitsgemeinschaft*)(CSA), led by the Lutheran pastor Theodore von Sass, participated in the elections to the Klaipėda Diet. Internal disagreements led to the formation of Ernst Neumann's more openly Nazi Socialist People's Union (Ger. *Sozialistische Volksgemeinschaft*), known as the Sovog. Erich Koch, then Gauleiter in East Prussia, persuaded the two groups to unite in late 1933. At their height, along with the storm trooper units modeled after the SA and trained in Germany, the Nazi groups in Klaipėda included almost 15,000 persons.

In February 1934 the Lithuanian Governor of Klaipėda Territory, Jonas Navakas, declared martial law and arrested hundreds of members of the irredentist Nazi front organizations. In December 1934, 126 Nazi conspirators were put on trial in

Kaunas for treason and ethnic incitement, creating a major crisis in Lithuania's relations with Berlin; as a result, a trade embargo was imposed on Lithuania by Germany. The Neumann-Sass trial created considerable interest in the European press and an outpouring of anti-Lithuanian propaganda in the Reich. Harsh punishments, including four death sentences, were handed down in March 1935, but French and British pressure for leniency, as well as the government's desire not to worsen relations with Germany, caused most sentences to be commuted by 1938. As Lithuanian control over Klaipėda Territory weakened during the late 1930s, Neumann and Sass' Nazis began operating in the open and seized complete control of local government after the annexation of Klaipėda to Germany in March 1939. During the German occupation (q. v.) of Lithuania in 1941-1944 Lithuanians were, as a rule, not eligible for admission into the Nazi Party, although a pro-Nazi political group, the Lithuanian Nationalist Party (q. v.), operated briefly between June and September 1941. See HOLOCAUST.

NAZI-SOVIET PACT (1939-1941). This pact actually consisted of three separate and, for Lithuania, fateful treaties, the first of which was one of the immediate causes of World War II and also a prelude to the Soviet occupation of the Baltic States.

The Soviet-German Non-Aggression Treaty of August 23, 1939 (also known as the **Molotov-Ribbentrop Pact**). In the spring of 1939 the Soviet government began to make overtures to both Germany and its western rivals, Britain and France, concerning a mutual security arrangement. When the Western powers proved reluctant to grant the Soviet Union wide-ranging political rights of intervention in eastern Europe, especially the Baltic States, Stalin concluded a deal with Berlin in the summer of 1939. Hitler, anxious for a free hand in Poland, was willing to grant the Soviets territorial gains in the Baltic, eastern Poland and Romania.

A final deal was negotiated on the night of August 23-24, 1939 during a dramatic visit of the German foreign minister, Joachim von Ribbentrop, to Moscow, where he held direct talks with Soviet

Foreign Commissar Vyacheslav Molotov and Stalin. The pact itself, while dated on the 23rd, was actually signed in the early morning hours of August 24, 1939, and is considered one of the most important diplomatic revolutions in the 20th century. The published text of the treaty prohibited the parties from attacking one another or participating in any hostile "grouping of powers" directly or indirectly aimed at the other. It obliged each side to maintain "continuous contact" with the other and settle disputes by arbitration. However, the most critical part of the agreement was the secret protocol in which the Germans and Soviets "discussed in strictly confidential conversations the question of the boundary of their respective spheres of influence in Eastern Europe." Aside from the stricture that it be kept secret, the protocol contained three provisions. The first partitioned the Baltic States, defined as Finland, Estonia, Latvia and Lithuania, into spheres of influence "in the event of a territorial and political rearrangement." The first three states went to the USSR, while Lithuania was to be included in the German sphere. The Lithuanian-Latvian border formed "the boundary of the spheres of influence of Germany and the USSR." Both sides declared that they recognized "the interest of Lithuania in the Vilnius area." The second secret agreement on spheres of influence partitioned Poland approximately along the Narva, Vistula and San Rivers. The final territorial provision of the protocol reaffirmed Soviet rights to Bessarabia. Formally, the Molotov-Ribbentrop agreement of August 23 was a nonaggression pact. However, given the strategic realities of this partition of eastern Europe, the pact actually triggered war and constituted a de facto alliance, which was to be realized in the subsequent economic, military and diplomatic cooperation between Hitler and Stalin during the 1939-1941 period.

The German-Soviet Boundary and Friendship Treaty of September 28, 1939. The German-Soviet attack on Poland in September 1939, especially the rapid advance of the German armies, created new realities that required a revision of the August 23 agreement. When the Lithuanian government refused to be drawn into a military alliance with Germany against Poland, Berlin decided to accept a Soviet offer of renouncing the German sphere of influence in Lithuania in return for territorial gains in central Poland. On September 28, 1939 Ribbentrop once again flew to Moscow to sign a new borders and friendship pact with the Soviet Union. Another secret protocol was negotiated, which redefined the German-Soviet partition of the Baltics. It noted that in exchange for Lublin and part of the province of Warsaw, "the territory of the Lithuanian state falls to the sphere of influence of the USSR." The agreement also stipulated that "as soon as the Government of the USSR shall take special measures on Lithuanian territory to protect its interests," the German-Lithuanian border would be corrected to cede a small patch of land to Germany. The strip of territory in question constituted 1,800 square kilometers and ran through Marijampolė (q. v.), the largest town in southwestern Lithuania; it is usually termed the "Suwałki strip." The secret protocol of September 28 also declared that the economic agreements in force between Germany and Lithuania would not be affected by the measures of the Soviet Union referenced in the agreement.

The German-Soviet Treaty of January 10, 1941. Despite growing tensions between Berlin and Moscow, a series of primarily economic German-Soviet agreements were concluded in January 1941, providing for further cooperation. For Lithuania, the relevant agreements were the provisions for the repatriation of Baltic Germans and the territorial adjustment in Suvalkija (q. v.). After the Soviet occupation of Lithuania, it proved politically impractical to complete the transfer of the Suwałki strip to German jurisdiction. On January 10, 1941 the last of the German-Soviet secret protocols renounced German claims to this border strip in return for $7,500,000, payable in precious metals.

Political Impact in the 1980s. The Nazi-Soviet treaties, especially the Molotov-Ribbentrop Pact of August 23, 1939 became a major issue in the Baltic republics during their drive for independence in the late 1980s. The Baltic delegates to the Soviet Congress of People's Deputies in Moscow, which convened in May 1989, opened the issue of the Molotov-Ribbentrop Pact. On June 4, 1989 the Congress announced the formation of a commission to evaluate the Molotov-Ribbentrop Pact, which included Sąjūdis leader Vytautas Landsbergis and other prominent Baltic reformers. In July 1989 the preliminary findings of the majority of the commission's working group condemned the German-Soviet treaties of 1939 and concluded that the Baltic States had been victims of aggression. On the 50th anniversary of the Nazi-Soviet Pact, in the largest political demonstration in Soviet history, more than a million persons linked hands in a 370-mile human chain from Tallinn to Vilnius called the "Baltic Way." The event dramatically revealed the popular support that the Baltic national movements were now able to command. See SĄJŪDIS; RUSSIA; URBŠYS, JUOZAS; ULTIMATUMS.

- P -

PAC (Lith. Pacas). Influential noble family which played an important role in the history of the Polish-Lithuanian Commonwealth (q. v.), especially in the latter part of the 17th century. The Pac name appears in historical sources in the 15th century; the last of the Pac's, Ludwik Pac (1780-1835), a commander of Polish forces in Napoleon's army, died in Paris in 1835. During the reign of King John Sobieski (1674-1696) (q. v.), the influence of the Pac family began to fade as the Sapieha (q. v.) clan gained power within Lithuania. **Nicholas Pac** (1570-1624) was bishop of Samogitia (q. v.) from 1609 to 1618 and the founder of a Jesuit college in the historic town of Kražiai (q. v.). He also used his family fortune to establish a seminary in Varniai. Nicholas was also the author of one of the earliest known Lithuanian-language texts published in the Grand Duchy of Lithuania, a 1589 welcoming address to King Sigismund Vasa (q. v.). **Christopher Sigismund Pac** (1621-1684), who had studied in Cracow and Italy, was the chancellor of Lithuania from 1658 until his death in Warsaw in 1684, and Lithuania's most powerful political figure during that time. Christopher was one of the most adamant defenders of Lithuanian interests within the Commonwealth and is remembered as the builder of one of the country's most impressive Baroque monuments, the Pažaislis monastery and church complex outside Kaunas (q. v.). **Michael Casimir Pac** (d. 1682), the Lithuanian grand hetman (1667-1682), was one of the Grand Duchy's most able military leaders who distinguished himself during the difficult wars with Muscovy (q. v.) and Sweden during the 1650s and 1660s, as well as against the Turks and Tatars (q. v.) in the 1670s. Along with the other Pac's, Michael Casimir achieved fame as a patron of religious institutions and the arts, building the famous Baroque masterpiece of SS. Peter and Paul in the Antakalnis section of Vilnius; he was interred in this church after his death on April 4, 1682.

PALECKIS, JUSTAS (1899-1980). Lithuanian journalist and politician, Acting President and Prime Minister of Lithuania, June 17-August 3, 1941, Chairman of the Supreme Soviet of the Lithuanian SSR from 1941 until 1967, born on January 22, 1899 in Telšiai. Paleckis grew up in the Lithuanian community of Riga and, after completing studies in journalism, joined the Lithuanian Peasant Populist Union (q. v), then was briefly head of the Lithuanian Telegraph Agency, ELTA in 1926-1927. He became known for his leftist views, and after a visit to the USSR in 1933, drew closer to the Communists, supporting the establishment of a Popular Front in Lithuania. In June 1940 Paleckis' leftist credentials and political inexperience made him a suitable candidate to head the pro-Soviet People's Government (q.v.) whose makeup and policies were dictated by the Soviet Ambassador to Lithuania, Nikolai Pozdniakov, and the Kremlin's special emissary, Vladimir Dekanozov. Paleckis was admitted into the Lithuanian Communist Party (q.v.) on August 16, 1940. As head of state of Lithuania during its Sovietization in 1940, Paleckis formally oversaw the incorporation of Lithuania into the USSR on August 3, 1940. As Chairman of the Supreme Soviet of the Lithuanian SSR between 1941 and 1967, Paleckis was its nominal head of state; at the same time, he served as Deputy Chairman of the USSR Supreme Soviet in Moscow and was a candidate member of the Central Committee of the CPSU. As head of the Soviet Lithuanian government, a frequent member of Soviet parliamentary and peace delegations abroad, a journalist and poet with an intellectual's reputation, Paleckis was perhaps the best-known Lithuanian Communist on the international scene, although he held little power within the LCP itself. Paleckis died in Vilnius on January 26, 1980. See PEOPLE'S DIET; PEOPLE'S GOVERNMENT.

PALECKIS, JUSTAS VINCAS (1942-). Lithuanian politician born on January 1, 1942 in Samara, Russia, the son of former Soviet Lithuanian President, Justas Paleckis (q.v.). After graduating from the diplomatic academy of the Foreign Ministry of the USSR, Paleckis served in Soviet embassies in Switzerland and West Germany as well as in the Soviet Foreign Ministry in Moscow. Between 1983 and 1989 he worked in the Central Committee of the Lithuanian Communist Party (q.v.), heading the culture and ideology departments. After the LCP's break with Moscow in December 1989, Paleckis was secretary of the Party's Central Committee. In 1990-1991 he was deputy chairman of the Lithuanian Democratic Labor Party (q. v.) but joined the Lithuanian Social Democratic Party in 1992. In 1994 Paleckis became President Algirdas Brazauskas' (q.v.) chief advisor on foreign affairs. In July 1996 he was appointed Lithuanian ambassador to the United Kingdom.

PANERIAI (Pol. Ponary). Southwest suburb of Vilnius. The area of Paneriai, which literally means "along the Neris River," became notorious in World War II as the most infamous of the Nazi killing fields in Lithuania during the Holocaust (q. v.). In 1941-1944 the German Security Police and a detachment under their control known as the Special Platoon (Lith. *Ypatingas būrys*) killed tens of thousands of civilians, primarily Jews, in the woods of Paneriai, better known outside Lithuania under the Polish or Yiddish names of Ponary and Ponar respectively. Estimates of the number of victims range from about 60,000 to as many as 100,000.

PARTITIONS OF POLAND-LITHUANIA, 1772-1795. A major realignment of territory and power in East Central Europe during the late 18th century, which resulted in the destruction of the Polish-Lithuanian Commonwealth (q. v.) and the subjugation of both Poland and Lithuania to foreign rule until after World War I. The partitions, which occurred in three stages in 1772, 1793 and 1795, were the outcome of continuing interference by Austria, Prussia (q. v.), and especially Russia (q. v.), in the internal affairs of the politically and militarily weak Polish-Lithuanian state, which they had come to view as their protectorate. Russia in particular was alarmed by the growing movement for political, social and economic reform in the Commonwealth which gained ground during the mid-18th century, fearing the emergence of a more powerful Poland-Lithuania.

The **First Partition** (1772) was the direct result of the Confederation of Bar (q. v.), which aimed to end Russia's interference in Commonwealth affairs and expel Tsarist troops stationed in Poland-Lithuania. During the fighting, Austrian and Prussian troops crossed the frontiers of Poland; in 1770 Frederick II of Prussia began negotiations with Catherine II of Russia to partition the lands of the Commonwealth. A secret partition agreement between Russia and Prussia was signed on February 6, 1772 and, after Maria Theresa of Austria was persuaded to join the process, a formal treaty between the three powers was concluded on August 5, 1772. Russia received all of the Grand Duchy of Lithuania east of the Dvina and Dnieper Rivers as well as eastern Livonia, annexing the cities of Polotsk, Vitebsk and Mogilev in present-day Belarus (q. v.), ending four centuries of Lithuanian control in the region. Austria acquired most of Galicia, while Prussia took control of Polish lands in the western part of the Kingdom. However, the first partition also strengthened the reform movement in the remainder of the Commonwealth, which in turn provoked a Russian invasion of Poland-Lithuania in 1792.

The Russian occupation of the Commonwealth stimulated new partition negotiations between Prussia and Russia, the former desiring compensation for her losses in fighting revolutionary France. Secret Russian-Prussian negotiations in St. Petersburg concluded with the signing of the **Second Partition** convention on January 23, 1793. Russia's share of Lithuania included all of the palatinate of Minsk and the eastern parts of the palatinates of Vilnius, Brest and Nowogródek (Bel. Novohudrok); Catherine also received the eastern regions of Polish Volynia and Podolia. Prussia acquired western Poland, including Poznań, Kalisz, Toruń and Gdańsk (Danzig). Under Russian pressure the Commonwealth's Diet ratified the second partition in September, 1793. The Russian-Prussian seizure of territory provoked a wave of patriotic indignation in both Poland and Lithuania, leading to the Kościuszko (q. v.) rebellion of 1794.

During the insurrection, Russia and Austria negotiated the **Third Partition** of the Commonwealth and on January 3, 1795 the two powers signed a partition agreement. On October 24, 1795 Frederick William of Prussia acceded to the Austro-Russian agreement after it had undergone revisions. The act of delimitation was formally accepted on December 5, 1796, and the final convention for the partition of the remainder of Poland and Lithuania was concluded by Austria, Prussia and Russia on January 26, 1797 in St. Petersburg. Russia acquired the remainder of Lithuania to the east of the Nemunas River as well as the rest of Volynia and Podolia. Prussia received southwestern Lithuania, known as the *Užnemunė* or Suvalkija (Suwałki) (q. v.) region, which included the towns of Augustów, Sejny and Marijampolė, along with central Poland. Austria obtained Little Poland (Pol. *Małopolska*), including Cracow.

The partitions of 1772-1795 were a decisive event in the history of both Poland and Lithuania. It ended their formal statehood for 123 years and, in the long run, fundamentally altered the relationship between the two nations of the former Common-wealth. The elimination of a large, historic European state came as a shock and unwelcome precedent to the international community, especially in France and Britain, giving rise to the "Polish Question" which complicated both the internal politics of the partitioning powers and international diplomacy during the 19th century. See POLAND; RUSSIA.

PEASANT POPULIST UNION, LITHUANIAN (Lith. *Lietuvos Valstiečių liaudininkų sąjunga*). Left-of-center political party established in 1922. The Populist Union had its origins among the more radical members of the Lithuanian Democratic Party founded by the adherents of the *Varpas* (q. v.) movement in 1902. After the evacuation of much of the Lithuanian population to Russia during World War I some of the non-Bolshevik left fell under the influence of the Russian Socialist Revolutionary (SR) movement, which advocated peasant socialism. In November 1917 these leftists established the Lithuanian Socialist Populist Party (Lith. *Lietuvos socialistų liaudininkų partija*), which had its first congress in Vilnius in August 1918. At the beginning of 1919 the group published its first program, calling for the establishment of an independent Lithuanian democratic republic and a socialist political system. The party emphasized land reform that would provide economic justice for landless peasants and smallholders.

On December 4-6, 1922 the Socialist Populists convened a joint congress with the Peasant Union (Lith. *Valstiečių sąjunga*), which had been established by the peasant members of the Great Assembly (diet) of Vilnius (q. v.) in 1905. Previously allied with the Lithuanian Democratic Party, the Peasant Union had become disenchanted with the socially conservative direction of the former and found its natural allies among the Socialist Populists. The December 1922 joint congress united the two agrarian organizations into the Lithuanian Peasant Populist Union, which now explicitly abandoned its socialist designation and approved private land ownership. As a centrist, peasant-oriented secular party, the Populist Union won a large part of the Lithuanian electorate during the democratic period of the Republic of Lithuania (1920-1926) and played an important rule in governing the country. During the May 1926 elections to the Seimas, the Populists won 22 of the 85 seats to the legislature and managed to form a government in coalition with the Social Democrats (q. v.) and the ethnic minorities, headed by their long-time leader, Mykolas Sleževičius (q. v.). The military coup of December 17, 1926 and the dissolution of the Seimas in April 1927 put an end to the period of the Populists' active participation in government. The Nationalist government harassed the Populists, accusing them of organizing an anti-government uprising in Tauragė in September 1927 and of fomenting the 1934 agrarian uprising of the peasants in Suvalkija. The Peasant Populist Union, along with the other parties, were banned in 1935. During the Soviet occupation many Populist leaders were arrested; others joined both the anti-Soviet and anti-Nazi underground movements. After World War II, the Populist party was active as a member of the Supreme Committee for the Liberation of Lithuania (VLIK) (q. v.) and continued its political activities in emigration, primarily the United States and Canada. See AGRICULTURE; CONSTITUENT ASSEMBLY.

PEOPLE'S DIET, July 21-August 25, 1940 (Lith. *Liaudies Seimas*). Communist-controlled parliament elected in July 1940 which formally initiated Lithuania's incorporation into the USSR. After the Soviet military occupation of Lithuania on June 15, 1940, and the installation of the Soviet-controlled People's Government (q. v.) headed by Justas Paleckis (q. v.) on June 17, the Soviets began preparations to create a Soviet Lithuanian regime and solve the legal problem of Lithuania's Sovietization. In late June and early July 1940, the Soviets exerted intense pressure on the Lithuanian government to call elections in order to determine the country's future status. On July 6, 1940, a law for elections to a Lithuanian People's Diet was promulgated. The election rules and political realities permitted campaigning and voting for only one slate: the hastily formed and Communist-controlled Lithuanian Union of Labor (Lith. *Darbo Lietuvos Sąjunga*). On July 11-12 Communist-controlled security forces arrested hundreds of prominent political and cultural leaders, thus undermining political opposition. The state media pressed the theme that those who did not vote would be exposed as "enemies of the people."

The elections were held on July 14-15; voters' internal passports were stamped as they entered the polling places. Despite the public campaign and the extension of the date by one day, allegedly because of inclement weather, it is not clear how many eligible voters actually cast ballots. It is obvious, however, that the turnout did not approach the Communist claim that 95.5 percent of eligible voters had cast nearly 99.2 percent of their ballots for candidates supported by the Union of Labor, which won all 79 seats to the Diet. Recent estimates indicate that, in some districts, as few as a third of the eligible voters may have actually cast valid ballots. The People's Diet met in Kaunas on July 21-24, 1940. During the Diet's first session, the deputies unanimously voted to proclaim a Soviet Socialist form of government and issued a declaration announcing their intention to seek the admission of Lithuania into the USSR as a Union Republic. On July 22-23 the Diet voted to nationalize land, banks and large enterprises, and appointed a delegation of government officials and writers to travel to Moscow to petition the USSR Supreme Soviet for Lithuania's admission to the USSR. On August 3, 1940, the Supreme Soviet of the USSR admitted the Lithuanian SSR into the Soviet Union. On August 25, 1940, the Lithuanian People's Diet declared itself the provisional Supreme Soviet of the Lithuanian SSR.

After the Soviet retreat from Lithuania in June 1941, a number of the former People's Diet deputies and other observers revealed a great deal of the coercion, overt Soviet control and the carnival atmosphere which marked the July 1940 elections to the Diet and the legislation by which it ostensibly legalized Soviet rule in Lithuania.

PEOPLE'S GOVERNMENT (Lith. *Liaudies Vyriausybė*), July 17-August 26, 1940. Communist-controlled government which over-saw Lithuania's incorporation into the USSR. As Soviet troops invaded Lithuania on June 15, 1940, President Antanas Smetona (q. v.) left the country, temporarily transferring presidential power to Prime Minister Antanas Merkys (q. v.). Under Soviet pressure, Merkys, as acting president, appointed Justas Paleckis (q. v.) Prime Minister on June 17 and asked him to form a government. Paleckis formed a cabinet which included: Vincas Krėvė-Mickevičius (q. v.), Deputy Prime Minister, Foreign Minister and Acting Minister of Education; Gen. Vincas Vitkauskas, Defense Minister; Povilas Pakarklis, Minister of Justice; Ernestas Galvanauskas (q.v.),

Finance Minister and Acting Minister of Communications; Matas Mickis, Minister of Agriculture and Acting Interior Minister; Leonas Koganas, Minister of Health. After the formation of the Paleckis government, Merkys resigned the presidency, thus making Paleckis acting president as well. While there is some doubt about whether this was a constitutional act, Paleckis became de facto President of Lithuania. On June 18 Paleckis announced a leftist political platform and friendship for the Soviet Union; his pro-Soviet regime declared itself the "People's Government." On June 27, the People's Government disbanded the parliament (Lith. *Seimas*) and on July 6 called new elections. While the first cabinet of the People's Government contained no Communist Party members, the real power in Lithuania was held by the Soviet Army and NKVD, as well as the leadership of the Lithuanian Communist Party (q.v.) headed by Antanas Snieĉkus (q. v.), who became head of Lithuania's State Security Department.

After the People's Diet (q.v.) declared Soviet rule in Lithuania in July 1940, the Paleckis government accelerated the reorganization of the country's administration, police and military along Soviet lines and enacted decrees on nationalization. On August 26, 1941, following the incorporation of Lithuania into the USSR, the Lithuanian Supreme Soviet replaced the People's Government with the Council of People's Commissars of the Lithuanian SSR chaired by Mečislovas Gedvilas, thus completing the Sovietization of Lithuania's government.

PHILOMATHS (Pol. *filomaty*, Lith. *filomatai*). A secret student association originating at the University of Vilnius during the early 1800s. The Philomath association was established in 1817 by students who supported Masonic and Enlightenment ideals and was closely tied to a companion group called the Philarets (Pol. *filareci,* Lith. *filaretai*). One of the prominent founders of the group was the Polish poet Adam Mickiewicz (q. v.). At its height the two groups united dozens of active students and intellectuals, along with several hundred sympathizers. While small in number, the Philomaths were important in propagating the ideas of Polish-oriented romantic nationalism and political liberalism in Lithuania. In 1824 Tsarist authorities sentenced over one hundred alleged members of the Philomath and Philaret associations for anti-Russian activities, although only twenty persons actually served brief terms of imprisonment and exile.

PIŁSUDSKI, JÓZEF (1867-1935). Polish military and political leader, born in Lithuania near Švenčionys on May 5, 1867. He graduated from a Vilnius secondary school and then attended the University of Kharkov. From 1887 to 1892 Piłsudski was exiled to Siberia for anti-Tsarist activities. He was one of the leaders of the Polish Socialist Party at the turn of the century, but eventually became more interested in the struggle for Polish independence. He was instrumental in organizing the Polish legions which fought on the German side in World War I. In his military career Piłsudski eventually achieved the rank of Marshal. In November 1918 he was named regent of the newly independent Polish state. He hoped to recreate the old Polish-Lithuanian Commonwealth within its 1772 boundaries as a Polish-led federation of Poland, Lithuania and Ukraine. Piłsudski was particularly adamant about including his native Vilnius region in the new Poland. When the federative plans collapsed, he authorized Gen. Lucjan Żeligowski (q. v.) to stage a mutiny and seize Lithuania's capital in October 1920. Piłsudski returned to private life in 1922 but a military coup in May 1926 brought him to power as prime minister and defense minister. He was virtual dictator of Poland until his death in Warsaw on May 12, 1935. In recognition of his sentiment for the land of his birth, Piłsudski's heart was buried together with his mother's remains in the Rasa cemetery in Vilnius. See POLAND.

POLAND. Lithuania's southern neighbor, an important cultural and political factor in the country's history, area 312,612 sq. km., population est. 38,363,000; capital Warsaw, pop. 1,700,000. Lithuanian-Polish relations date back to pre-Christian times when the Baltic tribes encountered the West Slavic groups who were the ancestors of the modern Polish nation. The term for one of these tribes, the Lech, is the Lithuanian term for "Poles" (Lith. *lenkai*). Medieval chronicles report that the Lithuanian and Old Prussian (q. v.) tribes made numerous forays into Polish lands. The Polish tribes were united under the Piast dynasty, beginning with Mieszko I, who inaugurated the country's Christianization in 966. The center of this state was in Gniezno, the site of the first Polish metropolitanate. Central power was strengthened under Casimir I (1034-1058) and Bolesław II (1058-1079), but the real foundations of the Kingdom of Poland as a power in Central Europe were laid by Casimir III (1333-1370).

Lithuanian relations with Poland improved during the time of Gediminas (q. v.), whose daughter Anne married Casimir. The crucial turning point in Polish-Lithuanian relations occurred in 1385 when the Treaty of Krėva (q. v.) established a dynastic alliance between the two states, provided for the Christianization of Lithuania, and led to the demise of the dangerous Teutonic Knights (q. v.). Jogaila (q. v.), who assumed the Polish crown as Władysław II, established the Jagiellonian dynasty, which ruled until 1572 and is generally considered to have inaugurated Poland's golden age of political power and cultural development. The Union of Lublin in 1569 transformed the Polish-Lithuanian dynastic alliance into the Polish-Lithuanian Commonwealth (q. v.), a federation of the Kingdom and Grand Duchy that survived until 1795. As a result of the Union, Poland acquired Ukraine from Lithuania. The influence of the Polish nobility and the Catholic Church (q. v.) were factors in strengthening the historic process of linguistic Polonization (q. v.), which defined Lithuania's cultural history until the early 20th century.

During the early period of Tsarist rule over the former Commonwealth (1795-1823), the Polish and Lithuanian nobility generally struggled together for a restoration of the former Commonwealth. However, after the insurrection of 1863 (q. v.), the increasingly assertive Lithuanian-speaking intelligentsia of peasant stock began to stake out a separate national identity in opposition to the Poles. The greatest conflict between Poles and Lithuanians erupted after World War I over the Vilnius Question

(q. v.). Poland and Lithuania remained in a state of war until 1927 and diplomatic relations between the two countries were not established until 1938 (see ULTIMATUMS). In October 1939 Lithuania regained control of Vilnius (q. v.) and, after the collapse of Poland in September 1939, accepted thousands of Polish refugees and military internees. However, during World War II Polish-Lithuanian relations were marred by the violent struggle between the underground Home Army and Lithuanian authorities in eastern Lithuania, which included atrocities against civilians by both sides. During the late 1940s almost 200,000 Poles as well as some Lithuanians who claimed Polish roots, repatriated to Poland as part of the Polish government's agreement with the Soviet Union.

Lithuania's independence since 1990 has transformed Polish-Lithuanian relations. Poland's President Lech Wałęsa and majority Polish public opinion supported the Lithuanian independence movement and relations between the two countries improved. Wałęsa's visit to Lithuania in 1994 and the visit of his successor President Aleksander Kwaśniecki in February 1996 have further strengthened Polish-Lithuanian ties. However, some problems remain, including accusations by Polish and Lithuanian nationalists that their respective national minorities (230,000 Poles in Lithuania; 15-20,000 Lithuanians in Poland) have not been granted equal rights. Some Lithuanian politicians unsuccessfully demanded that a formal statement denouncing the 1920 Polish occupation of Vilnius be included in the Polish-Lithuanian state treaty which was signed by Presidents Wałęsa and Brazauskas (q. v.) in April 1994. However, the treaty, ratified by the legislatures of both countries on October 13, 1994, reaffirms the existing boundary between Poland and Lithuania, thus, explicitly confirming Lithuania's right to Vilnius. See CATHOLIC CHURCH; COMMONWEALTH, POLISH-LITHUANIAN; POLONIZA-TION; VILNIUS QUESTION.

POLONIZATION. The term used by historians for the process by which Polish culture came to play an important and, at times, dominant role in Lithuanian history. The Baltic peoples had for centuries been neighbors of the West Slavic tribes. During the 14th century, there were a number of Lithuanian military incursions into Poland, but also peaceful contacts: in 1325 Grand Duke Gediminas' (q. v.) daughter Aldona (Anne) married Casimir the Great of Poland. The historic impact of Polish culture on Lithuania dates from the country's Christianization in 1387, which was an outcome of the Polish-Lithuanian dynastic alliance. With the exception of a few Czechs and Germans, Lithuania's clergy of the late 14th century was predominantly Polish and the newly-established Lithuanian Church was under the jurisdiction of the Archdiocese of Gniezno. The shortage of native priests led to Polish dominance of the Lithuanian Church; for this reason, later Lithuanian nationalists came to view Catholicism as the major Polonizing force in Lithuania.

Beginning in the 15th century, Lithuanian society underwent a long and gradual division into a Polish-speaking nobility and Lithuanian-speaking peasantry. The last Grand Duke known to have spoken Lithuanian was Jogaila's (q. v.) son Casimir (1440-1492). Spoken Polish came into wider use in the Grand Duke's court by the middle of the 16th century and radiated outward to the magnates and landed gentry. In 1697 Polish and Latin became the official languages of the Grand Duchy, replacing the Belarusan form of Old Church Slavic, which had been utilized as the language of documents in the Lithuanian chancellory since the 15th century. Spoken Lithuanian was still used in the courts and in administration, but, except for occasional oaths sworn by peasants, Lithuanian was not written in official documents, except in Lutheran East Prussia. Many of the lesser gentry and townspeople of the ethnographically Lithuanian regions of the Grand Duchy continued speaking Lithuanian until the 18th century when, except in Samogitia, they gradually switched to Polish. By the 19th century, Polish was established as the language of public life and social prestige in most of Lithuania even as the country fell under Tsarist rule. Russian efforts (see RUSSIFICATION) to replace Polish with Russian were generally unsuccessful.

With the emergence of the Lithuanian national movement in the second half of the 19th century, the process of cultural and linguistic Polonization was gradually reversed in much of Lithuania and practically came to an end with the establishment of the Republic of Lithuania in 1918. However, Polonization continued in the eastern parts of the country, especially the Vilnius region, which came under Polish rule in 1920-1939. During the 1930s the Polish authorities, led by governor Ludwik Bociański of Vilnius province, sought to suppress Lithuanian culture and language in the area, causing great bitterness among the Lithuanian inhabitants, as well as tensions between the governments of Poland and Lithuania. After Lithuania regained Vilnius in 1939, the authorities tried to reverse the Polonization process in the region through a policy of Lithuanianization with mixed success. Ethnic violence during World War II between the Polish Home Army and Lithuanian armed formations further inflamed tensions in the area. Since the war, and despite a treaty outlining minorities policy between Lithuania and Poland in 1994, disputes still continue over the treatment of the Polish minority in eastern Lithuania, and Lithuanians living in the Suwałki region of Poland. See CATHOLIC CHURCH; COMMONWEALTH, POLISH-LITHUANIAN; POLAND.

PONIATOWSKI, STANISŁAW AUGUST (1732-1798). Last King of Poland and Grand Duke of Lithuania (1764-1795), born on January 17, 1732. Poniatowski received his early schooling at the court of the Czartoryskis (q. v.) and then furthered his education in Germany, France, Holland and Europe; in later life he developed a reputation as a cultured and urbane patron of the arts. He served in the Commonwealth's Diet from 1752 and was appointed a member of the Polish-Lithuanian diplomatic mission in St. Petersburg from 1755 to 1758, where he became the lover of the future Catherine II, then wife of Tsar Peter III. With Russian support, Poniatowski easily won election to the throne of the Commonwealth in Warsaw on August 2, 1764 as King and Grand Duke Stanisław August II. The King, although eager to halt the decline of the Polish-Lithuanian state, soon found himself torn between the determination of Catherine's Ambassador, Nikolai Repnin, to keep the Commonwealth subservient to Russia, and the movement for reform supported by much of the Polish-Lithuanian gentry. The Confederation of Radom (q. v.) forced Stanisław August to abandon hopes for reform. In 1771 the supporters of the reform-minded Confederation of Bar (q. v.) attempted to kidnap Stanisław August, and after the first partition (q. v.) of 1772, the King's powers were even further reduced. Poniatowski vainly tried to secure a more independent position for the Commonwealth vis-à-vis Russia after the first partition. At first, Stanisław August accepted the decisions of the Four-Year Diet (1788-1792) which legislated serious reforms for the Commonwealth and supported the subsequent resistance to Russia; but, sensing defeat against superior Russian forces, in August 1792 he defected to the pro-Russian Confederation of Targowica (q. v.). However, in 1794 the King gave his blessing to the insurrectionary movement of Tadeusz Kościuszko (q. v.). After the rebellion's failure, Stanisław August was exiled by Catherine II to Grodno (q.v.) where he abdicated on November 25, 1795. In 1796 Poniatowski was invited to the coronation of Tsar Paul I and remained in St. Petersburg until his death on February 12, 1798.

POPULATION AND DEMOGRAPHY. **Before 1914.** At the height of territorial expansion in the early 15th century under Vytautas (q. v.), the lands of the Grand Duchy and its dependencies totaled over 900,000 sq. km. and a population variously estimated between two and four million, of whom perhaps a half-million were ethnic Lithuanians. In the mid-17th century the number of houses subject to taxation by the Grand Duchy was over a half-million, reflecting a population of about three or four million, but this number was considerably reduced by the wars with Muscovy between 1654 and 1667. The Great Northern War (1700-1721) and the plague of 1708-1711 were the greatest demographic disasters in Lithuanian history. In western Samogitia (q. v.) and East Prussia (q. v.), it is estimated that the majority of the population perished, although there was some recovery by the late 18th century. In 1860 the Russian administration estimated that there were about 1,500,000 Lithuanians living in the provinces of the historically Lithuanian lands, mostly in Kaunas, Vilnius and Grodno gubernias. At the same time, there were about a quarter million Lithuanians in East Prussia. The comprehensive Russian census of 1897 showed a marked decline in the number of people listed as Lithuanians, especially in the eastern parts of the country due to the Polonization (q. v.) and Russification (q. v.) of the region. Despite a high birth rate, the Lithuanian-speaking population remained stable during this period due to assimilation into surrounding Slavic communities and emigration, primarily to America. On the eve of World War I the population of the ethnic Lithuanian lands stood at about four million, of whom about a half-million were Jews.

1914-1941. In 1915 the retreating Russian forces evacuated nearly a half-million inhabitants, including about 300,000 ethnic Lithuanians, but the majority returned to Lithuania after 1918. The first detailed population census of the Republic of Lithuania in 1923 and the Klaipėda Territory count of 1925 revealed the following demographic breakdown for a total population of 2,164,199 (excluding Vilnius):

Nationality	Number	Percent
Lithuanians	1,739,489	80.6
Jews	154,321	7.15
Germans	88,568	4.10
Poles	65,628	3.04
Russians	50,727	2.35
Other	65,466	2.76

Occupation	Number	Percent
Agriculture	1,129,870	76.71
Industry/Crafts	94,731	6.43
Other	248,344	16.86

Lithuania's demographic structure underwent revolutionary change during the interwar period as the country experienced majority rule for the first time. The relative ethnic proportions within the population at large did not change significantly before the late 1930s, but the ratio of urbanites rose to nearly a fourth of Lithuanian citizens on the eve of World War II. The process of urban "Lithuanianization," the single most important demographic revolution in the country's modern history, was even more pronounced. Before the Great War, not a single city in Lithuania had a majority of Lithuanian speakers. During the two decades of independence, all of Lithuania's major cities acquired large majorities of ethnic Lithuanians (with the exceptions of Vilnius and Klaipėda). For example, in 1923 Kaunas had a 59 percent ethnic Lithuanian population and Šiauliai 70 percent (1897 figures were 6.6 percent and 27.8 percent respectively). During the 1930s, the Lithuanian share of the urban population continued to grow, both in the country's larger cities and the smaller towns, which had for centuries been bastions of Jewish, German and Polish economic and cultural influence. With the loss of Klaipėda and the addition of Vilnius in 1939, the Lithuanian population stood at just over three million; the percentage of Germans decreased, while that of Jews grew larger. It is estimated that in 1941 the Lithuanian SSR contained about 3,100,000 inhabitants.

Genocide, War and Postwar Stalinism, 1941-1953. Lithuania suffered one of the highest rates of population loss in Europe as a result of World War II and postwar violence. The extent of demographic losses has been a subject of controversy and, sometimes, the object of politically motivated claims intended to either increase or decrease the number of victims of deportation, massacre and postwar resistance to Soviet occupation. The opening of Soviet archives has allowed us to more accurately estimate the extent of population losses during this period although precise figures must await further research.

The Soviet occupation of 1940-1941 exacted a large number of victims of repression, culminating in the deportations of about 18,000 civilians to points east and the massacres of civilians by the retreating Red Army in mid and late June 1941; most of the victims were ethnic Lithuanians. The Nazi occupation and the Holocaust (q. v.) resulted in the deaths of at least a quarter million people, mainly Jews. The period of the first decade of the second Soviet occupation (1944-1953) was also extremely violent, resulting in mass deportations of Lithuanian civilians and an anti-Soviet guerilla war which killed tens of thousands before waning in the early 1950s. Many deportees and refugees perished during their journeys, while others survived and/or returned; thus, an accurate appraisal as to what extent deportations and displacement constituted actual population losses may never be possible. Scholars are still dealing with figures that can best be described as reasonable approximations. The categories and numbers of the population changes are listed in the chart below, with the understanding that they are still only estimates.

Estimates of Lithuanian citizens killed/murdered 1941-1953:

1941-1944/5

Soviet executions (includes 1940-1941 and killings of June 1941)	2,000
Lithuanian losses: anti-Soviet uprising of June 23-24, 1941	700
Nazi executions: Jewish Holocaust	200,000
Nazi executions: Other	2,500
Acts of war (Civilian Deaths)	25,000
Acts of war (Lithuanians in German and Soviet units)	35,000

1944/5-1953

Armed resistance (anti-Soviet)	20,000
Local Communist forces and Soviet activists/collaborators	10,000
Civilians killed by combatants	2,000
Soviet executions/pacification	5,000

Forced Deportations:

Soviet deportations, 1940-1941	20,000
Forced labor to Germany, 1941-1944	75,000
Soviet deportations, 1945-1953	150,000

Refugee Movements and Repatriation:

Repatriation to Germany, spring 1941	50,000
Refugees to USSR, June-July 1941	25,000
Refugees reaching West, 1944-1945*	100,000
Repatriation to Poland, 1947-1950	170,000

*Not including Germans fleeing Klaipėda (Memel) Territory

The Post-Stalin Period. It took a considerable time for Lithuania to recover from the demographic disasters of the 1941-1953 period. The Soviet estimate of the population in 1950 was 2,573,000, reflecting the wartime and postwar losses; by 1970 the population had recovered to its 1939 level. The most significant changes in Lithuania's demographic structure since the war were: first, the influx of nearly 300,000 mostly Russian settlers and, second, the urbanization of the populace:

Year	Total	Lithuanian (%)	Urban (%)
1959	2,711,000	79.3	38.6
1970	3,128,000	80.1	50.2
1979	3,339,000	80	60.7
1989	3,690,000	79.6	68
1997	3,705,000	81	67.5

A decreasing birthrate and the aging of the population have been worrying demographers for the last two decades, but there have been no significant demographic changes since independence in 1990. (Additional statistical information is contained in the "Introduction.") See RESISTANCE MOVEMENTS.

POŠKA (Pol. Paszkiewicz), DIONIZAS (1757-1830). Lithuanian writer and patron of Lithuanian studies, born near Šilalė in Raseiniai district on April 30, 1757. Poška came from the Samogitian petty gentry and, along with Simonas Stanevičius (q. v.), is the best-known writer of the early 19th-century Samogitian movement which sought to preserve and nurture Lithuanian-language culture. Poška studied at the college of Kražiai (q. v.) and gathered a circle of like-minded students from the University of Vilnius. He undertook archeological excavations and gathered material for the ethnographic study of Samogitian peasants. Poška is best-knon for, among other works, his long poem *Mužikas Žemaičių ir Lietuvos* (Lith. The Samogitian and Lithuanian Peasant), which was written between 1815 and 1820 and first published by *Aušra* (q. v.) in 1886. The work criticized serfdom, empathized with the peasants and romanticized the life and work of Lithuanian villagers. Poška died on May 11, 1830.

POW (Pol. *Polska Organizacja Wojskowa*). Underground Polish military organization, founded during World War I. In 1918 the POW established chapters in Vilnius and, later, in Kaunas. The POW leadership believed that Lithuania should be annexed to Poland since it could not survive as an independent state and would simply become a German or Russian outpost threatening Polish interests. During the spring and summer of 1919 the POW began to organize a rebellion seeking to overthrow the Lithuanian government, involving over 300 people in the conspiracy. On August 28, 1919 members of the POW staged a brief armed attack on Lithuanian installations and communications but the revolt was quickly suppressed by the Lithuanian Army; about 400 people were detained and 45 were sentenced to prison by military courts in December 1920, effectively ending POW activities in Lithuania. While the POW coup attempt never seriously threatened the Lithuanian government, it provoked considerable suspicion of Poland and further worsened Polish-Lithuanian relations. See CENTRAL LITHUANIA; POLAND; ŻELIGOWSKI, LUCJAN.

PRESS BAN in Lithuania, 1864-1904. Tsarist decree and policy which forbad the publication and possession of Lithuanian-language publications in the Latin alphabet. The idea of adapting the Russian Cyrillic alphabet, the so-called *grazhdanka*, to the Lithuanian language had been proposed by the Pan-Slavist Russian scholar Alexander Hilferding (1831-1872). He hoped that the Lithuanian peasantry could be drawn away from the influence of the anti-Tsarist nobility and Catholic Church (q.v.) by persuading Lithuanians to utilize their own language in Cyrillic form. The Polish-Lithuanian insurrection of 1863 (q. v.) convinced some Russian officials and educators, particularly Mikhail Muravyev (q. v.), the Governor-General of Vilnius, and Ivan Kornilov (1811-1901), the curator of the Vilnius educational district, that Polish cultural and political influence was the main obstacle to Russian domination in Lithuania. In 1864 Kornilov organized a commission to prepare Cyrillic Lithuanian books for publication by the government; the first book was a primer for schools in Samogitia published in the summer of 1864. In all, a total of about fifty Cyrillic Lithuanian books for the peasantry were published by the Russian government. At the same time, Governor-General Muravyev issued an administrative order forbidding the publication of Lithuanian textbooks in the Latin alphabet. On September 6, 1865, Governor-General C. P. Kaufman, Muravyev's successor, formalized the prohibition into a comprehensive press ban on all Latin-Lithuanian publications which was confirmed by Russian Interior Minister, P. A. Valuyev, on September 23, 1865 and extended to the whole Russian Empire. The only exceptions to the press ban were several academic books on Lithuanian songs and literature published in Kazan and St. Petersburg. The Tsarist government devoted considerable effort to enforcing the press ban, especially during its last two decades. Russian authorities reported that during 1891-1903 the Russian police seized nearly 200,000 volumes of illegal Latin-Lithuanian publications. However, by the turn of the century, many Russian officials had become convinced that the 1864-1865 ban was both futile and counterproductive. In 1902 and 1903 the Russian Senate declared the original executive decree of the press ban illegal. The outbreak of the Russo-Japanese war and the need for internal support persuaded Tsar Nicholas II to lift the ban on Lithuanian publications in the Latin alphabet on April 24, 1904.

The Tsarist press ban is considered one of the formative events of the Lithuanian national movement during the 19th century. On the whole, the Lithuanian-speaking peasantry rejected the government's Lithuanian books in the new alphabet. Furthermore, the Tsarist policy provoked a widespread resistance movement. During the 1860s and 1870s Bishop Motiejus Valančius (q. v.) organized the publication of Lithuanian books in East Prussia (q. v.), which were then transported into Russian Lithuania by smugglers popularly known as the "book-carriers" (Lith. *knygnešiai*). This pattern of illegal publication, which resulted in the dissemination of over a million pieces of popular literature in Lithuania during the forty-year period of the press ban, greatly contributed to the resistance against Russification (q. v.) and the growth of political activism within the Lithuanian national movement. See INSURRECTION OF 1863; RUSSIFICATION.

PRUNSKIENĖ, KAZIMIERA (1943-).   Economist and prime minister, born on February 26, 1943 in Švenčionys district. In 1971 she received a doctorate in economics and taught at the University of Vilnius. From 1986 to 1988 Prunskienė worked in the agriculture ministry of the Lithuanian SSR, and in 1989-1990 was the deputy prime minister of the republic. She was one of the founders of the Sąjūdis (q. v.) movement and was appointed prime minister of Lithuania in March 1990, becoming the first woman head of government in the country's history. In May 1990 Prunskienė visited President Bush in Washington, then traveled to London, Paris and Bonn seeking recognition for Lithuania's independence. She also attempted to persuade Gorbachev (q. v.) to accept compromises in Lithuania's crisis with the Kremlin. However, Prunskienė's relationship with President Vytautas Landsbergis (q. v.) became strained and in January 1991 she resigned under pressure, retaining her seat in the legislature. She is co-founder and head of the Lithuanian Women's Party, established in 1993.

PRUSSIA, PRUSSIANS. The region west of Lithuania between the Nemunas and Vistula Rivers and once the homeland of West Baltic tribes linguistically related to the Lithuanians. In historical literature the term Old Prussian is used to describe the original inhabitants who were settled in the region, probably by the time of the Bronze Age (about 1800 B. C.). Until medieval times, the Baltic Prussians maintained contacts with their Germanic and Slavic neighbors. Rich archeological finds of Roman coins and artifacts in the Sambia (or Semba) region of what today includes Kaliningrad (Ger. Königsberg) testify to a flourishing amber trade. The first extensive historical report on the Prussians dates to the Anglo-Saxon traveler Wulfstan in the ninth century. The Vikings are reported to have established a foothold in Sambia during the 11th century. In 997 St. Adalbert (in Czech, Vojtech) was martyred in Pomerania, the westernmost region of Old Prussia and in 1008 the Benedictine monk St. Bruno of Querfurt and eighteen companions were killed during a Prussian war with the now Christian Poles. In 1226 the Polish prince, Conrad of Mazovia, appealed to the Teutonic Knights (q. v.) to subdue and convert the Prussians who had been raiding Polish lands. The Teutonic Order's successful crusade against the Prussians in the 13th century, combined with steady German colonization, resulted in the disappearance of the Old Prussian language and culture by the 17th century. The name "Prussia" came to denote the state of the German settlers rather than the land of the original inhabitants. Glossaries and several religious texts of the 16th century have allowed scholars to reconstruct the basic characteristics of the Old Prussian language as a distinct West Baltic relative of Lithuanian and Latvian.

In 1466 the Teutonic Order lost considerable territory to Poland, mainly western Prussia, including Gdańsk (Danzig). In 1525 Grand Master Albert Hohenzollern converted to Lutheranism and became a vassal of the Polish crown: the Prussian lands of the

Teutonic Order became the secular Duchy of Prussia. In 1618 the Duchy of Prussia came under the Brandenburg line of the Hohenzollerns and in 1660 ended its dependence on the Polish crown. In 1701 Frederick I declared Brandenburg-Prussia a kingdom with its capital in Berlin. The Prussian Kingdom included the Lithuanian-speaking regions of **East Prussia** (Ger. *Ostpreussen*), which during the early 18th century encompassed the area between Königsberg and the present Lithuanian border, known among Lithuanians as **Lithuania Minor** (Lith. *Mažoji Lietuva*). The first Lithuanian books, mostly religious texts, were published in East Prussia during the Reformation; thus, Lithuanian East Prussia played an important role in the development of early Lithuanian literature (q. v.), especially through the works of Kristijonas Donelaitis (q. v.). The plague of 1708-1711 during the Great Northern War (q. v.) resulted in a depopulation which was compensated by large-scale immigration, primarily from southern Germany. Despite the demographic changes, the Prussian authorities widely utilized the Lithuanian language (q. v.) in the local offices, courts, schools and Lutheran churches of Lithuania Minor during the 18th and early 19th centuries. Official Germanization of all minorities intensified after the unification of Germany in 1871. In 1876 German was made the sole official language, which effectively confined the spoken Lithuanian language to church and home. This weakened, but did not destroy Lithuanian social and cultural life in East Prussia. Lithuanian cultural life remained stronger in the Klaipėda (q. v.) region, which came under Lithuanian rule between 1923 and 1939. The chauvinistic anti-Lithuanian campaign of the Nazis (q. v.) during the 1930s, as well as the massive population losses and transfers of the Second World War virtually obliterated Lithuanian culture in East Prussia.

The Potsdam agreements of 1945 divided East Prussia into northern and southern zones administered by the Soviet Union and Poland respectively. The Soviet zone became the Kaliningrad Oblast (district) of the RSFSR (now the Russian Federation). The local German and Lithuanian population was almost entirely replaced by Soviet, primarily Russian, settlers and all the German and Lithuanian place names were Russianized. The district was heavily militarized, containing Russian naval bases and air stations. After Lithuania's independence in 1990, Kaliningrad Oblast was geographically separated from the rest of Russia and transit rights for the Russian military became a major domestic and foreign policy issue for the Lithuanian government. Germany, Poland and Lithuania have all expressed interest in the future of this Russian enclave, stressing the need for demilitarizing Kaliningrad, although officially all three countries recognize Russian control of the region. Currently there are about 25,000 Lithuanians, mainly postwar immigrants, living in former East Prussia. See KLAIPĖDA; LITERATURE, LITHUANIAN; NAZIS.

- R -

RADOM, CONFEDERATION OF. Political movement of Polish-Lithuanian nobility and gentry established in the Polish town of Radom in the summer of 1767 in order to oppose the reform policies of King Stanisław August Poniatowski (q. v.) and the Czartoryski (q. v.) family. The Confederation of Radom was led by Karol Stanisław Radziwiłł (q. v.), the palatinate of Vilnius, and was encouraged by the Russian Ambassador in Warsaw, Nikolai Repnin, who feared that a reform of the Polish-Lithuanian Commonwealth's (q. v.) administrative and military system would strengthen the Polish-Lithuanian state. The King and reform party proved powerless to resist the Confederation when Russian troops were stationed in Warsaw. In July 1767 the Confederate Diet was convened in Warsaw with Russian support and was further reinforced by pro-Radziwiłł forces from Lithuania. The political result of the Radom Confederation was the passage of the so-called Cardinal Laws for the Commonwealth, which were guaranteed by Russia. These statutes reconfirmed the nobility's political rights, maintained free royal elections and retained the infamous *liberum veto*, thus perpetuating the political anarchy and international weakness that had come to characterize the Polish-Lithuanian

Commonwealth. At the same time, the Radom debacle and the overt interference of Russia in the Commonwealth's political affairs enraged much of Polish-Lithuanian society and provoked the anti-Russian Confederation of Bar (q. v.) which led to the first partition (q. v.) of Poland and Lithuania in 1772. See RUSSIA.

RADVILA (RADVILAS). See RADZIWIŁŁ.

RADZIWIŁŁ (Lith. Radvila, also Radvilas, Lat. Radivilius). The wealthiest, best-known and most powerful of Lithuania's noble magnate families, who dominated Lithuanian politics during the 16th and 17th centuries. The family originated from one Radvilas, a palatine of Trakai and royal courtier of the late 15th century, whose son Nicholas Radvilas (d. 1510) became chancellor of Lithuania. Increasingly, the family came to be known by its Polonized name, Radziwiłł, and embraced two major branches: one centered in the Biržai region of northern Lithuania, whose male line ended in 1669; the other centered in the Nesvizh region of what is now western Belarus, which still has living descendants. In 1547 the Radziwiłłs were made princes of the Holy Roman Empire and eventually they owned hundreds of estates, maintained a private army and, at times, were virtual rulers of the Grand Duchy of Lithuania. **Barbara Radziwiłł** (1520-1551) (q. v.), the second wife of Sigismund Augustus (q. v.), was the Queen of Poland and Grand Duchess of Lithuania. The Radziwiłłs included some of the most important statesmen, clerics and military leaders of early modern Lithuania: **Albert Stanisław Radziwiłł** (1573-1656) was chancellor of Lithuania between 1623 and 1656; **Christopher Radziwiłł** (1547-1603) was grand hetman of Lithuania; **George Cardinal Radziwiłł** (1556-1600) was bishop of Vilnius (1583-1591) and Cracow (1591-1600); **Janusz Radziwiłł** (1612-1655) led the Lithuanian attempt to forge a dynastic union with Sweden by the Treaty of Kėdainiai in 1655 (q. v.). In the 18th century, **Karol Stanisław Radziwiłł** (1734-1790) first led both the pro-Russian Confederation of Radom (q. v.) and then joined the anti-

Russian Confederation of Bar (q. v.). Perhaps, the best-known Radziwiłłs are **Nicholas Radziwiłł the Black** (q. v.) and **Nicholas Radziwiłł the Red** (q. v.), both of whom spearheaded the Reformation in Lithuania and Poland.

RADZIWIŁŁ (Lith. Radvilas), BARBARA (1520-1551). Queen of Poland and Grand Duchess of Lithuania, daughter of the Lithuanian Grand Hetman George Radziwiłł and sister of Nicholas Radziwiłł the Red (q. v.). After the death of his first wife, Elizabeth of Hapsburg, Sigismund Augustus (q. v.), the heir to the Polish-Lithuanian throne who resided in Vilnius during the mid-1540s, secretly married Barbara there in 1547. Despite opposition from the Polish court and nobility who feared the influence of the Radziwiłł family, Sigismund Augustus refused to annul the marriage. After the death of his father, Sigismund the Old, in 1548 and his own elevation to the Polish throne, Sigismund Augustus strove to have Barbara recognized as Queen of Poland (after the Lithuanian Council of Lords had already recognized her as Grand Duchess). She was finally crowned Queen in Cracow on December 7, 1550 but died soon thereafter, on May 8, 1551, and was buried in the Cathedral of Vilnius. There was suspicion that Barbara had been poisoned by her mother-in-law, Bona Sforza (q. v), who had adamantly opposed her son's second marriage. The drama surrounding the passionate love of Sigismund and Barbara and the consequent political intrigues have been favorite themes in Polish and Lithuanian literature and theater.

RADZIWIŁŁ (Lith. Radvilas), NICHOLAS THE BLACK (1515-1565). Lithuanian statesman and one of the leaders of the Polish-Lithuanian Reformation, born in Nesvizh (Pol. Nieśwież) on February 4, 1515. In 1542 Nicholas was appointed marshal of the royal court and became close to Sigismund Augustus (q. v.), heir to the Polish and Lithuanian thrones. In 1549 Nicholas was granted the title of prince by the Holy Roman Emperor. In 1550 he was appointed chancellor of Lithuania and directed much of his effort to resisting the designs of Ivan IV (The Terrible) on Lithuania's Russian lands; until his death, he was the acknowledged ruler of the Grand Duchy. During the mid-1560s Nicholas the Black led the Lithuanian delegation in their negotiations with Poland for a new union and gained a reputation as an advocate of Lithuanian equality with the Poles. Nicholas' historic reputation rests in large part on his role during the Reformation. He corresponded with John Calvin and other Protestant leaders and was instrumental in establishing the first Reformed congregation in Lithuania. In 1564 Nicholas commissioned the publication of the famous Bible of Brest, the first Polish translation of the Scriptures, which is considered a landmark in the development of modern Polish literature. Ironically, despite his devotion to Protestantism, Nicholas' sons eventually reconverted to Catholicism. He died on May 29, 1565. See REFORMATION.

RADZIWIŁŁ (Lith. Radvilas), NICHOLAS THE RED (1512-1584). Lithuanian statesman and military leader. After extended study in Germany and travels in Europe, Nicholas the Red, along with his cousin, Nicholas the Black (q. v.), were granted the title of prince in 1549. As brother-in-law of King Sigismund Augustus (q. v.), Nicholas the Red exerted great influence in Lithuania, but he also gained notoriety as a military leader in the wars against Muscovy, successfully fighting the forces of Ivan IV (the Terrible) in Livonia and gaining a famous victory against the Tsar at the Battle of Ula in 1564. During the Polish-Lithuanian negotiations preceding the Union of Lublin (q. v.) in 1569, Nicholas strongly opposed any attempts to diminish the Grand Duchy's autonomy and boycotted the final sessions of the diet which enacted the Union. After the death of Sigismund Augustus in 1572 (q. v.), Nicholas led an unsuccessful Lithuanian attempt to persuade Poland to restore the Grand Duchy's Ukrainian and other lands lost at Lublin and briefly obstructed King Stefan Batory's (q. v.) recognition as Grand Duke of Lithuania. Like his cousin Nicholas the Black of the Nesvizh branch of the Radziwiłłs, Nicholas the Red was an ardent promoter of Protestantism. He sponsored the classical school of Abraomas Kulvietis (q. v) in Vilnius in 1539 and also established Calvinist schools on his estate in Biržai. The descendants of Nicholas the Red remained loyal to the Reformed Church even after the successful Counter-Reformation in Lithuania. As a result, the Biržai area still contains the largest congregations of the Evangelical Reformed Church in Lithuania.

RAŠTIKIS, STASYS (1896-1985). Lithuanian military leader, born on September 13, 1896. After serving in the Russian Army in World War I and completing the Military Academy of Tbilisi in 1917, Raštikis returned to Lithuania and helped found the Lithuanian Army. In 1919 he was wounded and captured in the war against the Bolsheviks, but returned to Lithuania in 1921 and served both as an infantry officer and in the General Staff. In 1935 Raštikis was appointed commander of the Lithuanian Army and became known for his efforts at modernizing and reorganizing the armed forces; in 1938 he also served as defense minister. Raštikis' coolness towards the Nationalist regime and personal disagreements with President Antanas Smetona (q. v.) eventually led to his dismissal in January 1940. During the crisis of the Soviet ultimatum of June 14, 1940, Raštikis was proposed as prime minister, but his candidacy was rejected by Moscow. Fearing arrest by the NKVD, Raštikis fled to Germany in March 1941. Between June 23 and August 5, 1941, he served as defense minister of the LAF (q. v.) Provisional Government. In 1949 Raštikis emigrated to the United States where he taught at the Monterey Institute of Foreign Languages. Between 1956 and 1982 he published four volumes of memoirs, which are among the most important sources for the political history of interwar Lithuania. He died in Los Angeles on May 2, 1985. See ARMED FORCES.

REFORMATION in Lithuania. Historically, Protestantism penetrated Lithuania from the same direction as Catholicism. In 1525 Grand Master Albert Hohenzollern of the Teutonic Knights, under the personal influence of Martin Luther and aware that Protestant teachings were gaining ground in Prussia (q. v) and Livonia (q. v.), secularized the Order and became a prince in vassalage to the Polish crown. The monarchy and the Church made efforts to halt the Reformation: in 1520 King Sigismund the Old (q. v.) banned Luther's teachings from the Kingdom of Poland and in 1527 the diocesan synod of Vilnius attacked what it termed the Lutheran heresy. Lutheranism probably found its first adherents in Lithuania among German merchants and craftsmen; reportedly by 1540 Franciscans had begun preaching Protestant doctrines at St. Anne's in Vilnius, where services were held for the city's German community. One of the first known Lithuanian propagators of Lutheranism was Father Jonas Tartila who was forced to flee to Prussia in 1535. In 1537 King Sigismund forbade Lithuanian students from attending the Lutheran-oriented University of Wittenberg but this did little to stem the appeal of Protestantism. The best-known early Lithuanian teacher of Protestant doctrine was Abraomas Kulvietis (q. v.).

While Sigismund the Old held firm against Protestantism, his son Sigismund Augustus (q. v.), who became effective ruler of Lithuania in 1544, had been educated in the Italian humanist spirit and was more tolerant of Protestantism. It was during the reign of Sigismund Augustus (1548-1572) that the Reformation reached its height in Lithuania and, at the same time, Calvinism, rather than Lutheranism, became the dominant movement in the Grand Duchy. In 1554 and 1555 Calvin himself urged Sigismund Augustus to turn Poland-Lithuania away from Catholicism. Although Sigismund remained loyal to the Catholic cause, he also refused to suppress the Protestants: in 1563 the King gave equal rights to all Christians. The conversion to Calvinism of the two most powerful Radziwiłłs (Radvilas), Nicholas the Black (q. v.) and his cousin Nicholas the Red (q. v.), further strengthened Protestantism through the endowment of Reformed churches and schools. By the second half of the 16th century, the Reformation engulfed most of Lithuania: in 1563 the Lithuanian Council of Lords included 10 Calvinists out of 18 members. More radical Protestant groups also emerged, such as the Czech Brethren, the Anabaptists and the

Arians (also known in Lithuania as the Socinians or Antitrinitarians). The latter received support from John Kiška of Samogitia; some of the more militant Arians advocated the abolition of social classes, taxes and military service. During the Reformation groups of so-called Judaizers, fascinated by Jewish and Eastern learning, also appeared in Lithuania.

While it is difficult to gauge the real extent of the Reformation in Lithuania, at its height it appealed to a large part of the Lithuanian nobility and urban populace. The fragmentation of Protestantism in Lithuania and the strong Counter-Reformation (q. v.) movement spearheaded by the Jesuits (q. v.) led to the restoration of Catholicism as the dominant religion in Lithuania during the late 16th and early 17th centuries. Significant Reformed (Calvinist) communities survived in northern Lithuania around Biržai. Lutheranism remained dominant only in Lithuanian East Prussia and along the western border of the Grand Duchy. In general, despite occasional outbreaks of violence, Lithuania avoided the widespread religious civil wars and massacres that accompanied the Reformation in western Europe: religious toleration was reaffirmed by the Polish-Lithuanian Diet in 1573 and the Lithuanian Statute of 1588 (q. v.). However, during the 18th century Protestants, like the Orthodox, were classified as dissidents (q. v.) and increasingly became subject to discrimination. See CATHOLIC CHURCH; COUNTER-REFORMATION; KUL-VIETIS, ABRAOMAS; RADZIWIŁŁ, NICHOLAS THE BLACK; RADZIWILŁŁ, NICHOLAS THE RED.

RELIGION, PRE-CHRISTIAN. Archeological research has revealed considerable information about the material culture and social structure of the eastern Baltic region, but there is no certainty concerning the religious beliefs of the Lithuanians and the other Baltic peoples before their conversion to Christianity in the Middle Ages. The major reason for this is that early Baltic tribes left no written records of their own. In his work *Germania* from the first century A. D., Tacitus wrote of the peoples on the Baltic Sea as worshipping the "mother of the gods" and wearing emblems in the shape of a boar. In the 9th century, the Anglo-Saxon traveler Wulfstan described the society of the Old Prussians, but left little useful information about their religion.

Most of the first descriptions of pre-Christian religious rites in Prussia (q. v.) and Lithuania were written by Catholic (q. v.) observers, eager to either demonize or dramatize the cultural life of local pagans. Before the 20th century, historians had based their view of pre-Christian religion in the Baltic region on these obviously biased medieval Christian chronicles. Some of these sources, as well as 19th-century historians, such as Teodor Narbutt (q. v.), assumed the existence of a high priest, a caste of pagan "clergy," vestal virgins, and large temples, obviously evoking the religious structures of classical antiquity. This connection with Rome is evoked by the name of the sacred center of the early Baltic religion, the site of Romuva, which supposedly contained the headquarters of the high priest Krivis and the idols of a pagan trinity of gods (Patrimpas, Perkūnas, Pikulas), described in 14th and 15th-century chronicles. The existence of such an elaborate pagan religion was questioned by Lithuanian historians of the early 20th century, for example, Petras Klimas (q. v.) and Zenonas Ivinskis. Scholars then began to describe the early Lithuanians and other Balts as animists engaging in a kind of nature worship, deriving much of the evidence for this formulation from current folk beliefs, known to have survived from pre-Christian times. It is known that traditional Lithuanians reserved a special role for certain animals, for example, the grass snake (Lith. *žaltys*), who was a protector of the hearth, and the industrious bee. There is also evidence that early Lithuanians believed that their ancestors dwelt within nature, especially trees and certain animals, near the places where they had lived, and that ancestral spirits continued their existence in a mysterious realm called the *dausos*. Some scholars maintain that the popular custom of cemetery visitations on All Souls' Day reflects this ancestor cult. In addition, various pre-Christian supernatural beings inhabited the imagination of the Lithuanian peasantry into modern times: the *laumė*, a semidivine wood nymph, and the *aitvaras*, a mischievous being who could bring a person misfortune or luck.

The prominent Lithuanian archeologist, Prof. Marija Gimbutas (1921-1994) of UCLA, developed a vision of early Lithuanian religious life based on a matriarchal paradigm which reflected an Old European (as opposed to Indo-European) culture whose religion was dominated by female figures such as Žemyna, the Mother Earth, Laima, the giver of life, and Ragana, the goddess of destruction and regeneration. This culture is thought to have celebrated the unity, sacredness and fertility of life, characteristic of an egalitarian, peaceful society. Gimbutas' historical model presupposed a later Indo-European invasion which subsumed the Old European culture and brought new male gods to the ancestors of the Lithuanians: Dievas, the god of heaven, the Thor-like Perkūnas, god of thunder, and Velinas, the god of the underground, whose name became the root for the Lithuanian word for devil in Christian times.

Gimbutas' model has evoked debate in the West as well as in Lithuania. Excavations in Vilnius during the late 1980s which seem to have uncovered ruins of a pre-Christian temple, have renewed interest in the earlier emphasis on a well-developed and socially organized hierarchical religion, leading some to reevaluate the credibility of the once-discredited medieval sources. However, there is no unanimity concerning the details of the religious beliefs of the ancient Lithuanians, which, given the lack of reliable sources, is often based on informed speculation. See ARCHEOLOGY; BALTS; CATHOLIC CHURCH.

RENAISSANCE in Lithuania. The Renaissance had its greatest influence in Lithuania when the country was experiencing the intellectual ferment of the Reformation (q. v.). During the 15th century Lithuanian rulers took an increased interest in university education. A number of students from the Grand Duchy attended the Lithuanian college at the University of Prague, established by royal decree in 1397, as well as the University of Cracow revitalized during the reign of Jogaila (q. v.), or Władysław II. Sons of the higher nobility favored Italian universities, especially Bologna and Padua. The first extensive private libraries at the beginning of the 16th century belonged to the Lithuanian chancellor Albert Goštautas (Pol. Gasztowt) and Abraomas Kulvietis (q. v.). Influenced by the new emphasis on the Greek and Latin classics, the nobility adopted the theory that the Lithuanian nation was descended from the mythical Roman prince Palemon, who had fled to Lithuania to escape a tyrannical emperor. The idea that Latin was a parent tongue of the Lithuanian language greatly enhanced the popularity of Latin poetry in the Grand Duchy. Among the most prominent of the earlier Renaissance Latin poets in Lithuania were Nicolas Hussovianus, born ca. 1480, and the Spanish humanist Peter Roysius, who lived in Vilnius from 1551 to 1571. The influence of Renaissance culture in Lithuania grew during the reign of the Italian-born Queen Bona Sforza (q. v.), the wife of Sigismund the Old (q. v.).

In 1534 Italian masters Bernardino Zenobi, Giovanni Cini and Fillipo da Fiesole were commissioned to reconstruct the Cathedral of Vilnius, while other churches in Lithuania were built by Flemish and other West European architects. The influence of the Renaissance in Lithuania is still seen in some of the extant architecture, although it is mingled with the late Gothic tradition, which had prevailed until the 16th century. In the 17th century the Baroque style tended to dominate. The Muscovite sack of Vilnius in 1655 destroyed much of Lithuania's Renaissance architectural heritage. In art, portraiture of the royal court and nobility was the most common expression of Renaissance influence. Among the best-known paintings of Lithuania's Renaissance is the Virgin Mary of the *Aušros Vartai* (Pol. *Ostra Brama*), or Gates of Dawn Chapel. See ARCHITECTURE; ART.

RESISTANCE MOVEMENTS, World War II and postwar period. The successive foreign occupations of Lithuania in 1940-1945 spawned a variety of resistance movements. After the death of Stalin in 1953 a national and religious dissident movement continued the tradition of resistance to foreign (Soviet) rule.

Anti-Soviet Resistance in 1940-1941. During the first Soviet occupation of 1940-1941, the sigle most important anti-Soviet underground movement was the Lithuanian Activist Front (LAF) (q. v.). However, there were numerous smaller groups and spontaneous acts of passive resistance, such as the distribution of anti-Russian leaflets and the defacing of Communist symbols. On the morning of June 23, 1941, after the outbreak of the Nazi-Soviet war, the LAF initiated an anti-Soviet uprising which seized Kaunas from the Red Army and proclaimed a provisional government. In Vilnius, smaller units of the LAF attacked the Soviet army and took control of many public buildings. The rebellion spread spontaneously to many parts of Lithuania. Much of the population greeted the German Army as liberators from Soviet rule. The rebels' provisional government declared a restoration of the country's independence under the laws existing previous to June 15, 1940, the day of the Soviet occupation. However, the Germans disbanded the provisional government on August 5, 1941 and banned the LAF several weeks later.

Anti-Nazi Resistance, 1941-1944. In Lithuania, the history of resistance against the Nazis is complicated because it was divided into bitterly antagonistic movements. The Lithuanian non-Communist anti-Nazi underground was basically divided into the Lithuanian Front (Lith. *Lietuvių Frontas*) (LF), an outgrowth of the LAF, the Union of Lithuanian Freedom Fighters (Lith. *Lietuvos Laisvės Kovotojų Sąjunga*) (LLKS), and other groups. The LF represented a Catholic wing, while the LLKS can be described as a more militantly anti-German "secular" wing. These Lithuanian anti-Nazi groups eschewed armed resistance on the basis that nothing should be done to assist the Soviet military effort, instead hoping for Germany's defeat by the Western powers. They aimed to harbor the nation's strength in a future showdown with the Soviet Union to preserve Lithuania's independence. Thus, non-Communist resistance opposed such German policies as suppression of education, labor recruitment and attempts to create Lithuanian SS detachments.

In eastern Lithuania, while the Polish Home Army (Pol. *Armja Krajowa*) fought the Nazi occupiers, it turned against the local Lithuanian police and administration in 1943-1944, sometimes with German acquiescence. The Polish-Lithuanian struggle in eastern

Lithuania, which was accompanied by atrocities against civilians, was a continuation of the earlier conflict over Vilnius (q. v.). The Home Army also mistrusted Soviet designs on a future Poland. For their part the Soviet partisans, active primarily also in the forests of eastern Lithuania, began to operate in larger numbers in late 1942, reinforced by guerrillas sent from the Soviet side of the front, and in close cooperation with Soviet partisans in Belarus. There were also several Jewish partisan units, the United Partisans Organization (Yiddish: *Fareinikte Partisaner Organizatzie*), or FPO, established in Vilnius in 1942, and other groups which operated in forests east of the city. The Soviet and Polish partisans had limited appeal in ethnically Lithuanian areas because their movements were incompatible with Lithuanian national goals: the Soviets denied Lithuania's independence, while the Poles demanded Vilnius.

Postwar Anti-Soviet Partisans. The outbreak of armed resistance to Communist rule in 1944-1945 was encouraged by several factors, including the massive Soviet draft, which sent thousands of young men fleeing into the forests; the widespread belief that the Soviet presence was short-lived because the United States and Britain were committed to the restoration of Lithuanian independence; and memories of Soviet atrocities during 1940-1941. Armed resistance to Soviet power reached its height from 1946 to 1948 when the anti-Soviet partisans controlled much of the countryside and numbered about 20,000 men and women, enjoying considerable support from the populace. The major organizational units which sought to unify the resistance with limited success were the Lithuanian Freedom Army (Lith. *Lietuvos Laisvés Armija*) (LLA), and the United Democratic Resistance Movement (Lith. *Bendras Demokratinio Pasipriešinimo Sąjūdis*) (BDPS). The partisan movement was geographically divided into resistance districts (Lith. *apygardos*). The armed resistance began to weaken in 1948-1949 as hope for Western assistance faded, Soviet collectivization of the peasantry cut off food and supplies, and Soviet intelligence succeeded in penetrating the movement. At the height of the war, the Soviet security forces employed over 100,000 men, including NKVD units, interior ministry troops, regular army units and local pro-Soviet Lithuanian auxiliaries. The number of people who perished during the war can be roughly estimated at about 40,000 Soviet and Lithuanian combatants, and between 10,000 to 15,000 civilians. In 1947 the renowned partisan leader Juozas Lukša-Daumantas (1921-1951) managed to reach the West and then returned in 1950 with help from American intelligence, but he was killed in an ambush the following year. His book, *Partizanai* (Lith. Partisans), became a valuable source for the history of the Lithuanian guerillas. The armed resistance gradually waned, becoming increasingly demoralized and undisciplined, until it was discontinued in 1952; however, reports of sporadic armed clashes continued until the 1960s. A great deal of additional material on the postwar guerilla movement has been collected and published since the late 1980s.

National and Religious Dissent after Stalin. During the Hungarian Revolution of 1956, there were several anti-Communist demonstrations, the largest involving a mainly student protest in Vilnius on All Souls' Day (November 1, 1956). Anti-Soviet protest became more pronounced in the 1960s when Catholic dissenters began to agitate against religious persecution. In 1970-1972 four major Soviet show trials were held against dissident clergy. In May 1972 anti-Soviet riots erupted after the self-immolation of Romas Kalanta (q. v.). In November of the same year Lithuania received international attention when the Lithuanian sailor Simas Kudirka (1930-) was forcibly returned by Coast Guard officers after seeking asylum on the American ship *Vigilant* at Martha's Vineyard; Kudirka's trial in Vilnius further galvanized anti-Soviet dissent. Also in 1972 Catholic dissenters began circulating the underground *Lietuvos Bažnyčios Kronika* (Lith. The Chronicle of the Lithuanian Catholic Church); other samizdat publications followed. In November 1976 the Lithuanian Helsinki Committee was formed, which announced that it would monitor Soviet compliance with the human rights provisions of the 1975 Helsinki Accords. In November 1978 the Catholic Committee for the Defense of the Rights of Believers was announced at a press conference in Moscow, resulting in the imprisonment of the priests Alfonsas Svarinskas (1925-), Sigitas Tamkevičius (1938-) and others. Some of the Lithuanian dissenters, such as the poet Tomas Venclova (1937-) and the Catholic nun Nijolė Sadūnaitė (1938-), gained international support and recognition. Others, like Antanas Terleckas (1928-), the economist and founder of the Lithuanian Liberty League (Lith. *Lietuvos Laisvės Lyga*), and Balys Gajauskas (1926-), participated in Lithuanian politics after independence. While the active post-Stalin dissident movement involved only a few thousand persons with an unknown number of sympathizers, it provided an important impetus for the emergence of the pro-independence Sąjūdis (q. v.) movement in 1988. See NAZI-SOVIET PACT; NAZIS; RUSSIA.

REVOLUTION OF 1905. This Revolution in Lithuania consisted of a series of strikes, meetings, demonstrations and uprisings, which can be divided into three basic categories: the workers' movement in the towns, the peasant revolts and the Great Lithuanian Assembly (Diet) of Vilnius (q. v.) in December 1905. The workers' movement was weaker in Lithuania than elsewhere in the Empire since Lithuania was less industrialized and ethnic Lithuanians comprised only a small minority of the working class. A number of workers' strikes and demonstrations broke out in Lithuania after the news of the "Bloody Sunday" massacre in St. Petersburg on January 22, 1905 reached Vilnius and Kaunas. By January 25 there were about 5,000 striking workers in Vilnius alone. The strike movement reached its peak in October when twelve people were killed in Vilnius in clashes with the police. The Tsar's October Manifesto of 1905, and the repressions of 1906 which followed, effectively suppressed the unrest.

During the years 1905-1907 widespread rural unrest broke out in most of Lithuania, much of it fueled by economic issues, such as the peasants' demands for an end to the redemption payments imposed after the emancipation of 1861, more land, and higher wages for the landless agrarian workers. Protests against national and religious discrimination were also widespread and included two major demands: establishment of primary and secondary education in the Lithuanian language, and the appointment of

Lithuanian Catholics to local government offices. Peasant rallies and disturbances became numerous in the fall of 1905 and reached a peak in December of that year, especially in southwestern Lithuania, which was reported to be in complete anarchy. Armed bands of Lithuanian peasants attacked Russian officials and soldiers. Many Russian government schools, seen as centers of compulsory Russification (q. v.) and Orthodoxy, were also closed or sacked by the populace. In addition to protest, the peasantry undertook constructive action, beginning to conduct local government business in Lithuanian, setting up their own Lithuanian-language schools and curricula, and joining with Jews and Belarusans to demand equal national rights.

In November 1905 the Lithuanian press published an appeal for a Lithuanian national assembly to discuss the land question, taxes, and the problems of rural education and administration. On December 4-5, 1905 over 2,000 delegates, half of them peasants, attended what later became known as the Great Assembly (Diet) of Vilnius, the first modern Lithuanian political convention, which proposed an autonomous and democratic Lithuanian state. During the high point of the Revolution in late 1905, the governors of Vilnius and Kaunas gubernias had promised the introduction of the Lithuanian language into rural administration and permission for Catholics to hold office. However, as the revolution weakened in 1906, and with the appointment of Peter Stolypin (q. v.) as Russia's prime minister, repression was intensified. The imperial government sent out punitive expeditions into the countryside, including elements of the reactionary bands, the "Black Hundreds," Russian nationalists who terrorized non-Russians. On occasion, the Russian Army shelled population centers: the towns of Akmenė and Žagarė were devastated. Many of the Lithuanian intelligentsia and peasantry were imprisoned and deported, and by 1907 the uprising in Lithuania had been largely subdued. Despite the failure of the revolution, the events of 1905 accelerated the radicalization of the Lithuanian national movement, stimulating antagonism against Tsarism and encouraging the movement for Lithuanian independence. See RUSSIFICATION.

RIFLEMEN'S UNION (Lith. *Šaulių Sąjunga* or *šauliai*). Volunteer military organization, which served as a national guard in Lithuania between 1919 and 1940. Its founder and long-time leader was Vladas Putvinskis (1873-1929) who established the Lithuanian Riflemen's Union on August 20, 1919 in Kaunas. It served as a support organization for the beleaguered Lithuanian Army, which was then fighting the independence wars on several fronts. The Union became a popular and influential patriotic organization which sponsored cultural affairs and sports. In 1935 the *šauliai*, who had operated as local groups with elected commanders, were placed under the control of the Army. By 1939 the Union numbered over 60,000 members, including women and auxiliaries, and sponsored hundreds of choral groups, bands, reading rooms and sports clubs. In June 1940, following the Soviet invasion, the Riflemen's Union was disbanded. In 1991 the *Šaulių Sąjunga* was reestablished in Lithuania, although the organization has not regained its prewar importance.

RUSSIA, formally RUSSIAN FEDERATION, pop. 149,300,000, area 17,075,000 sq. km.; capital: Moscow, 9,000,000. Since the formal establishment of the Russian Empire in 1721, Russia has played a dominant role in the history of Lithuania (for the earlier period, see MUSCOVY). Even before the Partitions (q. v.) of the Polish-Lithuanian Commonwealth (q. v.) in 1772-1795, Russian military power, diplomatic influence and open interference in Poland-Lithuania's chaotic internal affairs had transformed the Commonwealth into a de facto Russian protectorate. In 1795 most of Lithuania came under Tsarist rule, and in 1807 the southwestern part of the country, known as Užnemunė or Suvalkija (q. v.), also came under the sovereignty of Russia as part of the autonomous Kingdom of Poland (q. v.). Until the insurrection of 1830-1831 (q. v.), the Russian government interfered little with Lithuania's social and cultural structures. However, the reactionary Tsar Nicholas I (1825-1855) attempted to integrate Lithuania more closely to the rest of Russia by persecuting Catholicism, suppressing education and Polish culture, and abolishing the

Lithuanian Statute in 1840. The very name of Lithuania was eradicated when the gubernias of the old Grand Duchy (Grodno, Vilnius, and Kaunas) were given the title, Northwest Territory (Rus. *Severo-zapadnyi krai*). A more intensive policy of Russification (q. v.) followed the insurrection of 1863 (q. v.), when a press ban (q. v.) forbad the printing of Lithuanian books in the Latin alphabet. Anti-Catholic repression culminated in the violent incident at Kražiai (q. v.) in 1893, which did much to turn Lithuanian public opinion against Russian rule. By the turn of the century, the Russian government, initially concerned only with combatting Polish influence in Lithuania, concluded that some accommodation with the growing Lithuanian national movement was desirable and canceled the press ban in 1904. After the Revolution of 1905 (q. v.) some rights were granted the Lithuanian language in schools and public offices; however, the liberalization was partly reversed during the government of the conservative Russian Prime Minister, Peter Stolypin (q. v.) (1907-1911).

In 1915 the Russian Army retreated from Lithuania in the face of the German offensive, thus ending over a century of Tsarist rule. After the revolutions of 1917, the successor state to the Tsarist Empire, Soviet Russia, signed a peace treaty (q. v.) with Lithuania on July 12, 1920, renouncing for all time Russian claims to Lithuania. Between the wars, Soviet-Lithuanian relations were generally friendly, as Moscow consistently supported, at least formally, Lithuania's position on the Vilnius Question (q. v.). After the Soviet occupation of Lithuania in June 1940 and the country's forcible incorporation into the USSR on August 3, 1940, the Kremlin attempted to integrate the Lithuanian economy and culture into the Soviet model, provoking both armed and passive resistance movements (q. v.). Soviet genocidal policies led to enormous population (q. v.) losses. After Boris Yeltsin's election to the presidency of the Russian Soviet Federative Socialist Republic (RSFSR) in June 1990, the Russian republic's government proved a useful counterweight to Soviet leader Mikhail Gorbachev's (q. v.) attempts to suppress the Lithuanian independence movement.

The establishment of the Russian Federation within the Commonwealth of Independent States has led to a new era in

Russian-Lithuanian relations. Since the formal independence of Belarus (q. v.), Russia no longer has an eastern border with Lithuania (although the Kaliningrad District of the Russian Federation borders the Republic on the west). A Russian-Lithuanian treaty led to the withdrawal of all Russian troops from Lithuania by September 1993. Economically, Lithuania remains dependent for much of her oil and natural gas on Russian supplies, although trade with Russia has decreased to less than half of Lithuania's foreign commerce as economic ties to the West have grown. Lithuania's stated desire to join NATO has led to vociferous Russian protests and even threats. For its part, the Lithuanian government has been unhappy with Moscow's reluctance to extradite officials and military personnel involved in the murders of Lithuanian civilians during the troubles of 1990-1991. However, the Lithuanian government's tolerant policy towards the small Russian minority (about 8.5 percent of the population), which has received easy terms for citizenship, has led to a much more positive relationship with Moscow than that of Latvia and Estonia. See NAZI-SOVIET PACT; PARTITIONS; PEOPLE'S DIET; PEOPLE'S GOVERNMENT; POPULATION AND DEMOGRAPHY; RESISTANCE MOVEMENTS; RUSSIFICATION; SĄJŪDIS.

RUSSIFICATION. Generally, the term used for the policy of suppressing indigenous cultures and imposing Russian culture. In Lithuania, Russification was official policy during the Tsarist period, especially the second half of the 19th century, and, in different form, during the Soviet periods of 1940-1941 and 1944-1990. Historically, resistance to Polonization (q. v.) and Russification (q. v.) provided the main focus of struggle for the Lithuanian national movement. During the first decades of Tsarist rule following theThird Partition (q. v.) of the Polish-Lithuanian Commonwealth (q. v.), the Russian government generally did not interfere with the religious, cultural and social structure of the Lithuanian Grand Duchy. This tolerant attitude began to change during the reign of Tsar Nicholas I (1825-1855) when a policy of

Official Nationality, which stressed autocracy, Orthodoxy and Russian values, was adopted. After the suppression of the insurrection of 1831 (q. v.), the government launched an attack on the Catholic Church and the Polish landowning nobility, the two forces it believed were inimical to Russian interests in Lithuania. Many churches, monasteries and schools, including the University of Vilnius, were closed and the lands of nobles who supported the insurrection were transferred to Russian officials. In 1840 the Lithuanian Statute (q. v.) was abrogated and Russian law introduced; the very name of Lithuania was formally eliminated and the country was now referred to as the Northwest Territory (Rus. *Severo-zapadnyi krai*). The Tsarist government proclaimed its intent to educate the youth of the land "in the Russian spirit."

This initial period of Russification, directed mainly at the Polish element, did not much affect Lithuanian culture, which actually experienced a renaissance during the 1840s and 1850s. A second and more intensive period of Russification followed the defeat of the insurrection of 1863 (q. v.) and its violent suppression by Governor-General M. N. Muravyev (q. v.). Initially, the Russian cultural officials known as the "Russifiers" (Rus. *obrusitely*), led by Ivan P. Kornilov (1811-1901), the curator of the Vilnius gubernia educational district, believed that by eliminating Polish and Catholic influence in Lithuania, the Lithuanian peasantry would become natural allies of Russia because of their inherent pro-Russian historic orientation (Rus. *russkoye nachalo*). The Russian press ban (q. v.) of 1864-1865 on Lithuanian publications in the Latin alphabet was initially intended to draw the Lithuanian national movement to the Russian side rather than destroy it. At the same time, the Russian government encouraged the settlement of thousands of Russian peasants, mainly Old Believer communities, in Lithuania. However, by the end of the 19th century, Russian authorities came to view the Lithuanian national movement and its intelligentsia as an anti-Tsarist and anti-Russian force; assimilationist policies now stressed linguistic Russification in the primary schools and attempts to halt the Lithuanian book-smuggling movement. The lifting of the press ban in 1904 and the Revolution of 1905 signified the failure of Tsarist Russification policy, which was also undermined by increasing skepticism about its effectiveness among Russian officialdom.

During the period of independence (1918-1940), Russian culture was of minor importance in Lithuania. The Soviet occupation of 1940 initiated a new period of Russification in Lithuania, which was especially marked after 1944. While Soviet national policy, in contrast to that of the Tsars, officially stressed the national cultural rights of the Lithuanian people, it also emphasized the preeminence of the Russian nation as an "elder brother" and stressed the importance of the Russian language. The latter was introduced as a compulsory subject from the early grades in all Soviet Lithuanian schools. In addition, official Russian-Lithuanian bilingualism was introduced into public life. The business of the large economic enterprises, and until 1988, the meetings of the Lithuanian Communist Party's (q. v.) Central Committee, as well as sessions of the Lithuanian Supreme Soviet, were conducted primarily in Russian. The mass immigration of at least a quarter million mostly ethnic Russian industrial workers into urban areas, especially Vilnius and Klaipėda, further promoted the Russification of the country. During the late 1950s and 1960s the use of Lithuanian became more prevalent in many public offices; however, pressure for the use of Russian continued, especially after the Tashkent Conference of 1975 which mandated more intensive Russian-language instruction in Soviet schools. In the history curriculum of Lithuanian schools and in academic scholarship, the progressive nature and benefits of Russian imperialism were stressed. In the late 1970s the government decreed that all doctoral dissertations in Soviet Lithuania, even those dealing with Lithuanian literature, were to be published in Russian. During the Brezhnev period (1964-1982), the Soviet government proclaimed the convergence (Rus. *sliyanie*) of the nations of the USSR into a single Soviet people as official long-term policy. The later Brezhnev years in particular witnessed an intensified campaign in favor of "internationalism," the code word for Russification.

The period of Gorbachev's perestroika (1985-1991) undermined Soviet Russification policy, as Russian cultural dominance became a publicly-debated issue and a source of national protest. The reestablishment of Lithuanian independence in 1990 ended compulsory bilingualism. The formerly omnipresent Cyrillic alphabet has largely disappeared from the country's streets and official buildings. The study of Russian is no longer required in Lithuanian-language schools; English and other Western languages have replaced Russian as the most popular foreign languages. History curricula have been revamped to reflect an emphasis on Lithuanian and world history rather than the Russian past. At the same time, the government has subsidized Russian-language schools and cultural institutions for the Russian minority, which in 1996 made up about 8.5 percent of Lithuania's population. See KRAŽIAI MASSACRE; MUSCOVY; RESISTANCE MOVEMENTS; RUSSIA.

- S -

SĄJŪDIS. Lithuanian national independence movement of the late 1980s and early 1990s. As a result of the more open political climate under Soviet leader Mikhail Gorbachev (q. v.), demands for reform and greater political autonomy acquired a public forum during the mid-1980s. On June 3, 1988, about 500 people, representing primarily the Lithuanian intelligentsia, gathered at the headquarters of the Lithuanian Academy of Sciences and agreed to form a 36-member Initiative Group for the Movement for Restructuring (Perestroika) in Lithuania, about half of whom were Party members. The initial stated purpose of the group was to encourage a program for reform (or perestroika) which was being obstructed by the conservative leadership of the Lithuanian Communist Party (q. v.). The group quickly articulated a program to end the privileges of the Party elite, the so-called *nomenklatura*; to make government accountable for its actions; to establish political and economic self-sufficiency for Lithuania; to broaden legal rights of the citizens; to halt the destruction of the environment; to save Lithuania's cultural heritage; and to provide an honest accounting of the "blank spots" in the country's history.

Influenced by the already strong popular front movements in Estonia and Latvia, the Initiative Group took action to make the movement a public force through mass demonstrations. The growing number of people around the group became popularly known in Lithuania and abroad as *Sąjūdis*, or simply, "the movement." At the same time, the Initiative Group began publishing *Sąjūdžio žinios* (Lith. News of Sąjūdis), the first independent periodical permitted by the Soviet authorities. The activists of the Initiative Group later formed the core of the executive council of Sąjūdis, including Vytautas Landsbergis (q. v.), Arvydas Juozaitis, and the poet, Sigitas Geda, among others.

On June 24, 1988 the Initiative Group sponsored a rally attended by tens of thousands of people to demand that the delegates leaving for the 19th Party Conference of the CPSU in Moscow represent Lithuanian interests. On July 9, 1988 about 100,000 people gathered at a rally organized by Sąjūdis, the largest political gathering in the country's history to that date. The prominent display of the prewar national tricolor flag and the speeches stressing national values indicated that Sąjūdis was now in the forefront of political change in Lithuania. On October 22-24, 1988 the nationally-televised founding congress of the Lithuanian Movement for Restructuring (Lith. *Lietuvos Persitvarkymo Sąjūdis*) took place in Vilnius and elected an executive council headed by Landsbergis. While the public platform of Sąjūdis did not yet demand outright independence for Lithuania, it formulated a program calling for a "juridical" Lithuanian state; economic autonomy; self-determination; social justice; establishing Lithuanian as the official language; equal rights and cultural autonomy for the national minorities; and close ties with the Lithuanian diaspora. Nevertheless, the leadership of Sąjūdis and the populace at large, including high-ranking Communists, commemorated Lithuanian Independence day for the first time since the war on February 16, 1989; afterwards, calls for Lithuania's outright independence became commonplace.

In the elections to the Soviet Union's Congress of People's Deputies in March 1989, Sąjūdis and Sąjūdis-supported candidates won an overwhelming majority. The participation of over a million

Baltic citizens in the human chain, stretching from Tallinn to Vilnius, to commemorate the 50th anniversary of the Molotov-Ribbentrop Pact (q. v.), earned Sąjūdis international attention as well as the enmity of the Soviet government. Sąjūdis now called for an independent Lithuanian state and organized massive demonstrations on the occasion of the highly publicized visit of Mikhail Gorbachev (q. v.) to Lithuania on January 11-13, 1990. On February 24, 1990, Sąjūdis, campaigning on an independence platform, won a majority in the elections to the Supreme Soviet of the Lithuanian SSR. On March 11, 1990 the Supreme Soviet, by a vote of 124-0, elected Vytautas Landsbergis chairman of the legislature and proclaimed the restoration of Lithuanian independence. Upon assuming Lithuania's presidency, Landsbergis resigned from the leadership of Sąjūdis, but remained an acknowledged force within the movement as well as its honorary chairman. Tensions within Sąjūdis between moderate and more militant nationalist elements resulted in the victory of the latter during the December 1991 congress of the movement in Vilnius. Much of the intelligentsia and the leadership of 1988-1989 abandoned the movement, and the emergence of political parties further reduced the membership and influence of Sąjūdis. See RESISTANCE MOVEMENTS.

ŠALKAUSKIS, STASYS (1886-1941). Lithuanian philosopher and academic, born in Ariogala on May 4, 1886. Šalkauskis graduated from the University of Moscow in 1911, where he studied philosophy and law. During World War I Šalkauskis continued his studies in philosophy at the University of Fribourg in Switzerland, writing his doctoral dissertation on the Russian philosopher Vladimir Solovyev. In 1922 he obtained a position at the Faculty of Theology and Philosophy of the University of Kaunas and in 1939 was appointed rector of the University. Šalkauskis was removed from his post after the Soviet occupation of June 1940. He died in Šiauliai on December 4, 1941.

Šalkauskis was arguably Lithuania's most influential philosopher of the interwar period and exerted great influence, particularly on Catholic intellectuals involved in the *Ateitis* (q. v.) movement. He was sharply critical of the Nationalist Union's (q. v.) political dictatorship under Antanas Smetona (q. v.). One of his basic notions was that Lithuania was in a unique position to act as a synthesizer of Western and Eastern cultures. His own ideas owed much to West European progressive Catholic thought, although he also espoused Thomistic principles. Šalkauskis was instrumental in fostering high standards of academic work and nurturing the growth of the country's Catholic intelligentsia. While his works were banned during the Soviet period, there has been renewed interest in his work since 1990.

SAMOGITIA (Lith. *Žemaitija*). Historically and ethnographically distinct region of western Lithuania. The Lithuanian term for the region, *Žemaitija*, literally means "Lowlands," and the people are called *žemaičiai*, or "Lowlanders." The Latinized form of the name, Samogitia, has come into wider use in English. Samogitia is bounded by the Latvian border to the north, the Baltic coast in the west, the Nemunas River in the south and the Nevėžis River in the east. Before the unification of the Lithuanian state in the 13th century, Samogitia was ruled as a separate principality. After the inclusion of Samogitia in the Lithuanian state, it played a key role in the wars against the Teutonic Knights (q. v.): the region constituted the territorial wedge between the Prussian and Livonian branches of the Order. Between 1345 and 1382, the Knights made some one hundred forays into Samogitia from Prussia and Livonia. In 1382 Jogaila (q. v.) gave up western Samogitia to the Order; then again, between 1398 and 1409, Grand Duke Vytautas (q. v.) was forced to cede most of Samogitia to the Knights. There were several large-scale Samogitian rebellions against the Order during 1401-1409. The Treaty of Melno in 1422 finally ended the Teutonic Knights' claims to Samogitia.

Within the Grand Duchy of Lithuania, Samogitia retained a degree of autonomy and was governed by an elder (Lith. *seniūnas*) elected by a diet of the local nobility. Serfdom was less entrenched here than in the rest of Lithuania and there were more freeholders.

During the pre-Christian period, a high proportion of Samogitia's population consisted of free men and nobles. Christianization and Polonization (q. v.) came later to Samogitia than to the rest of the Grand Duchy; by the early 19th century, this was the only region of the country where the Lithuanian language (q. v.) was still widely spoken outside the peasantry, primarily among the petty gentry and townspeople. During the first half of the 19th century, some members of the Samogitian gentry, such as Dionizas Poška (q. v.), Simonas Stanevičius (q. v.), and the historian Simonas Daukantas (q. v.), began to support the development of Lithuanian culture. Between the 16th and 19th centuries, most European maps showed Samogitia as a distinct entity within Lithuania. While Samogitia lost its separate administrative status in 1843, 19th-century ethnographers and scholars often treated the people and their distinctive dialect as separate from the Lithuanians. Periodically, separatist sentiments have emerged in Samogitia but, aside from the publication of a few periodicals in the Samogitian dialect and local ethnographic organizations, there has been no significant independence movement in modern times.

SAPIEHA (Lith. Sapiega). Lithuanian noble family and rivals of the powerful Radziwiłł (q. v.) and Pac clans, who played an important political role in the 16th and 17th centuries and also became one of the wealthiest landowning families of Poland in the 19th and 20th centuries. The most famous and powerful member of the family was **Leo Sapieha** (1557-1633), who studied classical languages at the University of Leipzig and, upon his return to Lithuania in 1581, was appointed royal secretary to King Stefan Batory (q. v.). He quickly rose to become chancellor, palatine of Vilnius and, finally, between 1625 and 1633, grand hetman of Lithuania. Sapieha became prominent for his insistence on safeguarding the autonomy of the Grand Duchy of Lithuania from Polish interference and as an able diplomat in dealings with Muscovy (q. v.). **Casimir Paul John Sapieha** (1637-1720), the grand hetman of Lithuania and palatine of Vilnius, and one of the richest men in Lithuanian history, was also known for his anti-Polish political attitude and opposition to King John Sobieski (q. v.).

SAULĖ or ŠIAULIAI, Battle of (1236). One of the most decisive early military clashes between the Lithuanians and the Germanic crusading orders. In February 1236 Pope Gregory IX issued a bull announcing a crusade against Lithuania. In September 1236 the Knights of the Sword organized a large expeditionary force of German knights and native auxiliaries from Latvia and Estonia. The crusading army was surprised by a defending Lithuanian force in marshes near a place called Saulė, which is thought to be near the present city of Šiauliai (q. v.). Little is known about the battle except that the master of the Livonian Order (q. v.) and many of his knights perished. Some historians consider that the battle was a sign of the increasing unity among the Lithuanian tribes against a common enemy and an important factor in furthering the unification of the Livonian (q. v.) Knights of the Sword with the Teutonic Order (q. v.) in Prussia.

ŠAULYS, JURGIS (1879-1948). Lithuanian statesman and diplomat, born in Tauragė district on April 23, 1879. After dismissal by Tsarist authorities from the Kaunas Theological Seminary in 1900, Šaulys joined the Lithuanian national movement. He became one of the founders of Lithuania's Democratic Party (q. v.) and an editor of *Varpas* (q. v.). He was elected to the Taryba (q. v.) and signed the 1918 declaration of Lithuanian independence. He spent most of the interwar period in the Lithuanian foreign service, developing a reputation as one of the country's most able diplomats. Šaulys was known for his liberal political philosophy and, as an expert on Polish affairs within the foreign ministry, was an influential advocate of a detente with Warsaw during the 1930s. He died in Lugano, Switzerland on September 18, 1948.

SERFDOM, or the personal bondage of the peasantry. In contrast to the decline of serfdom in Western Europe after the 14th century, in Eastern Europe the landowners expanded the demesne, which resulted in the strengthening of the *corvée* system of compulsory labor. During the 14th century the Lithuanian landed nobility employed the labor of slaves, usually war captives, and serfs who were descended from these slaves (Lith. *parobkai*). However, before the 15th century, the majority of the peasants in the ethnographically Lithuanian lands of the Grand Duchy were not yet serfs, but members of a large peasant community, the rural district (Lith. *valsčius*), which performed certain duties to the Grand Duke, but itself remained free. Gradually, the state transferred increasing power over the peasants to the landowners. Grand Duke Casimir's (q. v.) Privilege of 1447 gave authority over the peasants to their landlords and prohibited the escape of seignioral villagers to royal domains, beginning the process of tying the peasant permanently to the private landowners' estates. Eventually, most seignioral peasants lost all rights to leave their holdings in search of better conditions. Even on state lands the administrative functions formerly held by the peasant *valsčius* were abolished.

The Valakas or Volok (q. v.) Reforms begun in 1547 divided the peasantry into those who performed regular *corvée* labor (Lith. *lažas*) and formed a part of the estates' inventories, the true serfs; and those who paid money rent (Lith. *činšas*) and contributed a limited number of days of special labor, but were free to move to other estates or towns. By the 18th century this former category, the enserfed seignioral peasantry, constituted the majority of Lithuania's rural population. The very name for serfdom in Lithuanian, *baudžiava*, came to signify compulsory labor. One major reason for enserfdom were higher grain prices in Western Europe, which created a demand for East European grain, thus encouraging landowners to increase production on their estates by utilizing serf labor. Compulsory labor was not uniform in Lithuania, but it is estimated that in the 17th and 18th centuries the regular summer labor averaged about three days per week for an able-bodied peasant. During the later 18th century, estates increasingly assigned labor on the basis of household rather than on the area of a peasant's holding. In addition to the regular labor, there were numerous other seasonal and miscellaneous obligations, including intensive harvest work, construction labor, road repair and transportation duties.

Other feudal obligations included payments in kind and money, the *činšas*. Some peasants paid the *činšas* in place of the *corvée*, but the majority paid some money rent along with labor obligations. In addition to taxes to the state and Church, there were various fees for services, such as marriage licenses and hunting fees, as well as compulsory liquor monopoly purchases from the landowners' distilleries. Furthermore, the landowners and administrators of state lands called the economies (q. v.) had legal and administrative authority over the peasants. A lord could punish his serf by fine, imprisonment, mutilation, public flogging and, in rare cases, death. Officially, there were certain legal safeguards from excessive abuse, but these statutes were often disregarded.

Lithuania periodically experienced peasant revolts, such as the uprising of Samogitian peasants in 1418, the Merkinė uprising of 1483, and a number of outbreaks during the first half of the 16th century, especially in Samogitia (q. v.). The most famous of the peasant rebellions was the mass insurrection of 1769 which engulfed the large estates of the Šiauliai (q. v.) economy. Proposals to reform agrarian relations and abolish serfdom became more numerous among the gentry in the 18th and 19th centuries. Two of the early reformers were Pawel Brzostowski (1739-1827) and Ignatius Karp (1780-1809) who abolished labor obligations and emancipated thousands of peasants. The first widespread emancipation occurred in the Lithuanian-speaking lands of the Grand Duchy of Warsaw (in Suvalkija or Suwałki), where the peasants were emancipated without land in 1807. During the first half of the 19th century the Russian government initiated reforms intended to limit and regulate peasant obligations. Increasing agrarian unrest during the 1850s in Lithuania and throughout the Russian Empire persuaded the Tsarist government to consider the abolition of serfdom; much of the initiative for the emancipation of serfs in Russia came from the Lithuanian nobility. On February 19, 1861 Tsar Alexander II proclaimed his Emancipation Manifesto, mandating the abolition of serfdom after a two-year waiting period. The peasants were to receive title to their holdings through redemption payments scheduled over 49 years. The already emancipated Lithuanian peasants in Congress Poland (Suvalkija), received their holdings under the reform of 1864, which did not require redemption payments. While the emancipation made legal serfdom a thing of the past, it did not entirely end the landowners' exploitation of the peasantry who were still often forced to rent additional land from the nobility. The peasants were still subject to the military draft, excluded from significant government offices and not allowed to move without permission. Many of these restrictions were ended after the Revolution of 1905 (q. v.), but the last remnants of agrarian feudalism disappeared only after the Republic of Lithuania's Land Reform Bill of 1922, which parceled out most large estates. See AGRICULTURE.

SFORZA, BONA (1494-1557). Queen of Poland and Grand Duchess of Lithuania from 1518 to 1550, born in Milan on February 2, 1494. Bona was the daughter of the Duke of Milan and Bari, Giovanni Galeazzo Sforza; her mother Isabella was the daughter of Alfonzo II of Naples. Bona was known for her fine education and training in administration. In 1518 Bona was married in Cracow to Sigismund I, or the Old (q. v.). As Queen of Poland, she became renowned for her financial dealings during which she regained many royal estates and became one of the wealthiest rulers of the age. Bona was a driving force behind the Volok Reform (q. v.) begun in 1547, which radically transformed Lithuania's agrarian world. She also sponsored humanist learning at the royal court. Bona made great efforts to secure the throne for her son Sigismund Augustus (q. v.), born in 1520, but bitterly opposed his marriages to Elizabeth of Hapsburg and Barbara Radziwiłł (q. v.). Suspicion has lingered that Bona caused the deaths of both women, in 1545 and 1551 respectively. In 1556 Bona settled in Bari, Italy where she died on November 20, 1557, probably poisoned by her steward, Gian-Lorenzo Pappacoda.

ŠIAULIAI. Fourth largest city and important industrial center, located in northern Lithuania, pop. in 1995: 150,000. The first significant settlements here date to the eighth century; Šiauliai is mentioned in historical sources by the 14th century. The Battle of Saulė (Šiauliai) (q. v.) is thought to have taken place in the area in 1236. A parish was established in Šiauliai in 1445. Between the 16th and 18th centuries Šiauliai was the center of a large royal estate or economy (q. v.) governed by Count Tyzenhauz (q. v.) and, before the plague of 1708-1711, numbered over 1,000 inhabitants. In July 1769 the peasants of the Šiauliai economy rebelled against increases in labor obligations but were suppressed by Lithuanian, Courlandian and Russian troops. After the Third Partition (q. v.) of the Polish-Lithuanian Commonwealth, the city and its environs came under the rule of the Russian Count Platon Zubov. During the 19th century railroad connections and an increasing population led to industrial growth, mainly leather, tobacco and food-processing, as well as the founding of a number of schools. By 1914 the population stood at about 24,000. In addition to the plurality of Jews (nearly 45 percent), the town had about 30 percent ethnic Lithuanians, the highest such percentage of any urban center in Lithuania before the Great War. Most of the Jewish population of Šiauliai (known in Yiddish as Shavle), a fourth of the 1939 population of 31,600, was annihilated in 1944 during the liquidation of the city's ghetto. Heavy fighting during the Soviet capture of the city in July 1944 destroyed about 80 percent of Šiauliai. The city has grown considerably since the war with the construction of electronics, wood-processing, bicycle and other factories, and the development of public institutions, such as the Šiauliai Pedagogical Institute and a well-regarded theater.

SIERAKOWSKI (Lith. Sierakauskas), ZYGMUNT (1826-1863). Military officer and one of the leaders of the insurrection of 1863 (q. v.), born on May 17, 1826 in the Lutsk district of Volynia. Sierakowski studied at the University of St. Petersburg, where he befriended students from Lithuania, and then graduated from the Russian General Staff Academy in 1859. Between 1860 and 1862 he was sent to Western Europe with a Russian military mission where he became acquainted with such revolutionaries as Giuseppe Garibaldi and the Russian radical, Alexander Herzen. When the insurrection of 1863 erupted in Lithuania, Sierakowski defected from the Russian Army and accepted the Lithuanian rebels' offer to lead their military campaign. He hoped to secure the Baltic coast so that the insurgents could obtain foreign assistance. On April 27, 1863 Sierakowski was captured by the Russians during a battle near Biržai, brought to Vilnius and court-martialed. He was hanged on June 15, 1863 in Lukiškės Square in Vilnius; his wife, Apolonia Dalewska of Kėdainiai, was deported to Siberia.

SIGISMUND I, or SIGISMUND THE OLD (1467-1548). King of Poland (1507-1548) and Grand Duke of Lithuania (1506-1548), born in Cracow on January 1, 1467. Sigismund, the grandson of Jogaila (q. v.), was born to King Casimir (q. v.) and Elizabeth of Habsburg. In 1498 he traveled to Buda where his brother Władysław ruled as King of Bohemia and Hungary. From 1499 to 1506 Sigismund was the viceroy of Silesia. In October 1506, Sigismund journeyed to Vilnius to be crowned as Grand Duke of Lithuania, succeeding his brother Alexander (q. v.). In January 1507 Sigismund was crowned King of Poland in Cracow. In 1518 Sigismund married Bona Sforza (q. v.) of Milan and Bari. His reign was marked by three major wars with Muscovy during which Lithuania lost Smolensk (1514), one of the most important outposts between Moscow and Vilnius. In domestic affairs, Sigismund attempted to increase royal revenues but was forced to concede greater powers to the Polish diet, especially in the critical area of military finance; increasingly, the Polish-Lithuanian nobility preferred to rely on periodic levies for mercenaries. Just before Sigismund's death, his wife, Queen Bona, helped carry out the important agrarian transformation known as the Volok Reform (q. v.). Both Sigismund and Bona were generous patrons of the arts and thus encouraged the ideas of Renaissance humanism in Lithuania, which they visited frequently. While Sigismund officially disapproved of the Reformation and issued edicts protecting Catholicism, he displayed a politically prudent tolerance towards the spread of Protestantism. He died in Cracow on April 1, 1548.

SIGISMUND II, or SIGISMUND AUGUSTUS (1520-1572). Grand Duke of Lithuania (1544-1572) and King of Poland (1548-1572), born in Cracow on August 1, 1520. The only surviving son of Sigismund I (q. v.), or the Old, and Bona Sforza (q. v.), Sigismund Augustus was the last ruler of the Jagiellonian dynasty that traced its roots to the House of Gediminas (q. v.). During his youth Sigismund Augustus received the best education of any Lithuanian ruler to date and was reportedly fluent in Latin, German and Italian. Largely through the machinations of Queen Bona, the young Sigismund secured Lithuania's agreement to elect him Grand Duke. In 1543 Sigismund married Elizabeth of Hapsburg, the daughter of the future Holy Roman Emperor, Ferdinand I. In 1544 Sigismund Augustus came to Vilnius to govern Lithuania as his father's viceroy. He is credited with stimulating the city's trade and manufactories and encouraging Renaissance architecture, including the construction of an opulent palace for the Grand Duke, known as the Lower Castle, in the center of Vilnius. Sigismund Augustus was an enthusiast of Renaissance art and scholarship and played a decisive role in bringing Western European culture to Lithuania. In Vilnius Sigismund became friendly with the widow Barbara Radziwiłł (q. v.) whom he married in 1547 following the death of his wife Elizabeth. Upon the death of his father in 1548, Sigismund Augustus became King of Poland. His personal life was marked by drama and tragedy, especially the bitter conflicts with his mother, and the death of Barbara soon after her coronation as Queen of Poland in 1551. He married Catherine of Hapsburg in 1553 but the union was childless.

In foreign affairs, Sigismund Augustus was faced with a prolonged war in Livonia against Ivan IV (The Terrible) of Muscovy, until in 1561 much of the region was placed under Lithuanian control. However, he retained good relations with the Ottomans and Tatars. In domestic affairs, he continued the Volok

Reform (q. v.) and reformed the administration of the Grand Duchy by creating new palatinates, which were subdivided into districts. In 1566 the Grand Duke ratified the second Lithuanian Statute (q. v.). Like his father, Sigismund Augustus proved tolerant of religious diversity during the Reformation (q. v.). The major event of his reign was the ratification in 1569, after difficult negotiations, of the Union of Lublin (q. v.), which created the Polish-Lithuanian Commonwealth. Sigismund Augustus died on July 7, 1572 near Białystok.

SIGISMUND III, or SIGISMUND VASA (1566-1632). King of Poland and Grand Duke of Lithuania (1587-1632), King of Sweden (1594-1599), born on June 20, 1566 in Gripsholm, Sweden. He was the son of John Vasa, the Duke of Finland and Catherine, daughter of Sigismund I of Poland and Lithuania, who had been married in Vilnius in 1562. Sigismund III was thus the nephew of the last Jagiellonian ruler, Sigismund Augustus (q. v.). In 1568 John Vasa was crowned King of Sweden. In 1587, following the death of King Stefan Batory (q. v.), Sigismund was elected King of Poland and, with the support of the Lithuanians, was named Grand Duke after ratifying the third Lithuanian Statute (q. v.). After the death of his father John, Sigismund was crowned King of Sweden in Uppsala in 1594 but was deposed by the Swedish Diet, the Riksdag, in 1599, which then chose his uncle, Charles IX, as the new King. Sigismund was married twice: to Anne of Hapsburg in 1593, and then to her sister Constance in 1602.

Sigismund III's reign proved an especially turbulent time in the Commonwealth's foreign and domestic affairs. The King's insistence on pursuing his claim to the Swedish throne involved Lithuania in a destructive war with Charles IX and his successors in Livonia (q. v.), marking the beginning of Swedish domination in that region. During Muscovy's Time of Troubles (1598-1613), Sigismund also laid claim to the Muscovite throne, at first proposing his son Władysław as Tsar, but then attempting to seize Muscovy for himself. His refusal to accommodate Orthodoxy and his heavy-handedness aroused Russian resistance; thus, despite the brief occupation of Moscow by Polish-Lithuanian forces and Lithuania's recovery of Smolensk in 1611, Sigismund's Muscovite adventure was a failure in the long term. Domestically, the King's attempts to abolish the Diet's (q. v.) *liberum veto* and institute a hereditary monarchy provoked armed rebellion among the Polish-Lithuanian nobility. Sigismund also intensified religious conflict: raised as a Catholic, he vigorously attacked Protestantism. In 1596, fearing the political consequences of the establishment of the Muscovite patriarchate in 1589, he supported the conclusion of the Union of Brest (q. v.), which created the Greek Catholic, or Uniate Church, but proved divisive in Ukraine. In general, Sigismund failed to achieve most of his political goals. He died in Warsaw on April 30, 1632.

SIGISMUND (Lith. Žygimantas) KARIBUTAITIS (d. 1435). Lithuanian prince, son of Kaributas and grandson of Grand Duke Algirdas (q. v.). Sigismund is best known as the leader of a Lithuanian expeditionary force sent by his cousin, Grand Duke Vytautas (q. v.), to assist the Hussites of Bohemia against the Holy Roman Emperor, Sigismund I, in 1422. After declaring war against the Emperor, Sigismund Kaributaitis received the support of the Czech Taborite leader, Jan Žižka. In 1423 Sigismund was recalled from Bohemia, but in the following year, he returned there on his own, proclaimed himself a Hussite, and unsuccessfully attempted to claim the Bohemian throne. In 1434 Sigismund went to Livonia from where he supported Švitrigaila (q. v.) in the latter's civil war with Vytautas' brother and his namesake, Sigismund Kęstutaitis (q. v.). He was wounded in the Battle of Pabaiskas in 1435 and reportedly died in captivity.

SIGISMUND (Lith. Žygimantas) KĘSTUTAITIS (ca. 1365-1440). Grand Duke of Lithuania from 1432 to 1440, born about 1365 in Trakai, the son of Kęstutis (q. v.). Sigismund was a close ally of his older brother Vytautas (q. v.) during the civil strife that followed the death of their father in 1382, and reportedly spent much of that time as a hostage of either Jogaila (q. v.) or the Teutonic Knights (q. v.). After 1399 he was briefly the ruler of the principalities of Nowogródek (Bel. Novohrudok) and Starodub. Following Vytautas' death in 1430, and the seizure of power by Jogaila's brother Švitrigaila (q. v.) who was proclaimed Grand Duke, Sigismund was at first a supporter of the latter's struggle with Poland, but he was soon persuaded by the Polish nobility and Švitrigaila's Lithuanian enemies to switch sides. Sigismund overthrew Švitrigaila in 1432 and, with the support of Poland, sought to undermine Švitrigaila's support among the eastern, primarily Slavic and Orthodox, nobility of the Grand Duchy. In 1434 Sigismund issued an important decree, the so-called Privilege of Sigismund, granting equal rights to Lithuania's Orthodox nobility, due process to all gentry, and the transferring to the landowners dues that the peasants formerly owed the Grand Duke. Sigismund finally defeated the combined forces of the rebellious Švitrigaila and the Livonian Knights at the Battle of Pabaiskas, near Ukmergė, in 1435. After consolidating his rule, Sigismund schemed to break away from vassalage to Poland and even conspired with Holy Roman Emperor Albert II in an attempt to create an anti-Polish alliance. He also sought to roll back privileges granted the landowning nobility by strengthening the Grand Duke's power with the help of the lesser gentry. In 1440 Sigismund was assassinated in Trakai by a faction of the Lithuanian nobility who were opposed to his anti-Polish and centralizing policies.

SKIRGAILA (ca. 1353-1397). Lithuanian ruler of Kiev, son of Grand Duke Algirdas (q. v.) and a leading supporter of Jogaila's (q. v.) policies. While little is known of Skirgaila's early life, he is reported to have led a mission to the Teutonic Order and central Europe in 1379-1380 seeking support for his brother Jogaila's attempts to gain Lithuania's throne. After the death of Kęstutis (q. v) in 1382, Skirgaila ruled his uncle's lands in Trakai (q. v.). He was the leader of the Lithuanian delegation that traveled to Poland and Hungary to conduct the negotiations that resulted in the Treaty of Krėva (Pol. Krewo) (q. v.), which created the Polish-Lithuanian dynastic alliance. Afterwards, Skirgaila served as viceroy in Lithuania for his brother Jogaila, now King of Poland as Władysław II. However, Vytautas' (q. v.) agreement with Jogaila at Ostrovo in 1392 elevated the former to ruler of Lithuania; Skirgaila was demoted and sent to rule Kiev in 1394. Some historical sources indicate Skirgaila may have been poisoned there in 1397, reportedly because of his cruel and capricious ways.

SLADKEVIČIUS, VINCENTAS. Lithuania's first cardinal of the modern era, Archbishop of Kaunas and president of the Lithuanian bishops' conference from 1988 to 1993, born on August 20, 1920 in Kaišiadorys district. A graduate of the Kaunas Jesuit secondary school, he entered the city's seminary in 1939 and was ordained a priest in 1944. In 1958 Bishop Teofilius Matulionis of Kaišiadorys consecrated Sladkevičius and appointed him bishop without the approval of the Communist authorities. As a result, Sladkevičius was held under house arrest until 1982 when he was allowed to return to Kaišiadorys to assume his duties. In 1988 he became president of the Lithuanian bishops' conference and in June of that year was formally inducted into the college of cardinals in Rome. As Lithuania's leading prelate, Sladkevičius took an active role in the Lithuanian reform movement, especially during the period from 1988 to 1990, by advocating religious freedom and tolerance, criticizing the Soviet system and publicly proclaiming Lithuania's right to independence. In 1990 he was named Archbishop of Kaunas. In 1992 the new Archbishop of Vilnius, Audrius Bačkis, replaced Sladkevičius as president of the Lithuanian bishops' conference. See CATHOLIC CHURCH.

ŠLEŽEVIČIUS, ADOLFAS. Prime minister of Lithuania 1993-1996, and leader of the Lithuanian Democratic Labor Party (LDDP) (q. v.), born on February 2, 1948 in Šiauliai district. An economist by training, Šleževičius began his political career as deputy minister of the meat and dairy industry of the Lithuanian SSR between 1977 and 1981. From 1983 until 1989 he worked within the Central

Committee of the Lithuanian Communist Party (q. v.). During 1990-1991 Sleževičius was first deputy minister of agriculture. In 1991 Sleževičius headed a Lithuanian-Norwegian joint venture company and in 1992 was elected President of the Lithuanian Dairy Producers Association. In 1993 he was named chairman of the LDDP (q. v.). On March 9, 1993, President Algirdas Brazauskas (q. v.) appointed Sleževičius Prime Minister of Lithu-ania. During the fall of 1995 he was accused of a serious conflict of interest after withdrawing his personal funds only days before the government's closure of several major Lithuanian banks. After rejecting the President's calls for his resignation, Sleževičius was dismissed from office by the Seimas by a vote of 94-26. He was replaced by the new prime minister, Mindaugas Stankevičius (q. v.), on February 23, 1996.

SLEŽEVIČIUS, MYKOLAS (1882-1939). Lithuanian statesman, prime minister of Lithuania, 1918-1919 and in 1926, born in Raseiniai district on February 21, 1882. He studied law at the University of Odessa from 1902 to 1907, then returned to Lithuania where he joined the Lithuanian Democratic Party (q. v.). During World War I he served in Petrograd as an official of the Lithuanian Central Relief Committee. At the Lithuanian Conference in Petrograd in 1917, Sleževičius broke with some of the more radical socialists by insisting on immediate Lithuanian independence. After returning to Lithuania in 1918, Sleževičius headed the new republic's second cabinet from December 1918 to March 1919, and served again as prime minister and acting foreign minister from April to December, 1919, during the most critical months in the young republic's history. He was instrumental in organizing the fledgling Lithuanian Army and organizing resistance against successive Bolshevik, Bermondtist (q. v.) and Polish military attacks, and took the lead in negotiating Lithuania's de facto recognition in crucial talks with Poland and at the Paris Peace Conference. In 1920 Sleževičius was elected to Lithuania's Constituent Assembly (q. v.) and was a leader of the Peasant Populist Union (q. v.) in the Lithuanian parliament from 1920 to

1926; he was also chairman of the parliament's foreign affairs committee. When the coalition of Social Democrats and Populists won the elections of May 1926, Sleževičius headed the center-left government from June to December 1926, also serving as foreign minister and justice minister. The Sleževičius government's liberal domestic policies and its conclusion of a nonaggression pact with the Soviet Union in 1926 aroused right-wing and Christian Democratic opposition. On December 17, 1926 Sleževičius and President Kazys Grinius (q. v.) were removed from office by a military coup which placed the Nationalist leader, Antanas Smetona (q. v.), in power. Afterwards, Sleževičius served in the Kaunas city government and was one of the leaders of the Lithuanian Bar Association, and practiced law. He also led the Peasant Populist Union during the years of the Nationalist dictatorship. Sleževičius died in Kaunas on December 11, 1939. See TARYBA.

ŠLIŪPAS, JONAS (1861-1944). One of the liberal leaders of the Lithuanian national movement, born in Šiauliai district on February 23, 1861. In 1880-1883 he studied at the Universities of Moscow and St. Petersburg and then briefly at the University of Geneva. In 1883-1884 he edited *Aušra* (The Dawn) (q. v.) but left for the United States as a result of harassment by the German police. Šliūpas completed his medical studies at the University of Maryland in 1891 and worked as a doctor among the Lithuanian immigrants in Scranton, Shenandoah and the other communities of Pennsylvania's coal belt. He became one of the best-known leaders of the Lithuanian national movement in the United States as editor of a number of secular Lithuanian-language newspapers. Šliūpas was one of the first to urge Lithuanians to form separate ethnic Catholic parishes from the Poles, but is probably best remembered for his conflicts with the Catholic clergy because, as a publicist, he popularized secular liberalism and atheism. He became the acknowledged leader of the *laisvamaniai*, or Lithuanian free-thinkers. However, Šliūpas rejected the radical socialists' internationalist outlook, seeking to organize a liberal nationalist movement. Despite his materialist and atheist writings, Šliūpas befriended the Lithuanian Catholic leader, Rev. Antanas Burba (1854-1898), and was able to cooperate with those Catholic clergy who supported Lithuanian national causes. During World War I he was one of the major organizers of Lithuanian-American efforts to support Lithuania's independence. In 1921 Šliūpas returned to Lithuania where, in addition to teaching the history of medicine at the University of Kaunas, he continued to advocate the secularization of Lithuanian society and criticized the Nationalist authoritarian government. In 1933 he was elected mayor of the seaside resort of Palanga. Despite his atheist views in predominantly Roman Catholic Lithuania, Šliūpas was respected and honored for his pioneering efforts in fostering the Lithuanian national movement. Displaced by World War II, he died in Berlin on November 6, 1944. See NATIONALISM, LITHUANIAN.

SMETONA, ANTANAS (1874-1944). Lithuania's President, 1919-1920 and 1926-1940, leader of the country's Nationalist movement, born in Ukmergė district on August 10, 1874. While attending secondary school in Jelgava, Latvia, Smetona became involved in protests against Tsarist Russification policies. In 1902 he graduated from the University of St. Petersburg's Law School and then moved to Vilnius where he quickly became a prominent leader of the Lithuanian Democratic Party (q. v.), representing its more conservative wing. Smetona was elected to the presidium of the revolutionary Great Assembly of Vilnius (q. v.) in December 1905. He was editor of the weekly *Lietuvos Ūkininkas* (Lith. The Lithuanian Farmer) and was a prominent contributor to the first Lithuanian daily, *Vilniaus Žinios* (Lith. Vilnius News). Smetona left the Democratic Party in 1907 to establish a more conservative nationalist movement and, along with Juozas Tumas-Vaižgantas (q. v.), founded the periodical *Viltis* (Lith. Hope). Smetona provided a rallying point for Lithuanian intelligentsia opposed to Marxism's call for class struggle. After disputes with Catholic elements who were suspicious of Smetona's liberal secular views, in 1914-1915 he gathered, around the bi-weekly *Vairas* (Lith. The

Rudder), the core of what was to became Lithuania's Nationalist movement. During World War I Smetona gained prominence as the head of Lithuanian relief efforts in Vilnius.

In 1917 Lithuanian leaders persuaded the German occupation authorities to permit the establishment of the Lithuanian Council, the Taryba (q. v.), which elected Smetona as its chairman. Smetona favored accepting Berlin's demands for a Lithuanian state formally linked to Germany, but the majority of the Taryba rejected such a policy, leading to serious rifts within the Council and briefly forcing Smetona's resignation. However, Smetona was chosen chairman of the Taryba when it issued Lithuania's Declaration of Independence on February 16, 1918. Smetona left for Germany in December 1919 ostensibly to seek German assistance against the invading Red Army, provoking accusations that he was abandoning the country; this left Prime Minister Mykolas Sleževičius (q. v.) to cope with the crisis. Nevertheless, Smetona became the Republic's first President on April 4, 1919 and served until the convocation of the Constituent Assembly (q. v.) on June 19, 1920. Smetona's Nationalist movement failed to elect any deputies to Lithuania's parliaments between 1920 and 1926. He turned to journalism and became one of the government's most vocal critics. Smetona also taught Greek classics at the University of Kaunas and translated much of Plato into Lithuanian.

Smetona and two Nationalist colleagues won election to the Seimas in May 1926. On December 17, 1926 pro-Nationalist army officers, with the connivance of the Christian Democrats, overthrew the government of President Kazys Grinius (q. v.) and Sleževičius and chose Smetona President of Lithuania in a rump session of the Seimas. In April 1927 Smetona dissolved the parliament and dismissed the Christian Democrats from the government, initiating a Nationalist dictatorship. A new constitution (q. v.) of 1928 legitimized Smetona's rule and by September 1929 he had won his power struggle with his main rival among the Nationalists, the charismatic Prime Minister Augustinas Voldemaras (q. v.), replacing him with his brother-in-law, Juozas Tūbelis (q. v.). Smetona based his power on the Nationalist Union, the Army and a prosperous middle-class of farmers, business interests and professionals. While all political parties were banned outright in 1935, Smetona's regime reserved serious repression only for the political extremes: Communists and their allies on the left, domestic fascists and German Nazis on the right. Despite a personality cult which emphasized Smetona's role as the Leader of the Nation (Lith. *Tautos vadas*) and some superficial borrowings from Italian fascism, Smetona's authoritarian regime was neither totalitarian nor fascist. Smetona himself publicly condemned racism and anti-Semitism, while the government permitted considerable cultural, religious and ethnic diversity. During the 1930s Smetona's conservative leadership, especially on land reform and foreign affairs, came under increasing attack from younger Nationalist radicals. Others were dissatisfied with his aloof and cautious manner of rule, and even attacked him personally for having married into a family with allegedly Polish roots. Christian Democrat, Populist and other centrist leaders, as well as intellectuals like Stasys Šalkauskis (q. v.), criticized Smetona's repressive rule for creating a climate of political apathy and servility among the populace. During the international crises of 1939-1940 which threatened Lithuania's independence, Smetona reluctantly included opposition members in coalition governments.

In response to the Soviet ultimatum (q. v.) of June 14, 1940, Smetona advocated armed resistance, but when the majority of the cabinet demurred, he transferred his presidential powers to Prime Minister Antanas Merkys (q. v.) and, together with his family, escaped into Germany. He then traveled to Switzerland and Brazil, before arriving in the United States in March 1941, eventually settling in Cleveland. Smetona's public anti-Soviet statements led to problems with U. S. authorities and his attempts to create a government-in-exile failed. Smetona was killed in a fire in Cleveland on January 9, 1944. See NATIONALISM, LITHUANIAN; NATIONALIST UNION.

SNIEČKUS, ANTANAS (1903-1974). Long-time leader of the Lithuanian Communist Party (q. v.), born in Šakiai district, on January 10, 1903. Sniečkus was born into a well-to-do peasant family, but during his studies at the Lithuanian secondary school in Voronezh between 1915 and 1918, he began to participate in Marxist study circles. He returned to Lithuania and joined the LCP in 1920, beginning a long career in Lithuania's underground Communist movement. Sniečkus was arrested in 1921, but fled to Soviet Russia before his trial. He worked as a contributor to Lithuanian Communist youth periodicals in Smolensk between 1921 and 1925 and then studied economics for a year in Moscow, where he also worked in the Lithuanian section of the Comintern. Sniečkus returned to Lithuania in December 1926 and was coopted into the LCP's Central Committee; while in the underground, he edited the Party newspaper *Tiesa* (Lith. The Truth). He was sentenced to prison in 1930 but was sent to the USSR in 1933 in a prisoner exchange. He worked for the Comintern until 1936 when he again returned to Lithuania where he was appointed the LCP's First Secretary, serving another jail term in 1939-1940.

Sniečkus was released from prison in June 1940 following the Soviet occupation of Lithuania and was named Director of State Security in the People's Government (q. v.). He helped orchestrate the People's Diet (q. v.) vote for Lithuania's incorporation into the USSR after which he remained First Secretary of the LCP. From 1942 to 1944 Sniečkus was chief of staff of the Soviet partisans in German-occupied Lithuania. In addition to his leadership of the LCP, Sniečkus was a candidate member of the Soviet Communist Party's Central Committee from 1941 to 1952 and a full member of the CPSU Central Committee from 1952 to 1974. He was also a deputy to the USSR Supreme Soviet. While Sniečkus occupied no government post within Lithuania, he was the republic's most powerful politician and oversaw the enlargement and entrenchment of the LCP.

Sniečkus was in office longer than any other East Bloc party boss. The time he spent in Lithuanian prisons during the 1930s helped Sniečkus avoid Stalin's purges of the Lithuanian Communists in the USSR. Sniečkus' success in holding on to his position after 1940 can be credited to his tenacious loyalty to the Kremlin in suppressing any signs of national opposition to Soviet rule, as well as to his ability to anticipate political changes in

Moscow and deflect any challenges to his authority on the local level. For most Lithuanians of the postwar generation, he came to personalize the country's Sovietization. During Sniečkus' steward-ship, the postwar LCP acquired a majority of ethnic Lithuanians by the 1960s; thus, he was instrumental in shaping the Lithuanian nomenklatura. Sniečkus died in Druskininkai on January 22, 1974. See ANGARIETIS, ZIGMAS; KAPSUKAS, VINCAS.

SOBIESKI, JOHN (1629-1696). King of Poland and Grand Duke of Lithuania from 1674 to 1696, elected to the throne after the death of King Michael Wiśniowiecki (q. v.). His alliance with Louis XIV of France against Brandenburg Prussia in the 1670s proved only a slight advantage to the Commonwealth. Sobieski achieved fame when he gathered a Polish-Lithuanian army against the Ottoman Turks who were besieging Vienna. On September 12, 1683 the King led a combined relief force of 74,000 men, including the army of Charles of Lorraine, which attacked and routed Grand Vizier Kara Mustafa's Turkish troops. The Lithuanian army, led by Casimir John Sapieha, delayed its march and arrived in Austria only after the siege of Vienna had been broken; Sapieha then marched through Slovakia. Sobieski pursued and destroyed the Turks' rear guard near Esztergöm, opening the way for Hungary's liberation from the Ottomans. However, except for his fame as the savior of Europe, Sobieski proved unsuccessful in other areas. He failed to prevent Muscovy's control of Ukraine and his later anti-Turkish campaigns in Moldavia (Moldova) achieved only limited results. In domestic affairs, opposition from the Sapieha (q. v.) family and other Lithuanian nobles hindered the King's exercise of power. Sobieski died in Warsaw on April 17, 1696.

SOCIAL DEMOCRATIC PARTY, LITHUANIAN (Lith. *Lietuvos Socialdemokratų partija*). Lithuanian social democracy developed from Marxist roots in the early 1880s when Lithuanian socialists established the first links with George Plekhanov's Liberation of Labor (Rus. *Osvobozhdenie Truda*). In 1887 the Belarusan officer

Evgeni Sponti (1866-1931) established a study group of people interested in Russian populism and Marxism. There was no organized Marxist movement in the country until the early 1890s, when it gained strength primarily among Jewish workers in Vilnius, whose earliest leaders were Arkadi Kremer (1865-1935) and the skilled propagandist Samuel Gozhansky (1867-1943), and who were assisted by the noted Russian Marxist Julius Martov (1873-1923). The Vilnius-based General Jewish Workers' Union, commonly known as the Bund (q. v.), was founded in 1897 and, at the time, was one of the best organized social democratic groups in the Russian Empire. Among Gentile workers, socialism first developed among the Polish proletariat in Lithuanian towns; during the 1890s a chapter of the Polish Socialist Party (Pol. *Polska Partja Socjalistyczna*) was established in Vilnius. The Russian Social Democratic Labor Party, founded in Minsk in 1898, became active in Lithuania in 1901. At the turn of the century, Rosa Luxemburg's Social Democracy of the Kingdom of Poland and Lithuania (Pol. *Socjaldemokracja Królestwa Polskiego i Litwy*) briefly had some support among Lithuania's workers.

Socialist ideas developed slowly among ethnic Lithuanians who comprised a minority among the country's urban work force. Nevertheless, in 1896 Andrius Domaševičius (1865-1935) and Alfonsas Moravskis (1868-1941) founded the Lithuanian Social Democratic Party (LSDP) whose platform was influenced by the Erfurt Program of the German Social Democrats. The LSDP was broken up by the Tsarist police in 1897-1899 and was reorganized in 1900-1902. The LSDP published the first significant Lithuanian-language socialist periodicals, most notably *Darbininkų balsas* (Lith. The Workers' Voice) in 1902. Increasingly, the influx of ethnic Lithuanians into the party raised the national issue and led to an eventual split within the Lithuanian socialist movement between those supporting Lithuania's independence and opposing Polish predominance, and elements with a more internationalist outlook, the most radical of whom joined the Bolsheviks. By the time of the emergence of independent Lithuania in 1918, the Social Democrats had become a major force in the country's politics, achieving their greatest success in the May 1926 elections when the

Party won 15 of 85 seats in the Seimas and was able to form a left-of-center coalition government together with the Peasant Populists (q. v.) and the minority parties. After the military coup of December 1926, the LSDP was harassed by Smetona's Nationalist regime, but it is estimated that it had over 3,000 members and nearly 20,000 supporters within the youth movement and among trade unions between the wars. In June 1940 the LSDP was suppressed and its members joined other parties in resistance to both the Soviet and Nazi occupations. After 1944 the LSDP remained active in exile, led by Steponas Kairys (q. v.) and Kipras Bielinis (1883-1965). The Lithuanian Social Democratic Alliance in the United States published a popular Lithuanian-language weekly, *Keleivis* (Lith. The Traveler), in Boston between 1905 and 1979. After the restoration of Lithuania's independence in 1990, the LSDP has reappeared in Lithuania; the party won seven seats in the parliamentary elections of October 1992 and twelve seats in the elections of October-November 1996.

SOVIET-LITHUANIAN MUTUAL ASSISTANCE TREATY OF 1939. The Soviet-German Treaty of Friendship of September 28, 1939, or the second Nazi-Soviet (q. v.) agreement, contained a secret protocol amending the Molotov-Ribbentrop Pact of August 23 and assigning Lithuania to the Soviet sphere of influence in exchange for Lublin and part of the province of Warsaw. On October 3, 1939 Lithuanian Foreign Minister Juozas Urbšys (q. v.) was called to Moscow to begin negotiations with Stalin and Molotov. According to Urbšys' memoirs published in 1988, Stalin laid out a map of Lithuania on the table and bluntly told the visitors that Germany had agreed to transfer their country to the USSR's sphere of influence. Stalin and Molotov then proposed that Lithuania and the USSR sign two treaties: the first, dealing with the transfer of Vilnius to Lithuania (which had been foreseen in the Nazi-Soviet treaty of August 23) and a second, establishing a mutual assistance pact providing for Soviet military bases in Lithuania. On October 7 a larger Lithuanian delegation arrived in Moscow, which included Urbšys, the Commander of the Armed

Forces, Gen. Stasys Raštikis (q. v.), Deputy Prime Minister Kazys Bizauskas, and several experts. The Lithuanians carried proposals for a mutual assistance pact without the stationing of Soviet troops in Lithuania during peacetime. Despite Lithuanian objections, the prospect of the return of Vilnius, as well as overt threats from the Kremlin, persuaded Lithuania to sign the Treaty on the Transfer of Vilnius and on Soviet-Lithuanian Mutual Assistance on October 10, 1939. Stalin combined the treaties concerning Vilnius and the mutual assistance pact into a single treaty, which gave the appearance that the return of Vilnius was a reward for the acceptance of Red Army bases, an impression Lithuania had been anxious to avoid.

Article 1 of the Treaty proclaimed the transfer of Soviet-occupied Vilnius to Lithuania, since it had been "unlawfully wrested from Lithuania by Poland," and reaffirmed the Soviet-Lithuanian treaties of 1920 (q. v.) and 1926 as the basis for relations between the two countries. The mutual assistance provisions (Articles 2-9) mandated common defense in case of a military threat to Lithuania or the USSR "by any European power," and, most important, envisioned the stationing of Soviet land and air forces of "strictly limited strength" in Lithuania. The pact, it was emphasized, was not to "affect in any way the sovereign rights of the contracting parties, in particular their State organizations, economic and social system...," and was to respect "the principle of non-intervention in internal affairs generally." The Treaty, which was to run for fifteen years with a possible ten-year extension, was accompanied by a secret protocol, detailing the deployment and number of Soviet troops (20,000), as well as a map outlining that part of Vilnius territory that was being transferred to Lithuania. The area assigned to Lithuania was only a fraction of the territory granted to the Republic of Lithuania in the 1920 peace treaty with Soviet Russia; however, it did include the greater part of the Lithuanian-speaking area in the Vilnius region. A recent archival draft of a "secret protocol" to the 1939 Soviet-Lithuanian pact has been discovered, which allowed Lithuania to exercise neutrality, with the Kremlin's permission, if the USSR became involved in a war with a "third party." A similar condition had been extended to Estonia and Latvia as well. These protocols proved useful in enabling the Baltic States to avoid the humiliating and painful step of actively supporting the Soviet campaign against Finland in 1939-1940.

Public reaction to the Lithuanian-Soviet Mutual Assistance Pact differed significantly from that in Latvia and Estonia. Despite their basic antipathy to Communism, the establishment of Soviet bases in October 1939 was accompanied by the fulfillment of a cherished national dream for most Lithuanians: the return of Vilnius. Nevertheless, the Soviet-Lithuanian mutual assistance pact curtailed Lithuania's freedom of action in foreign affairs and proved a prelude to the Soviet occupation of the country in June 1940. See RUSSIA; VILNIUS QUESTION.

SOVIET-LITHUANIAN PEACE TREATY OF JULY 12, 1920. This treaty, signed in Moscow, formally renounced Russian sovereignty over Lithuania. The defeat of the Bolsheviks in Lithuania in 1919 led Lenin's government to propose armistice negotiations with the Lithuanian government on September 11, 1919, thus granting de facto recognition to the Republic of Lithuania. The peace negotiations commenced on May 7, 1920 and proceeded quickly since, at the time, Soviet Russia was hard-pressed in her war with Poland. In the first article of the treaty signed on July 12, 1920, Soviet Russia acknowledged Lithuania's independence "in perpetuity." Article 2 of the treaty assigned Lithuania generous boundaries, which encompassed parts of what is now Belarus and Poland, including such historic sites as Grodno (q. v.) and Augustów. These regions were once part of the Grand Duchy but ethnic Lithuanians there were now a minority. Article 4 committed both countries not to allow the formation of armed groups on its territory hostile to the other state. Another important provision of the 1920 treaty was Russia's promise to cancel the Lithuanian portion of any state debts incurred during the Tsarist period, to return cultural treasures, such as the Lithuanian Metrica (q. v.), and to compensate war damages. The 1920 borders envisioned in the treaty were never realized and the compensation provisions were only partially fulfilled. Nevertheless, the Lithuanians emphasized the Soviet-Lithuanian Peace Treaty of 1920 as the legal basis for defining Lithuania's relations with the USSR, particularly since the treaty was never abrogated. Some Lithuanians still claim the 1920 territorial provisions as the legitimate borders of the Lithuanian state, although the Republic of Lithuania has repeatedly stressed the inviolability of present borders. See RUSSIA.

STANEVIČIUS, SIMONAS (1799-1848). Lithuanian writer, born in Raseiniai district on October 26, 1799. Stanevičius, a member of the Samogitian petty gentry, graduated from the University of Vilnius in 1826 after which he obtained a position with the Plater family as their chief librarian. While Stanevičius wrote on a number of topics, including history, religion and linguistics, he is most remembered for his work in folklore. In 1829 he published *Dainos žemaičių* (Lith. Samogitian Songs), a highly regarded collection of Lithuanian folk songs. Stanevičius also produced fiction in the form of popular fables, exhorting his readers to love the Lithuanian language and take pride in the country's past. Along with Dionizas Poška (q. v.), Stanevičius is considered one of the most talented figures in the so-called "Samogitian movement" which fostered a renaissance in Lithuanian studies during the first half of the 19th century. He died on March 10, 1848 near Švėkšna.

STANISŁAW I, or STANISŁAW LESZCZYŃSKI (1677-1766). King of Poland and Grand Duke of Lithuania, 1706-1709, and in 1733, born on October 20, 1677 in Lviv, Ukraine. In 1699 Leszczyński was appointed palatine of Poznań. In 1704 the Polish-Lithuanian Electoral Diet deposed Augustus II (q. v.) and chose Leszczyński, Sweden's favorite candidate, as King. In 1706 Augustus agreed to Stanisław's election in the Treaty of Altranstädt with Sweden, but Leszczyński reigned only briefly. As a result of Russia's victory over Sweden in 1709, Augustus II was able to regain the throne with Russian help. Leszczyński fled to France, where he achieved some influence when his daughter Marie married King Louis XV; as a result, he acquired the Duchy of Lorraine and Bar. After the death of Augustus II in 1733, the Commonwealth's Diet once again elected Leszczyński King but within weeks the Russian government forced him to abdicate in favor of Augustus III (q. v.). Thus, during his brief reigns, Stanisław I was never able to really rule Poland-Lithuania. Returning to France, Leszczyński devoted himself to arts and letters at his ducal court in Lunéville, which gained fame as one of the centers of the Polish Enlightenment. Leszczyński himself published numerous works on politics and philosophy; in some of his writings, he criticized the systemic weaknesses of the Polish-Lithuanian state. He was the author of one of the most influential Polish reformist polemics of the time, *Głos wolny wolność ubezpieczający* (Pol. A Free Voice Insuring Freedom), published in 1749. Leszczyński died in France on February 23, 1766.

STANKEVIČIUS, LAURYNAS MINDAUGAS. Lithuania's prime minister during most of 1996, born on August 10, 1935 in Aukštadvaris. During the 1950s and 1960s Stankevičius worked as a senior economist at the Ministry of Finance of the Lithuanian SSR. From 1969 to 1978 he was deputy to Soviet Lithuania's representative in Moscow, and from 1978 to 1993 was deputy assistant to the chairman of the State Labor Committee. During 1993-1994 Stankevičius was minister of social security, and from 1994 to 1996 headed the Ministry for the Reform of Public Administration. Stankevičius was appointed head of government on February 23, 1996, after the dismissal of premier Adolfas Šleževičius (q. v.) on charges of corruption. It was widely anticipated that Stankevičius would essentially head a caretaker government as the country prepared for the October 1996 parliamentary elections. After the Conservative victory in these elections, he was indeed replaced by Gediminas Vagnorius (q. v.).

STOLYPIN, PETER (1862-1911). Russian prime minister 1906-1911, and Tsarist official in Lithuania 1887-1902, born in Dresden on April 14, 1862. The Stolypin family had extensive landholdings in Kalnaberžė and elsewhere in Kaunas gubernia. Stolypin held various administrative posts in Kaunas; between 1887 and 1902 he served as the chairman of the gubernia's nobility. In 1902 he was appointed governor of Grodno (q. v.) and then served as governor of Saratov, 1903-1906. In 1906 Stolypin was appointed Prime Minister by Tsar Nicholas II and became known for an ambitious agrarian reform, known as the Stolypin Reform, as well as the violent suppression of revolutionary activities in the Russian Empire, including the Lithuanian national movement, during the period 1905-1907. Stolypin was a strong supporter of Russification (q. v.) policies. He was assassinated in Kiev on September 18, 1911. See REVOLUTION OF 1905.

STULGINSKIS, ALEKSANDRAS (1885-1969). President of Lithuania from 1920 to 1926 and one of the country's prominent Catholic politicians, born in Tauragė district on February 26, 1885. Stulginskis attended the Kaunas Theological Seminary and then studied theology at the University of Innsbruck, but later enrolled in agricultural studies. He worked as an agronomist in Lithuania during World War I. He became one of the leaders of the Christian Democratic (q. v.) movement and in 1917 was elected to the Lithuanian Council, the Taryba (q. v.). Stulginskis was one of the signatories of the February 16, 1918 declaration of independence. Soon after, Stulginskis came to head the Lithuanian Farmers' Union (Lith. *Lietuvos Ūkininkų Sąjunga*), which together with the Christian Democrats, formed the basis for the Catholic Bloc in Lithuanian politics during the 1920s. In 1918 and 1919 Stulginskis served as deputy prime minister, as well as minister of the interior and minister of agriculture. In 1920 he was elected speaker of Lithuania's Constituent Assembly (q. v.) and, in effect, became head of state and the country's President. Under the terms of the Constitution of 1922 (q. v.), Stulginskis was formally chosen President by the Seimas and served in the office until June 1926 when he was replaced by Kazys Grinius (q. v.). As president, Stulginskis was remembered as a serious and hard-working executive who eschewed political ambition. After the coup of December 1926, he was again chosen speaker of the Seimas until its dissolution in April 1927. Thereafter, he retired to his farm in western Lithuania, occasionally appearing in public and stressing the need for democracy. In July 1941 Stulginskis and his wife were deported to eastern Siberia by the Soviets; they were allowed to return to Lithuania in 1956. Stulginskis died in Kaunas on September 22, 1969.

SUPREME COMMITTEE FOR THE LIBERATION OF LITHU-ANIA (Lith. *Vyriausias Lietuvos Išlaisvinimo Komitetas*, or VLIK). Lithuanian resistance group which claimed leadership in the efforts to restore Lithuania's independence. During the Nazi (q. v.) occupation the major non-Communist resistance and political groups sought ways to establish a body to coordinate efforts to restore Lithuania's independence. The sense of urgency was heightened by the perception of impending Allied victory and the approach of the Soviet Army in the wake of the German retreat. The Supreme Committee, which was to become better-known by its Lithuanian acronym, VLIK, was founded on November 25, 1943 and represented the Christian Democrats (q. v), the Peasant Populists (q. v.), Social Democrats (q. v.), the Nationalist Union (q. v.), the Freedom Fighters' Alliance and other groups. VLIK made its first public appeal on February 16, 1944, disseminated by the underground press, proclaiming the restoration of Lithuania's independence as its primary goal and declaring itself the legitimate provisional authority in Lithuania until a coalition government could be established; the group's head in 1944-1945 was the Social Democratic leader, Steponas Kairys (q. v.). In the spring of 1944 the Gestapo arrested VLIK's courier to Sweden, penetrated the resistance network and arrested nine of its leading members. In expectation of the return of the Soviet Army to Lithuania, VLIK appointed a group to work in the West where virtually all of its activity took place after 1945. Between 1945 and 1955, while

VLIK was headquartered in the American Zone of occupied Germany, it was led by Msgr. Mykolas Krupavičius (q. v.). In 1955 the headquarters of VLIK were transferred to New York. VLIK was initially the most active émigré political coalition seeking to restore Lithuania's independence, but its influence was undercut by persistent feuding between the constituent political factions and its often uneasy relationship with Lithuanian diplomatic representatives still accredited in Western countries. Moreover, after the 1960s other organizations, such as the Lithuanian Community (Lith. *Bendruomenė*) gained an increasing role among the postwar émigrés. VLIK was formally disbanded after the restoration of Lithuania's independence in 1990; its longtime leader, Dr. Kazys Bobelis, was elected to the Seimas in 1992 and headed the parliament's foreign affairs committee. See RESISTANCE MOVEMENTS.

SUVALKIJA (Pol. Suwałki). Region of southwestern Lithuania, located to the south and west of the Nemunas River. The region is often referred to in Lithuanian as Užnemunė, or literally, the Trans-Nemunas territory, as well as Sūduva, or the land of the Sudovians. Agricultural settlements appeared relatively late in southwestern Lithuania. Until the 13th century, Suvalkija was inhabited by the Sudovians (Lith. *sūduviai*), also known as the Yotvingians (Lith. *jotvingiai*) (q. v.), a Baltic tribe who spoke a dialect close to Old Prussian and who were, by the 14th century, either exterminated by the Teutonic Order (q. v.) or assimilated by Lithuanians. Most of the region reverted to wilderness which served as a buffer between the warring crusaders and Lithuanians. In the 15th century Lithuanian peasants increasingly penetrated Suvalkija from the north, while Slavic, predominantly Polish, settlers moved in from the south into the Augustów lake region. Towns and crown estates, later known as economies (q. v.) (Lith. *ekonomija*) were established in Suvalkija after the Volok Reform (q. v.) of the mid-16th century. The final partition of Poland-Lithuania placed Suvalkija under Prussian rule between 1795 and 1807 when it became part of the Duchy of Warsaw, one of Napoleon's protectorates. After 1815

Suvalkija came under the Kingdom of Poland, whose autonomy within the Russian Empire was restricted after 1831 and virtually abolished after the insurrection of 1863 (q. v.). Suvalkija was part of Augustów province until 1867 when it was included in the smaller Suwałki gubernia, with the town of Suwałki as its largest town and capital. The Russian imperial census of 1897 found that Lithuanians formed 52 percent of the population of Suwałki gubernia; during the 19th century the Czarna Hańcza River, which runs through Suwałki city, was the approximate ethnic dividing line between the Lithuanian and Polish populations. Since 1920 the region has been divided between Lithuania (independent and Soviet) and Poland. There are currently at least 10,000 ethnic Lithuanians living on the Polish side of the border, primarily around the towns of Puńsk and Sejny. The eastern edges of Lithuanian Suvalkija are inhabited by people of the *dzūkai* dialect (see DZŪKIJA), while the main part of the region belongs to the *suvalkiečiai*, or Suvalkian, dialect. The latter group are often stereotyped by other Lithuanians as industrious and thrifty to a fault.

Southwestern Lithuania played a crucial role in the development of the modern Lithuanian nation. The preponderance of royal estates in the region and the abolition of serfdom in 1807 led to better economic conditions for Suvalkija's peasantry compared to other regions of the country. During the late 19th century the majority of Lithuania's intelligentsia came from this region, most of them graduates of the Marijampolė (q. v.) secondary school and children of Suvalkija's prosperous peasantry, who formed the economic backbone of the Lithuanian national movement. The Lithuanian dialect of northern Suvalkija, that of the *kapsai*, became the basis for the creation of the modern Lithuanian literary language (q. v.) developed at the turn of the century, which is now the official language of the country.

SUWAŁKI DEMARCATION AGREEMENT. Polish-Lithuanian armistice agreement of October 7, 1920. After the capture of Vilnius by the Polish Army in April 1919, there were continuous clashes between Polish and Lithuanian forces, despite a number of armistice and demarcation agreements. The Red Army counter-attack of the summer of 1920 forced a Polish retreat from eastern and southern Lithuania. The Soviet Russian-Lithuanian Peace Treaty of July 12, 1920 (q. v.) transferred Vilnius to Lithuania; Lithuanian forces entered the city on August 26, 1920. In September 1920 Lithuanian and Polish delegations met in Suwałki to negotiate a demarcation agreement that would prevent future Lithuanian-Polish clashes. On October 7, 1920 the two sides signed an agreement to end the military conflict, exchange prisoners, and most important, draw a temporary line of demarcation to separate the two forces. The agreement left Vilnius in Lithuanian hands.

Almost immediately after the signing of the Suwałki agreement, a Polish force under the command of General Lucjan Żeligowski (q. v.) attacked the Lithuanian Army and on October 9 seized Vilnius. A renewed Polish-Lithuanian conflict broke out, which was ended by an armistice brokered by the League of Nations on November 29, 1920. At the time, Żeligowski's force was described as a mutinous army of renegade local troops, but Polish leader Marshal Józef Piłsudski (q. v.) later admitted that the general was acting under secret orders from Warsaw. Among Lithuanians, the violation of the Suwałki accord was a bitter turning point in relations with Poland. A copy of the violated Suwałki Agreement was placed on prominent display in the Military Museum in Kaunas, confirming the stereotype of the treacherous Pole among Lithuanians. More than any other event, the violation of the agreement and the Żeligowski invasion mobilized Lithuanian opinion around the Vilnius Question (q. v.); this irredentism dominated the political life of independent Lithuania between the wars and was the fundamental cause of Polish-Lithuanian conflict in the 20th century. See PIŁSUDSKI, JÓZEF; POLAND; VILNIUS QUESTION.

ŠVITRIGAILA. Grand Duke of Lithuania from 1432 to 1435. He was the youngest son of Grand Duke Algirdas (q. v.) and his second wife Juliana. Very little is known of Švitrigaila's early life. He is first mentioned as a signatory of the Treaty of Dubysa with the Teutonic Knights (q. v.) in 1382. In 1386 he was baptized in Cracow as Bolesław, although Švitrigaila is rarely mentioned by his Christian name. After the death of his mother Juliana, he became prince of Vitebsk, but was removed from that position by his cousin Vytautas (q. v.) when the latter came to power in Lithuania. Švitrigaila became a perennial pretender to the Lithuanian throne, dissatisfied with the lands that he was given to rule in western Podolia and Novgorod Seversk. At different times, Švitrigaila allied himself to the Teutonic Knights and the Muscovite Grand Duke Vasilii against Vytautas, who finally imprisoned Švitrigaila between 1409 and 1418. Švitrigaila escaped, but in 1419, after unsuccessful attempts to gain support in Hungary and at the Church Council in Constance, he made peace with Vytautas and was given to rule Lithuanian principalities in the Slavic eastern part of the Grand Duchy. Upon Vytautas' death in 1430, Švitrigaila was chosen Grand Duke. His election provoked a war with Poland over the issues of the Lithuanian throne and the Polish-Lithuanian territorial dispute in Volynia and Podolia. Švitrigaila fell out with Vytautas' younger brother Sigismund Kęstutaitis (q. v.) who overthrew Švitrigaila in 1432 with Polish support. Sigismund's coup provoked a costly civil war as Švitrigaila sought allies among Lithuania's eastern princes and the Livonian (q. v.) branch of the Teutonic Order. Švitrigaila's forces suffered a decisive defeat at Pabaiskas in 1435, although he continued a fruitless struggle against Sigismund in the Grand Duchy's south and east, which he controlled until 1437. After 1440 Švitrigaila ruled in Lutsk, seeking to assert Lithuanian authority in Volynia and Podolia. He died in Lutsk on February 10, 1452.

Švitrigaila was one of the most controversial and contentious rulers of medieval Lithuania and his career illustrated the fragile nature of the Polish-Lithuanian dynastic alliance of 1386. His opposition to union with Poland earned him the enmity of the Polish nobility and their Lithuanian supporters who accused him of favoring Russian Orthodoxy. At the same time, this gained him the reputation among Lithuanians as a kind of early patriot. In his attempts to strengthen the unity of the Lithuanian state, Švitrigaila tried repeatedly but unsuccessfully to unite the Catholic and Orthodox Churches in the Grand Duchy.

- T -

TARGOWICA, CONFEDERATION OF. One of the confederations (q. v.) of Polish-Lithuanian nobility established in 1792. Following the first partition of the Polish-Lithuanian Commonwealth in 1772, a reinvigorated reform movement sought to save the remainder of the state from foreign, especially Russian, interference. The culmination of the movement was the Four-Year Diet of 1788-1792 which adopted the Constitution of May 3, 1791 (q. v.) based on liberal, Enlightenment principles. Seeking to preserve Russian influence in the Commonwealth, Empress Catherine II encouraged the formation of an alliance of conservative Polish-Lithuanian gentry led by magnates who feared the loss of their feudal privileges and were opposed to a centralized state. Some of the Catholic hierarchy, mindful of the secularizing policies of the French Revolution, were also wary of the reform movement. In Lithuania, some of the nobility were unhappy with the provisions of the May 3 Constitution abolishing the Grand Duchy. After concluding her war with Turkey in 1792, the Russian Empress invited prominent Polish-Lithuanian conservatives to St. Petersburg in April 1792 where they ratified the requisite act of confederation. The actual document was proclaimed in the Ukrainian town of Targowica (in Ukrainian, Targovitsa), then part of the Kingdom of Poland, on May 14, 1792 under the leadership of Stanisław Potocki, Seweryn Rzewuski and other prominent landowners. Another similar act of confederation was proclaimed in Vilnius on June 25; here the most prominent leaders of the Targowica movement were Ignacy Massalski (q. v.), the Bishop of Vilnius, and the Kossakowski family. Later in 1792 the Polish and Lithuanian confederates united into a single movement, supported by the Russian Army which then invaded the Commonwealth.

King Stanisław II Poniatowski (q. v.) had initially sided with the reformers, but the royal force of 36,000 men proved no match for the superior Russian military. In August 1792 Poniatowski went over to the Confederation. A new Commonwealth Diet which reversed the reforms was convened in Grodno (q. v.) from June to October 1793; it was surrounded by Russian troops who arrested any deputies opposed to Catherine. The Confederation of Targowica initiated the death throes of the Polish-Lithuanian Commonwealth, inasmuch as the movement led directly to the second partition (q. v.) of the state between Russia and Prussia. The leaders of the Targowica movement, which provoked the desperate uprising of 1794 led by Thaddeus Kościuszko (q. v.), were widely viewed as traitors and some of them, like Massalski, were executed during the anti-Russian insurrection. In turn, the revolutionary events of 1794-1795 led to the final partition of the Polish-Lithuanian state and its disappearance from the map of Europe. See CONFEDERATIONS.

TARYBA (1917-1920). Name for the Lithuanian council which declared Lithuanian independence on February 16, 1918. In September 1917, seeking to neutralize growing anti-German sentiment in Lithuania and fearing the spread of revolution, the German military authorities permitted the convocation of a Lithuanian conference in Vilnius. Rather than become an advisory body to the German authorities, the four-day conference (September 18-22) set as its ultimate goal the establishment of an independent Lithuanian state, albeit with unspecified ties to Germany. On September 21 the conference elected the Council of Lithuania (Lith. *Lietuvos Taryba*), known as the Taryba, and headed by Antanas Smetona, which asserted that it was the legitimate representative of the people of Lithuania. In order to negotiate the structure of Lithuanian statehood, members of the Taryba traveled to Germany to consult with the Kaiser's government in October 1917 and attended conferences of Lithuanian representatives in Bern, Switzerland, and Stockholm in October and November. On December 11, 1917, under pressure from German authorities who were eager to use the Lithuanian card in their peace negotiations with the Bolsheviks at Brest-Litovsk, the Taryba declared Lithuania's conditional independence with "eternal" military and economic ties to Germany. In January 1918 several members of the Taryba, led by Steponas Kairys (q. v.), left the body in protest against what they considered the council's pro-German stance. By February 1918 the split in the Taryba was healed by a compromise, and on February 16, 1918 a new Declaration of Independence was signed without any reference to ties with Germany. The date of this declaration, announcing the restoration of the Lithuanian state based on a democratic political structure and the "severing of all ties that had bound Lithuania to any other nation in the past," has since been celebrated as Lithuania's national independence day. The new state was to have its capital in Vilnius, but the precise form of government was to be decided by a Constituent Assembly elected through universal suffrage. The Germans rejected the February 16 declaration, but on March 23, 1918, the Kaiser's government recognized Lithuania's independence on the basis of the Taryba's December 11 declaration. On July 11, 1918 the Taryba formally took the title of the Lithuanian State Council (Lith. *Lietuvos Valstybės Taryba*).

During 1918 the Taryba sought to neutralize Berlin's plans to make Lithuania a German protectorate. During the summer of 1918 the Council invited Prince William of Urach to assume a Lithuanian throne as King Mindaugas II, again provoking a walkout by leftist Taryba members. The plans for a monarchy became irrelevant upon Germany's defeat; on October 28, 1918 the Taryba created a three-man presidium to head the Lithuanian state, including Antanas Smetona, the Rev. Justinas Staugaitis (1866-1943) and Jurgis Šaulys (q. v.), which led to the creation of independent Lithuania's first government headed by Prime Minister Augustinas Voldemaras (q. v.) on November 11, 1918. In January 1919 the Taryba left Vilnius in the wake of the Bolshevik advance and transferred to Kaunas. In April 1919 the Council elected Smetona Lithuania's first president and it continued to operate as a kind of ad hoc parliament, helping create the foundations for the new Lithuanian state and seeking foreign recognition. The Taryba formally ended its existence with the convocation of Lithuania's Constituent Assembly (q. v.) on May 15, 1920.

TATARS, in Lithuania. The Tatars, sometimes incorrectly termed Mongols, emerged as a distinct Islamic people speaking a Turkic language during the 13th and 14th centuries when they began establishing powerful khanates in the eastern and southeastern regions of European Russia, exacting tribute from local Christian princes. A complex and ambiguous relationship developed between the Tatars and Lithuanians between the 13th and 16th centuries. The Lithuanian rulers came into contact with the Tatars during Lithuania's expansion into Russia; in 1254-1255 Mindaugas (q. v.) clashed with the Tatars over the Russian lands east of Lithuania. The Tatar military leader Burundai of the Golden Horde, the most powerful of the Tatar states, is known to have invaded Lithuania sometime in 1258-1260 and again, during the reign of Traidenis (q. v.). In later times, the Tatars were occasional allies of the Lithuanians against the Livonian and Prussian crusading orders as well as against the Muscovites. Beginning with the reign of Gediminas (q. v.), the Grand Duchy came into conflict with the Golden Horde over Ukraine. Some chronicles report that about 1360 Grand Duke Algirdas (q. v.) achieved an important victory over the Tatars at the Battle of Blue Waters (Rus. Sinye Vody), but there are few reliable sources on Lithuanian-Tatar relations until the late 14th century.

Grand Duke Vytautas (q. v.) attempted to exploit civil discord within the Golden Horde. In 1399 he launched an ambitious expedition of combined Lithuanian and Teutonic Knight forces against the Tatars in an attempt to place his protegé, Tamerlane's enemy Tokhtamysh, on the khan's throne and thus make the Golden Horde a Lithuanian vassal state. However, Vytautas' army was virtually annihilated by the Tatars at the decisive Battle of Vorksla: chronicles report that the Grand Duke himself barely escaped capture. In 1410 a Tatar detachment joined the Polish-Lithuanian force at the Battle of Grunwald (q. v.) against the Teutonic Knights. During the later 15th and 16th centuries

Lithuania continued to intervene in the Tatar states. After the disintegration of the Golden Horde, the Crimean khanate became an object of Lithuanian-Muscovite-Ottoman rivalry as each side sought the support of the Crimean Tatars. Eventually, the Ottomans gained decisive influence in the Crimea, while the Muscovites conquered the khanates of Kazan and Astrakhan in the mid-16th century. After these events, the Tatar role in Lithuanian policy diminished.

A number of Tatars, mainly soldiers and nobles who fled the civil wars of the Golden Horde, settled in the Lithuanian Grand Duchy during the 15th and 16th centuries. The majority were given the status of free people and, although their rights were somewhat restricted by the Lithuanian Statute (q. v.) of 1566, they served in separate detachments in the Grand Duchy's army. Among other Tatars, the Lithuanian branch came to be viewed as a distinct ethnic subunit of the Tatar nation. Small communities of Lithuanian Tatars have survived into the 20th century. During the interwar period there were three Muslim Tatar communities, including one in Kaunas, where a new mosque was constructed in 1930. In eastern Lithuania, the Tatar community was estimated at nearly 8,000 before World War II. The best-known settlement there is the Village of Forty Tatars, located near Vilnius. Most Lithuanian Tatars have linguistically assimilated into their surrounding Polish and Lithuanian communities; however, in recent years, the Lithuanian Tatar Association has become more active and has received government support in attempting to preserve the Tatars' unique cultural heritage.

TEUTONIC KNIGHTS. German crusading order which played a pivotal role in medieval Lithuanian history. The origins of the Teutonic Order reach back to the Third Crusade with the establishment of the Order of the Hospital of St. Mary of the Germans of Jerusalem in 1190. In 1198 the Order was reformed as a military organization whose elite was made up largely of knights, mostly friars, drawn from the German nobility; since then it has usually been referred to as the Teutonic Order. The Order was headed by a Master (later the Grand Master) elected by the Knights; it grew remarkably after the election of Master Herman of Salza in 1210. Much of the Teutonic Order transfered to Hungary where King Andrew enlisted their help against the pagan Cumans; but the Hungarians came to fear the power of the Knights and expelled them in 1225. The Holy Land remained the Order's concern until the fall of Acre in 1289.

In 1226 the Polish prince, Conrad of Mazovia, appealed to the Teutonic Knights for assistance against the Prussians (q. v.) and the first Knights arrived in the Baltic in 1230. The Teutonic Order acquired a charter from Holy Roman Emperor Frederick II, the Golden Bull of Rimini, granting the Grand Master the status of a prince of the Holy Roman Empire as well as title to the lands conquered during the crusade. Between 1230 and 1273 the Teutonic Knights, known among the Baltic tribes as the Knights of the Cross (Lith. *kryžiuočiai*), managed to conquer the Prussian tribes and, thus, laid the basis for the eventual Germanization of the region. In 1237, following the Lithuanian defeat of the Livonian Order (q. v.), or the Knights of the Sword, at the Battle of Saulė (Šiauliai) (q. v.), the Livonian crusaders joined the Teutonic Order as its Livonian branch. By the mid-13th century, the reconstituted Order became increasingly involved in war with the Lithuanians and Yotvingians (q. v.). Samogitia (q. v.), which geographically separated the territory of the Prussian and Livonian branches of the Order, became the main battleground. During the 14th century, the Knights began the practice of periodically augmenting their forces through appeals for assistance from knights in Western Europe, who joined the crusades attracted by the possibilities for exercising chivalry, while others were motivated by religious salvation and plunder. (One such knight is described in Chaucer's *Canterbury Tales*).

The power of the Teutonic Order, as well as the conflict with the Lithuanians, reached their peak during the 14th century, especially under the able and energetic Grand Master Winrich von Kniprode, who ruled from 1351 to 1382. Lithuania's interregnum and civil strife that followed the death of Algirdas (q. v.) in 1377 greatly facilitated the Knights' campaigns. After the Treaty of

Dubysa in 1382 in which Jogaila (q. v.) transferred most of Samogitia to the Order, the Knights' state for a time came to include virtually all of the eastern Baltic, extending from the Oder River to the Gulf of Finland. Kniprode also successfully transformed the Teutonic Order's domains into an economic power by fostering foreign trade: six Prussian towns, including Gdańsk and Königsberg, joined the Hanseatic League. However, Lithuania's dynastic alliance with Poland in 1386 and the Grand Duchy's subsequent acceptance of Roman Catholicism initiated the decline of the Order. Determined to regain Samogitia from the Order, Jogaila and Vytautas (q. v.) launched a war against the Knights in 1409 which culminated in the decisive Battle of Grunwald (q. v.) in July 1410. The Peace of Toruń in 1411 left Samogitia to Lithuania until the death of Vytautas, but in 1422 the Treaty of Melno established the Lithuanian-Prussian border for the next 500 years. The unsuccessful intervention of the Livonian Knights in the civil war between Švitrigaila (q. v.) and Sigismund Kęstutaitis (q. v.) in 1435 is generally considered the last serious military foray of the Teutonic Knights in Lithuania.

During the 15th century, the Teutonic Knights faced increasing opposition from Prussian towns, dissatisfied with the Order's political and economic dominance. The Thirteen Years' War (1453-1466) between the Order and the Prussian towns supported by the Poles, ended with the loss of considerable territory, including Gdańsk, to Poland, and the submission of the Grand Master as vassal to the Polish King on the territory that remained part of the Order. The gradual secularization of the governing institutions of the Order was finalized in 1525 with Grand Master Albert Hohenzollern's conversion to Lutheranism and his accession as the secular Duke of Prussia, albeit in vassalage to the King of Poland. Remnants of the Teutonic Knights survived on their German lands in Württemberg until their temporary suspension by Napoleon in 1809. In the 19th century the Order was an extension of the House of Hapsburg. During the 20th century, the Order provided priests for Germans in Italy, Slovenia and other states with small German communities. Revised statutes for the organization in 1929 transformed the Knights into a purely religious order under its original 1190 title and still including, as ceremonial dress, the white robe with a black cross on the left shoulder. See LIVONIA; PRUSSIA.

TILSIT (Lith. Tilžė, Rus. Sovetsk). Prussian border town on the left bank of the Nemunas River, now part of the Kaliningrad Oblast of the Russian Federation, pop. in 1995: 45,000. The city originated as a fortress of the Teutonic Knights (q. v.) in the 13th century. A town was built after the Treaty of Melno in 1422 and received a municipal charter in 1552. Tilsit became an important gateway to Lithuania and, later, the garrison town of the Lithuanian Dragoon Regiment of the Prussian Army. On June 25, 1807 Napoleon and Tsar Alexander I met on a raft near Tilsit to negotiate their peace treaty, providing for a Russian alliance with France against Great Britain. On the eve of World War II the town had nearly 60,000 inhabitants, most of whom fled or were killed during the Soviet attack into East Prussia in 1945. In 1946 Tilsit was renamed Sovetsk; most of its inhabitants are postwar ethnic Russian settlers.

Since the Reformation, Tilsit had been an important Lithuanian cultural center in Prussia and was the site of the first periodical in the Lithuanian language, *Nusidavimai apie Evangelijos Prasi-platinimą tarp Žydu ir Pagonių* (Lith. Stories about the Spread of the Gospel among Jews and Pagans), published between 1832 and 1914. Tilsit served as the main publishing center and transit point for Lithuanian-language publications, which were smuggled into Russian Lithuania during the Tsarist press ban (q. v.) of 1864-1904. During the early 20th century Tilsit was the center of Lithuanian Lutheran cultural life in East Prussia: the headquarters of the National Council of Prussian Lithuania were located here as was the residence of the philosopher and writer Vilius Storasta Vydūnas (q. v.). Lithuanian cultural activities in Tilsit were violently suppressed after the Nazis came to power in 1933. See PRUSSIA.

TRADE. Archeological evidence indicates that in prehistoric times the peoples of the Baltic littoral had extensive commercial ties both with their neighbors and distant lands. Evidence of the flourishing Baltic amber (q. v.) trade was found in the remains of one of the oldest known shipwrecks, dating back to ca. 1400 B. C., discovered in 1987 near Ulu Burun on Turkey's Mediterranean coast. Extensive archeological finds of Roman coins reveal that Baltic trade ties with the outside world continued during the classical period with links to the Danubian and Rhineland provinces of the Roman Empire. During the early medieval period the focus of trade shifted to the Scandinavian region. The discovery of 9th and 10th century Arabic coins also shows that trade ties had developed with the Near East. During the 13th century, largely as a result of the conquests of the Teutonic Knights (q. v.), German merchants became increasingly active in the eastern Baltic region. Lithuanians maintained particularly close ties with Riga, exporting furs, wax and other forest products in return for salt, iron and manufactured goods from Western Europe. A number of commercial treaties between Lithuanian rulers, such as Mindaugas (q. v.) and Gediminas (q. v.) have survived. During the 15th century Grand Duke Vytautas (q. v.) encouraged commerce between Kaunas and the Prussian centers of Gdańsk (Ger. Danzig) and Königsberg (Rus. Kaliningrad) (q. v.). Vilnius became the center of a lively trade between Western Europe and the Russian lands, including those bordering on the Black Sea. Between the 16th and 18th centuries West European demand for agricultural products stimulated Lithuanian export of grain and flax, primarily through Gdańsk and Riga. The destructive conflict with Muscovy (q. v.) and the Great Northern War (q. v.) of the early 18th centuries depressed Lithuanian trade, which experienced only a partial recovery, primarily due to grain exports, in the late 18th century. During Tsarist rule (1795-1915) Lithuanian grain and flax were exported mainly through Riga, while lumber was floated down the Nemunas River for shipment through Klaipėda; by the end of the 19th century, Lithuanian dairy products gained an increasing share of Russia's international trade. Since 1861 the expansion of the railroad system greatly facilitated exports.

Despite initial problems because of the need to reorient Lithuania's industry (q. v.) and trade following independence from Russia, foreign trade became a critical component of the country's economy during the 1918-1940 period. Foodstuffs, flax and live animals were the major exports. By the late 1930s Lithuania was the sixth leading exporter of butter in the world: in 1938 Lithuania shipped over 48,000,000 *litai* worth of butter, or 21 percent of total exports. Until the Nazi trade embargo of the 1930s, which grew out of Lithuania's conflict with Berlin over Klaipėda (q. v.) Territory, Germany had absorbed over half of Lithuanian exports; as a result of the embargo, Britain replaced Germany as Lithuania's leading trade partner after 1933. Commerce with the Soviet Union made up less than 10 percent of Lithuania's volume of trade between the wars. Industrial products, consumer goods such as automobiles and radios, and raw materials, especially coal and iron, made up the lion's share of Lithuanian imports between 1918 and 1940. In order to facilitate trade, the Lithuanian government made major improvements to the port of Klaipėda and expanded the country's merchant marine on the eve of Soviet occupation in 1940. During the 1918-1939 period Lithuania also gained earnings on transit of goods to and from the Soviet Union, although this was hampered by the German trade embargo of the 1930s; transit shipments slowed to a trickle after the outbreak of World War II.

The Soviet occupation and annexation of Lithuania in 1940 resulted in the nationalization of the Lithuanian economy, while the entire decade before 1950, characterized by war, Nazi occupation and the postwar guerilla resistance (q. v.) to Soviet rule, makes it impossible to speak of trade in the normal sense. The intense industrialization of Lithuania during the Soviet period of 1950-1990 resulted in the integration of the country's economy into the industrial, energy and communications system of the USSR. In as much as all foreign trade was controlled by Moscow, it is difficult to ascertain how much of Lithuania's total production was exported abroad, or how much was imported from foreign countries, primarily East Bloc European states. After the restoration of Lithuania's independence in March 1990, the country experienced considerable economic difficulties as the Soviet government embargoed vital supplies and raw materials to Lithuanian industry. During the mid-1990s Lithuania still depended on Russian supplies of petroleum and natural gas to fuel its industry. However, since Russian energy costs have practically reached world-wide market levels, and the country has one of the largest oil refineries in northern Europe at the town of Mažeikiai, the government planned to considerably reduce its reliance on Russian energy sources by constructing an oil terminal north of Klaipėda. In 1992 three-fourths of Lithuanian exports, estimated at 8.7 billion *litai*, were still directed to former Soviet states, primarily Russia, Latvia and Belarus. However, by the mid-1990s about half of trade went to Western countries, mainly Germany, and it is expected that this trend will continue in the future. (For current economic statistics, see "Introduction: The Government and Economy," pp. 3-4.) See AGRICULTURE; INDUSTRY.

TRAIDENIS. Grand Duke of Lithuania from ca. 1269 to 1282. Traidenis was one of the more prominent Lithuanian rulers between the death of King Mindaugas (q. v.) in 1263 and the accession of Grand Duke Gediminas (q. v.) in 1316. It is not entirely clear under what circumstances Traidenis came to power. The Livonian Chronicle mentions Kernavė as "the land of King Traidenis," although other sources indicate he may have resided primarily in what was to later become Vilnius (q. v.). Traidenis devoted most of his efforts to unifying the Lithuanian tribes against the incursions of the Teutonic Knights (q. v.) and encouraging other Baltic peoples, such as the Semigallians, Yotvingians (q. v.) and Prussians to resist the Order. He also continued Lithuania's expansion into the Slavic lands by acquiring the lands known as Black Rus', presently part of Belarus, for the Grand Duchy. Generally, Traidenis is credited with continuing the process of Lithuania's unification and with laying the foundations of the Lithuanian state, which was further consolidated by his successors.

TRAKAI. Town located in a lake region 23 km. southwest of Vilnius, pop. in 1995: 7,000, historically significant as the residence of medieval Lithuanian rulers who often lived there even after the establishment of Vilnius as the country's capital in 1322. Trakai gained fame as the island castle of Grand Duke Kęstutis (q. v.) and his son Vytautas (q. v.) and as a principality that occupied most of central Lithuania. An early 15th century account of the town and castle were provided by the Burgundian traveler Ghillebert de Lannoy. In the early 16th century, Trakai lost importance as a political and military center, especially after the construction of the royal residence in Vilnius during the time of Sigismund Augustus (q. v.). The town and castle were substantially destroyed during the Muscovite invasion of 1655-1666. Trakai was part of Poland between 1920 and 1939. In 1951 restoration of the island castle was begun and much of the former ducal residence has now been rebuilt, serving as a site for historical exhibits and artistic performances. The island castle of Trakai and its picturesque environs are visited by hundreds of thousands of domestic and foreign tourists every year. Trakai is also home to one of the last surviving communities of Lithuanian Karaim (q. v.), also known as Karaites, a people of Turkic language related to the Tatars but practicing a form of Judaism.

TRENIOTA (d. 1264). Grand Duke of Lithuania in 1263-1264, following the death of King Mindaugas (q. v.). One of the Samogitian notables, Treniota became a rival and opponent of Mindaugas, probably because of the latter's baptism and attempts to seek peace with the Teutonic Knights. Some scholars consider him the leader of the pagan opposition to the King. Treniota was involved in the assassination of Mindaugas in 1263, but his rule over Lithuania was brief as he himself was killed in 1264.

TŪBELIS, JUOZAS (1882-1939). Lithuania's prime minister from 1927 to 1938, born in Rokiškis district on April 18, 1882. Trained as an agronomist, he was Lithuania's first minister of agriculture in

1918-1919. Between 1920 and 1926 Tūbelis was a successful businessman involved in founding and directing some of Lithuania's largest companies owned by ethnic Lithuanians, such as the food concern, Maistas, and the dairy cooperative, Pienocentras. As a member of the Nationalist Union (q. v.), the brother-in-law and confidant of President Antanas Smetona (q. v.), he proved a compliant head of government. Tūbelis followed a conservative fiscal policy at home and was credited with maintaining a stable currency. He resigned in March 1938, following the crisis precipitated by the Polish ultimatum (q. v.) of that year. Tūbelis died in Kaunas on September 30, 1939.

TUMAS-VAIŽGANTAS, JUOZAS (1869-1933). Lithuanian writer and publicist, born in Rokiškis district on September 8, 1869. Tumas was educated at the Daugavpils secondary school where he became interested in literature. In 1888 he entered the Kaunas Theological Seminary and, after his ordination in 1893, worked in a number of parishes, often in trouble with Lithuania's Polonized hierarchy who were critical of Tumas' nationalist activities. Between 1896 and 1902, Tumas was the editor of *Tėvynės Sargas* (Lith. Guardian of the Fatherland), an illegal Catholic monthly, which became the core of the Lithuanian Christian Democratic Party (q. v.). During this time he became widely known as a fiction writer and publicist under the pen-name of Vaižgantas. After the Revolution of 1905 Tumas-Vaižgantas became increasingly involved in politics; he gained respect for his tolerance of diversity, which earned him the good will of a wide spectrum of Lithuanian political leaders. During the 1920s, in addition to his pastoral duties, Tumas-Vaižgantas taught Lithuanian literature at the University of Kaunas. He died in Kaunas on April 29, 1933; his funeral was attended by thousands of mourners.

Tumas-Vaižgantas is one of Lithuania's most popular and admired prose writers, unrivaled in his description of the Lithuanian village of the second half of the 19th century during the period of the national revival. In his novel, *Pragiedruliai* (Lith. Sunrays), Tumas-Vaižgantas painted a broad canvas of the social and economic transformation of Lithuania's rural world during the press ban (q. v.) period, providing colorful portraits of Lithuanian peasants, Jews and the Polonized gentry. Two other highly regarded works were the short story about a family tragedy during the Great War, *Rimai ir Nerimai* (Lith. The Rimas and Nerimas Families), which came out in 1915, and *Dėdės ir dėdienės* (Lith. Uncles and Aunts), a novel describing Lithuanian society at the turn of the century, published in 1920. See LITERATURE.

TYSZKIEWICZ (Lith. Tiškevičius). Prominent Lithuanian noble family of Ukrainian descent, who were particularly influential in the 17th century, but also produced some notable leaders in modern times. **George Tyszkiewicz** (1596-1656) was bishop of Samogitia (q. v.) and Vilnius (q. v.), known primarily as an energetic reformer of Catholic liturgy and monastic life. He was also the author of some early Lithuanian-language hymns and prayers. **Eustach Tyszkiewicz** (1814-1873) was one of the pioneers of Lithuanian archeology (q. v.), known for his initial explorations of barrow graves in the Vilnius and Minsk regions, publishing the first serious studies in Lithuanian archeology in 1850. He and his brother **Constantine Tyszkiewicz** (1806-1868) amassed a large collection of archeological finds. While most of the Tyszkiewicz family were culturally Polish, **Alexander Tyszkiewicz** (1866-1945), a landowner from Kretinga, became a prominent supporter of the Lithuanian national movement, leading protests against the Tsarist press ban (q. v.). **Alfred Tyszkiewicz** (1882-1930) assisted the Lithuanian delegation at the Paris Peace Conference in 1919 and was appointed Lithuanian minister to Great Britain (1920-1921).

TYZENHAUZ (Lith. Tyzenhauzas), ANTONI (1733-1785). Lithuanian count, statesman, and the crown treasurer of the Grand Duchy of Lithuania between 1765 and 1780. A close friend of King Stanisław August Poniatowski (q. v.), he was appointed administrator of Lithuania's royal estates or economies (q. v.) in 1765. Count Tyzenhauz attempted to transform the Grand Duchy's extensive crown economies into large and efficient state manorial farms through a series of economic reforms. He introduced the latest agricultural technology, organized the peasants' compulsive labor efficiently and dramatically increased the incomes of the state lands. Tyzenhauz utilized serf labor for numerous public projects, such as roads and bridges, which were intended to facilitate the expansion of a network of manufacturing enterprises employing compulsory labor. The largest of these industrial centers was Grodno (q. v.), which employed over 3,000 workers, including foreign specialists. Supported by King Stanisław, Tyzenhauz became the most powerful man in Lithuania by the late 1770s. However, despite Tyzenhauz's introduction of public schooling and health measures on the state lands, his reliance on new labor obligations to the villagers provoked resistance among royal peasants, some of whom were well-to-do rent payers who had been free of labor duties for generations. The most dramatic outbreak was the Šiauliai (q. v.) peasants' revolt of 1769. In addition to social unrest, business losses from his industrial works and political opposition from Lithuania's magnates led to Tyzenhauz's dismissal from public office on charges of corruption in 1780. He died in Warsaw on March 30, 1785. See AGRICULTURE; SERFDOM.

- U -

ULTIMATUMS OF 1938-1940. A period of foreign policy crises in Lithuania's relations with her three large neighbors, Poland, Germany and the Soviet Union, between 1938 and 1940. The ultimatums by the three powers undermined the international security, sovereignty and territorial integrity of the interwar Republic of Lithuania. Some Lithuanian historians have referred to these years as the "period of the three ultimatums."

The Polish Ultimatum of March 17, 1938. The immediate cause of the confrontation was a border incident on March 11, 1938, which resulted in the death of Polish soldier Stanisław Serafin. The Polish government, concerned about its deteriorating international position in view of German moves against Austria and Czechoslovakia, decided to utilize the incident to settle its conflict with Lithuania. On March 14 Lithuania's envoy to Estonia, Bronius Dailidė, proposed an immediate meeting of Polish and Lithuanian representatives to deal with the incident and to discuss procedures for eliminating future misunderstandings at the border. The Lithuanian minister in Paris, Petras Klimas (q. v.), was instructed to contact the Poles and arrange discussions concerning the establishment of diplomatic relations with Poland. Despite attempts to dampen the crisis, on March 17 the Polish mission in Estonia delivered Warsaw's ultimatum to Dailidė in Tallinn. The note stated that Lithuania's proposals suggesting talks were unacceptable and went on to demand "the immediate establishment of diplomatic relations without any...conditions." Diplomats in Kaunas and Warsaw were to be accredited no later than March 31; the Lithuanians were given only 48 hours to respond. Poland's ultimatum concluded with the threat that, in the event of a negative response, the Polish government would "guarantee the true interests of the state by its own means." At the same time, anti-Lithuanian public demonstrations in Poland escalated, while Nazi Germany adopted an openly hostile attitude to Lithuania. On March 19 the Lithuanian cabinet met to discuss the Polish demands. Foreign Minister Stasys Lozoraitis (q. v.) advised the government to accept the Polish ultimatum in its entirety, while the commander of the army, Gen. Stasys Raštikis (q. v.), explained that Lithuania could not face Poland alone. As a result, on March 19, Dailidė delivered Lithuania's acceptance of the Polish ultimatum. However, the attitudes created by decades of hostility changed only gradually. On March 31 Poland and Lithuania exchanged diplomats, but neither Franciszek Charwat nor Kazys Škirpa (q. v.), the Polish and Lithuanian envoys respectively, were known for their commitment to Polish-Lithuanian understanding. The new Lithuanian Constitution of 1938 (q. v.) emphatically named Vilnius as the country's capital. Both sides continued to accuse the other of mistreating ethnic minorities. Despite bilateral agreements on postal communications, transport and the opening of borders, trade talks moved slowly.

The German Ultimatum of March 22, 1939. A more assertive Nazi policy towards Lithuania, especially on the Klaipėda (q. v.) issue, became more evident after Hitler's success of March 1936 in the Rhineland. Lithuanian policy in Klaipėda during the late 1930s sought to placate Berlin through concessions to the local German elements. Pro-Nazi forces, campaigning under a so-called "German list," scored a decisive victory in the December 1938 elections to the Klaipėda Territory's diet, receiving nearly 87 percent of the vote. At the same time, Lithuania still sought outside political support for its formal sovereignty over the Territory both through efforts at closer ties with Poland, and attempts to persuade the Western Powers to intercede with the Reich on Lithuania's behalf. On December 12, 1938 Britain and France issued a joint demarche to Berlin on preserving the status quo in Klaipėda Territory; however, Paris and London also made it clear that the Western Powers would not intervene over the Klaipėda issue.

On March 12, 1939 Foreign Minister Juozas Urbšys (q. v.) left for Rome to attend the coronation of Pius XII. On March 20 Urbšys arrived in Berlin on his way to Kaunas, hoping to find a compromise with the Reich over the Klaipėda crisis, and was received by German Foreign Minister Joachim Ribbentrop on the same evening. Urbšys had no chance to present any proposals, because Ribbentrop curtly informed him that the situation in Klaipėda Territory had become dangerous and could result in the spilling of German blood. In such a case, he warned, the German Army would immediately enter Lithuania. The only solution to the problem, Ribbentrop told Urbšys, was the immediate transfer of Klaipėda to Germany. Lithuanian diplomats concluded that, in light of the treatment Hitler had just accorded the Czechs and the attitude of the signatories to the Klaipėda Convention, there was little hope of international support for Lithuania. On March 21 Urbšys returned to Kaunas and informed the government of the Reich's ultimatum. There was no question of military resistance to the Germans without outside assistance and the Cabinet quickly approved the transfer of Klaipėda to Germany. The urgency of the situation was heightened by a report that Hitler was already sailing to Klaipėda aboard a German warship. On the evening of March

21 the Lithuanian government approved a press release emphasizing that it was submitting to a threat of force rather than acknowledging Germany's rights to Klaipėda, but Kaunas suffered a further humiliation when a sharp German response persuaded the Lithuanians to shelve that statement.

On the morning of March 22 Urbšys flew to Berlin to negotiate the transfer of Klaipėda. Having acquired the territory, the Germans allowed the establishment of a free Lithuanian zone in the port of Klaipėda to soften the impact of the port's loss on the country's trade. In addition to the transfer of territory and the free trading zone, the March 22, 1939 agreement with Germany provided for a mutual non-aggression pact. While the treaty stipulated an orderly transfer, the actual withdrawal of Lithuanian police and officialdom from Klaipėda more closely resembled mass flight by government officials, Lithuanian civilians and Jewish refugees. Uniformed Nazi toughs harassed the evacuees, settling scores with those who had supported the Lithuanian cause in the Territory. German troops crossed into Klaipėda Territory on March 23 and, together with the local Nazi network, completed the seizure of power. Accompanied by a large fleet (which included the famous pocket battleship *Graf Spee*) Hitler sailed to Klaipėda on the same day aboard the cruiser *Deutschland*. He toured the city and made a brief speech, which reasserted the "Germanness" of Memel and boasted that the Third Reich had now righted a historic wrong. The annexation of Klaipėda Territory was Germany's last seizure of territory before the onset of World War II.

The Soviet Ultimatum of June 14, 1940. Despite previous reassurances that relations with Lithuania were satisfactory, in May 1940 Soviet authorities informed the Lithuanian government that several Soviet soldiers, stationed in Lithuania as part of the October 1939 Soviet-Lithuanian mutual assistance pact (q. v.), had been abducted by unnamed parties. On May 25, 1940 Foreign Commissar Vyacheslav Molotov presented a protest note to the Lithuanian envoy in Moscow, Ladas Natkevičius, concerning the killing of Red Army man G. Butayev and the disappearance of two more Soviet soldiers in Lithuania, claiming that these actions were being carried out under the protection of Lithuanian authorities.

On May 28, in an attempt to defuse the crisis, Kaunas informed the Soviet government that it had created a commission to investigate the charges and invited Soviet representatives to join the inquiry. At the end of May, the Soviet news agency TASS began to publicly air charges that Lithuania was mistreating Soviet soldiers.

In early June, the Kremlin sent for Prime Minister Antanas Merkys (q. v.), who met with Molotov on June 7. Molotov reintroduced the Butayev case, claiming the Soviet soldier had been murdered and insisted that the Lithuanian government and press were too anti-Soviet. After an inconclusive and acrimonious discussion, Merkys met with Molotov at the Kremlin again on the evening of June 9. Molotov now charged that Lithuania was "organizing a Baltic military alliance against the Soviets" in connivance with the other Baltic States. On June 11 Urbšys was sent to Moscow with a message from President Antanas Smetona (q. v.) to Soviet President M. I. Kalinin, expressing friendship to the Soviet Union. However, the Soviet attitude grew increasingly harsh. Molotov accused the Lithuanians of sympathizing with the Finns during the recently concluded Winter War. On June 12 Merkys returned to Kaunas, while Urbšys remained behind to continue the talks.

At midnight on June 14, 1940 Molotov called Urbšys to the Kremlin and announced an ultimatum to the Lithuanian government. The first part of the statement outlined the accusations against Lithuania, which were a summary of the recent press attacks about the mistreatment of Soviet soldiers and allegations of a Baltic alliance directed against the USSR. Molotov now also accused the Lithuanian government of "massive arrests" of personnel who serviced the Soviet garrisons. In the second part of the ultimatum, the Soviet government demanded the arrest of Interior Minister Kazys Skučas (1894-1941), and Augustinas Povilaitis (1900-1991), the chief of state security. Lithuania was then to immediately form a new government "capable and desirous of ensuring... the execution of the mutual assistance treaty between the Soviet Union and Lithuania, and resolutely suppressing the treaty's enemies." The third and final point of the ultimatum spelled out Lithuania's military occupation: Molotov demanded that the Soviet government immediately "assure the unhampered entry of units of the Soviet Army, which will be stationed in the most important centers of Lithuania and will be sufficiently numerous" to ensure the effective execution of the mutual assistance treaty and end the "acts of provocation" against the USSR. The Lithuanian government was given until 10:00 AM of June 15 to respond; if no reply were received, the Soviets would assume a Lithuanian refusal. The Lithuanian cabinet met in the early morning hours of June 15. President Antanas Smetona, along with a minority of the ministers, counseled armed resistance in order to preserve the country's honor. However, despite Smetona's urging, and earlier plans to offer armed resistance against foreign invasion, the majority of the ministers decided to accept the ultimatum. The fear of bloodshed and the hope that the entry of still more Soviet troops would curtail, rather than end, Lithuania's independence were major factors in discouraging organized resistance. President Smetona left Kaunas on the same afternoon, leaving Merkys as acting head of state. The first Soviet units arrived in Kaunas on the evening of June 15.

The Soviet ultimatum of June 1940 and the subsequent establishment of the People's Government (q. v.) initiated the process of Lithuania's Sovietization. Lithuanian diplomatic missions abroad and Lithuanian resistance organizations considered that the country was under foreign occupation as of June 15, 1940; thus, all state authority and legislation from that date until the formal restoration of Lithuania's independence on March 11, 1990 was seen as illegitimate. Most historians, including Soviet and Russian scholars since the late 1980s, consider the Soviet ultimatum of June 14, 1940 as an act of force based on trumped-up charges which served as a pretext for armed invasion, thus implementing the annexation of the Baltic States already foreseen in the Molotov-Ribbentrop Pact of August 1939. See NAZI-SOVIET PACT; RUSSIA.

UNIVERSITIES (see EDUCATION).

URBŠYS, JUOZAS (1896-1991). Lithuanian diplomat and foreign minister from 1938 to 1940, born in Kėdainiai district on February 29, 1896. During World War I Urbšys served in the Russian Army, then joined the Lithuanian Army in 1918, retiring from military service in 1922. He entered Lithuania's diplomatic corps, serving in Berlin (1922-1933), Paris (1933) and as envoy to Latvia (1933-1934). From 1934 to 1936 Urbšys was director of the political department of the Foreign Ministry and then its secretary general from 1936 to 1938. On December 5, 1938 Urbšys was appointed foreign minister in the coalition cabinets of General Jonas Černius (q. v.) and Antanas Merkys (q. v.). He served as foreign minister during the last two years of the interwar Republic, when Lithuania was confronted by Polish, German and Soviet ultimatums (q. v.). While maintaining a cautiously optimistic public stance and maneuvering to preserve Lithuania's formal sovereignty, Urbšys recognized the threats to Lithuania. On May 30, 1940 he secretly informed Lithuanian diplomatic missions that, in the event of a foreign occupation, Lithuanian envoy to Rome, Stasys Lozoraitis, Sr. (q. v.) should handle Lithuania's affairs. Following the Soviet occupation of Lithuania, Urbšys was removed as foreign minister on June 17, 1940. In July 1940 Urbšys and his wife were exiled to Tambov in Russia; in 1941-1954 he was imprisoned, much of the time in solitary confinement. Urbšys was allowed to return to Lithuania in 1956 where he earned a living by translating French literary classics. The publication of his memoirs about the 1938-1940 period of ultimatums (q. v.) in 1988 spurred public discussion about the Nazi-Soviet Pact (q. v.) and the Soviet occupation, which contributed to the undermining of the Soviet version of the events of 1939-1940.

- V -

VAGNORIUS, GEDIMINAS. Lithuanian politician and the country's prime minister, born in Plungė district on June 10, 1957. An economist by training, Vagnorius was elected to the Supreme

Council on the Sąjūdis (q. v.) ticket in 1990 and made his mark as a supporter of Lithuanian president Vytautas Landsbergis (q. v.). Following the resignation of Prime Minister Kazimiera Prunskienė (q. v.), and amidst the crisis that erupted during the Soviet military attack in Vilnius in January 1991, Vagnorius replaced the short-lived government of Prime Minister Albertas Šimėnas (January 10-13) on January 13, 1991. Vagnorius oversaw Lithuania's economic transition during 1991-1992, including the dismantling of the country's Soviet-era collective farm system and attempts to replace the ruble with a new national currency. In the face of increasing opposition and criticism over his economic policies, Vagnorius was replaced by Aleksandras Abišala in July 1992. After the defeat of Landsbergis' party in the Seimas elections of October 1992, Vagnorius emerged as one of the leaders of the Fatherland Union-Conservative Party (Lith. *Tėvynės Sąjunga-konservatoriai*), the largest opposition faction in the parliament. He again became prime minister on November 28, 1996, after the Conservatives had won a majority in parliamentary elections. See SĄJŪDIS.

VALANČIUS, MOTIEJUS (1801-1875). Bishop and writer, born in Kretinga district on February 16, 1801. Valančius' well-to-do peasant parents altered his birth record to the Polonized form, Wołonczewski, in order to indicate gentry origins. This allowed Valančius to graduate from the Vilnius Theological Seminary and to attend the University of Vilnius, where he met fellow Samogitians active in the Lithuanian national movement of the early 19th century, such as his friend, the historian Simonas Daukantas (q. v.). After his ordination in 1828 he was sent to a parish in Belarus until 1834 when he returned to Lithuania to teach in the secondary school in Kražiai. In 1840 he was assigned to the Vilnius Theological Academy where he lectured and also earned a doctorate in theology. In 1845 Valančius was appointed the rector of the Varniai Theological Seminary where he worked until 1850 when he was chosen Bishop of Samogitia; he proved acceptable to the Russian government which considered him apolitical. Valančius was the first bishop of Samogitia to come from peasant stock. He expanded and improved the Lithuanian-language parochial school system in the diocese and in 1858 inaugurated Lithuania's temperance brotherhoods (Lith. *blaivystės brolijos*), one of the largest social movements of 19th-century Lithuania, which eventually encompassed almost a million people. In 1860 the Russian finance minister sought to expel Valančius from the Empire in order to halt liquor-tax revenue losses caused by the brotherhoods. The movement greatly expanded the use of the Lithuanian language through anti-alcohol books, pamphlets and posters. While Valančius did not consciously seek to undermine Polish culture in Lithuania, he was the first bishop of Samogitia to consistently publish his pastoral letters in Lithuanian.

Valančius underwent a painful struggle during the insurrection of 1863-1864: while sympathetic to the rebels, he considered their war a lost cause and, under pressure from Governor-General M. N. Muravyev (q. v.), condemned the rebels, urging a halt to the bloodshed. This earned him the enmity of much of the anti-Russian nobility in Lithuania. In May, 1864 Valančius was transferred to Kaunas where his activities could be more closely observed by the Russian authorities. After the press ban (q. v.), Valančius began to resist the Tsarist government since he saw Russification (q. v.) as a threat to Lithuania's Catholic Church. Between 1867 and 1869 Valančius organized the publication of Latin-script Lithuanian books in East Prussia and their illegal transport into Russian Lithuania. Most of his booklets exposed the government's plan to Russify Lithuania and introduce Orthodoxy, urging the peasants to be loyal to their Catholic faith and native language. Valančius died in Kaunas on May 29, 1875.

An educator and able Church administrator, as well as a talented writer, historian and ethnographer, Valančius was the most versatile and dominant figure in modern Lithuanian history before the emergence of political nationalism in the late 19th century. Although he was concerned primarily with the defense of the Catholic Church, his promotion of popular Lithuanian culture and the struggle against the press ban made him one of the prime movers of the modern Lithuanian national movement. Valančius is also the father of modern Lithuanian prose, his contributions encompassing religious publications, scholarship and fiction. His well-documented two-volume history, *Žemaičių vyskupystė* (Lith. The Diocese of Samogitia), published in 1848 remains valuable to this day. His didactic fictional works are still considered outstanding literature. His best-known work, *Palangos Juzė* (Lith. Juzė from Palanga), a collection of picturesque tales told by an itinerant tailor, was the most widely read book of Lithuanian fiction in the 19th century. Valančius' descriptions of village life became models for subsequent Lithuanian realist writers. See CATHOLIC CHURCH; EDUCATION; NATIONALISM, LITHUANIAN.

VARPAS (Lith. The Bell). Lithuanian monthly published in East Prussia from 1889 to 1906. *Varpas* was established primarily through the efforts of its first editor, Vincas Kudirka (q. v.), and his colleagues in the Lithuanian students' association, *Lietuva* (Lith. Lithuania), at the University of Warsaw. Unlike the monthly *Aušra* (Lith. Dawn) (q. v.) (1883-1886), which featured Lithuanian history and culture, *Varpas* also emphasized current political and economic concerns which appealed to the emerging secular Lithuanian intelligentsia. In 1890 the founders of *Varpas* also began publishing the monthly, *Ūkininkas* (Lith. The Farmer), aimed at the less-educated peasantry. *Varpas* was the first Lithuanian periodical to promulgate a coherent modern political program for the Lithuanian national movement. The members of the movement which gathered around the monthly came to be called *varpininkai*. Generally, they advocated secular liberal and democratic ideas, emphasizing the need for Lithuanian-speaking society to enter government service, commerce and the professions, which until then were dominated by non-Lithuanians. This led the *varpininkai* to attack Polish landowning interests in the countryside and Jewish economic dominance in the towns as inimical to the economic and educational progress of the Lithuanian nation. However, under Kudirka's editorship between 1889 and 1899, the monthly reserved its harshest criticism for the Tsarist autocracy's Russification (q. v.) policies, especially the press ban (q. v.). *Varpas* was also the first to emphasize the problems created by mass emigration abroad, especially to America, and urged Lithuanians to create economic conditions that would stem the exodus.

The publication of *Varpas* coincided with the period of the secularization and politicization of the Lithuanian national movement that characterized the turn of the century. While it criticized Tsarist anti-Catholic discrimination, *Varpas* was often attacked by the more conservative clerical Lithuanian press for its secularism and criticism of the Church. In the decade before World War I the Lithuanian intelligentsia, which had gathered around *Varpas*, began to fragment into more clearly defined political parties reflecting Christian Democratic (Catholic), liberal nationalist and socialist orientations. As each of these groups began publishing their own periodicals, *Varpas* became less relevant and ceased publication in March 1906. Periodicals called *Varpas*, and claiming to embody the spirit of the original monthly, have been published irregularly since 1913. See DEMOCRATIC PARTY, LITHUANIAN.

VELIUONA. Originally known as Junigeda, a historic town in central Lithuania on the Nemunas River, one of the country's oldest settlements, pop. in 1995: 700. Archeological excavations reveal that Veliuona was an important trading center since the 13th century. The town contains two castle sites and four castle-hills, indicating that Veliuona was the site of major military construction. The name Veliuona appears in the chronicles of the Teutonic Knights (q. v.) since 1315. In the 14th century Veliuona became the most important fortification defending the western approaches to Kaunas against the incursions of the Teutonic Order. Some scholars believe, and popular tradition maintains, that Grand Duke Gediminas (q. v.), who reportedly hailed from the Veliuona region, may have been killed here in 1341 during a siege of the castle by the Teutonic Knights. In 1421 Grand Duke Vytautas (q. v.) built one of the first churches in Samogitia (q. v.) on the heights overlooking the Nemunas. In 1443 Veliuona received a town charter. The town remains a popular tourist attraction for Lithuanians interested in medieval history.

VILNIUS (Rus. Vilna, Pol. Wilno). The largest city and capital of Lithuania, located on hilly terrain at the confluence of the Neris and Vilija Rivers, pop. in 1995: 575,000. There is evidence of a settlement in what is now the capital's old town as early as the fifth century. By the 12th century a town had grown up and had become an important trading center. Recent excavations suggest that a church was constructed on the site of the present Cathedral of Vilnius as early as the reign of King Mindaugas (q. v.) in the mid-13th century. However, there is little reliable historical evidence concerning Vilnius until the early 14th century. The city is referred to as Lithuania's capital in Grand Duke Gediminas' (q. v.) diplomatic correspondence of 1323. In popular culture the legend of the Iron Wolf (Lith. *Geležinis vilkas*) (q. v.) also ties the founding of the city to Gediminas. The role of Gediminas is reflected in the naming of the city's central cathedral square (Gediminas Square) and the most prominent castle hill (Gediminas Hill).

Medieval chronicles indicate that, during the reign of Gediminas (1316-1341), Vilnius became the undisputed political and cultural center of the Grand Duchy. German and other foreign merchants resided here in large numbers and even before Lithuania's formal conversion to Christianity in 1386, the city hosted a number of Catholic and Orthodox churches. In 1387 Vilnius was placed under the Magdeburg Law and received additional municipal privileges in 1432 and 1536. Vilnius has always been a multinational city: in addition to the German and Russian communities and the influx of Poles beginning in the late 14th century, Tatars and Jews settled in Lithuania's capital in increasing numbers from the early 15th century. The cultural and economic development of Vilnius accelerated in the mid-16th century during the reign of Sigismund Augustus (q. v.) who completed the Renaissance-style grand ducal palace and brought in Italian artisans to help construct a series of churches, palaces and public buildings. The University of Vilnius opened as a Jesuit Academy in 1579.

While Vilnius and its central castle were besieged and heavily damaged a number of times, especially during the civil strife and wars with the Teutonic Order in the late 14th century, the city itself was first captured by foreign forces when it was razed during the Muscovite invasion of 1655. The capital recovered somewhat during the late 18th century with the construction of the present cathedral and city hall, but when the Grand Duchy passed to Russian rule in 1795, the population of Vilnius had declined to less than 20,000 inhabitants. Under the Tsars, Vilnius became the seat of the Governor-General of the Northwest Territory (Rus. *Severozapadnyi krai*), which included most of the Lithuanian-speaking lands of the former Grand Duchy. The population grew to 64,000 by 1869 and to nearly 200,000 by 1914. Since the 18th century Vilnius has gained fame as a center of Jewish culture, largely because of the learned Elijah Ben Solomon (q. v.), known as the Gaon of Vilnius, and the establishment of YIVO, the Institute for Jewish Research, in 1925. By the 19th century, Jews (q. v.) had become a plurality (about 40 percent) of the city's population. Polish speakers and Russians constituted most of the remainder; ethnic Lithuanians made up only two percent of the city's population before World War I. However, Lithuanians have always considered Vilnius as the legitimate historic capital of the country.

The German Army occupied Vilnius between September 1915 and January 1919 after which the city changed hands between Lithuanian, Soviet and Polish forces until October 9, 1920 when General Lucjan Żeligowski's (q. v.) Polish troops captured Vilnius from the Lithuanians; it then became the capital of the rump state of Central Lithuania (q. v.). International efforts to resolve the Vilnius Question (q. v.) proved unsuccessful and in March 1922 Vilnius and its environs were incorporated into Poland over Lithuanian protests. The Soviet-Lithuanian Mutual Assistance Treaty (q. v.) of October 10, 1939 formally transferred sovereignty over Vilnius to Lithuania and the Lithuanian Army took possession of the city on October 28, 1939. While there was an influx of Lithuanian officials, students and others into Vilnius after the fall of 1939, the greatest demographic changes in Vilnius occurred after June 1941. During the Nazi occupation of 1941-1944 the city's Jewish population was ghettoized and virtually annihilated, mainly at the killing site of Paneriai (q. v.). After World War II, Vilnius' Polish population became proportionately smaller as a result of repatriation to Poland and a massive influx of Lithuanians and Russians; for the first time since the late Middle Ages, Lithuanian speakers made up a slight majority of Lithuania's capital. The process can be seen in the figures below:

Population of Vilnius in the 20th Century (percentages)

Nationality	1916	1941	1959	1994
Lithuanians	2.1	28.1	33.6	52.5
Russians	1.6	3.6	29.4	19.3
Poles	50.1	50.7	20.0	19.1
Jews	43.5	16.2	7.0	.8
Others*	2.7	1.4	10.0	8.3
Total Population	140,800	186,300	236,100	584,400

* Mostly Belarusans and Ukrainians

Vilnius was at the center of the Lithuanian independence movement in 1988-1991 and was the site of the massacre of Lithuanian demonstrators at the city's TV tower by Soviet troops on January 13, 1991, which killed fourteen persons and injured hundreds. See JEWS; POLAND; VILNIUS QUESTION.

VILNIUS QUESTION. The dispute between Poland and Lithuania concerning the status of Vilnius (q. v.) and its environs. The problem of Vilnius is rooted in a historic paradox. Since the 14th century the city had been the capital of the Grand Duchy of Lithuania and the administrative center of the Lithuanian lands during the Tsarist period (1795-1918). At the same time, by the beginning of World War I Vilnius had become the center of Polish and Jewish culture with only a small population of ethnic

Lithuanians. However, Lithuanians consistently claimed Vilnius on the grounds that any restored Lithuanian state was a historic successor to the Grand Duchy and only this city could serve as its capital. During the early 20th century the Lithuanian intelligentsia sponsored cultural and Catholic organizations in Vilnius and began publication of the first Lithuanian-language daily, *Vilniaus Žinios* (Lith. Vilnius News), in 1904. Vilnius was also the site of the Great Assembly of Vilnius (q. v.) in December 1905 and the February 16, 1918 Declaration of Independence by the Taryba (q. v.). A further complication regarding Vilnius was that, while the population of the city was predominantly Polish, Jewish and Russian, much of the surrounding countryside was inhabited by ethnic Lithuanians and Belarusans. In addition, some Belarusan nationalists also laid claim to Vilnius during the early 20th century.

The Polish-Lithuanian dispute over Vilnius intensified during 1918-1919 with the reemergence of Poland and Lithuania as independent states. The Lithuanian government insisted on Poland's recognition of Lithuania as an independent state with Vilnius as its capital. Polish leaders, including Józef Piłsudski (q. v.), preferred that Lithuania federate with Poland, while most local Polish politicians in the Vilnius region were adamantly opposed to Lithuanian rule. Polish-Lithuanian talks during 1919-1920 failed to resolve the impasse over Vilnius, although the Soviet-Lithuanian Peace Treaty of July 12, 1920 (q. v.) granted the city to Lithuania. Despite the Suwałki agreement (q. v.), which left Vilnius on the Lithuanian side, Polish troops under the command of Gen. Lucjan Żeligowski (q. v.) captured the city on October 9, 1920. Between April and December 1920 Belgian diplomat Paul Hymans led the League of Nations efforts to resolve the dispute. The Hymans Plan called for a loose Polish-Lithuanian confederation with Vilnius as part of Lithuania. On December 24, 1920 Lithuania officially rejected the Hymans proposals. In March 1922 Poland annexed Vilnius and on March 15, 1923 the Conference of Ambassadors announced that the current Polish-Lithuanian armistice line, leaving Vilnius to the Poles, was the de jure boundary between Poland and Lithuania. On April 16, 1923 Lithuanian Prime Minister Ernestas

Galvanauskas (q. v.) formally notified the Conference of Lithuania's rejection of this decision.

Lithuanian diplomacy officially maintained the position that Vilnius was the sole legitimate capital of the Republic even after it was compelled to normalize relations with Poland by the ultimatum of March 17, 1938 (q. v.). The issue of Vilnius galvanized Lithuanian public opinion during the interwar period and the goal of regaining the country's capital united virtually the entire political spectrum. With over a half-million members and supporters, the Union for the Liberation of Vilnius (Lith. *Vilniui Vaduoti Sąjunga*) was one of the most popular organizations in independent Lithuania. After the fall of Poland to German and Soviet invasions, the Soviet-Lithuanian Mutual Assistance Pact of October 10, 1939 (q. v.) transferred Vilnius and surrounding territory (6,880 sq. km.) to the Republic of Lithuania. Poland's government-in-exile in London asserted Poland's rights to its pre-1939 borders, including Vilnius, but this position became irrelevant after the war. In 1989 Soviet leader Mikhail Gorbachev (q. v.) once again raised doubt about the status of Vilnius in an attempt to convince Lithuanians not to seek independence. Since the late 1980s there has been some heated rhetoric about the history of Polish-Lithuanian relations in the press of both countries; however, the Polish-Lithuanian state treaty of 1994 formally reasserted Lithuania's sovereignty over Vilnius. There is currently no serious international challenge to Lithuanian sovereignty over Vilnius, although some nationalist elements in Poland and Belarus still attempt to raise the issue. See CENTRAL LITHUANIA; POLAND; VILNIUS.

VOLDEMARAS, AUGUSTINAS (1883-1942). Lithuanian statesman and political leader, born in Švenčionys district on April 4, 1883. In 1910 Voldemaras received his degree in history and classics at the University of St. Petersburg. In 1914-1915 he furthered his studies in Italy and Sweden after which he returned to Russia where he taught briefly at the University of Perm. In 1917 Voldemaras was appointed Lithuanian representative to Ukraine's governing council, the Rada, in Kiev. He joined the Lithuanian State Council, or Taryba (q. v.), upon his return to Lithuania in the summer of 1918. Voldemaras formed the first government of independent Lithuania on November 11, 1918 in which he served as both prime minister and foreign minister. In December 1918 Voldemaras led the Lithuanian delegation to the Paris Peace Conference and was subsequently replaced as prime minister. From 1920 to 1926 Voldemaras taught at the University of Kaunas and became a prominent publicist in the nationalist press. In 1926 he was elected to the Third Seimas as a member of the Nationalist Union (q. v.). After the Nationalist coup of December 17, 1926, Voldemaras became prime minister under President Antanas Smetona (q. v.). During the late 1920s he negotiated a series of important agreements with Germany, Poland and the Vatican. At the same time, Voldemaras and his radical Nationalist supporters came into conflict with the more moderate Smetona. He was dismissed from the government in September 1929 and was exiled to Zarasai, a town in eastern Lithuania, thus ending his active political career. After an unsuccessful military coup tried to restore Voldemaras to power in June 1934, he was imprisoned and in February 1938 was forced to leave the country. In August 1939 Voldemaras returned to Lithuania from France and was again exiled to Zarasai; in January 1940 he was allowed to leave the country. On June 19, 1940 Voldemaras returned to Kaunas and was immediately arrested by the Soviets who exiled him to Ordzhonikidze in the Caucasus where he reportedly died on December 16, 1942.

Despite his brief tenure in office, Voldemaras was a major political player in interwar Lithuania. An ambitious and charismatic politician, he was the focus of the radical right-wing nationalists who became known as the Voldemarists (Lith. *voldemarininkai*) and was revered by the clandestine extremist nationalist society, the Iron Wolf (q. v.). Although he was admired for his obvious intellectual ability, Voldemaras was hampered by his ambition and penchant for impulsive behavior, such as his inexplicable decision to return to Soviet-occupied Lithuania in June 1940 despite warnings from Lithuanian diplomats. See NATIONALIST UNION; SMETONA, ANTANAS.

VOLOK, or VALAKAS REFORM. The reform of the agrarian economy and society of the Grand Duchy of Lithuania during the 16th century, so called because of the unit of land (Rus. *volok*, Lith. *valakas*, Pol. *włóka*) that the state assigned to the average peasant household. Until the early 16th century, Lithuania's land tenure system was chaotic and there existed no uniform system of rural administration. The Volok Reform, encouraged by Queen Bona Sforza (q. v.), was initiated during the rule of Sigismund Augustus (q. v.) in 1547 and then finalized in statutes published in 1557 which introduced the comprehensive restructuring of agriculture known as the Volok system. The land reform delineated the boundaries of the crown domains and private estates, assigning to the state those lands to which the nobility did not have clear title. The statutes compelled the peasants to settle in street villages on the Western model, while government surveyors measured and recorded the peasant holdings. The amount of peasant feudal obligations was then based on the size of the household's holding and calculated according to the unit of land, the *volok*, which consisted of smaller units called *margai* in Lithuanian (Pol. *morgi*). The Lithuanian volok, somewhat larger than the Polish *włóka*, averaged about 30 *margai* (1 *margas* = .712 hectares or 1.75 acres, 1 *volok* = approx. 21.36 hectares). The main economic goals of the reform were to increase the revenues of the Grand Duchy's treasury through efficient taxation of the land, and to regulate and systematize the obligations of the peasantry. One measure of the effectiveness of the reform was the four-fold increase in income generated from the crown lands between 1547 and 1588. The Volok Reform also stimulated productivity by introducing the three-field system of cultivation on the large manorial farms of Lithuania, thus transforming Lithuanian agriculture. To a considerable degree, the Volok Reform defined the structure of Lithuania's agrarian world well into the 19th century. See AGRICULTURE; ECONOMICS; SERFDOM.

VYDŪNAS. Pen name of Vilius Storasta (1868-1953), philosopher and writer, born on March 22, 1868 in Šilutė district. Vydūnas graduated from the Ragainė (Ger. Ragnit) teachers' college in 1892, then taught French and English at the Tilsit (q. v.) gymnasium until 1912. During his studies at the universities of Leipzig and Berlin Vydūnas mastered Sanskrit and became a devotee of Indian philosophy. Between 1917 and 1919 he taught Lithuanian language and literature at the University of Berlin During the interwar period Vydūnas became the best-known Lithuanian cultural figure and community leader in East Prussia. His activities in fostering Lithuanian-language theater and music, his criticism of the Germanization of East Prussia's Lithuanians, as well as his historical study, *Sieben hundert Jahre deutsch-litauischer Beziehungen* (Ger. 700 Years of German-Lithuanian Relations), published in 1932, provoked the anger of German nationalists and led to Nazi repression. Lithuanian cultural organizations sponsored by Vydūnas were banned by 1935 and he was imprisoned by the Nazis in 1938. He died in West Germany on February 20, 1953.

Virtually all of Vydūnas' historical work and literature are imbued with Eastern religious thought, including pantheism and reincarnation, as well as a romantic view of medieval Lithuania's pagan culture, as portrayed in his dramas *Prabočių šešėliai* (Lith. Shadows of the Ancestors) (1908) and *Amžina ugnis* (Lith. The Eternal Fire) (1912). Vydūnas is remembered as the leading proponent of a synthesis between Eastern mysticism and Lithuania's pre-Christian tradition.

VYTAUTAS (Rus. Vitovt, Pol. Witold). Grand Duke of Lithuania between 1392 and 1430, often called Vytautas the Great in Lithuanian historical literature, and widely acknowledged as medieval Lithuania's most important ruler. Vytautas was born about 1350, probably in Trakai, the oldest son of Kęstutis (q. v.). He first achieved prominence as an ally of his father in the struggle for power that followed the death of his uncle, Grand Duke Algirdas (q. v.). Following the death of his father, Grand Duke Kęstutis, in 1382, possibly murdered by Algirdas' son Jogaila (q. v.), Vytautas was imprisoned in the castle of Krėva (q. v.). He quickly escaped and sought refuge with the Teutonic Knights (q. v.) with whose support he waged a lengthy campaign against his cousin Jogaila, who had seized the grand ducal throne. In 1383 Vytautas was baptized and added the Christian name Alexander to his signature. In 1384 he secretly reached a reconciliation with Jogaila and turned against the Teutonic Order; back in Lithuania Vytautas was given the lands of Grodno, Brest-Litovsk and Podlachia, later acquiring Volynia as well. Vytautas was a prominent participant in the signing of the Act of Krėva (q. v.), Jogaila's coronation as King of Poland in 1386, and the formal re-Christianization of Lithuania in 1387. However, Jogaila's decision to appoint his brother Skirgaila (q. v.) as viceroy in Lithuania provoked a fierce rebellion from Vytautas who once again turned to the Teutonic Knights for assistance, initiating a destructive civil war which ended with the Treaty of Astravas (Rus. Ostrov) in 1392. By this agreement Vytautas was given to rule the Grand Duchy of Lithuania as Jogaila's vassal, but he later took the title of Grand Duke and, in effect, ruled Lithuania without any significant interference from his cousin.

During the 1390s Vytautas undertook the Grand Duchy's expansion to the east. In 1390 his daughter Sophia married Grand Prince Vasili I (1389-1425) of Moscow; Vytautas then shored up Lithuanian power in Smolensk and extended the Grand Duchy's influence to Riazan and Tula. But Vytautas' plans to subdue the Golden Horde were undone when his army suffered a crushing defeat at the hands of the Tatars (q. v.) at the Battle of Vorksla in 1399. Muscovy took this opportunity to roll back some of Lithuania's gains in the Russian lands, but Vytautas renewed his campaigns in the east, and by 1408 had recovered the territories lost after Vorksla. In order to pursue his ambitions in the east, Vytautas had ceded Samogitia (q. v.) to the Teutonic Order in 1398 but in 1409 a massive rebellion of the Samogitians against the Knights elicited his support and led to a joint Lithuanian-Polish campaign against the Order culminating in the decisive victory over the Knights at Grunwald (q. v.) on July 15, 1410. The Peace of Toruń in 1411 proved inconclusive and, supported by the Holy Roman Emperor Sigismund, the Order continued to claim

Samogitia which led to Vytautas' alliance with the Hussites of Bohemia in their war against the Emperor. A new Polish-Lithuanian campaign against the Teutonic Knights in 1422 led to the Treaty of Melno which established the Lithuanian-Prussian border for the next five centuries.

In his relations with Poland, Vytautas always sought to rule Lithuania independently. He achieved this by the Act of Radom in 1401, which made Vytautas supreme ruler of Lithuania during his own lifetime, and the Act of Horodło (q. v.) in 1413. During the 1420s Vytautas' relations with Poland grew more acrimonious as the Grand Duke began to entertain the idea of acquiring a royal crown, a plan supported by Emperor Sigismund but opposed by the Poles. However, Vytautas died on October 27, 1430 amidst preparations for his coronation. He was married twice, first to Princess Anne, who bore him Sophia, and in 1418 to Juliana, who was childless. Since Vytautas left no male heirs, the Lithuanian throne once again became an object of contention. Vytautas' struggle to break free of the union with Poland was continued by his brother Sigismund Kęstutaitis (q. v.).

During the reign of Vytautas, Lithuania reached its greatest territorial expansion and influence, stretching from the Baltic to Black Seas. He succeeded in ending the centuries-old Teutonic threat and redefined Lithuania's relationship with Poland. In domestic affairs, the ethnographically Lithuanian lands began an irreversible Christianization during his reign. Vytautas constructed a number of churches and oversaw the introduction of ecclesiastical administration. He also strengthened the nobility by granting them lands and peasants in return for their loyalty and military service. Vytautas fostered trade and encouraged Jews (q. v.) to settle in Lithuania by granting them extensive privileges.

VYTENIS (d. 1315 or 1316). Grand Duke of Lithuania, ca. 1295 to ca. 1315, brother of Gediminas (q. v.). According to chronicles he was probably the son of Pukuveras and the exact dates of his reign are unknown, although the period 1295-1315 is generally accepted. Vytenis is best known for his diplomatic and military struggle against the Teutonic Knights (q. v.), especially his alliance with the archbishop and burghers of the Hanseatic town of Riga against the Order. In 1298 Vytenis joined forces with Riga in a long military campaign against the Teutonic Knights. A Lithuanian garrison was stationed in Riga until 1313. In 1295 and 1306 Vytenis intervened on behalf of Bolesław of Mazovia in the struggles for the Polish throne. While Vytenis remained faithful to traditional Lithuanian religion, he allowed Catholic monks and churches to operate in the Grand Duchy and seems to have been interested in creating an Orthodox metropolitan see in Lithuania. Thus, Vytenis established the basic outlines of Lithuania's policy of defense in the west and expansion in the east which was continued by his successors in the 14th and 15th centuries.

- W -

WIŚNIOWIECKI, MICHAEL (1638-1673). King of Poland and Grand Duke of Lithuania between 1669 and 1673. After the abdication of John Casimir Vasa in 1668, the Commonwealth's Diet rejected foreign contenders and elected Michael Korybut-Wiśniowiecki, a descendent of Grand Duke Algirdas' (q. v.) son, Kaributas. King Michael's brief reign was marked by a series of unsuccessful wars against the Ottoman Turks and Cossacks; in Lithuania, it was a period of the ascendance of the Pac (q. v.) family, which controlled the Grand Duchy's chancellory and army. He died near Lviv during a military campaign on November 10, 1673.

WŁADYSŁAW II. See JOGAILA.

WŁADYSŁAW IV VASA (1595-1648). King of Poland and Grand Duke of Lithuania from 1632 to 1648, the son of King Sigismund III Vasa (q. v.) and Anne of Hapsburg, born on April 19, 1595.

During Muscovy's Time of Troubles (1598-1613), Władysław was elected Tsar by the boyar assembly in 1610 under threat of the Polish-Lithuanian army, which was then encamped in Moscow; however, Russian resistance to this project and Władysław's father's machinations led to the enthronement of the Romanovs instead. After his father's death in 1632, he was elected King and Grand Duke as Władysław IV in an unusually peaceful royal election, the last of its kind. In domestic affairs, Władysław followed a policy of religious toleration towards the Orthodox and Protestants. In foreign affairs, he succeeded in holding off Muscovite attacks on Smolensk, but failed in his bid to gain the throne of Sweden and unite it with the Commonwealth. Władysław's attempts to initiate political and social reform in the Commonwealth in the 1630s and 1640s foundered because of chaos in the Commonwealth's diets (q. v.), where the *liberum veto* was ever more frequently invoked to obstruct royal decrees. During Władysław's last years growing rebellion among Cossacks in the Ukraine pushed Poland-Lithuania towards a major conflict with Muscovy. Władysław died in Merkinė, Lithuania on May 20, 1648. He was succeeded by his brother John Casimir Vasa (q. v.).

WOMEN, in Lithuanian history. Little is known about the social status of women in Lithuania before historical records. In a recent interpretation, the renowned Lithuanian archeologist and feminist scholar Marija Gimbutas (1921-1994), in her ground-breaking study, *The Civilization of the Goddess*, assumed a matriarchal culture in Lithuania before the advent of the patriarchal warlike Indo-European invasion. While some scholars disputed her findings, Gimbutas pointed out the evidence that this culture had been dominated by female goddesses and that relicts of this matriarchal orientation had survived in later Baltic, including Lithuanian, culture. Medieval sources give us the first real historical view of the role of women in Lithuanian society. In 1447 Grand Duke Casimir (q. v.) issued a privilege granting noble women the right of inheritance, which was also confirmed in the Lithuanian Statute (q. v.) of 1529; however, these property rights were more circumscribed than those of men. In terms of criminal law, the Statute punished assaults on women twice as hard as attacks on men. In the 16th century the Lithuanian commentator, Michalo Lituanus (Lith. Mykolas Lietuvis), wrote a tract portraying Lithuanian women as possessing excessive political and economic clout and envying the Grand Duchy's Muscovite and Tatar neighbors who kept women subjugated. In general, despite the legal protection enjoyed by women in the Grand Duchy of Lithuania, their social status in the culture subordinated them to men. As in the rest of Europe, albeit on a relatively smaller scale, witch hunts, primarily against lower class Lithuanian women, were conducted between the 16th and 18th centuries.

Lithuanian women became increasingly active during the 19th century: Emilia Plater was one of the leaders of the 1830-1831 insurrection (q. v.) against Russian rule. During the period of the Tsarist press ban (q. v.) between 1864 and 1904 Lithuania's rural women established a network of illegal underground schools which became the basic means of educating children in the native language. The image of Lithuanian mothers teaching their children to read by the spinning wheel was immortalized in perhaps Lithuania's most popular sculpture, *Vargo mokykla* (Lith. The School of Hardship), by Petras Rimša (1881-1961). By the late 19th century Lithuanian women became an increasingly important component in the development of Lithuanian culture, especially in literature. Since educational opportunities for peasant women were limited before 1918, most Lithuanian women writers came from the Polonized gentry, including Žemaitė (q. v.), Gabrielė Petkevičaitė-Bitė (1861-1943), Marija Pečkauskaitė (1878-1930), better known as Šatrijos Ragana and the sisters Sofija Pšibiliauskienė (1876-1926) and Marija Lastauskienė (1872-1957), who wrote under the collective pseudonym Lazdynų Pelėda. During the Revolution of 1905 (q. v.) the first Lithuanian women's organization, The Lithuanian Women's Association (Lith. *Lietuvos moterų susivie-nijimas*), was founded with the purpose of promoting women's rights within a future Lithuanian state. In December 1905 the Congress of Lithuanian Village Women convened in Šiauliai and urged women to form their own organizations to fight for equal rights. Other secular and Catholic women's groups, led by proponents of women's rights such as the pedagogue Ona Brazauskaitė-Mašiotienė (1883-1949), were formed during the critical period of the Great War (1914-1918).

The restoration of an independent Lithuanian state in 1918 finally created the conditions for the full legal equality of women and their increasing participation in public life. In 1920 the provisional Constitution (q. v.) or Basic Law of Lithuania mandated equal rights for men and women; in that year, Lithuanian women voted for the first time during the elections for the Constituent Assembly (q. v.), whose first sessions were opened and chaired by Gabrielė Petkevičaitė-Bitė. In 1922 at the initiative of the women members of the Seimas, Lithuania's civil code was amended to grant women full property rights. The 1918-1940 period also saw the emergence of the first generation of university-educated ethnic Lithuanian women who were able to enter the professions, especially teaching, medicine, the arts and government service. Sofija Kymantaitė-Čiurlionienė (1885-1958), the widow of Lithuania's best-known artist Mikalojus Čiurlionis (q. v.) and a prominent author, was a member of the Lithuanian delegation at the League of Nations in the late 1920s. The first Lithuanian-language periodicals for women also appeared between the wars. In December 1937 the second Lithuanian Women's Congress gathered about 1,000 delegates who issued a public appeal to translate the legal principles of equality between the sexes into economic and social justice for women. After 1940 most Lithuanian women's organizations were banned or reorganized as Soviet-style associations. During the Nazi occupation of 1941-1944 women constituted a conspicuously large percentage of the Gentiles who assisted Jews. Women also were prominent in the anti-Soviet resistance and dissident movements after 1944.

The nearly five decades of Soviet rule left a mixed legacy to Lithuania's women. Women became a majority in the medical and teaching professions and were showcased in such assemblies as the Lithuanian Supreme Soviet, although, as in the rest of the USSR, very few women actually achieved status within the real power elites, such as the Communist Party's Central Committee or

Politburo. In some ways, the Soviet years were a setback for women: as many women entered the work force, including industrial and mechanized agricultural labor, they were also held responsible for the traditional domestic chores, creating an exhausting and stressful social and family situation. The numerous women's publications and official organizations such as the Congress of Soviet Lithuanian Women did little to alleviate the situation. During the late 1980s women actively participated in the growing Lithuanian independence movement and, in February 1990, fourteen women were elected to the Supreme Council which declared the restoration of the Lithuania's independence on March 11, 1990. Kazimiera Prunskienė (q. v.) became the country's first prime minister (March 1990-January 1991) and the first woman to head a government in Eastern Europe. She achieved international prominence for her diplomatic tour of the United States and European capitals in the spring of 1990 during the difficult days of the Soviet economic blockade against Lithuania. Ten women were elected to the first postwar Seimas (legislature) of the Republic in October 1992.

Recent statistics indicate that the percentage of women in top government, managerial and business positions is decreasing, partly due to the general economic recession that has followed the collapse of the Soviet system. However, many women active in the more than 20 non-governmental women's organizations have begun raising their voices against what they term patriarchal and traditional stereotypes that exclude women from positions of power and subordinate them to men. For example, while most school teachers are women, there are few women school principals and directors, especially in the larger secondary schools. The situation of Lithuania's women has encouraged the beginnings of a Western-style feminist movement. In 1995 the Lithuanian Women's Party (Lith. *Lietuvos moterų partija*) was established under the leadership of Ms. Prunskienė to encourage direct political action by women. Other women have been prominent in relief work, for example, the Catholic Caritas organization. See LITERATURE, LITHUANIAN; ŽEMAITĖ.

- Y -

YČAS, MARTYNAS (1885-1941). Lithuanian lawyer and statesman, born in Biržai district on November 13, 1885. A 1911 law graduate of the University of Tomsk (Siberia), he returned to Lithuania in 1912 and was elected to the Duma, Russia's legislature, where he frequently lobbied for Lithuanian interests. Yčas became one of the few prominent non-Russian members of the liberal Constitutional Democrat, or Kadet, Party. He was active in the February Revolution 1917 which overthrew Tsarism and briefly became viceminister of education in Russia's Provisional Government. In 1918 Yčas returned to Lithuania and was appointed minister of commerce in the Lithuanian government. He also served with the Lithuanian delegation at the Paris Peace Conference in 1919 and presided over the commission to settle the Lithuanian-Latvian border in 1921. During most of the interwar period he engaged in private business. Yčas was also a longtime head of the Lithuanian synod of the Reformed Church. He died in Rio de Janeiro on April 5, 1941.

YELTSIN, BORIS (1931-) See GORBACHEV, MIKHAIL.

YOTVINGIANS, or Sudovians. Western Baltic tribe, related to the Prussians (q. v.), whose name first appears in a Kievan chronicle describing Prince Vladimir's campaign of 983, although it is almost certain that they were the *Soudinou* mentioned by the Greek scholar Ptolemy in the second century as the neighbors of the Slavs and Goths. In Lithuanian historical literature the term Sudovians (Lith. *sūduviai*), also used in some medieval chronicles, has recently gained greater acceptance as the correct term for the people who inhabited the region now known as Suvalkija (q. v.), Sūduva or Užnemunė, that is, the land to the south and west of the Nemunas River. In constrast to Lithuanian, there is no written record of the

Yotvingian language except for proper names preserved in medieval documents, but prevailing opinion among linguists is that Yotvingian was a dialect of Old Prussian. The Yotvingians were weakened by persistent invasions of their land from Kievan Rus' and its successor state of Volynia-Galicia. The tribe was finally exterminated or Germanized by the Teutonic Knights (q. v.) in the early 14th century. The southern lands of the Yotvingians were settled by Poles, Belarusans and Ukrainians, while the northern region, now generally called Suvalkija, was largely wilderness until the 16th century when Lithuanian peasants began to settle the area. See PRUSSIA.

YOUNG LITHUANIA (Lith. *Jaunoji Lietuva*). A popular nationalist Lithuanian youth organization. The Young Lithuanians (Lith. *jaunalietuviai*), as they were commonly called, were founded in 1927 at the initiative of the nationalist student fraternity Neo-Lithuania, which recognized a need to include the youth of Lithuania's villages and towns in a broader nationalist movement. The Union of Young Lithuania (Lith. *Jaunosios Lietuvos Sąjunga*) was formally an independent social organization but in practice constituted the youth wing of the Lithuanian Nationalist Union (q. v.). In 1936 the Nationalists formalized their relationship with Young Lithuania by allowing its members to join the Nationalist Union without the required candidacy period. At its height, Young Lithuania had about 40,000 members and operated numerous sports, cultural and educational clubs. Young Lithuanians openly declared their allegiance to authoritarian principles and Smetona as the nation's leader. The group's intense nationalism, emphasis on the leader principle, uniforms and the penchant for paramilitary-style drilling gave it a radical aura. Young Lithuania was banned in June 1940 after the Soviet occupation but was reestablished in 1990, albeit on a much smaller scale.

- Z -

ŻELIGOWSKI, LUCJAN (1865-1947). Polish military leader and politician, born in Oshmyany (Belarus) on October 17, 1865. He graduated from the Riga Polytechnic Institute and served in the Russian Army during World War I. In 1918 he helped organize the Polish Army and served as a general in Poland's war against the Bolsheviks. In September 1920 Żeligowski received secret instructions from Polish leader Józef Piłsudski (q. v.) to organize a military operation for the occupation of Vilnius. When the Polish-Lithuanian Suwałki Agreement (q. v.) of October 7, 1920 assigned Vilnius to the Lithuanian side of the demarcation line, Żeligowski, in a ruse to bypass the accord, declared a mutiny on the following day. His forces, called the Lithuanian and Belarusan Division, were supported by additional Polish Army units in an attack on Lithuanian troops. At the same time Żeligowski announced a manifesto, proclaiming that the inhabitants of Vilnius, rather than the Entente or League of Nations, would decide the fate of eastern Lithuania. After capturing Vilnius on October 9, Gen. Żeligowski's forces continued their invasion of Lithuania but their advance was halted by the Lithuanian Army in fierce battles at the towns of Giedraičiai and Širvintos, north of the capital. An armistice brokered by the League of Nations Control Commission was proclaimed on November 21, 1920. As supreme commander of the army of Central Lithuania (q. v.) during 1920-1922, Żeligowski controlled this ministate before its formal incorporation into Poland. In 1925-1926 he was Poland's minister of defense and served as a member of the Polish parliament from 1927 to 1939. Żeligowski died in London on July 9, 1947. See VILNIUS QUESTION.

ŽEMAITĖ. The pen name of Julija Žymantienė née Beniuševičiūtė (1845-1921), Lithuanian writer, born on May 31, 1845 in Plungė district. Žemaitė was raised in a family of poor Samogitian gentry and was tutored at home, receiving no formal schooling. Like most Lithuanian gentry women, she was raised in Polish culture, but attained a command of the Samogitian dialect through her close contacts with peasants. In 1865 she married Laurynas Žymantas, with whom she lived in poverty for nearly twenty years. After the couple's circumstances improved, Žemaitė became interested in Lithuanian literature in part through her acquaintance with the student (and later editor), Povilas Višinskis (1875-1906), who encouraged her literary efforts and suggested her pen name, meaning "The Samogitian Woman." Her first short story, *Piršlybos* (Lith. Matchmaking), was published in 1895 and was followed by scores of short stories and sketches of contemporary Lithuanian life. Žemaitė was a pioneer in developing secular, non-didactic prose fiction in the Lithuanian language. In 1911 she moved to Vilnius and during 1913-1915 worked as a newspaper editor. In 1916 Žemaitė came to the United States to raise funds for Lithuanian war victims; while here, she wrote primarily for the Lithuanian socialist press. While Žemaitė joined the Social Democrats in 1917 and expressed anticlerical attitudes, she was sharply critical of Bolshevism. She died in Marijampolė on December 7, 1921 soon after her return from America.

Žemaitėoccupies a unique niche in the history of Lithuanian literature. In contrast to the contemporary fashion of idealizing Lithuanian village life, she penned powerful descriptions of the backwardness, ignorance and social injustice of rural Samogitia, based on her own experiences and written in the rough speech of the local peasantry. While she portrayed the Polonized gentry as an alien and demoralizing exploiter of the peasants, Žemaitė also revealed the roots of narrowness and provincialism in Lithuanian society itself, whether among the peasants or intelligentsia. Žemaitė was the only Lithuanian writer of the period to consistently address the problem of the subjugation of women as a major social issue; she is thus one of the earliest proponents of equality for women in Lithuania. See LITERATURE.

ŽEMAITIJA. See SAMOGITIA.

BIBLIOGRAPHY

Introduction

In compiling a historical bibliography on Lithuania for the English-speaking reader, one immediately encounters the issue of language. There is a particular problem with primary sources: except for Lithuanian-speaking East Prussia before World War I, the official documents that are available for the period before the early 20th century were issued in Latin, the Belarusan form of Old Church Slavic, Polish, German or Russian. There are few English-language translations of primary sources, although there is a more extensive selection of translated memoirs. However, for those readers familiar with Slavic languages, and for students of medieval and modern European history, I have listed the more important collections of primary sources in the major languages listed above. Regarding reference books and atlases, I have also included some titles in non-Western languages if they contain useful bibliographies, maps, art, statistical charts or summaries in English or other Western languages that can be accessed by those with some foreign-language skills. For the non-Western languages, I have indicated the language of the work and provided a translation of the title; for Cyrillic titles, I have used a simplified version of the Romanization system employed by the U. S. Bureau of Standards.

Before 1945 historical studies and monographs dealing with Lithuanian history were published primarily in German, Russian, Polish and, since the early 20th century, Lithuanian. It is only in the last quarter-century that the quality and quantity of historical works on Lithuania in English and the major Western languages has improved substantially. I have included not only the most important Western-language secondary works, but also some Russian and

Polish entries, if the latter contain extensive bibliographies or can otherwise be useful to the student with a smattering of Polish and/or Russian. While there is an extensive scholarly historical literature in Lithuanian dating from the early 1900s, I have not, as a rule, included such secondary works: they would be beneficial only to those with a command of Lithuanian and thus of little use to most readers of this *Dictionary.*

Finally, while I have excluded most blatantly propagandistic works which have little pedagogical or scholarly value, the reader must note that not all publications listed below are of equal merit regarding their level of historical scholarship or objectivity. Common sense should make it relatively easy to distinguish the more objective studies from the polemical tracts.

Organization

The bibliography is organized according to the following chronological and topical categories:

REFERENCE WORKS

1. Bibliographies
2. Western-Language Periodicals Relating to Lithuania
3. Encyclopedias
4. Research Aids and Guides to Collections
5. Government Reports and Statistical Publications
6. Atlases and Other Guides

HISTORICAL SOURCES

7. Primary Sources: Documents
8. Primary Sources: Diaries and Memoirs

HISTORICAL STUDIES (CHRONOLOGICAL DIVISIONS)

9. General
10. Prehistoric and Ancient Lithuania, Folklore, Tradition, Pre-Christian Religion
11. The Earlier Medieval Period (ca. 1200-1387)
12. The Later Medieval Period (1387-1569)
13. The Polish-Lithuanian Commonwealth (1569-1795)
14. Tsarist Rule (1795-1863)
15. Tsarist Rule (1863-1914)
16. The Great War and the Struggle for Independence (1914-1920)
17. The Democratic Republic (1920-1926): Domestic Affairs
18. The Authoritarian Republic (1926-1940): Domestic Affairs
19. The Independent Republic (1918-1940): Foreign Affairs
20. Soviet Lithuania (1940-1941)
21. The Nazi Occupation (1941-1944)
22. Soviet Lithuania: The Postwar Stalin Years (1944-1953)
23. Soviet Lithuania After Stalin (1953-1988)
24. Sąjūdis and the Independence Movement (1988-1990)
25. The Republic of Lithuania Since 1990

HISTORICAL STUDIES (TOPICAL DIVISIONS)

26. Art, Language and Culture
27. Literature
28. Women's History
29. Jewish History and the Holocaust
30. Emigration and Diaspora Communities
31. Lithuanian East Prussia (Lithuania Minor)

REFERENCE WORKS

1. Bibliographies

Adomonienė, Ona. *Bibliografiya istorii Litvy: 1971-1975.* [Bibliography of the History of Lithuania, 1971-1975]. Vilnius: Biblioteka Akademii Nauk Litvy, 1992. (In Russian).

_____. *Lietuvos TSR istorijos bibliografija, 1966-1970.* [Bibliography of the History of the Lithuanian SSR, 1966-1970]. Vilnius: Lietuvos TSR MA Istorijos Institutas, 1980. (In Lithuanian).

Balys, Jonas. "Retrospective and Current Lithuanian Bibliographies," *JBS,* 6, 4 (Winter 1975): 329-332.

_____. *Lithuania and Lithuanians: A Selected Bibliography.* New York: Praeger, 1961.

_____. *Lithuanian Periodicals in American Libraries: A Union List.* Washington, DC: Library of Congress, 1982.

Biržiška, Vaclovas. *Lithuanian Publications in the United States, 1874-1910.* Ed. Stasė Vaškelis. Chicago: Institute of Lithuanian Studies, 1994.

Dundulis, Bronius. "A Historiographic Survey of Lithuanian-Polish Relations," *Lituanus,* 17, 4 (Winter 1971): 5-34.

Jakštas, Juozas. "The 1863 Revolt in Soviet Lithuanian Historiography," *Lituanus,* 9, 4 (Winter 1963): 145-148.

Kantautas, Adam and Filomena Kantautas. *A Lithuanian Bibliography: A Check-list of Books and Articles Held by the Major Libraries of Canada and the United States.* Edmonton: The University of Alberta Press, 1975.

_____. *Supplement to a Lithuanian Bibliography: A Further Check-List of Books and Articles Held by the Major Libraries of Canada and the United States.* Edmonton: The University of Alberta Press, 1979.

Krapauskas, Virgil. "Marxism and Nationalism in Soviet Lithuanian Historiography," *JBS,* 23, 3 (Fall 1992): 239-260.

Mažeika, Rasa. "The Grand Duchy Rejoins Europe: Post-Soviet Developments in the Historiography of Pagan Lithuania," *Journal of Medieval History*, 21 (1995): 289-303.

Szameitat, Max. *Bibliographie des Memellandes.* Würzburg: Holzner-Verlag, 1957.

Ulpis, Antanas et al, eds. *Lietuvos TSR Bibliografija. Serija A. Knygos lietuvių kalba.* T. 1: 1547-1861 [Bibliography of the Lithuanian SSR. Series A. Vol. 1: 1547-1861]. Vilnius: Mintis, 1969.

Vėbra, Rimantas. *Bibliografinė rodyklė: 1957-1991.* [A Bibliographical Guide: 1957-1991]. Vilnius: R. Vėbra, 1991.

2. Western-Language Periodicals Relating to Lithuania

Acta Baltica. (Königstein im Taunus). Irregular. 1960/61- .

Baltic Forum. Semiannual. 1981-1989.

Baltic Independent. Vilnius. Weekly. 1991- .

Baltic Observer. Riga. Weekly. 1992- .

Baltic Review. New York. Irregular. 1953- .

Baltistica. Vilnius. Semiannual. 1965- .

Bridges. Brooklyn, NY. Monthly. 1989- .

Bulletin of Baltic Studies. Brooklyn, NY. Quarterly. 1970-1971.

East and West. London. Quarterly. 1954-1961.

Journal of Baltic Studies. Quarterly. 1971- .

Lietuvos TSR Mokslų Akademija [The Academy of Sciences of the Lithuanian SSR]. Series A. Vilnius. Semiannual. 1955-1990.

Lithuanian Bulletin. New York. Irregular. 1943-1951.

Lithuanian Days: Lietuvių Dienos. Los Angeles. Monthly. 1946-.

Lituanistikos darbai. Lithuanian Studies. Chicago. Annual. 1970- .

Lituanus. Chicago. Quarterly. 1954- .

Revista Baltica. Buenos Aires. Semiannual. 1957- .

Revue Baltique. Tallinn. Quarterly. 1940.

Studi Baltici. Rome. 1931-1940, 1952-1961.

Vytis. The Knight. Chicago. 1915- .

3. Encyclopedias

Banevičius, Algirdas. *111 Lietuvos valstybės 1918-1940 politikos veikėjų enciklopedinis žinynas.* [An Encyclopedic Directory of 111 Political Figures of the Lithuanian State, 1918-1940]. Vilnius: Knyga, 1991. (In Lithuanian).
Lietuvių enciklopedija [Lithuanian Encyclopedia]. 37 vols. Boston: Lithuanian Encyclopedia Press, 1953-1985. (In Lithuanian).
Sužiedėlis, Simas, ed. *Encyclopedia Lituanica.* 6 vols. Boston: Lithuanian Encyclopedia Press, 1970-1978. (In English).
Zinkus, Jonas, ed. *Lithuania: An Encyclopedic Survey.* Vilnius: Encyclopedia Publishers, 1986.

4. Research Aids and Guides to Collections

Cadzow, John F. "The Lithuanian Periodical Holdings in the Kent State Library," *JBS,* 5, 3 (Fall 1974): 264-275.

Dwyer, Joseph D. "The Lithuanian Collection of the University of Pennsylvania Libraries," *JBS,* 4, 3 (Fall 1973): 298-299.

Grimstead, Patricia Kennedy. *Archives and Manuscript Repositories in the USSR, Estonia, Latvia, Lithuania and Belorussia.* Princeton, NJ: Princeton University Press, 1981.

_____. *The 'Lithuanian Metrica' in Moscow and Warsaw: Reconstructing the Archives of the Grand Duchy of Lithuania, Including an Annotated Edition of the 1887 Inventory Compiled by Stanisław Ptaszycki.* Cambridge, MA: Harvard Ukrainian Research Institute, 1984.

Higher Education and Research Institutions in Lithuania: A Short Guide. Vilnius: Lithuanian Information Institute, 1993.

Koressaar, Victor. "Baltic Studies and Library Resources," *Bulletin of Baltic Studies,* 2 (1970), 3-5.

Nollendorfs, Valters and Betty J. Zeps. "Research Materials in Baltic Studies: A Survey of Availability and Need," *JBS,* 11, 4 (Winter 1980): 283-314.

Paulauskas, Vaclovas. *Who's Who in Lithuania.* Vilnius: Politika, 1993.

Šešplaukis, Alfonsas. *Lituanica Collections in European Research Libraries.* Chicago: Lithuanian Research and Studies Center, 1986.

Ziplans, Emilija E., et al, comps. "Baltic Material in the University of Toronto Library," *JBS,* 4, 3 (Fall 1973): 279-280.

5. Government Reports and Statistical Publications

Čepaitė, Zita, Daila Gudavičiūtė, Solveiga Daugirdaitė, comps. *Lithuania: Women in a Changing Society.* Vilnius: Lithuanian Non-Governmental Women's Organization, 1995.

Constitution of the Republic of Lithuania, 1992. Vilnius: Publishing House of the Seimas, 1993.

Lietuvos moterys. Lithuania's Women. Vilnius: Lietuvos Statistikos departamentas, 1994. (In English and Lithuanian).

Lietuvos vaikai. Lithuanian Children. Vilnius: Lietuvos Statistikos departamentas, 1994. (In English and Lithuanian).

342 / Bibliography

Lithuania. Washington, DC: International Monetary Fund, 1993.

Lithuania: Women in the Changing Society. Report Compiled by Lithuanian Non-Governmental Women's Organizations to be Presented at the United Nations Organization Fourth Women's World Conference in Beijing, 1995. Vilnius: Pradai, 1995.

Navikas, A. *Lithuania: Partner in a World Economy.* Vilnius: Lithuanian Ministry of Foreign Affairs, 1994.

Royal Institute of International Affairs. *The Baltic States: A Survey of the Political and Economic Structure and the Foreign Relations of Estonia, Latvia and Lithuania.* London: Oxford University Press, 1938. Reprinted Greenwood Press, 1970.

United States Congress. *Baltic States Investigation. Hearings Before the Select Committee to Investigate the Incorporation of the Baltic States into the U.S S.R.* Washington, DC: Government Printing Office, 1954.

_____. Select Committee on Communist Aggression. *Baltic States Investigation. Hearings Before the Select Committee to Investigate the Incorporation of the Baltic States into the U.S.S.R., November 30-December 11, 1953.* Washington, DC: Government Printing Office, 1953.

_____. Select Committee on Communist Aggression. *Investigation of Communist Takeover and Occupation of Poland, Lithuania and Slovakia. Sixth Interim Report of Hearings before the Subcommittee on Poland, Lithuania and Slovakia of the Select Committee on Communist Aggression.* Washington, DC: Government Printing Office, 1954.

United States Central Intelligence Agency. *The Baltic States.* Washington, DC: Central Intelligence Agency, 1994.

United States. Department of State. Office of Public Communication. *Background Notes: Lithuania.* Washington, DC: U.S. Dept. of State, Government Printing Office, 1994.

Women in Lithuania: The National Report to the Fourth UN World Conference on Women in Beijing 1995. Vilnius: Danielius, 1995.

6. Atlases and Other Guides

Augustinas, Vytautas. *Lithuania.* Brooklyn, NY: Ateitis, 1955.

Harrison, Ernest J., ed. *Lithuania, 1928.* London: Hazell, Watson & Viney, 1928.

Karys, Jonas K. *Nepriklausomos Lietuvos pinigai* [The Currency of Independent Lithuania]. New York: Franciscan Fathers Press, 1953. (In Lithuanian).

Lietuvos TSR Aukščiausiosios Tarybos Prezidiumo Organizacinis-Informacinis Skyrius [The Information-Organization Section of the Presidium of the Supreme Soviet of the Lithuanian SSR]. *Lietuvos TSR administracinis-teritorinis suskirstymas 1959 m. vasario 1 dienai.* [The Administrative-Territorial Arrangement of the Lithuanian SSR as of February 1, 1959]. Vilnius: VPMLL, 1959. (In Lithuanian).

Macijauskas, Aleksandras. *My Lithuania.* New York, NY: Thames and Hudson, 1991.

Pocius, Jonas. *Present-day Lithuania in Figures.* Vilnius: Gintaras, 1971.

Pugevičius, Casimir and Marian Skabeikis, eds. *World Lithuanian Roman Catholic Directory.* New York: Franciscan Press, 1981. (In English and Lithuanian).

Twinning, David T. *Guide to the Republics of the Former Soviet Union.* Westport, CT: Greenwood Press, 1993.

HISTORICAL SOURCES

7. Primary Sources: Documents

Consultations of MM. de Lapradelle, Louis de Fleur and Andre Mandelstam Concerning the Binding Force of the Decision of the Conference of Ambassadors of March 15, 1923. London: Hazell, Watson and Viney, 1929.

Deveikė, Jonė, trans. *Didžiosios Lietuvos Kunigaikštijos 1529 metų Statutas* [The 1529 Statute of the Grand Duchy of Lithuania].

Intro. Aleksandras Plateris. Chicago: Morkūnas Printing Press, 1971. (Text of the statute in old Belarusan and Lithuanian.)

Documents Concerning the Dispute Between Poland and Lithuania. Geneva: League of Nations, 1920.

Kaslas, Bronius J, ed. *The USSR-German Aggression Against Lithuania.* Intro. and Foreword by Bronis J. Kaslas. New York: R. Speller, 1973.

La Lithuanie et la Seconde Guerre mondiale: recueil des documents. Paris: G.-P. Maisonneuve et Larose, 1981.

Lithuania, 1991.01.13: Documents, Testimonies, Comments. Vilnius: State Pub. Center, 1992.

Lazutka, Stanislav. *Privilegiya evreiyam Vitautasa Velikogo 1388 goda.* [The Jewish Privilege of Vytautas the Great of 1388]. Moscow: Evreiskii universitet v Moskve, 1993. (In Russian).

Lazutka, Stasys and Edvardas Gudavičius, eds. *Pirmasis Lietuvos Statutas.* Vol. 1, Part 2: *Paleografinė ir tekstologinė nuorašų analizė* [The First Lithuanian Statute. Vol. 1, Part 2: A Paleographic and Textual Analysis of the Copies]. Vilnius: Mintis, 1983. (In Lithuanian and Russian).

Lazutka, Stasys and Edvardas Gudavičius, eds. *Pirmasis Lietuvos Statutas.* Vol. 1, Part 2: *Dzialinskio, Lauryno ir Ališavos nuorašų faksimilės* [The First Lithuanian Statute: Vol. 1, Part 2: Facsimiles of the Dzialiński, Laurynas and Ališava (Olszewski) Copies]. Vilnius: Mintis, 1985. (In Lithuanian and Russian).

Le Saint-Siege et la situation religieuse en Pologne et dans les Pays Baltes, 1939-1945. 3 vols. Vatican City: Libreria Ed. Vaticana, 1967.

Lietuvos gyventojų trėmimai: 1941, 1945-1952. Dokumentų rinkinys [The Deportations of Lithuania's Inhabitants: 1941, 1945-1952]. Vilnius: Mokslo ir enciklopedijų leidykla, 1994.

Pashuto, Vladimir and Shtal, I., eds. *Gedimino laiškai.* [The Letters of Gediminas]. Vilnius: Mintis, 1966. (In Lithuanian, Russian and Latin.)

Rabikauskas, Paulius, ed. *The Foundation of the University of Vilnius (1579): Royal and Papal Grants.* Rome: Lietuvių Katalikų Mokslo Akademija, 1979.

Rozauskas, Eusiejus, ed. *Documents Accuse.* Compilation and commentary by Boleslavas Baranauskas and Kazys Rukšėnas. Vilnius: Gintaras, 1970.

Sontag, Raymond James and James Stuart Beddin, eds. *Nazi-Soviet Relations 1939-1941: Documents from the Archives of the German Foreign Office.* Washington, DC: Department of State, 1948.

Sužiedėlis, Saulius. "An OSS Report on Wartime Population Changes in the Baltic," *Lituanus,* 27, 3 (Fall 1981): 67-80.

The Road to Negotiations with the USSR. 2nd rev. ed. Vilnius: State Pub. Centre, 1991.

Vaitkevičius, Bronius, Juozas Žiugžda et al, eds. *Bor'ba za sovetskuyu vlast' v Litve 1918-1920. Sbornik dokumentov* [The Struggle for Soviet Power in Lithuania 1918-1920. A Collection of Documents]. Vilnius: Mintis, 1967. (In Russian)

8. Primary Sources: Diaries and Memoirs

Armonas, Barbara. *Leave Your Tears in Moscow.* New York: Harper & Row, 1961.

Garbštienė, Onutė. *Hell in Ice.* Trans. Raimunda K. Bartuška. Intro. Alfred Erich Senn. Vilnius: Mintis, 1992.

Kudirka, Simas. *For Those Still at Sea: The Defection of a Lithuanian Sailor.* Written with Larry Eichel. New York: The Dial Press, 1977.

"Lithuanians by the Laptev Sea: The Siberian Memoirs of Dalia Grinkevičiūtė (translated by Laima Sruoginytė)," *Lituanus,* 36, 4 (Winter 1990): 37-67.

Mekas, Jonas. *I Had Nowhere to Go.* New York: Black Thistle Press, 1991.

Pasek, Jan Chryzostom. *Memoirs of the Polish Baroque: The Writings of Jan Chryzostom Pasek, a Squire of the Commonwealth of Poland and Lithuania.* Catherine S. Leach, ed. Berkeley: University of California Press, 1976.

Stanke, Alain. *So Much to Forget: A Child's Vision of Hell.* Agincourt, Ont.: Gage Publishing, 1977.

Yla, Stasys. *A Priest in Stutthof: Human Experiences in the World of the Subhuman.* Trans. Nola M. Zobarskas. New York: Manyland books, 1971.

HISTORICAL STUDIES (CHRONOLOGICAL DIVISIONS)

9. General

Allworth, Edward, ed. *Nationality Group Survival in Multi-Ethnic States: Shifting Support Patterns in the Soviet Baltic Region.* New York: Praeger, 1977.

American Lithuanian Literary Association. *Lithuania, Past and Present.* New York: American Lithuanian Literary Association, 1965.

Backus, Oswald P. "The Impact of the Baltic and Finnic Peoples Upon Russian History," *JBS*, 4, 1 (Spring 1973): 1-10.

Biržiška, Vaclovas. "Provisional Governments in Lithuanian History," *Lituanus*, 8, 1-2 (Spring 1964): 3-10.

Bourdeaux, Michael. *Land of Crosses.* Chulmleigh, Devon, UK: Augustine, 1980.

Chase, Thomas G. *The Story of Lithuania.* New York: Stratford House, 1946.

Clemens, Walter C., Jr. *Baltic Independence and Russian Empire.* New York: St. Martin's Press, 1991.

Ekmanis, Rolfs. "Russia, the West and the Baltics," *Lituanus,* 41, 4 (Winter 1995): 5-28.

Forgus, Silvia P. "Manifestations of Nationalism in the Baltic Republics," *Nationalities Papers*, 7, 2 (Fall 1979), 197-212.

Fitzmaurice, John. *The Baltic. A Regional Future?* New York: St. Martin's Press, 1992.

Gerutis, Albert, ed. *Lithuania: 700 Years.* 3rd rev. ed. New York: Manyland Books, 1969.

Greimas, Algirdas. *La Lithuanie, un des pays baltes.* Kaunas: Baltos Lankos, 1993.

Harrison, Ernest J. *Lithuania: Past and Present.* London: T. F. Unwin, 1922.

Johnston, Hank. "The Comparative Study of Nationalism: Six Pivotal Themes from the Baltic States," *JBS,* 23, 2 (Summer 1992): 95-104.

Jurgėla, Constantine R. *Lithuania: The Outpost of Freedom.* St. Petersburg, FL: Valkyrie Press, 1976.

_____. Kazys Gečys and Simas Sužiedėlis. *Lithuania in a Twin Teutonic Clutch: A Historical Review of German-Lithuanian Relations.* New York: Lithuanian-American Information Center, 1945.

Jurgėla, Kostas. *History of the Lithuanian Nation.* New York: Lithuanian Cultural Institute, 1948.

Kasulaitis, Algirdas. *Lithuanian Christian Democracy.* Chicago: Leo XIII Fund, 1976.

Kirby, David. *The Baltic World 1772-1993: Europe's Northern Periphery in an Age of Change.* London: Longman, 1995.

Kirch, Aksel, Marika Kirch and Tarmo Tuisk. "Russians in the Baltic States: To Be or Not to Be?" *JBS,* 24, 2 (1993): 173-188.

Končius, Joseph B. *History of Lithuania.* Chicago: Lithuanian Catholic Press, n. d.

Lange, Falk. "The Baltic States and the CSCE," *JBS,* 25, 3 (Fall 1994): 233-248.

Lieven, Anatol. *The Baltic Revolution: Estonia, Latvia, Lithuania and the Path to Independence.* 2nd ed. New Haven: Yale University Press, 1994.

Litauen und seine Deutschen: Beiträge zur litauischen Geschichte sowie über die deutsche Volksgruppe in Vergangenheit und Gegenwart. Würzburg: Holzner-Verlag, 1955.

Loeber, Dietrich Andre, ed. *Regional Identity under Soviet Rule: The Case of the Baltic States.* Kiel: Institute for the Study of Law, Politics and Society of Socialist States and AABS, 1990.

Luntinen, Pertti. *The Baltic Question, 1903-1908.* Helsinki: Suomalainen Tiedeakatemia, 1975.

Manning, Clarence A. *The Forgotten Republics.* New York: Philosophical Library, 1952.

348 / Bibliography

Meissner, Boris, Dietrich A. Loeber and Egil Levits, eds. *Die Wirtschaft der baltischen Staaten im Umbruch.* Cologne: Verlag Wissenschaft und Politik: 1993.

Misiūnas, Romuald and Rein Taagepera. *The Baltic States: Years of Dependence 1940-1990.* 2nd rev. ed. Berkeley: University of California Press, 1993.

Ney, Gottlieb. "Lebensraum und Schiksalswandlungen der Völker des Baltikums," *Acta Baltica,* 1 (1960/61), 9-58.

Oakley, Stewart P. *War and Peace in the Baltic, 1560-1790.* London: Routledge, 1992.

Ochmański, Jerzy. *Historia Litwy* [History of Lithuania]. 2nd ed. Wrocław: Ossolineum, 1982. (In Polish).

Penkaitis, Norbert. *Agrarentwicklung in Litauen: 1918-1992.* Berlin: Duncker & Humblot, 1994.

Rauch, George von. *The Baltic States: The Years of Independence, 1917-1940.* University of California Press: Berkeley, 1974. Reprinted New York: St. Martin's Press, 1995.

Rezun, Miron, ed., *Nationalism and the Breakup of an Empire: Russia and Its Periphery.* Westport, CT: Praeger, 1992.

Šapoka, Adolfas. *Vilnius in the Life of Lithuania.* Trans. E. J. Harrison. Toronto: Lithuanian Association for the Vilnius Region, 1962.

Smith, Graham. *The Baltic States: The National Self-Determination of Estonia, Latvia, and Lithuania.* New York: St. Martin's Press, 1994.

_____, ed. *The Nationalities Question in the Soviet Union.* London and New York: Longman, 1990.

Smith, Inese A. and Maria V. Grunts. *The Baltic States: Estonia, Latvia and Lithuania.* Oxford: Clio Press, 1993.

Sprudzs, Adolf, ed. *The Baltic Path to Independence. An International Reader of Selected Articles.* Buffalo, NY: William S. Hein, 1994.

Stanke, Alain. *Lituanie: l'independance en pleurs ou en fleurs.* Montreal: Editions internationales A. Stanke, 1990.

Sužiedėlis, Saulius A. *The Sword and the Cross: A History of the Church in Lithuania.* Huntington, IN: OSV Press, 1988.

Thaden, Edward C. with Marianna Forster Thaden. *Russia's Western Borderlands, 1710-1870.* Princeton, NJ: Princeton University Press, 1984.

Trapans, Jan Arveds, ed. *Toward Independence: the Baltic Popular Movements.* Boulder, CO: Westview Press, 1991.

Vakar, Nicholas P. *Belorussia: The Making of a Nation.* Cambridge, MA: Harvard University Press, 1956.

Ziedonis, Arvids, ed. *Problems of Mini-Nations: Baltic Perspectives.* San Jose, CA: AABS, 1973.

10. Prehistoric and Ancient Lithuania, Folklore, Tradition and Pre-Christian Religion

Bagdanavičius, Vytautas. "The Lithuanian Legends of Laumės (Fairies) as a Remnant from a Stone Age Culture," *Lituanus*, 18, 1 (Spring, 1972): 73-80.

Gimbutas, Marija. *The Balts.* New York: Praeger, 1963.

_____. *The Civilization of the Goddess.* San Francisco: Harper, 1991.

_____. *The Goddesses and Gods of Old Europe, 6500-3500 BC: Myths and Cult Images.* New and updated ed. London: Thames and Hudson, 1982.

_____. *The Language of the Goddess.* San Francisco: Harper, 1991.

Greimas, Algirdas Julien. *Of Gods and Men: Studies in Lithuanian Mythology.* Trans. Milda Newman. Bloomington, IN: Indiana University Press, 1992.

Jaskanis, Danuta. *The Balts: The Northern Neighbours of the Slavs.* Warsaw: State Archeological Museum, 1981.

Mugurēvičs, Ēvalds. "A Historical Survey and Present Problems of Archaeological Science in the Baltic States," *JBS*, 24, 3 (Fall 1993): 283-294.

Noonan, Thomas. "Dirhan Hoards from Medieval Lithuania," *JBS*, 23, 4 (Winter 1992): 395-414.

Puzinas, Jonas. "In Search of the Origins of the Lithuanian People," *Lituanus*, 3, 1 (March 1957): 7-11.

Todd, Joan M. and Marijean H. Eichel. "A Reappraisal of the Prehistoric and Classic Amber Trade in the Light of New Evidence," *JBS,* 5, 4 (Winter 1974): 295-314.

Vėlius, Norbertas. *The World Outlook of the Ancient Balts.* Vilnius: Mintis, 1989.

Vycinas, Vincent. *The Great Goddess and the Aistian World.* New York: P. Lang, 1990.

11. The Earlier Medieval Period (ca. 1200-1387)

Christiansen, Eric. *The Northern Crusades: the Baltic and the Catholic Frontier, 1100-1525.* Minneapolis: University of Minnesota Press, 1980.

Gidžiūnas, Viktoras. "The Introduction of Christianity into Lithuania," *Lituanus,* 3, 4 (December, 1957): 6-13.

Giedroyć, Michał. "The Arrival of Christianity in Lithuania: Baptism and Survival (1341-1387)," *Oxford Slavonic Papers,* 22 (1989): 34-57.

_____. "The Arrival of Christianity in Lithuania: Early Contacts (Thirteenth Century)," *Oxford Slavonic Papers,* 18 (1985): 1-30.

_____. "The Arrival of Christianity in Lithuania: Between Rome and Byzantium (1281-1341)," *Oxford Slavonic Papers,* 20 (1987): 1-33.

_____. "The Ruthenian-Lithuanian Metropolitanates and the Progress of Christianisation (1300-1458)," *Nuovi studi storici,* 17 (1992): 315-342.

Kajackas, Algimantas. "The History and Recent Archeological Investigations of the Vilnius Cathedral," *Lituanus,* 36, 1 (Spring 1990): 49-58.

Kasekamp, Andres. "Characteristics of Warfare in the Times of Henry of Livonia and Balthasar Russow," *Lituanus,* 36, 1 (Spring 1990): 27-38.

Łowmiański, Henryk. *Studia nad dziejami Wielkiego Księstwa Litewskiego.* [Studies in the History of the Grand Duchy of

Lithuania]. Poznań: Adam Mickiewicz University, 1983. (In Polish and Russian.)

Mažeika, Rasa. "Of Cabbages and Knights: Trade and Trade Treaties with the Infidel on the Northern Frontier, 1200-1390," *Journal of Medieval History,* 20 (1994): 63-76.

_____. "Was Grand Prince Algirdas a Greek Orthodox Christian?" *Lituanus,* 33, 4 (Winter 1987): 35-55.

Mažeika, Rasa and S. C. Rowell. "Zelatores Maximi: Pope John XXII, Archbishop Frederick of Riga and the Baltic Mission 1305-1340," *Archivum Historiae Pontificiae,* 31 (1993): 33-68.

Nikžentaitis, Alvydas. "Die friedliche Periode in den Beziehungen zwischen dem Deutschen Orden und dem Grossfürstentum Litauen (1345-1360)," *Jahrbücher für Geschichte Osteuropas,* 41 (1993): 1-22.

Pashuto, V. T. *Obrazovanie litovskogo gosudarstva* [The Formation of the Lithuanian State]. Moscow: AN SSSR, 1959. (In Russian).

Roesdahl, Else, and David Wilson, eds. *From Viking to Crusader: Scandinavia and Europe 800-1200.* New York: Rizzoli, 1992.

Rowell, S. C. "A Pagan's Word: Lithuanian Diplomatic Procedure 1200-1385," *Journal of Medieval History,* 18 (1992): 145-60.

_____. "Between Lithuania and Rus': Dovmont-Timofey of Pskov, His Life and Cult," *Oxvford Slavonic Papers,* 25 (1992): 1-33.

_____. "Of Men and Monsters: Sources for the History of Lithuania in the Time of Gediminas," *JBS,* 24, 1 (Spring, 1993): 73-112.

_____. "Pagans, Peace and the Pope 1322-1324: Lithuania in the Centre of European Diplomacy," *Archivum Historiae Pontificiae,* 28 (1990): 63-98.

_____. "Pious Princesses or the Daughters of Belial: Pagan Lithuanian Dynastic Diplomacy, 1279-1423," *Medieval Prosopography,* 15 (1994): 3-77.

_____. "The Letters of Gediminas: 'Gemachte Lüge?' Notes on a Controversy," *Jahrbücher für Geschichte Osteuropas,* 41 (1993): 321-360.

_____. *Lithuania Ascending: A Pagan Empire within East Central Europe 1295-1345.* Cambridge: Cambridge University Press, 1994. [Cambridge Studies in Medieval Life and Thought, 25]

Sayers, William. "Scapulimancy in the Medieval Baltic," *JBS,* 23, No. 1 (Winter 1992): 57-62.

Urban, William. "Medieval Livonian Numismatics," *JBS,* 24, 1 (Spring, 1993), 37-52.

_____. *The Baltic Crusade.* DeKalb, IL: Northern Illinois University Press, 1975.

_____. *The Livonian Crusade.* Washington, DC: University Press of America.

_____. *The Prussian Crusade.* Lanham, MD: University Press of America, 1980.

_____. *The Samogitian Crusade.* Chicago: Lithuanian Research and Studies Center, 1989.

12. The Later Medieval Period (1387-1569)

Backus, Oswald P. "The Problem of Unity in the Polish-Lithuanian State," *Slavic Review,* 22, 3 (Fall 1963): 411-455.

Backus, Oswald P. *Motives of West Russian Nobles in Deserting Lithuania for Moscow 1377-1514.* Lawrence, KS: University of Kansas Press, 1957.

Halecki, Oscar. *Jadwiga of Anjou and the Rise of East Central Europe.* Ed. Thaddeus V. Gromada. Boulder, CO: East European Monographs, 1991.

Jakštas, Juozas. "Długosz About the Battle of Tannenberg: Vytautas and the Lithuanians Through the Eyes of a Chronicler," *Lituanus,* 7, 4 (Winter 1961): 120-123.

Jurgela, Constantine R. *Tannenberg (Eglija - Grunwald) 15 July 1410.* New York: Lithuanian Veterans Association Ramove, 1961.

Koncevičius, Joseph B. *Russia's Attitude Towards Union with Rome.* Washington, DC: Canorma Press, 1927.

Lazutka, Stasys. *I Litovskii Statut: Feodal'nyi kodekds Velikogo Kniazhestva litovskogo* [The First Lithuanian Statute: A Feudal Code of the Grand Duchy of Lithuania]. Vilnius: Ministry of Education of the Lithuanian SSR, 1974. (In Russian).

Ochmański, Jerzy. *Biskupstwo wileńskie w średniowieczu: ustrój i uposażenie.* [The Vilnius Diocese in the Middle Ages: Its Organization and Funding]. Poznań: Adam Mickiewicz University, 1972. (In Polish).

Picheta, Vladimir I. *Belorussiya i Litva XV-XVI vv.: issledovaniya po istorii sotsial'no-ekonomicheskogo, politicheskogo i kultur'- nogo razvitiya.* [Belarus and Lithuania in the 15th and 16th Centuries: Studies in Social-Economic, Political and Cultural Development]. Moscow: AN SSSR, 1961. (In Russian).

Sruogienė-Sruoga, Vanda. "Jogaila (1350-1434)," *Lituanus,* 33, 4 (Winter 1987): 23-34.

Sužiedėlis, Saulius. "The Meaning of 1387," *Lituanus,* 33, 4 (Winter 1987): 8-11.

Sužiedėlis, Simas. *Der heilige Casimir, 1458-1484: zum Gedächtnis seines 500. Todestages.* Christiana Verlag: Stein am Rhein, 1984.

Urban, William. "The Conversion of Lithuania 1387," *Lituanus,* 33, 4 (Winter 1987): 12-22.

White, William. "The Baltic as a Common Frontier of Eastern and Western Europe in the Middle Ages," *Lituanus,* 19, 4 (Winter 1973): 5-39.

13. The Polish-Lithuanian Commonwealth (1569-1795)

Dembkowski, Harry E. *The Union of Lublin: Polish Federalism in the Golden Age.* Boulder, CO: East European Monographs, 1982.

Frost, Robert I. *After the Deluge: Poland-Lithuania and the Second Northern War 1655-1660.* Cambridge: Cambridge University Press, 1993 [Cambridge Studies in Early Modern History]

Kirby, David. *Northern Europe in the Early Modern Period: The Baltic World 1492-1772.* London: Longman, 1990.

Lisk, Jill. *The Struggle for Supremacy in the Baltic, 1600-1725.* New York: Minerva Press, 1968.

Misūnas, Romuald J. "The Šventoji Project: 18th Century Plans for a Lithuanian Port," *JBS,* 8, 1 (Spring 1977): 28-50.

Picheta, Vladimir I. *Agrarnaya reforma Sigizmunda-Avgusta v litovsko-russkom gosudarstve.* [The Agrarian Reform of Sigismund August in the Lithuanian-Russian State]. Moscow: AN SSSR, 1958. (In Russian).

Plateris, Aleksandras. "The Codification of Law in the Grand Duchy of Lithuania," *Lituanus,* 11, 2 (Summer 1965): 28-44.

Trumpa, Vincas. "The Disintegration of the Polish-Lithuanian Commonwealth: A Commentary," *Lituanus,* 10, 2 (Summer 1964): 24-32.

14. Tsarist Rule (1795-1863)

Aleksandravičius, Egidijus. "Political Goals of Lithuanians,1863-1918," *JBS,* 23, 3 (Fall 1992): 227-238.

_____. "Hebrew Studies at Vilnius University and Lithuanian Ethnopolitical Tendencies in the First Part of the 19th Century," *Lituanus,* 37, 2 (Summer 1991): 5-22.

Cizauskas, Albert. "The Unusual Story of Thaddeus Kosciusko (1746-1817)," *Lituanus,* 32, 1 (Spring 1986): 47-66.

Fajnhauz, Dawid. *Ruch konspiracyjny na Litwie i Białorusi.* [The Conspiratorial Movement in Lithuania and Belarus]. Warsaw: PWN, 1965. (In Polish).

Koniukhova, T. A. *Gosudarstvennaya derevnya Litvy i reforma P. D. Kiseleva:1840-1857 gg.(Vilenskaya i Kovenskaya gubernii).* [The State Village in Lithuania and the Reform of P. D. Kiselev: 1840-1857 (Vilnius and Kaunas Provinces)]. Moscow: Izdatel'stvo Moskovskogo universiteta, 1975. (In Russian).

Sužiedėlis, Saulius. "Language and Social Class in Southwestern Lithuania Before 1864," *Lituanus,* 27, 3 (Fall 1981): 35-57.

Trumpa, Vincas. "Simonas Daukantas, Historian and Pioneer of Lithuanian National Rebirth," *Lituanus,* 11, 1 (Spring 1965): 5-17.

Ulashchik, N. N. *Predposylki krest'yanskoi reformy 1861 g. v Litve i zapadnoi Belorussii.* [The Preconditions for the Peasant Reform of 1861 in Lithuania and Western Belarus]. Moscow: Nauka, 1965. (In Russian).

15. Tsarist Rule (1863-1914)

Hellmann, Manfred. "Die litauische Nationalbewegung im 19. und 20. Jahrhundert," *Zeitschrift für Ostforschung*, 2, 1 (1953): 66-106.

Kahk, Juhan. "The East European Agrarian Reforms of the Middle of the Nineteenth Century in a New Historical Perspective," *JBS*, 23, 1 (Spring 1992): 23-28.

Ochmański, Jerzy. *Litewski ruch narodowo-kulturalny w XIX wieku.*[The Lithuanian National and Cultural Movement of the 19th Century]. Białystok: Białostockie Towarzystwo Naukowe, 1965. (In Polish).

Sabaliūnas, Leonas. *Lithuanian Social Democracy in Perspective 1893-1914.* Durham and London: Duke University Press, 1990.

Senn, Alfred E. *Jonas Basanavičius: Patriarch of Lithuania's National Rebirth.* Newton, MA: Oriental Research Partners, 1980.

_____. "Tsarist Authorities and Lithuanian Book-Smuggling," *JBS,* 11, 4 (Winter 1980), 334-340.

Strazhas, A[belis] S. "From *Auszra* to the Great War: The Emergence of the Lithuanian Nation," *Lituanus*, Vol. 42, No. 4 (Winter 1996), 34-73.

_____. "Lithuania 1863-1893: Tsarist Russification and the Beginnings of the Modern Lithuanian National Movement," *Lituanus,* Vol. 42, No. 3 (Fall, 1996), 36-77.

Weeks, Theodore. "Lithuanians, Poles and the Russian Imperial Government at the Turn of the Century," *JBS,* 25, 4 (Winter 1994): 289-304.

16. The Great War and the Struggle for Independence (1914-1920)

Butkus, Zenonas. "Great Britain's Mediation in the Lithuanian-Latvian Frontier," *JBS*, 24, 4 (Winter 1993): 359-368.

Danahar, David C. "Lithuania through German-Polish Eyes: An Austro-Hungarian State Paper and the Lithuanian Question, 1915-1917," *JBS*, 4, 1 (Spring 1973): 57-73.

Demm, Eberhard. "Anschluss, Autonomie oder Unabhängigkeit? Die deutsche Litauenpolitik im Ersten Weltkrieg und das Selbstbestimmungsrecht der Völker," *JBS*, 25, 2 (Summer 1994): 195-200.

Eidintas, Alfonsas. "Views on Foreign Policy within the Lithuanian State Council 1917-1919," *Studia Baltica Stockholmiensia*, 8 (1991), (Acta Universitatis Stockholmensis), 373-380.

Fischer, Fritz. *Germany's Aims in the First World War.* Intro. by Hajo Holborn. New York: W. W. Norton, 1967.

Foglesong, David. "The United States, Self-Determination and the Struggle Against Bolshevism in the Eastern Baltic, 1918-1920," *JBS*, 26, 2 (Summer 1995): 107-144.

Gabrys, Juozas. *La Lituanie sous le joug allemand 1915-1918; le plan annexioniste allemand en Lituanie.* Lausanne: Librairie centrale des nationalités, 1918.

Hiden, John. "From War to Peace: Britain, Germany and the Baltic States, 1918-1921," *JBS*, 19, 4 (Winter 1988): 371-378.

Jurgėla, Constantine R. *Lithuania and the United States: the Establishment of State Relations.* Chicago: Lithuanian Research and Studies Center, 1985.

Linde, Gerd. *Die deutsche Politik in Litauen im ersten Weltkrieg.* Wiesbaden: Otto Harrasowitz, 1965.

Lithuanian Information Bureau. *The Lithuanian-Polish Dispute.* 3 vols. London: Eyre and Spottiswoode, 1921-1923.

Lopata, Raimundas. "Lithuanian-Polish Cooperation in 1918: the Ronikier-Voldemaras Treaty," *JBS*, 24, 4 (Winter 1993): 349-358.

_____. "The Second Spring of Nations and the Theory of Reconstruction of the Grand Duchy of Lithuania," *Lituanus,* 39, 4 (Winter 1993): 68-78.

Łossowski, Piotr. *Stosunki polsko-litewskie w latach 1918-1920.* [Polish-Lithuanian Relations in the Years 1918-1920]. Warsaw: Książka i Wiedza, 1966. (In Polish).

Misiūnas, Romuald J. "Versailles and Memel," *Lituanus*, 14, 1 (Spring 1968): 65-93.

Navickas, Konstantinas. *Litva i Antanta v 1918-1920 gg.* [Lithuania and the Entente in 1918-1920]. Vilnius: Mintis, 1970. (In Russian).

Page, Stanley W. *The Formation of the Baltic States: A Study of the Effects of Great Power Diplomacy Upon the Emergence of Lithuania, Latvia, and Estonia.* New York: Howard Fertig, 1970.

Senn, Alfred Erich. "Comparing the Circumstances of Lithuanian Independence, 1918-1922 and 1988-1992," *JBS,* 25, 2 (Summer 1994): 123-129.

_____. *The Emergence of Modern Lithuania.* New York: Columbia University Press, 1959.

_____. *The Great Powers, Lithuania and The Vilna Question.* Leiden: E. J. Brill, 1966. [Studies in East European History, 11].

Trapans, Jan Arveds. "The West and the Recognition of the Baltic States: 1919 and 1991: A Study of the Politics of the Major Powers," *JBS*, 25, 2 (Summer 1994), 153-173.

Urbaniak, George. "French Involvement in the Polish-Lithuanian Dispute 1918-1920," *JBS,* 16, 1 (Spring 1985): 52-60.

Vitas, Robert A. "The Recognition of Lithuania: Completion of the Legal Circle," *JBS,* 24, 3 (Fall 1993): 247-262.

Wheeler-Bennett, John W. *Brest-Litovsk: The Forgotten Peace, March 1918.* London: Macmillan, 1938.

White, James D. "The Revolution in Lithuania, 1918-1919," *Soviet Studies*, 23, 2 (October 1971): 186-200.

17. The Democratic Republic (1920-1926): Domestic Affairs

Eidintas, Alfonsas. "Aleksandras Stulginskis: President of Lithuania, Prisoner of the Gulag," *Lituanus*, 41, 4 (Winter 1995): 29-46.

Krivickas, Vladas. "The Lithuanian Populists and the Agrarian Question, 1918-1926," *JBS*, 6, 4 (Winter 1975): 259-271.

_____. "The Polish Minority in Lithuania, 1918-1926," *Slavonic and East European Review*, 53 (January 1975): 78-91.

Kučas Antanas. *Archbishop George Matulaitis*. Trans. Joseph Boley. Boston: Lithuanian Catholic Press Society, 1975.

Simutis, Anicetas. *The Economic Reconstruction of Lithuania after 1918*. New York: Columbia University Press, 1942.

Vardys, V. Stanley. "Democracy in the Baltic States, 1918-1934: The Stage and the Actors," *JBS*, 10, 4 (Winter 1979): 323-336.

18. The Authoritarian Republic (1926-1940): Domestic Affairs

Misiūnas, Romuald J. "Fascist Tendencies in Lithuania," *Slavonic and East European Review*, 48, 110 (January 1970): 88-94.

Sabaliūnas, Leonas. "Lithuanian Politics Under Stress: Ideological and Political Developments Before the Soviet Occupation," *Lituanus*, 14, 3 (Fall 1968), 29-42.

_____. *Lithuania in Crisis: Nationalism to Communism 1939-1940*. Bloomington: Indiana University Press, 1972.

Taagepera, Rein. "Civic Culture and Authoritarianism in the Baltic States, 1930-1940," *East European Quarterly*, 7, 1 (January 1974): 407-412.

19. The Independent Republic (1918-1940): Foreign Affairs

Anderson, Edgar. "Military Policies and Plans of the Baltic States on the Eve of World War II," *Lituanus*, 20, 2 (Summer 1974): 15-34.

Čeginskas, Ebba. "Die baltische Frage in den Grossmächte-verhandlungen 1939," *Commentationes Balticae,* 12/13, 2 (1967): 3-46.

Crowe, David. *The Baltic States and the Great Powers 1938-1940: Foreign Relations.* Boulder, CO: Westview Press, 1993.

Hiden, John and Thomas Lane, eds. *The Baltic and the Outbreak of the Second World War.* Cambridge, UK: Cambridge University Press, 1992.

Hoover, Karl D. "The Baltic Resettlement of 1939 and National Socialist Racial Policy," *JBS,* 8, 1 (Spring 1977): 79-89.

Kancevičius, Vytautas, ed. *Lithuania in 1939-1940: The Historic Turn to Socialism.* Vilnius: Mintis, 1976.

Kaslas, Bronis J. "The Lithuanian Strip in Soviet-German Diplomacy, 1939-1941," *JBS,* 4, 3 (Fall 1973): 211-225.

Kirby, David. "A Great Opportunity Lost? Aspects of British Commercial Policy Toward the Baltic States, 1920-1924," *JBS,* 5, 4 (Winter 1974): 362-378.

Kriaučiūnienė, Živilė. "Contacs politiques et culturels franco-lituaniens en 1918-1920," *JBS,* 26, 1 (Spring 1995): 57-66.

Lautenschläger, Karl. "Plan 'Catherine': The British Baltic Operation, 1940," *JBS,* 5, 3 (Fall 1974): 211-221.

Łossowski, Piotr. *Litwa a sprawy polskie 1939-1940.* [Lithuania and Polish Problems]. Warsaw: PWN, 1982. (In Polish).

Makowski, Bronisław. *Litwini w Polsce 1920-1939.* [Lithuanians in Poland 1920-1939]. Warsaw: Państwowe Wydawnictwo Naukowe, 1986. (In Polish).

Meiksins, Gregory. *The Baltic Riddle: Finland, Estonia, Latvia, Lithuania—Key Points of European Peace.* New York: B. Fischer, 1943.

Meissner, Boris. "Die Beziehungen zwischen der Sowjetunion und den baltischen Staaten von der deutsch-sowjetischen Interessenbegrenzung bis zum sowjetischen Ultimatum," *Zeitschrift für Ostforschung,* 3, 2 (1954): 161-179.

Myllyniemi, Seppo. *Die baltische Krise, 1938-1941.* Trans. by Dietrich Assmann. Stuttgart: Deutsche Verlags-Anstalt, 1979.

Ruffmann, Karl-Heinz. *Deutsche und Litauer in der Zwischen-kriegzeit. Errinerungen enies Memelländers: überlegungen eines

Historikers. Lüneburg: Verlag Nordostdeutsches Kulturwerk, 1994.

Senn, Alfred Erich. "The Polish Ultimatum to Lithuania, March 1938," *JBS,* 13, 2 (Summer 1982): 144-156.

Slavėnas, Julius P. "Lithuania, Klaipėda and Hitler," Ziedonis, Arvids, William L. Winter and Mardi Valgemae, eds. *Baltic History* (Columbus, OH: Ohio State University Press, 1974), 257-260.

_____. "Lithuanian-German Friction over Klaipėda-Memel in the Early 1930s," *Lithuanian Studies,* 3 (1973), 219-229.

Sužiedėlis, Saulius, ed. *History and Commemoration in the Baltic: The Nazi-Soviet Pact, 1939-1989.* Chicago: Morkūnas Publishing Co., 1989.

_____. "The Secret Protocols: A Question of Authenticity," *Baltic Forum,* 6, 2 (Fall 1989): 32-42.

Tarulis, Albert N. *Soviet Policy Toward the Baltic States, 1918-1940.* Notre Dame, IN: Notre Dame University Press, 1959.

Tauber, Joachim. *Die deutsch-litauischen Beziehungen im 20. Jahrhundert.* Lüneburg: Verlag Nordostdeutsches Kulturwerk, 1993.

Toynbee, Veronica M. "German-Lithuanian Relations, 1937-1939, and the Transfer of Memel to Germany, March 1939," *Survey of International Affairs,* 3 (1953): 357-390.

_____. "Relations Between Poland and Lithuania, 1937-1939," *Survey of International Affairs,* 3 (1953), 342-357.

Vitas, Robert A. "The Polish-Lithuanian Crisis of 1938: Events Surrounding the Ultimatum," *Lituanus,* Vol. 30, No. 2 (Summer, 1984): 43-73.

_____. *The U. S. And Lithuania: The Stimson Doctrine of Non-Recognition.* New York: Praeger, 1990.

Vizulis, Izidors. *The Molotov-Ribbentrop Pact of 1939: The Baltic Case.* New York: Praeger, 1989.

Waldren, Stephen. *Lithuania, the Impact of the Stimson Doctrine.* Sandy Bay, Tasmania: Lithuanian Studies Society, 1993.

Žalys, Vytautas. *Ringen um Identität: warum Litauen zwischen 1923 und 1939 im Memelgebiet keinen Erfolg hatte.* Lüneburg: Verlag Nordostdeutsches Kulturwerk, 1993. (In Lithuanian and German)

Žiugžda, Robertas. *Lithuania and the Western Powers, 1917-1940.* Vilnius: Mintis, 1987.

Zwischen Staatsnation und Minderheit. Litauen, das Memelland und das Wilnagebiet in der Zwischenkriegzeit. A special issue of *Nordost-Archiv. Zeitschrift für Regionalgeschichte.* Lüneburg: Institut Nordostdeutsches Kulturwerk. Neue Folge. 2, 2 (1993).

20. Soviet Lithuania (1940-1941)

Anderson, Edgar. "British Policy Toward the Baltic States, 1940-1941," *JBS,* 11, 4 (Winter 1980): 325-333.

Budreckis, Algirdas Martin. *The Lithuanian National Revolt of 1941.* Boston: Lithuanian Encyclopedia Press, 1968.

Hough, William J. H., Jr. "The Annexation of the Baltic States and its Effects on the Development of Law Prohibiting Forcible Seizure of Territory," *New York Law School Journal of International and Comparative Law,* 6, 2 (Winter 1985), 300-533.

Ivinskis, Zenonas. "The Lithuanian Revolt Against the Soviets in 1941," *Lituanus,* 12, 2 (Summer 1966): 5-19.

Juda, Lawrence. "The United States' Nonrecognition of the Soviet Union's Annexation of the Baltic States: Politics and Law," *JBS,* 6, 4 (Winter 1975): 272-290.

Pajaujis-Javis, Juozas. *Soviet Genocide in Lithuania.* New York: Manyland Books, 1980

Senn, Alfred. "The Sovietization of Lithuanian Sports (1940-1941)," *JBS,* 23, 1 (Winter 1992): 73-80.

21. The Nazi Occupation (1941-1944)

Broszat, Martin. "Die nationale Widerstandsbewegung in Litauen im zweiten Weltkrieg, 1941-1944," *Gutachten des Instituts für Zeitgeschichte*, Vol. 2 (1966: Stuttgart), 35-64.

Kochavi, Alrieh. "Britain, the Soviet Union, and the Question of the Baltic States in 1943," *JBS,* 22, 2 (Summer 1991): 173-182.

Mackevičius, Mečislovas. "Lithuanian Resistance to German Mobilization Attempts, 1941-1944," *Lituanus,* 32, 4 (Winter 1986): 9-22.

Myllyniemi, Seppo. *Die Neuordnung der baltischen Länder 1941-1944.* Helsinki: Historiallisia tuktimukisa, 90, 1973.

Pavalkis, Victor. "The Attitude of the Vatican toward the German Church Policy in Lithuania During Its Occupation (1941-1944)," *JBS,* 4, 2 (Summer 1973): 130-134.

Raštikis, Stasys. "The Relations of the Provisional Government of Lithuania with the German Authorities, June 23-August 5, 1941," *Lituanus,* 8, 1-2 (1962): 16-22.

Sužiedėlis, Saulius. "The Military Mobilization Campaigns of 1943 and 1944 in German-Occupied Lithuania: Contrasts in Resistance and Collaboration," *JBS,* 21, 1 (Spring 1990): 33-52.

22. Soviet Lithuania: The Postwar Stalin Years (1944-1953)

Daumantas, Juozas. *Fighters for Freedom: Lithuanian Partisans Versus the U.S.S.R, 1944-1947.* Trans. E. J. Harrison. New York: Manyland Books, 1975.

Remeikis, Thomas. *Opposition to Soviet Rule in Lithuania 1945-1980.* Chicago: Institute of Lithuanian Studies Press, 1980.

Tauras, K. V. [pseud.] *Guerilla Warfare on the Amber Coast.* New York: Voyages Press, 1962.

Vardys, V. Stanley. "The Partisan Movement in Postwar Lithuania," *Slavic Review,* 22 (1963): 499-522.

23. Soviet Lithuania After Stalin (1953-1988)

Dauknys, Pranas. *The Resistance of the Catholic Church in Lithuania Against Religious Persecution.* Rome: Pontificia Studiorum Universitas, 1981.

Idzelis, Augustinas. "Response of Soviet Lithuania to Environmental Problems in the Coastal Zone," *JBS,* 10, 4 (Winter 1979), 299-308.

Kinsella, David and Rein Taagepera. "Religious Incident Statistics for Soviet Lithuanian Schools," *JBS,* 15, 1 (Spring 1984): 27-47.

Namsons, Andris. "Die Lage der katholischen Kirche in Sowjetlitauen," *Acta Baltica,* I (1960/61), 120-130.

Rukšėnas, Algis. *Day of Shame: The Truth About the Murderous Happenings Aboard the Cutter Vigilant During the Russian-American Confrontation off Martha's Vineyard.* New York: David McKay, 1973.

Vaitiekūnas, Vytautas. *A Survey of Developments in Captive Lithuania in 1965-1968.* New York: The Committee for a Free Lithuania, 1970.

Vardys, V. Stanley. "How the Baltic Republics Fare in the Soviet Union," *Foreign Affairs,* 44, 3 (April 1966): 512-517.

_____. "Human Rights Issues in Estonia, Latvia and Lithuania," *JBS,* 12, 3 (Fall 1981): 275-298.

_____. "Modernization and Baltic Nationalism," *Problems of Communism,* 24 (September-October, 1975): 32-48.

_____. "Soviet Colonialism in the Baltic States," *Baltic Review,* 29 (1965): 11-26.

_____, ed. *Lithuania under the Soviets: Portrait of a Nation, 1940-1965.* New York: Praeger, 1965.

_____. *The Catholic Church, Dissent and Nationality in Soviet Lithuania* Boulder, CO: East European Quarterly, 1978.

24. Sąjūdis and the Independence Movement (1988-1990)

Dobriansky, Paula J. *The Baltic States in an Era of Soviet Reform.* Washington, DC: U. S. Department of State, 1989.

Juozaitis, Arvydas. *The Lithuanian Independence Movement and National Minorities.* Frankfurt am Main: Peace Research Institute, 1992.

Senn, Alfred Erich. "Lithuania's Path to Independence," *JBS,* 22, 3 (Fall 1991): 245-250.

_____. *Gorbachev's Failure in Lithuania.* New York: St. Martin's Press, 1995.

_____. *Lithuania Awakening.* Berkeley, CA: University of California Press, 1990.

Vardys, V. Stanley. "Lithuanian National Politics," *Problems of Communism,* (July-August 1989): 60-75.

25. The Republic of Lithuania Since 1990

Burant, Stephen R. "Overcoming the Past: Polish-Lithuanian Relations, 1990-1995," *JBS,* 27, 4 (Winter 1996), 309-330.

_____. "Polish-Lithuanian Relations: Past, Present, and Future," *Problems of Communism,* (May-June 1991): 67-84.

Olcott, Martha Brill. "The Lithuanian Crisis," *Foreign Affairs,* 69, 3 (Summer 1990): 30-46.

Senn, Alfred. "Lithuania's First Two Years of Independence," *JBS,* 25, 1 (Winter 1994): 81-88.

Statteika, E. "Ethnic Minorities (Russians) in Lithuania," *Nationalities Papers,* 23, 3 (1995): 401-404.

Vėbra, Rimantas. "Political Rebirth in Lithuania, 1990-1991," *JBS,* 25, 2 (Summer 1994), 183-188.

HISTORICAL STUDIES (TOPICAL DIVISIONS)

26. Art, Language and Culture

Baltrušaitis, Jurgis. *Lithuanian Folk Art.* Munich: T. J. Vizgirda, 1948.

Dunn, Stephen P. *Cultural Processes in the Baltic Area Under Soviet Rule.* Berkeley, CA: Institute of International Studies, 1966.

Ford, Gordon B., Jr. *The Old Lithuanian Catechism of Martynas Mažvydas (1547).* Assen: Van Gorcum, 1971.

_____. *Old Lithuanian Texts of the Sixteenth and Seventeenth Centuries, With a Glossary.* The Hague: Mouton, 1969.

_____. *The Old Lithuanian Catechism of Baltramiejus Vilentas: A Phonological, Morphological and Syntactical Investigation.* The Hague: Mouton, 1970.

Johnston, Hank. "Religion and Nationalist Subcultures in the Baltics," *JBS,* 23, 2 (Summer 1992): 133-148.

Krikštopaitis, Juozas. "The Subjection of Lithuanian Sciences to the Soviet State System: Consequences and Prospects," *JBS,* 22, 2 (Summer 1991): 169-172.

Kudirka, Juozas. *The Lithuanians: An Ethnic Portrait.* Vilnius: Lithuanian Folk Culture Centre, 1991.

Piročkinas, Arnoldas. "The Lithuanian Language: Hostage of Foreign Powers," *Lituanus,* 42, 2 (Summer 1996), 44-59.

Sabaliauskas, Algirdas. *Noted Scholars of the Lithuanian Language.* Chicago: Akademinės Skautijos Leidykla, 1973.

_____. *We, the Balts.* Trans. by Milda Bakšytė-Richardson. Vilnius: Science and Encyclopedia Publishers, 1993.

Šilbajoris, Rimvydas, ed. *Mind Against the Wall: Essays on Lithuanian Culture Under Soviet Occupation.* Chicago: Institute of Lithuanian Studies Press, 1983.

Venclova, Tomas. "Four Centuries of Enlightenment: A Historic View of the University of Vilnius," *Lituanus,* 27, 2 (Summer 1981): 5-50.

Zinkevičius, Zigmas. *The History of the Lithuanian Language.* Trans. Ramutė Plioplys. Vilnius: Mokslo ir enciklopedijų leidykla, 1996.

27. Literature

Donelaitis, Kristijonas. *The Seasons.* Trans. Nadas Rastenis. Los Angeles: Lithuanian Days Publishers, 1967.

Kelertas, Violeta, ed. *'Come Into My Time': Lithuania in Prose Fiction 1970-1990.* Urbana, IL: University of Illiois, 1992.

––––––––––. "The Image of the German in Soviet Lithuanian Fiction," *JBS*, 10, 4 (Winter 1979): 345-351.

Krėvė, Vincas. *The Temptation.* Trans. Raphael Sealey, Intro. Charles Angoff. New York, Manyland Books, 1965.

––––––––––. *The Herdsman and the Linden Tree.* Trans. Albinas Baranauskas, Pranas Pranckus and Raphael Sealey, Intro. Charles Angoff. New York: Manyland Books, 1964.

Matulis, Anatole C. *Lithuanian Culture in Modern German Prose.* Vienna: R. Spies and Co., 1966.

Meras, Icchokas. *Stalemate.* Trans. Jonas Zdanys. New York: Farrar, Straus, Giroux, 1980.

Miłosz, Czesław. *The Issa Valley.* Trans. Louis Iribrane. New York: Farrar, Straus, Giroux, 1981.

Norkeliūnas, Kazys. "Jurgis Baltrušaitis as Rescuer of Russian Poets and Artists from Bolshevik Persecution," *Lituanus*, Vol. 42, No. 4 (Winter 1996), 26-33.

Pachmuss, Temira. *Russian Literature in the Baltic between the World Wars.* Columbus, OH: Slavica, 1988.

Rubulis, Aleksis. *Baltic Literature: A Survey of Finnish, Estonian, Latvian and Lithuanian Literatures.* Notre Dame: University of Notre Dame Press, 1970.

Shner-Nishmit, Sara. *The Children of Mapu Street: A Novel.* Philadelphia: Jewish Publication Society, 1970.

Skrupskelis, Alina, ed. *Lithuanian Writers in the West: An Anthology.* Chicago: Lithuanian Library Press and Loyola University Press, 1979.

Sruoga, Balys. *Forest of the Gods*. Trans. Aušrinė Byla. Vilnius: Vaga, 1996.
Vėlaikis, Jonas [pseud. Bronius Vaškelis]. "Lithuanian Literature Under the Soviets," *Lituanus*, 12, 3 (Fall, 1966): 25-43.

28. Women's History

Thorborg, Marina, ed. *Women Around the Baltic Sea. Part I: Estonia, Latvia and Lithuania. Work Report on Baltic Issues. (1) October, 1993.* Lund: Lund University Department of Education, 1993.
Udrėnas, Nerijus. "Women in the Ethnic Processes of Sixteenth-Century Lithuania," *Lituanus*, 42, 2 (Summer 1996), 16-26.

29. Jewish History and the Holocaust

Agranovskii, G. *Litovskii Ierusalem: Kratkii putovoditel' o pamiatnym mestam evreiskoi istorii i kul'tury v Vil'niuse.* [The Jerusalem of Lithuania: A Short Guide to Memorable Places of Jewish Culture and History in Vilnius]. Vilnius: Lituanus, 1992. (In Russian).
Arad, Yitzhak. "The 'Final Solution' in Lithuania in the Light of German Documentation," *Yad Vashem Studies*, 11 (1976), 234-272.
_____. *Ghetto in Flames: The Struggle and Destruction of the Jews in Vilna in the Holocaust.* New York: Holocaust Library, 1982.
_____. *The Partisan: From the Valley of Death to Mt. Zion.* New York: Holocaust Library, 1979.
Atamukas, Solomonas. *Evrei v Litve* [The Jews in Lithuania]. Vilnius: Lituanus, 1990. (In Russian).
Berdichevsky, Norman. "The Baltic Revival and Zionism," *Lituanus,* 38, 1 (Spring 1992): 69-78.
Dawidowicz, Lucy S. *From That Place and Time: A Memoir, 1938-1947.* New York: W. W. Norton, 1989.

Eckman, Lester Samuel and Chaim Lazar Litai. *The Jewish Resistance: the History of the Jewish Partisans in Lithuania and White Russia during the Nazi Occupation, 1940-1945.* New York: Shengold Publishers, 1977.

Faitelson, Aleks. *Heroism and Bravery in Lithuania, 1941-1945.* New York: Gefen Books, 1996.

Frome, Frieda. *Some Dare to Dream: Frieda Frome's Escape from Lithuania.* Ames, IA: Iowa State University Press, 1988.

Ganor, Solly. *Light One Candle: A Survivor's Tale from Lithuania to Jerusalem.* New York: Kodansha International, 1995.

Gefen, Aba. *Defying the Holocaust: A Diplomat's Report.* San Bernardino, CA: Borgo Press, 1993.

_____. *Unholy Alliance.* Tel-Aviv: Yuval, 1973.

Gordon, Harry. *The Shadow of Death: The Holocaust in Lithuania.* Lexington, KY: University Press of Kentucky, 1992.

Greenbaum, Masha. *The Jews of Lithuania: A History of a Remarkable Community, 1319-1945.* Jerusalem: Gefen, 1995.

Gringauz, Samuel. "Jewish National Autonomy in Lithuania (1918-1925)," *Jewish Social Studies*, 14 (1952), 225-242.

Levin, Dov. "The Participation of the Lithuanian Jews in the Second World War," *JBS,* 6, 4 (Winter 1975): 300-310.

_____. *Baltic Jews Under the Soviets, 1940-1946.* Jerusalem: Hebrew University, 1994.

_____. *Fighting Back: Lithuanian Jewry's Armed Resistance to the Nazis, 1941-1945.* Trans. Moshe Kohn and Dina Cohen. New York: Holmes & Meier, 1985.

_____. "The Jews and the Election Campaigns in Lithuania, 1940-1941," *Soviet Jewish Affairs*, Vol. 10, No. 1 (February 1980), 39-51.

_____. "The Jews in the Soviet Lithuanian Establishment," *Soviet Jewish Affair*, Vol. 10, No. 2 (May 1980), 21-37.

_____. "The Jews and the Socio-economic Sovietization of Lithuania (Part I)," *Soviet Jewish Affairs*, Vol. 17, No. 2 (1987), 17-38.

_____. "The Jews and the Socio-economic Sovietization of Lithuania (Part II)," *Soviet Jewish Affairs*, Vol. 17, No. 3 (1987), 25-38.

_____. *The Lesser of Two Evils: Eastern European Jewry under Soviet Rule 1939-1941.* Philadelphia: Jewish Publication Society, 1995.

Levin, Nora. *While Messiah Tarried: Jewish Socialist Movements, 1871-1917.* New York: Schocken Books, 1977.

"Lithuania." *Encyclopaedia Judaica.* Vol. 11, 1971. 361-390.

Mishell, William W. *Kaddish for Kovno: Life and Death in a Lithuanian Ghetto 1941-1945.* Chicago: Chicago Review Press, 1988.

Oshry, Efraim. *The Annihilation of Lithuanian Jewry.* New York: Judaica Press, 1995.

Rabinowitsch, Wolf Zeev. *Lithuanian Hasidism from Its Beginnings to the Present Day.* London: Valentine and Mitchell, 1970.

Ran, Leizer. *Yerusholayim de-Lita. Jerusalem of Lithuania.* 3 vols. n. p.: 1974. (In Hebrew and English).

Ronn, J. Michel. *The Dworskys of Lazdei: The History of a Lithuanian Jewish Family from the Mid-1700s until the Present.* Brooklyn, NY: J. M. Ronn, 1990.

Sachar-Gertner, Sheina. *The Trees Stood Still.* Framingham, MA: Holocaust Survivors, 1981

Shochat, Azriel. "Jews, Lithuanians and Russians 1939-1941," Vargo, Bela and George L. Mosse, eds. *Jews and Non-Jews in Eastern Europe 1918-1945.* New York: John Wiley, 1974, 301-314.

_____. "The Beginnings of Anti-Semitism in Independent Lithuania," *Yad Vashem Studies on the European Jewish Catastrophe and Resistance,* 2 (Jerusalem, 1958), 7-48.

Schoenburg, Nancy. *Lithuanian Jewish Communities.* New York: Garland, 1991.

Shulman, Yaacov. *The Vilna Gaon: The Story of Rabbi Eliyahu Kramer.* New York: CIS Publishers, 1994.

Sužiedėlis, Saulius. "Icchokas Meras and the Holocaust: Terror and Salvation in Contemporary Lithuanian Literature," *Lituanus,* 27, 3 (Fall 1981): 5-7.

Tobias, Henry Jack. *The Jewish Bund in Russia from its Origins to 1905.* Stanford, CA: Stanford University Press, 1972.

Tory, Avraham. *Surviving the Holocaust: the Kovno Ghetto Diary.* Trans. Jerzy Michalowicz. Cambridge, MA: Harvard University Press, 1990.

Zingeris, Emanuelis, ed. *Atminties Dienos. The Days of Memory: International Conference on the 50th Anniversary of the Liquidation of the Vilnius Ghetto.* Vilnius: Lithuanian State Jewish Museum, 1995.

30. Emigration and Diaspora Communities

Aušra, Valdas. "Lithuanian Lutherans in North America," *Lituanus*, 41, 2 (Summer 1995): 5-18.

Danys, Milda. *DP Lithuanian Immigration to Canada After the Second World War.* Toronto: Multicultural History Society of Ontario, 1986.

Fainhauz, David. *Lithuanians in the USA: Aspects of Ethnic Identity.* Chicago: Lithuanian Library Press, 1991.

————. *Lithuanians in Multi-Ethnic Chicago until World War II.* Chicago: Lithuanian Library Press and University of Loyola Press, 1977.

Friedlander, Judith. *Vilna on the Seine. Jewish Intellectuals in France since 1968.* New Haven, CT: Yale University Press, 1990.

Gaida, Pranas et al, eds. *Canada Ethnica.* Vol. 5: *Lithuanians in Canada.* Ottawa and Toronto: Time Press, 1967.

Gedmintas, Aleksandras. "Organizational Relationships in the Development of the Binghampton Lithuanian Community," *JBS*, 11, 4 (Winter 1980): 315-324.

Greene, Victor R. *For God and Country: The Rise of Polish and Lithuanian Ethnic Consciousness in America, 1860-1910.* Madison, WI: State Historical Society of Wisconsin, 1975.

Gudelunas, William A. "The Lithuanians of Pennsylvania's Lower Anthracite Region: A Study in the Persistence of Ethnic Identification," *Lituanus,* 32, 3 (Fall 1986): 79-87.

Kezys, Algimantas. *Lithuania through the Wall: Diary of a Ten-Day Visit to My Native Land.* Chicago: Loyola University Press, 1985.

Kriščiūnas, Raymond G. "The Emigrant Experience: The Decision of Lithuanian Refugees to Emigrate, 1945-1950," *Lituanus,* 29, 2 (Summer 1983): 30-39.

Kučas, Antanas. *Lithuanians in America.* Trans. Joseph Boley. Boston: Encyclopedia Lituanica, 1975.

Šilbajoris, Rimvydas. *Perfection of Exile: Fourteen Contemporary Lithuanian Writers.* Norman, OK: University of Oklahoma Press, 1970.

The Baltic Peoples in Australia: Lithuanians, Latvians, Estonians. Melbourne: AE Press, 1986.

Van Reenan, Antanas. *Lithuanian Diaspora: Königsberg to Chicago.* Lanham, MD: University Press of America, 1990.

White, James D. "Scottish Lithuanians and the Russian Revolution," *JBS,* 6, 1 (Spring 1975): 1-8.

Wolkovich-Valkavičius, William L. *From the Nemunas to the Assabet: A History of the Lithuanians and Lithuanian-Americans of Hudson, Massachusetts.* Hudson, MA: Hudson Lithuanian History, 1966.

_____. *Bay State Blue Laws and Bimba: A Documentary Study of the Anthony Bimba Trial for Blasphemy and Sedition in Brockton, Mass., 1927.* Brockton, MA: Forum Press, 1973.

_____. "Religious Separatism Among Lithuanian Immigrants in the United States and their Polish Affiliation," *Polish-American Studies,* 40, 2 (Autumn 1983): 93-123.

_____. *Lithuanian Fraternalism: 75 Years of U. S. Knights of Lithuania.* Brooklyn, NY: Knights of Lithuania, 1988.

_____. *Lithuanian Pioneer Priest of New England: The Life, Struggle and Tragic Death of Reverend Joseph Zebris, 1860-1915.* Brooklyn, NY: Franciscan Press, 1980.

_____. *Lithuanian Religious Life in America: A Compendium of 150 Roman Catholic Parishes and Institutions. Vol 1: Eastern United States.* Norwood, MA: Lithuanian Religious Life, 1991.

_____. *Lithuanian Religious Life in America: A Compendium of 150 Roman Catholic Parishes and Institutions. Vol 2: Pennsylvania.* Norwood, MA:Lithuanian Religious Life, 1996.

_____. *Lithuanians of Norwood, Massachusetts: A Social Portrait in a Multi-Ethnic Town.* Norwood, MA: Author, 1988.

31. Lithuanian East Prussia (Lithuania Minor)

Brakas, Martin, ed. *Lithuania Minor: A Collection of Studies on Her History and Ethnography.* New York: Lithuanian Research Institute, 1976.

Broszat, Martin. "Die memelländischen Organisationen und der Nationalsozialismus," *Vierteljahrshefte für Zeitgeschichte,* 5, 3 (1957): 273-278.

Gornig, Gilbert-Hanno. *Das Memelland: gestern und heute. Eine historische und rechtliche Betrachtung.* Bonn: Kulturstiftung der deutschen Vertriebenen, 1991.

Plieg, Ernst-Alfred. *Das Memelland 1920-1939: Deutsche Autonomiebestrebungen in litauischen Gesamstaat.* Würsburg: Holzner-Verlag, 1962.

Smith, Raymond A., "The Kaliningrad Region: Civic and Ethnic Models of Nationalism," *JBS,* 24, 3 (Fall 1993): 233-46.

Stephens, David. "The German Problem in Memel," *Slavonic Review,* 14 (1935-36), 321-331.

APPENDIX 1

PRONUNCIATION OF LITHUANIAN NAMES AND TERMS

The modern Lithuanian language is written in the Latin alphabet and is modeled in part on the Czech script. The following are the most frequently encountered letters and letter combinations that differ from English usage.

Lithuanian	English Equivalent
a, ą	a as in father
e, ę	e as in ever
ė	ay as in hay
u	u as in put
ū, ų	long vowel as in boot
i	i as in hit
į, y	ee as in sheep
o	long vowel as in oar
č	ch as in chair
c	ts-sound as in cuts
d	d as in endure

j	an initial y-sound, as in **y**es
l	l as in **l**et
š	sh as in **sh**eep
t	t as in **t**ier
ž	z as in a**z**ure
ius	as Latin **ius**, or as "yoos", but shorter
ie	single sound (diphthong) as in **y**ear
au	single sound (diphthong) as in **ou**t
ai	single sound (diphthong) as in p**ie**
uo	single sound (diphthong) as in sh**o**re
io	"yo" as in **yo**gurt

APPENDIX 2

LITHUANIAN RULERS 1251-1572[a]

Mindaugas (ca. 1251-1263), King of Lithuania

Pagan Rulers 1263-1316

Treniota (1263-1265)

Vaišvilkas (1265-1268)

Švarnas (1268-1269)

Traidenis (1270-1282)

Daumantas (ca. 1282-1285)

Pukuveras, Butigeidas (ca. 1285-1295)[b]

Vytenis (1295-1316)

Grand Dukes of the House of Gediminas

Gediminas (1316-1341)

Jaunutis (1341-1345)

Algirdas (1345-1377)

Kęstutis of Trakai (1377-1378)

Jogaila (1378-1401)[c]

Vytautas (1401-1430)[d]

Švitrigaila (1430-1432)[e]

Sigismund Kęstutaitis (1432-1440)[e]

Grand Dukes-Kings of the Jogaila Dynasty (Jagiellonians)

Jogaila (Władysław II)	Grand Duke of Lithuania (1378-1401) King of Poland (1386-1434)
Casimir IV	Grand Duke of Lithuania (1440-1492) King of Poland (1444-1492)
Alexander	Grand Duke of Lithuania (1492-1506) King of Poland (1501-1506)
Sigismund I (the Old)	Grand Duke of Lithuania (1506-1548) King of Poland (1506-1548)
Sigismund II (Augustus)	Grand Duke of Lithuania (1544-1572) King of Poland (1548-1572)

[a]For the oft-used Slavic (Polish and Russian) versions of these names, see entries under "The Dictionary."

[b]The historicity of these figures is uncertain.

[c]Jogaila, Gediminas' grandson, was formally Grand Duke of Lithuania from 1378 to 1401; however, the period of 1377-1386 was also one of interregnum and civil war.

[d]De facto ruler of Lithuania 1390-1430.

[e]Period of 1432-1435 was one of civil war and conflicting claims to the throne.

APPENDIX 3

RULERS OF THE COMMONWEALTH PERIOD
(1569-1795)

Kings of Poland, Grand Dukes of Lithuania, 1572-1795

Henry Valois (1572-1574)

Stefan Batory (1575-1586)

The Vasa Dynasty

Sigismund III (1587-1632)

Władysław IV (1632-1648)

John Casimir (1648-1668)

1668-1795

Michael Wiśniowiecki (1669-1673)

John III Sobieski (1674-1696)

Augustus II (the Strong) of Saxony (1697-1706, 1709-1733)

Stanisław I Leszczyński (1706-1709, 1733)

Augustus III of Saxony (1733-1763)

Stanisław II August Poniatowski (1763-1795)

APPENDIX 4

LITHUANIAN POLITICAL LEADERS SINCE 1918

Presidents of the Republic of Lithuania 1918-1940:

Antanas Smetona (1919-1920)

Aleksandras Stulginskis (1920-1926)

Kazys Grinius (May-December 1926)

Antanas Smetona (1926-1940)

Prime Ministers of the Republic of Lithuania 1918-1940:

Augustinas Voldemaras (November-December 1918)

Mykolas Sleževičius (December 1918-March 1919)

Pranas Dovydaitis (March 1919-April 1919)

Mykolas Sleževičius (April 1919-October 1919)

Ernestas Galvanauskas (October 1919-June 1920)

Kazys Grinius (June 1920-January 1922)

Ernestas Galvanauskas (February 1922-June 1924)

Antanas Tumėnas (June 1924-January 1925)

Vytautas Petrulis (February 1925-September 1925)

Leonas Bistras (September 1925-May 1926)

Mykolas Sleževičius (June 1926-December 1926)

Augustinas Voldemaras (December 1926-September 1929)

Juozas Tūbelis (September 1929-March 1938)

Vladas Mironas (March 1938-March 1939)

Jonas Černius (March 1939-November 1939)

Antanas Merkys (November 1939-June 1940)

Justas Paleckis (June 1940)[a]

Vincas Krėvė-Mickevičius (June-July 1940)[b]

First Secretaries of the Lithuanian Communist Party 1940-1990:

Antanas Sniečkus (1940-1974)

Petras Griškevičius (1974-1987)

Ringaudas Songaila (1987-1988)

Algirdas Brazauskas (1988-1990)

Heads of State-Presidents Since 1990:

Vytautas Landsbergis (March 1990-February 1993)[c]

Algirdas Brazauskas (February 1993-)

Prime Ministers of the Republic of Lithuania Since 1990:

Kazimiera Prunskienė (March 1990-January 1991)

Albertas Šimėnas (January 1991)

Gediminas Vagnorius (January 1991-July 1992)

Aleksandras Abišala (July 1992-December 1992)

Bronislavas Lubys (December 1992-March 1993)

Adolfas Šleževičius (March 1993-February 1996)

Mindaugas Stankevičius (February 1996-November 1996)

Gediminas Vagnorius (November 1996-)

---

[a]Prime Minister and Acting President of the Soviet-controlled People's Government.

[b]Acting Prime Minister of the Soviet-controlled People's Government.

[c]Head of State as Chairman of the Legislature.

APPENDIX 5

FREQUENTLY ENCOUNTERED PLACE NAMES IN LITHUANIAN AND OTHER LANGUAGES

Cities

Lithuanian	*Polish*	*Russian*	*German*
Vilnius	Wilno	Vilna	Wilna
Kaunas	Kowno	Kovno	Kauen
Klaipėda	Kłajpeda	Klaipeda	Memel
Šiauliai	Szawle	Shaulyay	Schaullen
Tilžė	Tilsit	Sovetsk	Tilsit
Ukmergė	Wilkomierz	Ukmerge	Ukmerge

Geographical Formations

Nemunas	Niemen	Neman	Memel
Kuršių Marės	Kurszy	Kurskii zaliv	Kurisches Haff

ABOUT THE AUTHOR

Saulius Sužiedėlis is Associate Professor of History at Millersville University of Pennsylvania. He was born in Gotha, Germany in 1945 and grew up in the Lithuanian community of Brockton, Massachusetts. After two years of service with the Peace Corps in Ethiopia from 1967 to 1969, he received his M. A. in Russian history from the University of Maryland in 1972 and a Ph. D. from the University of Kansas in 1977. In 1974 and 1975 Prof. Sužiedėlis conducted his doctoral research at the University of Warsaw under a grant from the International Research and Exchanges Board (IREX). Between 1982 and 1987 Prof. Sužiedėlis was a research historian for the United States Department of Justice and during 1989-1990 worked as a radio journalist and commentator for the Voice of America, a division of the United States Information Agency. Prof. Sužiedėlis is author of *The Sword and the Cross: A History of the Lithuanian Church* and a number of scholarly articles on Lithuanian history published both in the United States and Lithuania. In recent years Prof. Sužiedėlis has delivered a series of public lectures and history courses in Lithuania and has been a guest scholar at the History Institute of the Lithuanian Academy of Sciences. Prof. Sužiedėlis is the current editor of the scholarly quarterly, *The Journal of Baltic Studies*. At present he is also working on a history of Lithuania during World War II.